PROMISED VERSE

Promised Verse

POETS IN THE SOCIETY
OF AUGUSTAN ROME

Peter White

Harvard University Press
Cambridge, Massachusetts
London, England
1993

Copyright © 1993 by the President and Fellows of Harvard College
All rights reserved
Printed in the United States of America

This book is printed on acid-free paper, and its binding
materials have been chosen for strength and durability.

Library of Congress Cataloging-in-Publication Data
White, Peter, 1941–
Promised verse: poets in the society of
Augustan Rome/Peter White.
p.   cm.
Includes bibliographical references and index.
ISBN 0-674-71525-X (alk. paper)
1. Latin poetry—History and criticism.   2. Augustus, Emperor of
Rome, 63 B.C.–14 A.D.   3. Rome—History—Augustus, 30 B.C.–14 A.D.
4. Literature and society—Rome.   5. Authors and patrons—Rome.
6. Poets, Latin—Biography.   7. Rome in literature.   I. Title.
PA6047.W4 1993
871'.0109—dc20
93-9190
CIP

To the three families I belong in

Contents

Preface

In this book I describe how the Augustan poets and Roman poets generally were integrated into the social order which sustained Roman literary life. I discuss how poets served and were served by the leaders of society, how that symbiosis complemented their relationships with a wider public, and how they positioned themselves to address civic or political themes as well as more private ones. The challenge of the task has been to try to bring a mass of literary and anecdotal particulars into a clean alignment. The pleasure of seeing the patterns into which they fall is what more than anything else I hope to pass along to readers.

Readers will also see how circumscribed the perspective of this book is. It is concerned with poets and poetry only, not with literature in general. I have not set out to elucidate what makes Latin poetry universal, but rather the opposite: the imprint it carries of a particular social matrix is what interests me. Although from time to time I interpret passages of poems or relate them to a historical or ideological context, critics will not find the argument literary and historians may not consider it properly historical. As a rule I do not review competing interpretations of texts brought up for comment, and that also limits the generality of this inquiry. The one sense in which I hope it is comprehensive despite these limitations is that I have tried to see as far as can be seen from the vantage point I have adopted. Roman poetry seems socially bound to an unusual degree, as anyone knows who has tried to teach it to non-classicists. A book that ponders why it is so deeply embedded in Roman social life cannot help dealing with important issues.

The book consists of two parts, which are each subdivided into three chapters. Part One describes how poets interacted with the magnates and groups who made up almost the entirety of the Roman literary milieu, and it concludes with a discussion of the influence that readers and supporters exerted over verse addressed to them. Part Two concerns the lopsidedly influential role which the emperor acquired over poets and poetry. But the argument starts from the premise that, in the case of Augustus at least, the emperor conceived his role as parallel to the role played by his aristocratic peers. In Chapter 4 the interpretation which ascribes a political intent to Augustus' literary interventions is traced back to seventeenth-century France and eighteenth-century Britain and is shown to be conceptually determined by political institutions of that era. In Chapter 5 I reexamine testimony in classical sources which has been thought to support a political interpretation of Augustus' literary role and argue that the support is illusory. In Chapter 6 I study how four themes with political implications are handled by different Augustan poets.

Augustan poets occupy the foreground of this study because the age of Augustus is the most brilliant, best documented, and most controversial in the history of Roman literature. But I have allowed for some depth of field by drawing in other poets from Ennius to Juvenal. What those poets who come into the discussion have in common is that they established or tried to establish ties with wealthy and powerful persons in Rome; not coincidentally, most of them already enjoyed a modicum of respectability in their own right. They are the poets about whom we tend to know most. It is unclear to me how well the following account would apply to those poets (the dramatists of the third and second centuries B.C. and the writers of mime and pantomime thereafter) who could appeal directly to mass audiences. Their careers and often their very existence are too poorly illuminated by the sources for us to perceive how they were integrated into the literary milieu. Another problem of which I have slowly become aware is that as a matter of procedure, I had to accept the literary traditions about the lives of Latin poets wherever possible. Not that I privately subscribe to the position of those who practice a rigorous agnosticism toward ancient literary biography (or of those who hold that Latin poetry cannot yield autobiographical data about its authors); such an epistemology would foreclose any possibility of a study like this one. Still, it is undeniable that the literary tradition does sometimes present details which are questionable if not outright false. And yet my readers would find less use in this study if I were constantly to pick and choose among the sources or to construe them arbitrarily than if I do my best to accept them.

The remaining caveats all have to do with format. In order to make this discussion of Roman poets more inviting to adepts of other literatures, I have translated passages of Latin and eliminated most technical terms (in the text, but not in the notes). The notes have been relegated to the back of the book. The argument is fully unfolded in the text and was written to be read through without reference to the notes; the numerical superscripts scattered en route may be regarded provisionally as caltrops. For the most part, the notes do no more than assemble citations of multiple or cumbersome sources, add refinements which would otherwise clutter the exposition, and occasionally take positions on controversies. Also at the back are three appendixes which contain material not elsewhere brought together that supports the argument of Chapters 1 to 3.

Finally, with no more than a handful of exceptions, I have referred to secondary sources in the text and in the notes only where they contained primary materials or where by the nature of the argument they themselves constituted primary sources, as in Chapter 4. This choice is not meant to convey a message that prior scholarship is nugatory, irrelevant, or superseded. The whole direction of this inquiry obviously owes much to the spate of books and articles about patronage that have been published by scholars within and beyond the field of classics during the last two decades. But I have opted not to cite secondary sources for three principal reasons. One is that a conscientious acknowledgment of relevant criticism would have burst the notes, particularly in Chapters 5 and 6. The majority of texts adduced there are chestnuts with a history of controversy that reaches back farther, I suspect, than many scholars realize. Nor did it seem practicable to debate counter-interpretations at every step of the way while trying to develop a viewpoint that I thought could accommodate all the passages in question. (Accordingly, I do not claim to have offered necessary interpretations but only a series of possible interpretations which have a certain cumulative consistency.) Finally, I wanted to construct in this book an argument resembling Horace's image of the sage, whole in himself and smooth and round. In light of that design, not to appeal to external authorities was a form of discipline. It meant that whatever arguments existed to support my case had to be fully declared right here, without reliance on proxies. But Appendix 2 on the friends of the Augustan poets does contain references to sources that provide fuller prosopographical information. And readers who desire some orientation to recent writing about patronage, the social context of Roman literary life, and the problem of politics in Augustan poetry will find it in the Bibliographical Note.

The debts which this book and its author have accumulated begin with that to the American Council of Learned Societies and to the Division of Humanities of the University of Chicago, which together supported the year of research in which the project was begun. My Division subsequently supported another quarter of leave in which to complete the book and supplied funds to help publish it. I am also indebted to classics faculty and students at the University of Texas, Princeton, and Harvard who graciously submitted to lectures that were cruder samples of this argument. Barbara Gold, Jasper Griffin, Michael Murrin, and Arnaldo Momigliano contributed written comments on portions they had read; I regret that all of them cannot see now how much I profited from their advice. The strictures of Richard Saller, who has since become a colleague, spurred me to look beyond my discipline for a framework in which to think about social relations, a needed lesson which I have come to appreciate. Nicholas Horsfall, Robert Kaster, Peter Wiseman, and James Zetzel read through a complete draft a year ago and indicated how short it fell of being the final draft. I was especially helped by Nicholas Horsfall and Robert Kaster, who responded with more than thirty sheets of closely spaced complaints, advice, and rescue work that have affected many more of the following pages than mention their names. At Harvard University Press Margaretta Fulton plied her sugar of praise and goad of censure until another twenty percent of the manuscript had melted away. René Pomerleau extracted a laser printout from the antiquated hardware and software on which I was reliant. And my manuscript editor, Mary Ellen Geer, efficiently raked out quirks and errors that had persisted in spite of many previous readings.

Where so many have contributed improvements, the reader too is assured of finding exercise.

Abbreviations

In the notes (and in parentheses in the text) the names and works of classical authors are usually given in the abbreviated notation of either the *Oxford Latin Dictionary* (pp. ix–xx) or the *Oxford Classical Dictionary* (2nd ed., pp. ix–xxii). The names of a few journals to which reference is made have also been abbreviated, in this case according to the system set out in the front pages of *L'Année Philologique*. Shortened citations are employed for the following editions or works of reference as well:

Adler	*Lexicographi Graeci*, vol. 1: *Suidae Lexicon*, ed. A. Adler (Leipzig, 1928–1938)
ANRW	*Aufstieg und Niedergang der römischen Welt: Geschichte und Kultur Roms im Spiegel der neueren Forschung*, ed. H. Temporini and W. Haase (Berlin and New York, 1972—)
Bayer	*Vergil-Viten*, ed. K. Bayer, in *Vergil: Landleben: Bucolica, Georgica, Catalepton*, ed. J. and M. Götte (Munich, 1970)
Brummer	*Vitae Vergilianae*, ed. J. Brummer (Leipzig, 1912)
CIL	*Corpus inscriptionum Latinarum* (Berlin, 1863—)
Clark	*Q. Asconii Pediani orationum Ciceronis quinque enarratio*, ed. A. C. Clark (Oxford, 1907)
Clausen	*A. Persi Flacci saturarum liber*, ed. W. Clausen (Oxford, 1956)
Courtney	*P. Papini Stati Silvae*, ed. E. Courtney (Oxford, 1990)
FGrHist.	*Die Fragmente der griechischen Historiker*, ed. F. Jacoby (Leiden, 1957—)

FPL	*Fragmenta poetarum Latinorum epicorum et lyricorum praeter Ennium et Lucilium,* ed. W. Morel (Leipzig, 1927); ed. K. Büchner (Leipzig, 1982)
Georgii	*Tiberi Claudi Donati ad Tiberium Claudium Maximum Donatianum filium suum interpretationes Vergilianae,* ed. H. Georgii (Leipzig, 1905)
GL	*Grammatici Latini,* ed. H. Keil (Leipzig, 1857)
Gow-Page	*The Greek Anthology: The Garland of Philip and Some Contemporary Epigrams,* ed. A. S. F. Gow and D. L. Page (Cambridge, 1968)
Green	*The Works of Ausonius,* ed. R. P. H. Green (Oxford, 1991)
Hardie	*Vitae Vergilianae antiquae,* ed. C. Hardie (Oxford, 1966)
Helm	*Eusebius Werke,* vol. 7: *Die Chronik des Hieronymus,* ed. R. Helm (Berlin, 1956)
Hosius	*Lucanus: De bello civili,* 3rd ed., ed. C. Hosius (Leipzig, 1913)
IGRR	*Inscriptiones Graecae ad res Romanas pertinentes,* ed. R. Cagnat (Paris, 1911–1927)
ILS	*Inscriptiones Latinae selectae,* ed. H. Dessau (Berlin, 1892–1916)
Jal	*Florus: Oeuvres,* ed. P. Jal (Paris, 1967)
Lenz-Galinsky	*Albii Tibulli aliorumque carminum libri tres,* 3rd ed., ed. F. W. Lenz and G. K. Galinsky (Leiden, 1971)
Lindsay	*Sexti Pompei Festi de verborum significatu quae supersunt cum Pauli epitome,* ed. W. M. Lindsay (Leipzig, 1913)
———	*M. Val. Martialis epigrammata,* 2nd ed., ed. W. M. Lindsay (Oxford, 1929)
———	*Nonii Marcelli De compendiosa doctrina,* ed. W. M. Lindsay (Leipzig, 1903)
Lloyd-Jones and Parsons	*Supplementum Hellenisticum,* ed. H. Lloyd-Jones and P. Parsons (Berlin and New York, 1983)
Luck	*Albii Tibulli aliorumque carmina,* ed. G. Luck (Stuttgart, 1988)
Marx	*C. Lucilii carminum reliquiae,* ed. F. Marx (Leipzig, 1904–1905)

OGI	*Orientis Graeci inscriptiones selectae*, ed. W. Dittenberger (Leipzig, 1903–1905)
Page	*Further Greek Epigrams*, ed. D. L. Page (Cambridge, 1981)
RIC	*The Roman Imperial Coinage*, rev. ed., ed. C. H. V. Sutherland and R. A. G. Carson, vol. 1 (London, 1984)
Riese	*Anthologia Latina*, vol. 1.1: *Carmina in codicibus scripta*, ed. A. Riese (Leipzig, 1894)
———	*Geographi Latini minores*, ed. A. Riese (Heilbronn, 1878)
Roth	*C. Suetoni Tranquilli quae supersunt omnia*, ed. K. L. Roth (Leipzig, 1858)
RRC	M. H. Crawford, *Roman Republican Coinage* (Cambridge, 1974)
SB	*Anthologia Latina*, vol. 1.1: *Carmina in codicibus scripta*, ed. D. R. Shackleton Bailey (Stuttgart, 1982)
———	*Cicero's Letters to Atticus*, ed. D. R. Shackleton Bailey (Cambridge, 1965–1970)
———	*Cicero: Epistulae ad familiares*, ed. D. R. Shackleton Bailey (Cambridge, 1977)
———	*Cicero: Epistulae ad Quintum fratrem et M. Brutum*, ed. D. R. Shackleton Bailey (Cambridge, 1980)
———	*Horatius: Opera*, ed. D. R. Shackleton Bailey (Stuttgart, 1985)
———	*M. Valerii Martialis epigrammata*, ed. D. R. Shackleton Bailey (Stuttgart, 1990)
Skutsch	*The Annals of Quintus Ennius*, ed. O. Skutsch (Oxford, 1985)
Stangl	*Ciceronis orationum scholiastae*, ed. T. Stangl (Vienna, 1912)
Sudhaus	*Philodemi volumina rhetorica*, ed. S. Sudhaus (Leipzig, 1892–1896)
Thilo-Hagen	*Servii grammatici qui feruntur in Vergilii carmina commentarii*, ed. G. Thilo and H. Hagen (Leipzig, 1881–1902)
Vahlen	*Ennianae poesis reliquiae*, 2nd ed., ed. J. Vahlen (Leipzig, 1928)

van den Hout *M. Cornelii Frontonis epistulae*, ed. M. P. J. van den Hout (Leiden, 1954)

Vorsokr. *Die Fragmente der Vorsokratiker*, 6th ed., ed. H. Diels and W. Kranz (Berlin, 1951)

PART ONE

Poets and Roman Social Life

1

The Poet as Companion and Protégé

Vergil, Horace, Tibullus, Propertius, and Ovid each boast attachments to one or two important persons who occupy more of their attention than their other acquaintances among the Roman elite. These relationships form a pattern that can be paralleled both before and afterward. In the previous century Ennius and Lucilius had been linked with the Scipios, and a century later Martial and Statius were still panning among Rome's great houses in the hope of making comparable strikes. Although not every poet formed such attachments, they are evidently one of the more durable and characteristic features of Roman literary history.

What is immediately noticeable about these relationships is how deeply the poet is drawn into the private life of his important friend. Ennius inserted into the *Annals* an extended sketch of the companion with whom one of the poem's heroes "shares his table, conversation, and thoughts on personal affairs" (*Ann.* 268–270 Skutsch = 234–236 Vahlen). Since the beginning of scholarly commentary on the *Annals* in the half-century after the poet's death, it has been believed that this description was modeled on Ennius' own intercourse with Roman aristocrats.[1] Horace cherished a similar image of Lucilius' relations with Scipio and Laelius, who at the end of a day's business "would loosen up and kid around with him until the greens were cooked" (*Serm.* 2.1.71–74). In his own life Horace found occasion to chafe at Maecenas' reluctance to allow him holidays on his own (*Epist.* 1.7.25), and he says he is fussed at for failing to have his nails properly manicured (*Epist.* 1.1.104–105). Writing to a poet friend who craves acquaintance with the well-to-do, he warns that one must expect to be kept busy with hunting parties by day and drinking parties at night, and to be saddled at all times with the burden of the great man's confidences (*Epist.* 1.18). In the century after Horace a notable who has taken up a poet declares that "no one is more intimately linked to me both through the exercise of friendship and by constancy of association" (Tac. *Dial.* 5.2). Sources typically speak of poets as "living together" and enjoying "habitual contact" *(usus)* with their great friends, and the implications of that language are confirmed by the visits, trips, and parties which are the context of so much occasional verse.[2]

Although a Roman magnate might desire his protégé's company as he circulated around town or traveled abroad, it was the fixed elements of his routine which mainly structured their relationship. Many of these, like the morning reception and the dinner, naturally took place at home, and the great man's house *(domus)* therefore came to symbolize the very spirit of intercourse with the rich and powerful. The literature emanating from this milieu is filled with evocations of the house and its approaches—the threshold, the door, the hall. Martial squeezes almost the whole lexicon into a short envoi bidding a book of his poems "to visit the illustrious abode *(lares)* of Proculus." After directing the book up the Palatine and past the shrine of Cybele, Martial continues:

> Head toward the bright-walled dwelling *(Penates)* and the hall *(atria)* of the lofty mansion *(domus)* just to the left. Go up to it. You need not fear disdain and a haughty threshold *(limen):* no door *(ianua)* is swung more fully open on its jamb *(postis)*, nor is there any door to which Apollo and the learned sisters are nearer and dearer.
>
> Mart. *Epigr.* 1.70.1–15[3]

That the mansions of the great are idealized as nurseries of poetry is entirely consistent with the tendency of much Roman verse to celebrate the domestic and social preoccupations of the upper class. Yet if poets often focus on private themes, it is not from hostility or indifference toward public ones. This is obvious especially in the case of the Augustans, for example, all of whom dealt with national or public or civic themes as well as with love and other cares of private life. Even as late as the principate of Augustus, activities of public life were a steady counterpoint in the daily rhythms of Rome's inhabitants. Electoral and legislative assemblies were held outdoors, judicial proceedings were conducted in the fora, and entertainment was staged at state expense for mass audiences in the open air. Many poets and all their important friends had commitments in the public sphere by virtue of possessing equestrian or senatorial status. Public and private were thus complementary, and when a Roman poet celebrated the society of the great man's house, his purpose was not to exalt the latter over the former.

The distinction which poets actually invoke in this connection, and invoke repeatedly, is not so much between public and private as between the serious activities and the pastimes of their great friends. In the catch phrase this distinction is posed as a contrast of *seria* and *lusus* or *iocus*.[4] But it can appear in many other guises, as in a well-known passage in which Horace protests that his acquaintance with Maecenas has brought him no knowledge of affairs of state:

> Maecenas included me among his friends only to the extent that he would take me in his carriage when he traveled and share trivialities like "What time is it?" "Can Chickie the Thracian stand up to the Syrian?" "The frost these mornings nips you if you don't watch out."
>
> Hor. *Serm.* 2.6.41–45[5]

Behind these self-deprecating demarcations of light and serious there is a strategy. In the Roman taxonomy of human endeavor it is axiomatic that poetry belongs to an area set apart from serious concerns as the domain of leisure *(otium)*. A poet qua poet can have no basis for sharing that side of a friend's life which has to do with his capacity as an official or orator or jurist, but he can fittingly play a role in his off-duty life. By stressing the separation between pastime and profession, poets are claiming time that their friends can feel no compunction about reserving for poetry, and the poems fix attention on the dwelling-places of the great because that is where they retire to relax.

The Status of Poets

I emphasize the house setting and its connection with the distinction between business and leisure because these motifs point up important facts about the status of poets. (Orientation to the leisure requirements of the elite also affects the poetry itself, of course, and to this aspect of the matter I will return in Chapter 3.) In the first place, a poet who can organize his life to fit the domestic routines of the well-to-do must be essentially at leisure himself; he cannot owe his maintenance to work or a position that requires a broad and scheduled commitment of time. This presumption is generally borne out in the lives of those writers who created our corpus of Latin poetry. With rare exceptions, nothing in what they say about themselves or in what ancient sources report about them indicates that they practiced occupations which supported them.[6] One finds nothing approximating the modern pattern whereby a poet may double as an academic or editor or insurance company executive.

This leisure obviously has economic implications: poets who did not work had to have other sources of income.[7] Many of them were in a position to live at least in part off the income from capital invested in land and loans, exactly as their wealthier friends lived, if not as lavishly. This is most clear in the case of those poets (including Horace, Tibullus, and Ovid among the Augustans) who were knights *(equites),* since everyone who qualified as a knight had to declare assets worth at least 400,000 sesterces.[8] If the distribution of wealth among the population as a whole could be measured, it is probable that this sum would locate the *equites* near the top end of the scale. It is certain that it put them on a footing of basic self-sufficiency. At an annual return of 6 percent, capital of 400,000 sesterces would produce an income of 24,000.[9] Although figures about the cost of living are sparse and anecdotal, like all data about the Roman economy, there are enough to show that a man could live frugally at Rome within that budget. It would have provided adequately for housing. In the middle of the first century B.C., Cicero's rakehell client Caelius Rufus had been able to rent rooms in the smartest part of town for between 10,000 and 30,000 sesterces a year.[10] This range is consistent with a statement by Velleius from the year A.D. 30. Whereas a century and a half earlier, he says, a leading senator had incurred official censure for paying 6,000 to rent a house, nowadays "if someone rents for that amount, he scarcely cuts a figure as a senator" (Vell. Pat. 2.10.1). It is clearly implied that a man less concerned to maintain appearances could still rent for 6,000. As recently as the civil war years, there had been a substantial number of properties in Rome renting for under 2,000 a year.[11]

Other consumer expenses are harder to gauge, but nothing suggests that they were out of line with the cost of housing. The biographer of Cicero's friend Atticus reports that despite his wealth and a reputation for hospitality, Atticus was a frugal manager who "according to his logbook used to average no more than three thousand a month on expenses" (Nep. *Att.* 13.6).[12] To some extent Atticus may have been able to supply himself with wine, meat, and produce from his estate outside Rome, in which case his monthly outlay would represent a budget more for occasional needs or luxuries than for staples.[13] Nevertheless it bears comparison with a figure quoted in a similar context a century and a half later. In *Epigrams* 3.10, Martial caricatures a young wastrel who spent each day the amount his father had fixed as a monthly allowance; the presupposition of the piece is that 2,000 sesterces a month (or 24,000 a year) should have been ample. Elsewhere (*Epigr.* 12.36.3–4) Martial says that for a man in his own position a gift of a few *aureoli,* worth 100 sesterces apiece, might last two months. And finally, for comparison, a figure that indicates what a relatively lavish standard of living would be: in 45 B.C., when Cicero's son took up residence in Athens, Cicero arranged for him to receive an annual allowance of 80,000 sesterces. In his own eyes at least it was not a modest sum: Cicero was aware that as a consular's son Marcus had a certain position to maintain, and he wanted Marcus to live comfortably. What makes it precisely relevant to a consideration of the cost of living at Rome is that Cicero happens to add that with the 80,000 Marcus "would easily have been content if he were to live and rent a house in Rome (which was his plan)" (*Att.* 12.32.2 = 271 SB).[14] To rent a townhouse—not rooms—and to live in a style befitting a consular's son would have cost no more than three or four times what even the poorest knight could afford to spend.

The correlation between cost of living and the equestrian census that can be deduced from these various figures is drawn explicitly in one of our sources. At the end of a tract against the pursuit of riches, Juvenal asks: "What level of wealth is adequate?" and offers three alternatives. Strictly speaking, human needs can be satisfied for as little as the great moralists Socrates and Epicurus expended on them. But if that limit seems too drastic, he says, "then throw in some more according to our Roman scale of values," and raise the level to the amount of the equestrian census. If you still wrinkle your nose at that, raise it to two or three times the equestrian census (to the senatorial census, in other words). And if you cannot be satisfied with that, there is obviously no amount that can satisfy you (*Sat.* 14.316–329). On a scale which Juvenal clearly meant to represent a progression from subsistence to luxury, the equestrian census stands as the benchmark of medium comfort.

Yet even if it is true that an income of 24,000 sesterces was adequate to meet the ordinary expenses of living in Rome, the figures I have quoted suggest that it would leave little extra. I do not wish to exaggerate the resources of poets who were knights, or to leave an impression that they had no use or desire for other income. For the moment, however, let me emphasize an economic issue which I think is prior: possession of the equestrian census explains how some poets were free to devote so much time to the arduous camaraderie which was a prerequisite for gaining favor with the great.

Two questions naturally present themselves at this point. Were all poets in that case knights? And is it certain that their equestrian capital was acquired before rather than through their connections with rich friends?

The dramatists and writers of epic who created the earliest Latin poetry were of course outsiders to the city and its social hierarchy. But from the end of the second century B.C., Roman knights and senators make up an ever-increasing proportion of those poets whose background can be determined. To convert this assertion into a statistic is more complicated than might be imagined, however. If everyone known to have written any kind of Latin verse were counted, dilettanti would greatly outnumber mainstream writers and the results would not seem true to literary history as most of us understand it. Instead of the totality of verse-writers, let me present two samples which more fairly represent the mainstream. Quintilian names thirty-one poets (not counting the reigning emperor) in a survey of Latin poetry in book 10. The social status of slightly under half of these cannot be determined.[15] Five can be identified as certainly or almost certainly neither equestrian nor senatorial, and all of these were dramatists active in the second century B.C.: Accius, Caecilius, Ennius, Plautus, and Terence. Eleven are certainly or probably senators or knights: Albinovanus Pedo, Cornelius Gallus, Horace, Lucan, Lucilius, Ovid, Persius, Pomponius Secundus, Tibullus, Valerius Flaccus, and Varro. All of these except Lucilius were active well after the first group. The criteria underlying this classification by status are narrow and precise. Everyone I have identified as an *eques* or a senator either is explicitly named as such in the sources, or else held some position for which equestrian or senatorial rank is known to have been a prerequisite. (In Appendix 1 Albinovanus Pedo's equestrian status is marked as uncertain not because the status criterion is vague—there is no question that Pedo was an *eques*—but because it is merely probable rather than absolutely certain that Pedo the *eques* is Pedo the poet.) It does not follow, therefore, that all those about whom such information is lacking can be presumed to be non-equestrian. On the contrary, it has often been surmised that Afranius, Catullus, and Propertius were knights, and Saleius Bassus, Varius, and Vergil acquired enough or more than enough wealth to satisfy the equestrian census requirement. But no

Table 1   Poets of Quintilian's Canon

Status level	Certain	%	Probable	%	Certain plus probable	Percentage of total known statuses	Percentage of total entries
Senatorial	4	13%	—	—	4	25%	13%
Equestrian	6	19%	1	3%	7	44%	23%
Combined senatorial and equestrian	10	32%	1	3%	11	69%	35%
Non-equestrian	5	16%	—	—	5	31%	16%
Total known (= certain + probable) statuses					16	(100%)	52%
Unknown statuses					15	—	48%
Total entries					31		

Table 2   Poets of Quintilian's Canon, 40 B.C. to A.D. 80

Status level	Certain	%	Probable	%	Certain plus probable	Percentage of total known statuses	Percentage of total entries
Senatorial	3	16%	—	—	3	33%	16%
Equestrian	5	26%	1	5%	6	67%	32%
Combined senatorial and equestrian	8	42%	1	5%	9	100%	47%
Non-equestrian	—	—	—	—	—	—	—
Total known (= certain + probable) statuses					9	(100%)	47%
Unknown statuses					10	—	53%
Total entries					19		

matter how one reckons with the uncertain cases, poets from the upper orders make up an impressive percentage of the whole, as Tables 1 and 2 make clear. If we count only those poets whose status is documented, 69 percent (eleven out of sixteen) are either senators or knights; of those active between about 40 B.C. and A.D. 80, 100 percent (nine out of nine) are senators or knights. If on the other hand we count both certain and uncertain cases, poets belonging to the upper orders still make up 47 percent (nine out of nineteen) of those who were active from the middle of the first century B.C. on. Or to sum up in another way, senators and knights constitute between 47 percent and 100 percent of the poets

Quintilian thought had been important during the century and a half before he wrote.

Against the writers of Quintilian's canon, let us now set a much larger group, consisting of all named poets whose work survives independently in manuscripts or who are represented by quotations in collections of fragments. The names of the latter I have taken from Ribbeck's two corpora of dramatic fragments and from Morel's (now Büchner's) collection of hexameter and lyric fragments, plus Lucilius and Varro; I have also set a chronological limit, excluding anyone active after roughly the year A.D. 140. The sample which results, assembled as Appendix 1, consists of 121 poets, almost four times as many as Quintilian names. Apart from size, this sample has the further merits of being selected on a principle relatively independent of the issue I wish to examine, of including every Latin poet about whose work anything can be known, and of presenting us with poets whose oeuvre was known, copied, or cited by at least one reader beyond the author. This last criterion helps keep down the number of mere dilettanti, though the distinction between professional and dilettante cannot be pressed very far in Rome. (That epigraphically attested verse does not necessarily possess the quality of being known to readers is one reason I have not included it.)

As with the first group, half the writers have identifiable backgrounds and half do not. Let it be noted, however, that in this sample the uncertainties tend to run deeper. For a quarter of the 121, we know no more than their names, and that they predate the texts which quote them. Where backgrounds are known, the social composition is very like that of the group Quintilian names, as Tables 3 and 4 indicate. If we count only those poets about whose status something definite is known, senators and *equites* make up 81 percent of the total (fifty out of sixty-two). For the period from about 40 B.C. to A.D. 140, they make up 94 percent of the total (thirty-one out of thirty-three). If, on the other hand, for the same 180 years we exclude no one from the count, identifiably upper-class writers still make up 55 percent (thirty-one out of fifty-six) of the total. There are of course far too many uncertainties here to recover even the approximate ratio of senatorial and equestrian poets to non-equestrian poets during the period. It is possible to establish only a range, but the range implies that the upper class was preponderant. From about 40 B.C. on, senators and knights constitute at least 55 percent of those poets of whose verse any trace remains, and they may have approached 94 percent.

Table 3   Poets Represented by Texts or Fragments to A.D. 140

Status level	Certain	%	Probable	%	Certain plus probable	Percentage of total known statuses	Percentage of total entries
Senatorial	32	26%	3	2%	35	56%	29%
Equestrian	11	9%	4	3%	15	24%	12%
Combined senatorial and equestrian	43	36%	7	6%	50	81%	41%
Non-equestrian	10	8%	2	2%	12	19%	10%
Total known (= certain + probable) statuses					62	(100%)	51%
Unknown statuses					59	—	49%
Total entries					121		

Table 4   Poets Represented by Texts or Fragments, 40 B.C. to A.D. 140

Status level	Certain	%	Probable	%	Certain plus probable	Percentage of total known statuses	Percentage of total entries
Senatorial	16	29%	3	5%	19	58%	34%
Equestrian	10	18%	2	4%	12	36%	21%
Combined senatorial and equestrian	26	46%	5	9%	31	94%	55%
Non-equestrian	1	2%	1	2%	2	6%	4%
Total known (= certain + probable) statuses					33	(100%)	59%
Unknown statuses					23	—	41%
Total entries					56		

To respond now to the first of the questions I posed earlier, not all poets were knights. Quite apart from the fact that in the larger sample knights are considerably outnumbered by senators—it is in the nature of Roman society that senators leave more tokens of their identity than *equites*—there are a few poets who do not belong to either class. The mimographer Publilius Syrus, Tullius Laurea, and the fabulist Phaedrus were freedmen, and Florus, though not a freedman, manifestly lacked the capital a knight would have. And it is not unlikely that among those poets whose status is unknown there were other freedmen and some impecunious literati like Florus. Yet given the predominance of senators and knights where we do have information about status, the presupposition must be that the unknowns too were mostly upper-class. As it happens, there is a witness who confirms that this inference is correct, at least for the Augustan period. Toward the end of the *Art of Poetry,* Horace marvels that unlike a bumbler at sports, who will stay off the playing field for fear of being laughed at, an incompetent poet will feel no inhibition about composing verse. "But of course, why not?" the satirist continues. "He is free and born in freedom, and more than that, he meets the equestrian requirement, and has no blot upon his record" (*Ars* 382–384). Here as so often Horace parodies the viewpoint of his contemporaries, confounding the accidentals with the substance of a poetic vocation. But the sociological fact must have been that would-be poets usually had an equestrian income or better.

Whether they acquired this income before or precisely through their connections with the rich is much harder to determine; the glimpses which our sources allow us of their status rarely reveal when it was achieved. But if we may judge by the Augustan poets, whose lives are better known than most, it is at least not obvious that poets must have owed their upper-class credentials to the intervention of their friends. Ovid pointedly contrasts the equestrian rank his family had enjoyed for generations with the new knighthoods dispensed during the civil wars (*Am.* 3.15.5–6). Horace was commissioned as a military tribune during the civil war (*Serm.* 1.6.48), which means that he passed as a knight before he ever met Maecenas, and even after the debacle of the Republican cause, he evidently retained enough capital to procure a clerkship which established him on the fringes of the equestrian order. According to the Vergilian lives, before the poet was befriended by either Pollio or Maecenas he had resources adequate to support a career of study in Cremona, Milan, Rome, and Naples (Don. *Vita Verg.* 6–7 and 11 Hardie). How much if at all the family fortunes were subsequently impaired by government land seizures in north Italy we do not know. Cornelius Gallus was supposedly raised from lowliest estate by Augustus (Suet. *Aug.* 66.1), yet from the moment his activities are first documented and before he has entered Augustus' orbit, he is found hobnobbing with Cicero, discharging administrative functions in conjunction with Asinius Pollio, and serving—surely as an equestrian officer—in the army.[16] If as is widely thought the Albius to whom Horace writes *Epistles* 1.4 is the poet Tibullus, he was financially well-off from the time he was born. Propertius portrays himself as a gentleman of leisure in his first book of poems, which predate any mention of Maecenas, and he even felt secure

enough to turn down an opportunity of improving his finances by joining the staff of a governor posted to Asia (1.6). Although some at least
of the Augustan poets did benefit enormously in later life from the generosity of their friends, there is not one who can be plausibly seen as
disadvantaged when he started out.

Up to this point, the focus of my argument has been economic. I
have emphasized the status of poets because status points to material
resources which met their basic needs and afforded them leisure to share
in the pastimes and domestic life of the elite. Now I shall shift the focus
and consider another way in which poets' status relates to social activity.
Although relationships with poets normally belong to that area of a
great man's life which is private rather than public, poets obviously fall
into a different category from many others who have intimate access
to him. They socialize with him on very different terms than do slaves,
freedmen, family dependents, or agents, for example. They eat and revel
with him, accompany him on trips, enjoy his hospitality in villas and
vacation resorts; sometimes they even take up residence in his home in
town. They act and are treated as friends, in fact, and how they act is
consistent with what they say about their relationship.

It is now generally recognized that in Latin sources language expressing friendship, affection, and love typifies the discourse between poets
and the great, that such language is used when the two parties speak to
each other face to face, when they speak about each other to third parties, and when third parties speak about them, and that it is not subsid-
iary to some other representation of the relationship, but is itself the
preeminent expression of it.[17] Yet *we* do not ordinarily speak of friendship in discussing these relationships. There is one very practical reason
for eschewing the Latin terminology. "Friendship" is as elastic a concept
in Latin as it is in English, and it can and does cover such a range of ties
that it ceases to have much definitional force. But I believe that it is not
so much the looseness of the term that makes us uncomfortable with
it as an implication it is felt to carry. According to both Aristotle and
contemporary social scientists, friendship in the truest sense is a relationship which obtains between equals. Since poets like Horace and Tibullus
hardly seem to stand on a par with men like Maecenas and Messalla, we
find it difficult to think of them as truly friends.

But here again it is important to appreciate the level which poets
occupy in Roman society overall. Though far from equal to their great
friends in wealth or dignity, they too generally belong to a social and

economic upper class. They have had a similar education, engage in many of the same pursuits, and move in the same orbit.[18] Sharing a similar background, they hold similar values. This convergence of values is implicit in the theme of choosing worthy friends that is so frequently sounded in our sources. Friendship as Roman writers present it is based not so much on personal chemistry or economic parity as on ethical congruence: one chooses friends whose ideals and morals parallel one's own.[19] The importance of a common background in creating friendships is evident also in the patterns of association one sees. Whereas upper-class Romans often befriend poets or philosophers, they rarely establish such connections with those artists and intellectuals whose origins and formation diverge radically from their own: musicians, actors, painters, sculptors, and even the schoolmaster-scholars known as *grammatici*.

It is in terms of social and cultural affinities that poets can count as the equals of great men like Maecenas and Messalla and can practice the kind of reciprocity which we associate with friendship.[20] Thus a genuine ground of rapport does exist between them, and the affect-laden language which pervades their discourse is probably to be interpreted as an effort by both parties to neutralize those status differences which do still stand between them. In any society the category of "friend" often functions in opposition to ascriptive categories, contrasting self-selected relationships with those given by kinship or other institutional identities. In a Roman context, the emphasis on friendship serves to blunt the consciousness which each of the two parties has of belonging to a particular lineage, census-class, or order, and to refocus attention on particular pursuits and ideals which they share. Just as the emphasis on leisure defines an area in which poetry can be the legitimate concern of a gentleman, the emphasis on friendship defines an area in which differences between greater gentlemen and lesser gentlemen become inoperative.

The Pattern of Exchange

Although some aspects of the interaction between poet and protector have inevitably been noticed in the preceding discussion, the focus has been one-sided. In talking about leisure, livelihood, and class identity, I have concentrated on details which would clarify the position of the poet. It is time now to look more closely at the relationship the two parties have with each other, and here I take my cue from the sociologists who analyze relationships as structures of exchange. This approach may have one disadvantage, in that "exchange" for many of us is a strongly economic metaphor which might suggest that only material goods were in play. But we can forestall confusion by accepting the term in the sense in which many exchange analysts use it, to cover any interaction between parties. The possible ambiguity of the terminology is more than compensated by the usefulness of an approach that invites us to study a range of transactions which characterize the relationship between poets and their great friends.

What the great friends were able to contribute to the relationship has been discussed often, and naturally it is material benefits that have attracted the most attention. Monetary gifts are often alluded to and must have been important.[21] Yet the pattern of largesse is not easy to discern from the information we have. The most specific anecdotes are problematic in that they concern sums dispensed by the emperors.[22] While the emperor's behavior toward poets has much in common with that of other aristocrats, it is not identical. All his actions tend to take on quasi-public and exemplary meanings, even in areas of life which for other men would be considered private. The emperor is also wealthier than other members of his class and therefore is expected to practice generosity on a more grandiose scale. And because he is beset with a greater number and a greater variety of claims upon him than other men, he has more occasion to present gifts out of considerations other than personal friendship. (Hence perhaps it is in the context of imperial gifts that we find the most direct exchange of cash for poems.) For all these reasons we must be wary of inferring what ordinary magnates do from what the emperor does.

One thing which is clear, however, and worth emphasizing, is that no matter who bestows them, cash gifts come in the form of large lump sums rather than periodic installments.[23] Long-term subsidies in the form of a pension or allowance, though familiar from later epochs, seem foreign to the Roman literary milieu. No doubt one reason is that most Roman poets did not have to rely on others to finance their basic expenses, but probably value perceptions were even more important. Payment of a subsidy might have seemed to reduce the benefactor's munificence to the dimensions of a salary, and poets to the level of workers for hire.

Large, isolated gifts of money tend to be selective. They are not capriciously dispensed, but tied to particular occasions or given with particular ends in view. This is evident even in some of our testimonia, which generally reveal little about the circumstances under which gifts were made to poets. Yet it is clear, for example, that Ovid anticipated and received financial help when he was sent into exile (*Tr.* 4.5.7–8, *Pont.* 4.5.37–38). Martial received from Pliny funds offered under the category of travel money as he was preparing to retire from the capital to his native Spain (Pliny *Epist.* 3.21.2). A number of gifts from other benefactors probably came to Martial in the form of testamentary bequests. This inference is based not simply on the fact that in Roman society bequests are by far the most commonly mentioned vehicle for bestowing money on friends, but also on a legal privilege Martial is known to have acquired. The patent of triple paternity *(ius trium liberorum),* which had to be obtained from the emperor, was an excrescence from the Augustan marriage laws. It conferred on childless and even unmarried persons all the exemptions and prerogatives normally reserved to a married man who had fathered three children. Although most of its provisions were targeted to the senatorial class, it also held one great attraction for non-senators like Martial in that it removed a bar against accepting legacies from persons outside one's family. Martial's concern to obtain it points almost certainly to legacies as a recurring source of income.[24]

By contrast, one situation which may not have triggered regular disbursements was the actual presentation of verse to great friends. It is true that the emperors sometimes gave out large sums on such occasions, but these rewards usually involved persons with whom they had no continuing relationship. We have no record of such direct exchanges between poets and the other grandees they cultivated. Still, we have far too little information to insist that poems were never rewarded at the moment they were presented. That this was atypical seems indicated by Roman etiquette regarding generosity: to expunge a favor received by promptly doing a favor in return was held to be bad manners.[25] But it must be admitted that post-Augustan poets do speak at times as though they expected some cash return for what they wrote.[26] Perhaps the proprieties were changing, as they had already changed in another area of social relations when orators gained the right to demand fees for services.

Another benefit in the power of rich friends to bestow, and no less valuable than money, was property. Horace's poems have made the Sabine farm he received from Maecenas the most famous example, but it has parallels before and afterward, and in the Silver Age gifts of property loomed large in the fantasies that poets spun about their prospects.[27] Connections with the well-to-do also opened doors to positions and appointments that carried valuable emoluments. During the Republic, poets whose friends took up commands or governorships abroad were sometimes invited along to glean the harvest of rapine and administration.[28] The potential for gain dwindled as the emperors began to limit the initiative of legates and proconsuls and to regularize the boundaries of the empire. But new bureaucracies which took charge in the palace, the capital, the army, and the provinces greatly increased the number of possible openings. Most entailed long-term service, but there were some sinecures as well. Though senators still had minor positions to award, their more effective role now was to mediate appointments in the emperor's keeping.[29] By pulling other strings, the friends of poets could also help to arrange financially advantageous marriages. That prospect may not have appealed to every poet, but it was important to Ovid, who acquired his third wife through his connection with a prominent noble house (*Pont.* 1.2.136–139).

Gifts of cash, estates, emoluments, and dowries by no means constitute the totality of goods which the well-connected and the well-to-do were able to confer on poets they befriended. But among the benefits which at least some poets are known to have received, these were the most substantial. And since they have in common that, once conferred, they could not be readily withdrawn or terminated, they were valuable also in the sense that they left the recipient relatively independent of the giver. Not that literary independence was a specific objective of the generosity shown to poets; their benefits were no different from the benefits that non-literary friends received. Nevertheless, it is important to perceive that support was not directly keyed to literary output. In a later chapter we shall see that Roman grandees showed correspondingly little interest in prescribing what their poet friends should write.

Without dwelling on particular gifts, poets often emphasize the solidity and steadiness of the position to which their great friends have helped them. Thus, for example, the great friend is hailed as the "bulwark" or "fortress" (*praesidium*) of the poet's interests.[30] This metaphor lends itself to many applications, but in the context of social relationships it often points to economic assistance. A man who puts the finances of another on a solid footing protects him by guaranteeing his place in society.[31] Almost as common as the bulwark metaphor is the image of guardianship (*tutela*) associated with benefactors, which can likewise have an economic application.[32] Images that combine ideas of height and security—the friend as high citadel (*arx*) and as ridgepole or capstone (*columen*) of the poet's affairs—hint at the prestige the friendship confers as well as at its material rewards.[33] Imagery which poets apply to themselves also testifies to the benefits they have received. That is certainly what Ovid means by calling himself the "work" or "creation" *(opus)* of Sextus Pompeius, and it may be what is implied when in discourse with their great friends poets style themselves "your poet."[34] None of this language is meant to communicate anything specific about benefits conferred, but it does intimate that they were of decisive and lasting importance in the life of the recipient. And we have no reason to discount these testimonials as overblown.[35]

Important as material goods were, however, they did not outweigh the more intangible but everyday rewards which the leaders of society were in a position to bestow. The two aspects of the great friend's favor are commonly acknowledged in paired expressions extolling him as both the bulwark and the glory of his protégé. Though poets appropriate and vary them, these formulas are not peculiar to poetry, but echoes of the politesse which was practiced in real life.[36]

The glory which a protégé enjoyed was the reflected glory of identification with one of society's luminaries. Put more prosaically, it was visibility. Roman society was conservative and hierarchical, and offered few opportunities for a neophyte to rise by relying on his own resources. In addition to personal endowments, one needed the chrism of approbation by a social superior with prestige to lend. The loan of status was especially important for anyone who hoped to mix with the elite in the activities that filled their leisure.

Poets knew that in order to ply their art effectively they had to be taken up in this milieu, and that what launched their reputation in it was the reputation of their sponsors. Naturally the writers who most frankly convey their need of a piggyback are young beginners. The anonymous author of the *Panegyric of Messalla* tells the dedicatee that he yearns to "inscribe my name on your great deeds" (line 38) and is determined that "my book should not go without so great a name" (27). Still more direct is what the author of the *Encomium of Piso* says to the recipient of his poem: "I will rise higher if you open to me the road of fame, if you pull away my obscurity" (lines 223–224). But even more established poets confess that fame accrues from illustrious connections. Propertius, imagining what he will write as his relationship with Maecenas grows closer, anticipates consequences for his reputation as well: "Such is the glory you extend to me, Maecenas, and it is through your involvement that I too shall have been counted among your set" (3.9.59–60).[37] In another of his poems he calls Maecenas "my just glory in life and death" (2.1.74), as Vergil proclaims him to be "my ornament and, in fairness, chief portion of my fame" (*G.* 2.40).

Fame is the effect of various things the great friend does. In part it is simply the cachet which rubs off on all that the leaders of fashion elect to notice, whether they undertake a real commitment or not. Yet often they do perform specific services for the poets they take up. Because the great man almost always commands a large following, he can deliver a partisan audience for readings and generate interest in new books. By providing introductions to his peers, he can help to diffuse his protégé's reputation throughout other networks that set the tone of social life. Services of this sort will be considered more fully in the following chapter on poets in relation to groups.

If identification with prominent citizens met one obvious professional need by guaranteeing visibility, at a more profound level it had an impact on what poets wrote. The importance of understanding that influence is the one justification I can offer for subordinating discussion of the poems to discussion of their social background throughout this book. Again and again I will have occasion to comment on ways in which Roman poetry was affected by the absorption of poets in the life of the elite. But here at the outset let me insist that that influence, whose negative effects are all too patent, also had its positive side. Latin poets suffered a great handicap by comparison with the Greek poets from whom they had absorbed their convictions about poetry. Whereas much Greek poetry was incorporated into the civic and religious life of the city and other forms of song were fostered by the vitality of music in private life, the Roman environment gave relatively little stimulus to poetry. Music was no more a part of Roman education than physical culture; comedy and tragedy were in decline as forms of popular entertainment by the first century B.C.; and only at infrequent intervals was there any call for poetic texts in the celebration of religious ceremonies. Even the itinerant praise-singers of Greece found in the festival circuit they traveled a surer institutional niche than any poet of Rome. Involvement with the elite therefore offered Roman poets a source both of legitimation and of subject matter available almost nowhere else. It is in this sense that the great friend's expectations of his protégé must be recognized as a benefit of the same order as material support and publicity.

Poets allude to this benefit as they do to the others. They lap themselves in the authority of their friends when they claim to be writing at their behest, to be delivering on promises made to them, or to have garnered their critical approval.[38] Often the friend's role is described in far more fanciful terms: he is a font of creativity *(ingenium),* whom the poet entreats to assist, inspire, and strengthen him as he composes.[39] Such tropes persist even as the emperor comes to acquire a near monopoly over divinizing language during the principate. In the reign of the repressive and vainglorious Domitian, Statius still betrays no concern about saying to a lesser noble:

> I shall not call on Phoebus, though my strings be mute without him, nor on the nine Aonian goddesses together with Athena, nor on the gentle nurslings of Tegea or Dirce. You yourself, the subject of my song, come to me and confer fresh strength and heart . . . Let the thirsty bard be kept from the mystic Piplean font, let him be denied knowledge of Pirene: better in my eyes the water quaffed in copious draughts from your springs, as you essay prose in free measures or as your sweet eloquence is bound to art and heeds the laws of poetry . . . Spurn not the homage of a lesser lyre.
>
> Stat. *Silvae* 1.4.19–36

It is apparent that traditional imagery connecting creativity with superhuman intervention has been redeployed to interpret the influence of powerful but human friends. No doubt this trivializes the concept of inspiration, but Roman poets would not have resorted to such extravagant language if they were not trying to articulate a central fact of their experience. I will take up the issue again in Chapter 3. But one truth which the inspiration metaphor conveys is that, in the absence of any institutional stimulus, poets counted on the spoken and unspoken preferences of society friends to help them identify what was worth writing about.[40]

The benefits that prominent Romans could bestow were so immense that one cannot help wondering how poets could possibly reciprocate. Yet it can be taken as certain that alliances between them would not have developed so often if they did not benefit both parties. What the greater partner gained is difficult to perceive because he tends to be a silent partner. Maecenas, Messalla, and their peers left little or no testimony about their literary relationships, and consequently we have less to lead us than in the preceding pages.

But we can begin with a benefit that both ancients and moderns invariably credit poets with the power to bestow: the gift of poetic immortality. When Cicero championed the poet Archias' claim to Roman citizenship in the middle of the first century B.C., his closing argument was that only poets could fire the best efforts of statesmen like himself and satisfy "the need for the memory of our names not to pass away together with our lives but to encompass all future generations" (*Arch.* 29). The kind of poems that Cicero envisioned were epics that would portray in depth the "purposes and merits" *(consilia et virtutes)* of consuls and generals (*Arch.* 30). Yet it is a striking fact that Latin poets did not scale back their assurances of immortality even after grand forms like epic became the preserve of the imperial house and other men lost their eligibility for heroization. Early in the second century A.D. a verse compliment of Martial's elicited this reaction from the honorand: "Martial granted me the utmost that he could, intending more had he been able. And yet, what greater thing can be given to a man than glory and praise and immortality?" (Pliny *Epist.* 3.21.6). The poem to which Pliny refers (Mart. *Epigr.* 10.20) is an envoi of twenty-one lines written to accompany a selection of the epigrammatist's work. The immortal tribute amounts to five lines comparing Pliny's judicial eloquence with Cicero's. Pliny himself seems conscious of a discrepancy between convention and reality here, since he immediately adds, "You may say that what he wrote will not be everlasting: perhaps not, but Martial wrote as though it would be." And yet there is no sign that the shrunken compliments of the imperial period were any less coveted than the epic Cicero wanted from Archias. How could the promise of eternal glory, so disproportionate now to the poetry which was to produce it, have remained believable?

Perhaps the reason is that the elite were at bottom more concerned to promote their glory in the here and now than in time to come, and still found poetry effective in that dimension. Under the principate their opportunities to boost their status relative to one another were more narrowly circumscribed than they had been during the Republic. The emperor in one way or another controlled careers in the army, in oratory, and in jurisprudence, and these traditional avenues to distinction also took men less far than formerly. The lines of personal authority were more firmly set as well, now that civil strife no longer cast up intruders from the lower echelons of society to confuse them. The one arena in which the struggle for precedence went on as aggressively and even more aggressively than ever was social life. Here it was still possible to gain advantage over others by dominating fashion. And since verse remained the favorite dress for popular as well as serious literature, to be celebrated by poets had as much publicity potential as the cornering of artistic treasures, the building of palatial residences, the display of exotic pets, or innovations in cuisine or sex. The concern with publicity is the point at which the symbiosis between poets and the leaders of society seems most evident. While the latter to a great extent controlled the networks which set fashions and established reputations, they depended on their writer friends to give them a good press, just as writers depended on them for access to an audience.

Even if notables of the principate had enjoyed the option of being glorified in epic, no one poem, however grand, would have kept them in the public eye for very long. What they needed was serial publicity, whether the poems which advertised them were long or short, frivolous or serious. The slightness of a piece may actually have worked to advantage since the more topical it was, the more quickly it circulated. Content had so little importance that many poems say next to nothing about the persons they profess to honor. The compliment consists in the mere mention of their name, as poets were increasingly prone to claim. In an allocution that leads off one of the *Eclogues,* Vergil declines to celebrate the martial exploits of the dedicatee, but promises to ensconce him in pastoral verse with the assurance that "there is no page more pleasing to Apollo than one captioned with Varus' name" (*Ecl.* 6.11–12). Varus has not the least relevance to the rest of the poem, which proceeds without further reference to him. What he is told in the seven lines reserved to him is that a cameo appearance can be as glamorous as an entire poem in his honor. Later poets, taking the point as won, speak simply of "setting down," "inserting," or "weaving in" a complimentary mention in their books.[41]

The power to impart the plumes of chic if not immortality was a resource that Roman grandees clearly valued in poets. Yet it must also be obvious that they cannot have cultivated poets solely for publicity purposes. The majority of Latin poems we have, perhaps even a majority of occasional poems, do not compliment anybody, and no single individual is featured in more than a fraction of any given poet's oeuvre. Just as on the other side of the exchange, intangible services that poets provided were no less important than their poems. One young hopeful concludes a pitch for Messalla's friendship by promising:

> Not only will you be granted Pierian honors. For you I would venture over the rapacious waves, though the wintry sea be swollen by adverse winds; for you I would dare to stand alone before a mass of troops, or cast my puny self into the fire of Aetna. All that I am is yours.
>
>

Panegyricus Messallae 192–197

Though poets were rarely called on for sacrifices so flamboyant, the non-celebratory services they did provide can, like those tendered to Messalla, be roughly classified under the heading of companionship.

Aristotle observes that a lack of friends with whom to share one's life suits the rich even less than the poor (*Eth. Nic.* 8.5.3 1157b20–22), and his dictum certainly applies as much to Romans as to Greeks. The accumulation of companions by upper-class Romans can be seen as a form of consumption encouraged by the vast quantities of leisure at their disposal. The daily routine of one elderly consular happens to be described for us by Pliny in *Epistles* 3.1: he rises late, takes a three-mile stroll with any friends who may be visiting, and on his return makes himself comfortable with a book or more conversation. A long carriage ride follows during which the conversation continues, then a shorter walk. After that he sits down again with friends or closets himself with his muse until it is time to exercise and bathe. After the bath he and his guests have something light read to them as they wait for dinner, and dinner itself is accompanied by further readings and more conversation. The routine Pliny describes is for a day in the country rather than in Rome, and he also makes the point that his friend was retired and therefore entitled to his enviable leisure. Nevertheless, the consular's day must have had much in common with that of many senators and knights who had not opted for a career in the imperial service or in oratory. Even the pursuit of those careers could leave substantial blocs of time uncommitted. Consider the portrait of a senator and orator in his prime which is painted in the *Encomium of Piso*. Having borne due witness to Piso's mastery in court, the author passes to activities which engage him "when turbulent disputes have subsided during recess" (lines 85–86) or when "the furrowed brow of eloquence begins to pall" (139–140). Piso tosses off display orations in Greek and in Latin, writes poems, plays the lyre, practices sports, and demonstrates his skill in board games, trailed the while by troops of admirers (84–96, 137–208).

It is no accident that in their leisure hours both Piso and Pliny's consular friend were ringed by companions. To them and to their contemporaries, possession of an entourage was a visible sign of one's importance. As another magnate expresses it:

> To a spirit that is free and noble and born for upright pleasures, what can be sweeter than to see one's home always filled and bustling with a host of illustrious callers, and to know that this is due not to wealth or to childlessness or to the discharge of some offical function, but to oneself alone?
>
> Tac. *Dial.* 6.2

And if illustrious companions were not to be had, humbler ones would serve: the important thing was to be fortified by a retinue of some sort wherever one went.[42]

Yet it was not only for the sake of show that companions were recruited. The great man also turned to them for relief and amusement whenever he could extricate himself from the serious business of contending with peers and rivals. From at least the time of Terence, off-duty aristocrats had shown a notable predilection for the company of poets. Among countless opportunists who were only too eager to dedicate their attentions to the rich, poets took priority because they were seen as the stewards of a relatively scarce good. In the first place, they incarnated a value to which everyone paid at least lip service. Poetry was the foundation of Roman schooling, the one non-practical study with which every educated person had been thoroughly imbued. To associate with poets as an adult, therefore, signified a continuing commitment to a certain ideal of the liberal arts. Nor was the commitment strictly ceremonial. Poetry had an authentic place in the cultural experience of adults in that it offered (by way of epigram, elegy, lyric, and satire) the only literary means of exploring many realities of personal and social life. Finally, the company of poets was particularly welcome to those among the elite who themselves wrote verse. Not all who befriended poets had aspirations in that line, but many did, including the four most prominent angels of the Augustan Age: Maecenas, Messalla Corvinus, Asinius Pollio, and Augustus himself.[43] Such men both knew enough about technique to appreciate what professionals could achieve and were in a position to profit from their example and advice. Horace wrote his *Art of Poetry* for the instruction of a noble and his two school-age sons; part of what makes it so disappointing to a modern reader is that he sticks to discussing the conventional forms of poetry he assumed they would write rather than what he wrote himself. But poets were not recruited only to be consultants. Verse-writing was to some degree a sport in which the participants vied with or spelled one other, reciting and criticizing by turns.[44] It was an activity for which wealthy players wanted company, and they had no patience for any who were *less* competent than they.

The good offices that poets rendered as talismans of culture, interpreters of life and manners, and literary consultants or exercising-partners may seem paltry by comparison with the social rewards which their great friends could bestow on them. But that was not the calculation which would have presented itself to the great friend. The worth of a poet's services to him was measured not so much in relation to what he was able to offer in return as against services available from other would-be companions. In that perspective, poets looked very attractive. At any rate, that is the viewpoint which the author of the *Encomium of Piso* confidently imputes to Piso:

> Your whole house echoes with the varied arts of its visitants and a spirit of culture pervades all. You have no use for a crude, brute mass of clients that know only how to shove a path for you through crowds by dint of grim exertion. What you admire is talent in all its aspects.
>
> *Laus Pis.* 133–137

There is a catch not acknowledged here which draws ample comment elsewhere, however. Although poetic ability opened doors in Roman society, there was more to the task of literary friendship than the performance of literary services. Once welcomed into the great man's house and life, a poet was expected to attend on him as faithfully as any other companion, whether the day's agenda featured an outing or a literary reception, partying or moping. It is the open-endedness of their obligations to society friends that poets complain about, much more than about the nuisance of writing verse to order. Horace aired the difficulties of the situation in three of his literary epistles (*Epist.* 1.7, 1.17, and 1.18), and it was as exasperating as ever for Martial more than a century later. To a rich man attempting to claim a greater portion of his time he protests:

To hang by your door night and day is not the only way to be a friend—
besides, poets cannot afford that loss of time. By the rites of the Muses
which I practice, by all the gods, I swear I am your friend even if I do not
pay court to you.

Mart. Epigr. 10.58.11–14

But few poets achieved enough social independence to limit their services to great friends as Martial tried to do.

The idea of exchange both helps to organize our understanding of
Roman literary relationships and alerts us to nuances of behavior which
might otherwise go unnoticed. But it must be emphasized that the kind
of exchange I have described is only one of the processes that can connect players in the literary milieu. I have focused mainly on relationships
between poets who pursued no career but poetry and littérateurs with
superior social and economic resources at their disposal. To single out
these relationships for study is legitimate in that they are well documented and particularly problematic: we want to know what constraints
lie behind the work of major writers who become obligated to powerful benefactors.

But it would certainly be a mistake to imagine that all relationships
which poets established in Roman literary society can be reduced to a
single pattern of exchange. Even where actions seem similar, the relationships can be diverse. Ovid's behavior toward Messalla and his sons
resembles in several ways Horace's behavior toward Maecenas: he frequented their house, he wrote poems to celebrate events in their lives,
he claims to have looked to them for literary guidance, and he accepted
valuable gifts from them. Yet socially and economically he stood closer
to Messalla than Horace did to Maecenas, and it is unlikely that he and
Messalla enjoyed essentially the same kind of intercourse as Horace and
Maecenas. To take another example, for several months in 54 Cicero
busied himself in writing an epic on Julius Caesar's campaign in Britain.[45]
Although this project was anything but disinterested, the interests in play
would not be much illuminated by adducing as a parallel, say, the epic
which Archias proposed to write for Cicero. A similar point can be
made about the lyric lament which Tiberius composed on the death of
Augustus' adopted son Lucius in A.D. 2 (Suet. *Tib.* 70.2). Whatever literary debt Tiberius may have owed to models like Propertius' elegy for
Augustus' son-in-law Marcellus (3.18), he and Propertius had very
different social motivations for writing.

There are many cases, moreover, in which the exchange implicit in literary relationships is complicated by the fact that the poet is himself the party in control of superior social and economic resources. In his advice on poetry to the wealthy Pisos, Horace warns that possession of great riches can make it impossible for a poet to elicit honest criticism of his work (*Ars* 419–437). Little as he may have empathized with the plight of rich poets, Horace must have seen how their ranks were increasing. In the century after he wrote, the most celebrated poets were to be rich men of senatorial status: Pomponius Secundus, Seneca, Lucan, Silius Italicus, and Valerius Flaccus (not to mention the prince Germanicus and the emperor Nero). When such men took up poetry, they also established literary relationships which were as lively and necessary as those formed by poets who were less affluent. In Horace's own day, Asinius Pollio, who pioneered the formal poetry recital, was one of the city's richest and most distinguished men. Obviously the form of exchange in his relations with literary friends will have differed from that in Horace's.

Because the advantage in wealth and status was just as likely to lie on the side of the poet as with persons whom he befriended, the Roman literary milieu cannot usefully be differentiated into blocs, either of artists and patrons or of professionals and amateurs. Poetry was a communal pursuit in which the roles of creator, connoisseur, and supporter were constantly interchanged. Hence in utterances emanating from this milieu what is emphasized is not the division of roles but the commitment all have to the Muses. This projection of collegiality takes us back to a point made earlier, that Latin sources tend not to distinguish between poet and patron but speak of both alike as friends. Beyond intimating that the two parties have much in common economically, socially, and culturally, such language reflects the truth that in one sphere of activity they regard themselves as intimate collaborators.

Names and Representations

There are also other aspects of the relationship which are best appreciated when we take seriously its representation in our sources as simple friendship. In the first place, no matter what the balance of wealth and status between two parties, the nature of their commitment to each other was formally undefined. A friendship could have a definite beginning and reach a definite end, but what was tendered or withdrawn at those points was the possibility of intimacy, not the performance of specified actions. In contrast to many other relationships into which a Roman could enter (as parent, spouse, master, soldier, or maker of a contract, for example), friendship carried no legal consequences. It could not even be translated into a definite set of rights and duties which were morally if not legally prescribed.[46] Friends offered each other and expected in return many a gesture of regard, but they operated according to an almost completely situational ethic.

That friendship was essentially undefined is the reason it so easily became an open-ended commitment for the weaker partner, as we have seen. Often it is handy to speak of a "literary friendship" or a "literary relationship" when we mean that two persons were connected more by mutual interest in poetry than, say, by politics or regional loyalty. But these phrases create a false impression if they suggest that literary friends exercised their friendship only in relation to literary pursuits. Maecenas once had four poets keep him company on a slow journey to Brundisium, yet to judge by Horace's account in *Satires* 1.5 the subject of poetry did not arise during the entire trip. In a society in which so many of the principal actors enjoyed nearly unbounded leisure, friendship did not lend itself to compartmentalization.

Another point to be made about the attachment between Roman poets and their friends may seem and indeed is somewhat at odds with what has just been said. But however difficult it may have been for poets to cope with a great man's demands for companionship, in principle friendship was not exclusive. To be taken up by one man did not preclude having more or less similar attachments elsewhere. Admittedly a certain dissonance between reality and representation is apt to be heard in poetic discourse at this point. A society poet stands as much to gain as a love poet by declaring that there is one only to whom his troth is plighted. In some cases the protestations may even correspond to facts, since through choice or circumstance it was possible to remain bound within the orbit of one individual. While the ethic of friendship does not preclude having more than one such relationship, it does not necessitate it either. Yet any objective reading of Augustan poetry will show that most poets did cultivate more than one person at a time. Vergil in the *Eclogues* pays homage to both Varus and Pollio; Propertius' *Monobiblos* gives us glimpses of the poet consorting with a variety of young aristocrats including Gallus and Volcacius Tullus; Ovid in his exilic poems invokes the loyalty of at least a half dozen longtime friends. The structure of Roman society was such that a kind of networking effect was even the likely consequence of friendship, as we shall see in the next chapter.

Finally, let me try to correct a false impression I may have left about exclusivity in another sense. Having discussed only relationships in which poets are involved, I may seem to have been describing a phenomenon which is in some crucial sense literary. From a Roman perspective, however, the relationships between poets and their prominent friends looked no different from a mass of other relationships in upperclass society which presented subtly compounded elements of parity and inequality. All alike go by the name of friendship. We are certainly entitled to focus on a particular set of socio-literary interactions and to point out if we can the differentia which set them apart. But we cannot understand them properly without considering why the Romans did not categorize them separately in the way we now do. Nor should we set aside the language in which the Romans did speak of them until we have explored its implications. Broad as the concept of *amicitia* may be, there is no other term that more helpfully fixes the mentality governing relationships between Roman poets and the elite.

Though friendship was the name conventionally applied to attachments between socialites and the companions who shared their pastimes, the two parties were liable to be characterized in more invidious ways as well. Whether the affiliation was literary or otherwise, the more powerful friend could be dubbed the "king" *(rex)*, "master" or "lord" *(dominus)*, or *patronus*, while the weaker partner was sometimes likened to a client, a parasite or *scurra*, or a slave.[47] All these words occur far less often than the vocabulary of *amicitia*, however. I cannot provide a statistical survey, but my impression is that, taken all together, they would account for well under 20 percent of references to the kinds of attachments which are formed in Roman social life. Furthermore, some of them are clearly metaphors in this context. The terms at either end of the series— king, master, and slave—denote roles which in a literal sense can have no application to voluntary two-party relationships. "Parasite" is evidently metaphorical as well; transliterated from Greek, it did not take deep root as a Latin word and for most of its history clung to its theatrical associations as the type name for the flattering, wisecracking cadger of meals who inhabited the plots of comedy. All these words are loaded terms in the sense that their use tends to be strongly marked. This is especially noticeable when they are uttered by one of the principals in a relationship rather than by third parties: then either they are exploited to emphasize the deference of the one partner and the grandness of the other, or they are reprobated as being untrue or unwelcome representations of the relationship.

Like friendship language, these alternative representations offer clues to the position poets occupied in the life and leisure of the well-to-do. But what they give us are partial, negative, or distorted images. To style the dominant partner as "king" testifies to his wealth and power, of course, but it also draws attention to the gulf between him and his minions and to the multiplicity of the latter. The attentions of a dependent who is called a parasite or *scurra,* on the other hand, are stamped as being crass, insincere, self-serving, and grotesque. If the interaction between two persons is likened to that between master and slave, the effect is to exaggerate the dependence of the weaker partner or to disallow his actions any element of dignity or choice. One who is a "client" rather than a friend is conceived of as having access and responsibilities to an important person without enjoying the give-and-take of real intimacy. The term "patron" highlights the inequality of the parties or insinuates that the exchange between them rests not on spontaneous and unqualified affection but on some colder claim.

In modern criticism this last pair of terms has become not just an eccentric representation of the relationship between poets and their great friends, but the paradigm which defines it. The shift in usage and understanding warrants a closer look. Patron–client ties appear to have constituted one of the basic lines along which archaic Roman society was stratified, but by the time narrative accounts of the period become available, the origins of the relationship are so murky that much about it remains in dispute. Whatever the stages that preceded, however, in the first century B.C. and the century following the word *patronus* was current in three applications which account for the great bulk of its occurrences: it signified an orator who undertook to plead someone's case (and by an easy extension the proponent of any sort of verbal defense), the ex-master who had granted a slave his freedom, or a person of standing who had accepted an invitation to interest himself in the fortunes of a town or corporate body.[48] The senses of *cliens* roughly corresponded. It did not denote the freed slave, who was almost always termed a *libertus,* but it was applied both to the party on whose behalf a man pleaded a case and more generally (and more often) to any person beholden to a social superior for some service. In the plural it regularly denoted the people of a town or organization which had placed itself under a great man's protection, and also the sum total of dependents whom he had bound to himself individually.[49] Without trying to reduce these relationships to a uniform schema, one can observe in them an ethos which is not typical of intercourse between friends. For one thing, they are more frankly oriented toward the discharge of services than is friendship, in which sentiments are primary and services incidental. No Roman moralist would disallow to patronage the utilitarian element which is so often decried in discussions of friendship. Patronage also involves greater formality than friendship. Client bodies strike plaques recording their covenant with the patron and set up statues to honor him; individual clients at least present themselves at his open house and make an act of submission to his care; the slave who is freed during his master's lifetime undergoes a ceremony in the presence of a magistrate. There is also a temporal counterpart to the formality of the proceedings: the tie which freedmen and clients establish with their patron is supposed to last throughout his lifetime and then pass to his descendants. But friends are not expected to make such commitments to each other, much less to each other's descendants. Last and perhaps most important, the majority of those whom a patron recognizes as his clients do not enjoy an intimate, quotidian relationship with him, whereas his friends do. If on the evidence of terminology and practice two sorts of relationship can fairly be distinguished here, and if in sources of the classical period pairs like Horace and Maecenas or Tibullus and Messalla are regularly described as friends rather than as client and patron, and if their behavior also conforms to behavior elsewhere associated with friends rather than with patrons and clients, it seems proper to conclude that, by Roman standards of the classical period, "friends" were what they were and not "client" and "patron."

But the clanking of a sentence being drawn into defensive position cannot help but give rise to suspicions. Two qualifications on what I have said are best admitted outright. If in theory it was possible to distinguish friends from clients, in practice there must have been a certain range of persons in any great man's entourage about whom he would have been hard put to say whether they were lesser friends or particularly assiduous clients. (In this respect, our formula "friends and acquaintances" is similar: an acquaintance is not the same as a friend, but in particular cases the determination is not always easy to make.) An exchange that was badly balanced over time might also work to clientize a friend. And so it is not possible to draw a clear distinction in every case.

The other limit on what I have said is chronological. Although the categories of friendship and patronage are infrequently conflated in literary sources down to the end of the first century A.D., there are signs of a convergence after that. The transition can be neatly documented with the help of a passage from Horace. The first of the *Epodes* leads off with an allocution to Maecenas, whom Horace salutes in the idiom of his time as "friend" *(amicus)*. This evident familiarity earns the poet a rebuke from his commentator Porphyrio (who is thought to have written sometime in the third century): "It seems out of place for Horace to call himself the friend of Maecenas when he ought to say 'client.'" Porphyrio clearly conceives of the word "client" not as an eccentric or invidious substitute for "friend," but as the proper name for the relationship.[50] How this change of perception came about I am not able to chart or explain, but some other symptoms of it are worth noting. In inscriptions and literary sources from the second century on, *patronus* is used more and more often by persons of status as a respectful title for those of still higher status.[51] The word *dominus,* which is sometimes coupled with *patronus* in such contexts, shows a parallel development beginning even earlier: it too became an honorific. And perhaps the inflation which made these words into courtesy titles can in turn be related to the crystallization of a distinction between "lower statuses" *(humiliores)* and "higher statuses" *(honestiores)* toward the end of the second century. The pullulation of honorific formulas is in general a hallmark of Latin of the later empire.

To return now to the era which is the focus of this study, the fact that the Romans so rarely applied the language of patronage to literary relationships creates a certain quandary for the student of Latin literature. The Romans undeniably had a concept of patronage, and so if they did not invoke it in this context the reason should be, according to the present argument, that it did not appear to them to fit. Yet any modern who tries to explain how writers and artists gain access to needed resources thinks almost automatically in terms of patronage. How is this contradiction to be resolved?

One solution would be to accept the contradiction and affirm that patronage as we use the term is something different from what the Romans meant by it. The word itself carries an obvious trace of postclassical developments, since "patronage" does not come to us by way of the Latin nouns *patrocinium* or *patronatus* but was a new coinage of French. It is bound to have picked up some new connotations in the course of being applied in many settings over many centuries after the disintegration of Roman society. Under the circumstances there can be no objection to treating "patronage" as a term of art, whose meaning is tied not to any historical manifestation but only to the definition arbitrarily assigned to it. Of course this approach is not without difficulties. It is more confusing to operate with a concept for which the people we seek to study had a separate meaning of their own than with categories like "bureaucracy" which they did not have at all. And if we are not careful, the definition we assign may import an unconsidered and possibly unwanted bias into our observations. In many modern applications of the term "patronage," for example, the emphasis is on the provision of material benefits (such as jobs, land, loans, or subsidies), whereas Roman sources regularly emphasize services over material goods.[52] Still, careful definitions can be formulated, and it must be accepted that every analysis commits us to some degree of abstraction. Right from the start it is artificial to have isolated the social relations of Roman poets and to be discussing them as though they had some objective reality as a distinct set. There is no reason then to balk at using an ahistorical definition of patronage if that is what is needed to help us understand these relationships.

The real question is whether the idea as now understood retains enough power to illuminate them. Sociologists and to a lesser extent anthropologists appeal to patronage models in order to explain interactions in modern times between landowners and peasants in central Italy, the workings of political machines in large American cities, Mafia organizations, and national political parties in Latin America (to take but a few examples from a long list). Systems of patronage have often sprung up in times past as well and have played an important and acknowledged role, for example, in the medieval European church and in eighteenth-century England. Informally we give the word still wider application; at any rate, I have heard it claimed that patronage-like practices exist in universities and law firms. The personal relationships which are at the center of these many systems are extremely diverse. The status of the principals varies, relative both to each other and to the rest of society, and there are even greater variations in the nature of the goods exchanged and in the way they are exchanged. Patronage cannot lightly be defined in such a way as to exclude any of these relationships if it is to have the universality proper to an analytic tool. But the consequence has been a series of definitions so neutered and redundant that they have little power to organize the facts of any actual situation. I offer one illustration of the problem as it relates to my own inquiry. Among most patronage systems which have been studied, intimate, sustained contact between the principals is not common, and so that is not taken to be a defining feature of the relationship. Yet in my opinion at least, such contact is at the heart of the relationships between Roman poets and their great friends. A concept of which it is no part seems of doubtful relevance.

The vagueness of what is meant by patronage is apparent as soon as it is set beside a term like "slavery" or "the family." And perhaps the reason for this weakness can be identified. In most, perhaps all, situations to which the term is applied, patronage is relational in two senses at the same time. It both denotes a relationship between two actors and implicitly opposes their interaction to personal or group interactions within some non-particularistic, institutional framework (or frameworks). What has made patronage such a handy word is the second aspect: it repeatedly functions as a kind of shorthand or negative term for relations *not* mediated through some system one has in mind. Definitions of patronage, however, are invariably preoccupied with the first aspect. In the effort to reduce the multiplicity of its manifestations to some common essence, the at least equally important correlative aspect is left out of the formulation.

At this point I can neither affirm nor deny the relevance of a properly defined concept of patronage to the social relations of Latin poets. But given my uncertainty that the word carries a useful positive meaning, I have determined to get along without it. In lieu of a concept let me offer a summary. The relationships between poets and Roman magnates with which this chapter has been concerned have been arbitrarily isolated from a mass of virtually indistinguishable relationships in upperclass society. These attachments were not hereditary but voluntary on both sides; they were intimate and sustained but not necessarily exclusive. Although the two parties were unequal in wealth and status, both generally belonged to a socioeconomic upper class, and they shared a similar cultural background. They exchanged goods which partly overlap but are mostly different, and which are partly material and partly not.

But important as such individual relationships were to many Roman poets, they are not the only axis on which their position in society should be seen. In the next chapter we will look at certain groups of which they also had to take account.

2

Group Attachments

In spite of the homage paid to figures like Maecenas and Messalla, the true constant in Roman literary life was not the enlightened protector, but the plethora of amateurs and professionals and sympathizers and rivals who crowded in around any poetic endeavor. Not all poets secured or even sought the kind of intimate attachment which Horace established with Maecenas. And whether they formed such attachments or not, poets were always engaged on other fronts. Horace and Propertius invoke the solidarity of comrades who share their pursuits, just as Catullus and Ovid do. The *Eclogues* and the *Satires* project artistic feuds that mattered little to notables honored in the poems. This chapter is devoted to collectives with which poets were involved, within and beyond the house of the great friend.

The Society of the Great House

Any poet who gained the friendship of a great man inevitably became associated with others in his following. Friendship with the great meant joining in a round of activities which were for the most part communal, from morning levee to evening potation. The fellow-habitués of these occasions were therefore one of the groups with which a poet most readily came in contact. But their impact as a group is problematic.

In the first place, while poets often refer to others who happen to have entrée into the same house, they rarely express a sense of group identity with them. As far as possible, they present their association with the great man as though it were an exclusive, two-party relationship, with "my king" and "my bulwark" on one side, "your bard" on the other. I know of only two instances in which the protégés of a luminary with literary tastes are described as forming an organized group. That is the picture which Horace paints for the would-be gate-crasher in *Satires* 1.9.48–52, extolling Maecenas' entourage as a harmonious sodality in which everyone has his proper role. And that is how a nameless author envisions the company of talents assembled around Calpurnius Piso in the *Encomium of Piso,* lines 109–137. But in both cases the group aspect may have been exaggerated for purposes of argument. Horace is making the point that his pushy acquaintance would not fit in with everybody else, whereas Piso's encomiast is an outsider arguing that he would fit in perfectly.

It is not simply for reasons of self-aggrandizement that poets tend to skirt the communal features of their attachment to great houses. Although Latin has a well-developed vocabulary for the phenomena of friendship, words which denote a plurality of friends and imply a fellowship between them are poorly represented in it.[1] On this point, Latin usage runs counter to modern parlance, in which we habitually speak of the "circle" around men like Maecenas or Messalla. "Circle" is a metaphor, and carries connotations which require scrutiny. As I understand the word, it implies a center, some sort of closure or identity among the people forming the circle, and the existence of links which unite them with one another as well as with the principal whose friendship they share. Hardly a moment's reflection is needed to see the difficulty of applying these notions to Roman social relations.

There is to begin with the problem that, although we can single out scores of friends whom Horace and Ovid mention, we have much less information about the associates of Maecenas and Messalla. If we were to fill in the "circle of Maecenas" with known elements, it would look fairly vacant by comparison. But paradoxically, we would have almost as much trouble defining it if Maecenas' life were as richly documented as Cicero's or Pliny's. One hardly ever hears talk of a "circle of Cicero" because it is obvious that Cicero's contacts encompassed vast numbers of contemporaries at every level of society. Cicero would surely have rejected the idea of a Ciceronian circle, in fact, if it meant that his sphere of influence took in only a portion of the society at large. Like any Roman magnate, he strove to maximize his network of personal relations among peers as well as dependents, and he was prepared to invoke some sort of friendship with all but a handful of personal enemies.[2]

There is every reason to think that if we possessed the correspondence of Maecenas and Messalla, it would show that they had as diverse a set of associates, if not quite as many, as Cicero. Even from the modest information we do possess, it is apparent that their literary avocations led them into friendly intercourse with each other and with like-minded leaders of society. Asinius Pollio lent his presence to a poetic reading which Messalla staged for one of his own protégés. Messalla and Maecenas debated the merits of Vergilian lines, and Maecenas composed a dialogue in which the featured speakers included Messalla as well as himself, Horace, and Vergil.[3] Poets who were identified with one or another of these men often mixed freely with the others as well. Horace and Vergil advertised their ties not only to Maecenas but to Pollio, and Horace's network also took in Messalla and many others among Rome's elite. Ovid, like Horace, testifies to multiple contacts within the aristocracy: with Messalla and his sons, with Paullus Fabius Maximus and his wife Marcia, and with Sextus Pompeius, for example.[4] The thrust of Roman social life was centripetal, and the movements of the principal players intersect to such a degree that it is difficult if not impossible to identify independent sets or circles.

The circle metaphor skews our perception in another way by insinuating that the associates of Maecenas (or of anyone else) were also associated with one another. The information we have about Maecenas' connections comes down to a sketchy list of persons whose involvement with him happens to be documented. Not only does this list not fully represent his milieu, but it presents us with a set of relationships which in many cases remain quite obscure. We have no means of knowing when Maecenas became friends with the poet Domitius Marsus or the consular Marcus Lollius, for example, or how intimate the friendship was; the circumstances of his connection with Propertius are hardly less obscure. It would be fanciful to suppose that a tie about which we know next to nothing automatically constituted a ground of rapport with Maecenas' other friends, and in fact many considerations tell against that assumption. In the course of his travelogue satire (*Serm.* 1.5.51–70) about a trip with Maecenas, Horace strives to work up a little humor at the expense of a city sophisticate named Sarmentus. The reason Sarmentus happened to be included in the travel party, though Horace never mentions it, was undoubtedly that Sarmentus was a freedman of Maecenas. He was moreover a secretarial colleague of Horace himself, though Horace does not mention that fact either.[5] In *Satire* 2.8 a prosperous knight who entertained Maecenas at a dinner party is targeted for an even more mordant sketch. Certain silences of Horace also hint at fissures within the ranks of Maecenas' associates. Though over a long career he found occasion to mention some fourscore friends, he never says anything about Domitius Marsus or Melissus or Propertius, although all had ties with Maecenas and all enjoyed some reputation as poets.[6] We know that it was physically impossible for one important friend to have had any regular part in the social life which flourished around Maecenas. According to the Donatan *Life,* Vergil "very rarely" visited Rome, preferring to sojourn in Campania and Sicily.[7]

But what more than anything else should inspire doubt about the degree of solidarity among Maecenas' associates is that solidarity would be just the opposite of normal. To the picture of amity Horace paints in *Satire* 1.9, the interlocutor responds with astonishment: "That's some story: hardly believable" (line 52). His own experience of the world had led him to the very different assessment of Maecenas' society which he offers in lines 43–48 and 56–57. Though his sentiments are meant to be repugnant, they cannot be dismissed as naive. Horace himself testifies repeatedly to the division and spite which prevailed in the lower echelons of his milieu, and his testimony parallels that of many other sources.[8] Rather than exempt relations among Maecenas' protégés from normal patterns of intercourse, it makes more sense to suspect that Horace's picture in *Satire* 1.9 is greatly idealized.

The last problem with the circle metaphor has to do with the idea of a center. Important persons in Roman society certainly attracted other men whose movements came to revolve around their own. If that is all it means to talk about the "circle of Maecenas," the figure does no harm. But if it has an ideological overtone, implying that Maecenas was the source of projects, causes, and directions pursued by his writer friends, that proposition calls for challenge and ultimately rejection. I will discuss in the next chapter the extent to which the friends of poets guided the activity of their protégés. Here where our attention remains focused on externals, it will suffice to note that the raw facts of literary output give little hint of an organizing force at the center of either Maecenas' or Messalla's "circle."

To take the latter first, if Messalla encouraged a particular direction in poetry, the evidence of it should surface in the Tibullan Corpus. That this collection by at least four different hands has one element of consistency is undeniable: it is mostly made up of love poems in elegiac distichs.[9] Beyond that its unity is far to seek. The protagonists whose amours are recounted include a woman and two men, engaged with partners who are heterosexual and homosexual, upper-class and lower-class, singles and spouses. The poems relate both ostensibly autobiographical experiences and the love affairs of others. There are a couple of pieces in which a poet seems to be impersonating the lover whose passion is described. The poems exhibit different styles and levels of talent, and range from full-scale elegies of nearly a hundred lines to quatrains which are little more than epigrams. The contributors to this small collection evince greater diversity in their treatment of love than we find between the books of Tibullus, Propertius, and Ovid. Interspersed with the erotic pieces are three poems in honor of Messalla (including the longest piece in the collection) which have nothing to do with love.[10] The most that could be said about Messalla's influence is that he was particularly receptive to a variety of poetry which was then very much in vogue.

Virtually every genre known is represented in the output of poets associated with Maecenas: epic, elegy, lyric, epigram, satire, pastoral, didactic, tragedy, and comedy. The surviving works are of a singularly high quality, but just as remarkable is the commitment to experimentation they show. Propertius, Horace, and Vergil all modified their aims substantially during their poetic careers, and Horace changed direction several times. How these manifold enterprises would be related to impulses from Maecenas is not apparent. They seem to have nothing in common with his own endeavors in literature. As the author of dialogues and other works in prose, he was notorious for a style that was febrile and precious in the extreme. The fragments of his poetry show an unshaken allegiance to the meters and manner of Catullus, whom Maecenas' own protégés were rendering obsolete.[11]

If in spite of the considerable literary divergences among Maecenas and his friends we nevertheless consider him a kind of mentor, it is because his protégés do show a similar orientation on another front. Most of them are known to have written verse in praise of Augustus. This tendency seems all the more salient if they are compared with the writers of the Tibullan Corpus, none of whom makes the slightest nod toward Augustus. The last chapter of this book will deal with the question of political poetry at some length. But it should be observed right now that Maecenas' imprint on the politics of his poet friends may have been less forceful than the antithesis I have just drawn would make it seem. The meager testimony we have about Plotius Tucca, Melissus, and Fundanius does not indicate whether they celebrated Augustus or not. But since

Melissus and Fundanius won fame as comic poets, they are unlikely to have found much scope for panegyric.[12] Vergil, on the other hand, must have arrived at his Caesarean sympathies without benefit of Maecenas' tutelage. They are already explicit in the *Eclogues,* which preceded his relationship with Maecenas. Varius also was writing poetry with political overtones in the latter 40s. We do not know that it was pro-Caesarean, but we do know that it was anti-Antonian. Even Horace in some of his *Epodes* seems to have addressed political themes, though not from a partisan standpoint, before he became Maecenas' friend. In all these cases, Maecenas may have encouraged attitudes which his protégés expressed, but he did not have to inculcate them.

Moreover, the argument that Maecenas' politics do not necessarily explain the political sympathies of his poet friends applies in reverse to Messalla and the poets of the Tibullan Corpus. It is most improbable that the silence of these poets about Augustus represents the opinion of their protector. Messalla and his sons were thoroughly integrated into the Augustan establishment, receiving early consulships, priesthoods, and other preferments as well as great material benefits. In 2 B.C. it was Messalla who moved in the senate that Augustus be given the long-coveted title "Father of the Fatherland."

My contention in the preceding paragraphs has been that the people who gathered around men like Maecenas and Messalla did not form closely knit groups pursuing distinctive ideologies. Groups in some sense unquestionably did form around them, and it is likely that the composition of each varied according to the education, predilections, and social ambitions of the principal. But until evidence to the contrary can be produced, I would suggest that their importance for the poets who belonged to them was more practical than ideological. They served two purposes in particular.

First, they supplied a nucleus of partisans around whom the poets could begin to assemble a public following. If the ethos of the group was slanted toward literary affairs, a poet could count on receiving a certain amount of informed and sympathetic attention as he worked. I am not thinking here only of the reaction to public recitations (about which more will be said below), but also of earlier stages when poets circulated drafts of their poems to other members of the group or consulted them at trial readings. Even where literary interests did not dominate discourse, a writer friend of the great man was likely to receive a more attentive hearing from other insiders than from people outside. The effect of a sign from the top must have been to some extent automatic: Seneca the Elder provides a glimpse of a rhetor who campaigned for Maecenas' good will by working Vergilian set-pieces into his declamations (*Suas.* 3.4–5). Not that the great man's enthusiasms were signaled only in code. Maecenas and Messalla plumped aggressively for poets they had taken up, and Pliny can be seen doing the same for his protégés more than a century later.[13] In a fashion-sensitive society with few facilities for mass communication, word of mouth was one of the most effective means of generating fame, and the leaders of society controlled the networks through which word of mouth was spread. Aspiring poets made no secret of their expectation that the great man would use his connections to puff them and their books.[14]

The network of friends around an important person was also a good location in which to scout out prospective benefactors. Our sources throw only fitful light on efforts by poets to coopt the friends of friends, but there was nothing unusual about the process. Writers of letters of introduction often urge the recipients, not merely to assist the person being introduced, but to adopt him into their entourage.[15] In some cases we get glimpses of these lateral movements as they are under way. Through Cicero, the young jurist Trebatius obtained an appointment on Caesar's staff which developed into a closer relationship than the original tie with Cicero.[16] Horace through his friendship with Maecenas gained access to Augustus, who eventually invited him to accept a secretarial position in the palace; conversely, Augustus offered to introduce a rhetor whom he had taken up to an eminent practitioner in the field of oratory.[17] Pliny introduced two of his literary acquaintances to each other and later learned that they had become fast friends, a development that parallels the tie which formed between Statius and the best friend of one of his important friends.[18] Martial often asks recipients of his books to show them to third parties: some of these requests may be first steps toward establishing relations of his own with the ulterior friends.[19]

Lateral recruitment also operated in the opposite direction. Those who had penetrated the house of the great man were sometimes able to bring in friends from outside. Valerius Maximus takes credit for having channeled to the advantage of his associates some of the influence he had enjoyed with his late benefactor Sextus Pompeius. Vergil and Varius introduced Horace to Maecenas, and Horace, who includes a lesson on mutual support in his advice to would-be companions, illustrates one of the complications in a satiric sketch of a self-styled friend angling for an introduction to Maecenas.[20]

However, one pattern of recruitment we might have expected to observe turns out to be rare. Except for freedmen (for whom intra-family connections always remained important), literary figures do not on the whole inherit literary relationships or extend them from one member of a family to another. Along one path of descent, to be sure, the possibility of inherited literary connections was largely precluded. Of the 121 poets of whose verse some trace remains and who are catalogued in Appendix 1, only seven (Licinius Calvus, Seneca, Statius, Sulpicia, Augustus, Asinius Gallus, and the younger Pliny) are known to have had parents active in their own right as writers of either prose or verse. It is something of a stretch to assemble even as many as seven cases of literary succession. Asinius Gallus' only known qualification as a poet is a two-line lampoon, and Augustus' verse output was limited mostly to his youth. Nor can all of the seven be convincingly viewed as the issue of literary families. It is not quite certain that Sulpicia's father was the Servius Sulpicius attested as the author of erotic verse, and we can assign a literary lineage to Augustus and Pliny only if we count adoptive rather than natural parents. To identify poets whose offspring took up poetry is even harder than to find poets who had literary parents. Only three of the 121 are known to have had children who produced so much as a line of verse: Abronius Silo, Caesar (as the adoptive parent of Augustus), and Asinius Pollio. Poetry at Rome appears to have been almost always an individual calling rather than (as sometimes in Greece) a matter of family tradition, which is perhaps not surprising.

What *is* surprising is the dearth of evidence for persistent family involvement on the other side of the relationship, in the houses of those who took up poets. Horace, who invokes the names of from sixty to a hundred friends, only once gives any sure indication of being on familiar terms with both a father and a son (namely, Calpurnius Piso and his two sons, recipients of the *Art of Poetry*). Even in this case, the depth of the poet's relationship with the sons is doubtful, since the elder is spoken of in a way that suggests he is still a boy at school.[21] Only twice do fathers and sons turn up among the thirty to sixty people Ovid knows. The poet's career was launched, he says, by the good offices of Messalla Corvinus, and thirty years later he was still cultivating Messalla's sons Messalinus and Cotta. The other father-and-son pair to whom Ovid refers occupied a late and marginal place in his life. While in exile at Tomis, he praised the Thracian king Rhoemetalces for repelling raiders from across the Danube, and he later wrote to the king's son Cotys imploring continued vigilance against the barbarian. Tibullus has, among several poems directed to Messalla, one piece (2.5) about Messalla's son which celebrates his reception into the priestly College of Fifteen and presages that he will one day have a triumph to be sung about. But the poem does not show us a son in the process of acceding to his father's role as Tibullus' protector. Messalinus was only about sixteen years old at the time of his installation in the priesthood, and Tibullus died shortly afterward, before any relationship with him could mature. The poem is rather to be seen as a compliment to the father through the son.[22] Propertius alludes to adolescent sons and a young daughter in his elegy for the aristocratic matron Cornelia (4.11.63–67 and 85–96), but such references to survivors are conventional in funeral poetry and do not imply a personal acquaintance on the part of the poet.[23]

It is also uncommon to find poets extending their connections laterally within a family, to brothers of someone they have befriended. In only five instances does Horace's network appear to have drawn in brothers. In the *Satires* he expressed the hope that his poetry would win the approbation of Messalla and his brother and of the two Visci.[24] The remaining cases are less convincing. Late in his career Horace wrote the *Art of Poetry* for the benefit of Calpurnius Piso's two sons, yet it is clear (from line 366 on) that the poem is directed more to the older than the younger son. Horace also composed poems in honor of both Tiberius and his brother Drusus. But whereas Tiberius is complimented in several pieces, Drusus' name is featured only in connection with a military operation which Augustus had expressly requested Horace to write about.[25] Finally, Horace refers to two brothers in the book business who were responsible for marketing one of his verse collections. Writers sometimes established personal ties with the dealers who sold their books, and that may but need not be the case with Horace and the Sosii.[26]

Among Ovid's associates two sets of brothers can be discerned, and the poet gives us a closer view of his relationships with them than we usually get in the case of Horace's friendships. All the brothers are prominent citizens who Ovid hopes will exert their influence to ameliorate the rigor of his exile. M. Valerius Messalla Messalinus and M. Aurelius Cotta Maximus are the sons of Messalla Corvinus, but whereas Ovid

says he has enjoyed a close relationship with Cotta almost since the latter's birth (*Pont.* 2.3.69–82), he admits he has had only meager contact
with Messalinus (*Pont.* 1.7.15–26, 55–60). Messalinus also received only
half as many letters from Ovid as Cotta. A similar gradation is apparent
in Ovid's relationship with the brothers Pomponius, who held consul-
ates in A.D. 16 and 17. With Graecinus, to whom he wrote three letters,
he had a connection going back to the era of the *Amores.* To Graecinus'
younger brother Flaccus he wrote only one short letter asking him to
join Graecinus in working on Ovid's behalf.[27] Both in the case of Messalla's sons and of the brothers Pomponius, it is obvious that in normal
times Ovid maintained an active relationship with only one brother. Not
until the crisis of exile did he attempt to mobilize the weaker connection.

Evidence for Propertius' cultivation of sibling links is practically non-
existent. The only poem that even adverts to them is the elegy for Cornelia, which contains a compliment to Cornelia's consular brother and
lengthier passages about her two sons.[28] The latter at least were too
young (probably less than sixteen years old) for either brother to have
enjoyed any significant association with Propertius.[29]

Although the friends and family surrounding a great man seem to
have exerted a limited influence over poets artistically and socially, it
would be a mistake to leave the impression that their importance was
not real. In the competitive environment of the capital they constituted
a primary community in which a poet could find a base, and which in
turn served to identify him in the eyes of the outside world. Though far
from homogeneous, each following had a particularity deriving ultimately from the prestige of the man who held it together. This made
these groups better defined socially than any other group in which a
poet was likely to have a foothold.

It may be a misconception to think of them as life-long affiliations,
however. At least the most successful poets must have outgrown an identification with any one grouping as they kept connecting with friends
of friends and as they themselves came to be sought out by socialites
with literary leanings. In the self-portrait which Horace draws at the end
of his first book of *Epistles,* he boasts that he has gained favor, not only
with Maecenas or even Augustus, but with "*the foremost* of the city in
war and peace" (*Epist.* 1.20.23). The generalizing plural is meant to convey the breadth of his acquaintance in society.[30] He has in mind notables
like those he names in *Satire* 1.10.84–86, who stand outside Maecenas'

sphere of influence but whose literary support Horace nevertheless claims to enjoy. Martial indicates unmistakably that the multiplication of friends leads to the weakening of attachment to anyone in particular. In an epigram about a holiday on which friends were supposed to exchange presents, he calls to mind that "huge and oppressive host in which each person considers himself my first and special friend" (*Epigr.* 9.55.3–4), and decides it is safest to send no gift to anyone. That the epigram is a joke does not falsify the picture Martial gives of his manifold attachments.

Peers and Comrades

Often in Augustan poetry our attention is drawn to unnamed friends on whom the poets evidently look as peers and comrades. Propertius addresses himself to sympathetic observers throughout the cycle of elegies in which he rehearses his experience of love, and "Lygdamus" in the Tibullan Corpus is conscious of a comparable ring of onlookers.[31] Horace in his early satires claims to be practicing a method of self-improvement that will render him more amiable to his friends.[32] Vergil's early poems are at least in some measure *poésies à clef* in which personalities and attitudes of the poet's own milieu are teasingly compounded in the personae of harmonious rustics. These hovering comrades are not likely to have been identical with people met in the houses of great society friends. The *Eclogues* give no sign that Vergil has as yet made the acquaintance of Maecenas and his entourage (though the jousting rustics of the *Third Eclogue* do evidently claim to belong to Pollio's set). It is clear that Propertius' anonymous friends are primarily coevals. They doubtless include scions of the elite like Gallus, but represent a stratum wider than the personal following of any one man. Furthermore, among the friends of those poets who happen to supply a number of names and details, definite categories begin to emerge. Some of Vergil's earliest associates—Quintilius, Plotius Tucca, Alfenus Varus, and probably others—came from his home region of north Italy.[33] Among Horace's friends we can detect at least two who were resident in Athens when he was studying there and perhaps a half-dozen who in 43 rallied along with him to the cause of Brutus and the Liberators.[34] In Ovid's case, an important nexus of associations is centered on his wife.[35]

Such affiliations—friends from home, fellow-students, comrades-in-arms, age-mates, in-laws—are precisely those which articulate the background of well-documented personages like Cicero and Pliny. To dispose of them is a corollary and a mark, not just of free birth, but of gentility. Obviously they do not all loom equally large in the lives of all the Augustan poets, who range in status from the near-freedman Horace to the near-senator Ovid (to specify only major and extant talents). Among Horace's many friends, for example, the almost complete lack of ties to his home region of southeast Italy is surely no coincidence, but a consequence of his father's freedman origins (much more than of Horace's own upbringing in Rome). It is also at least in part a function of social gradation that Horace never evinces an inclination to marry, whereas Propertius is conscious of some pressure, and Ovid gets married three times. What is significant, however, is not that the poets do not show the full array of peer-connections one encounters at the highest levels of society, but that all poets identify with some set of friends whom they treat as equals. In proportion as they have or acquire such ties, they define themselves as free agents, capable of playing a direct role in literary and social life without the mediation of social superiors.[36]

Moreover, as poets acquire prestige (society and literary society being largely indistinguishable), the companions that they have or collect sometimes slip into the status of protégés. A poet can thus acquire an entourage of his own, made up of persons in any way beholden to him. Martial boasts during his celebrity years of exerting influence to obtain citizenship for several persons (*Epigr.* 3.95.11–12) and complains after his retirement of having to make time for calls from clients (*Epigr.* 12.68). Ovid says that once upon a time, before the disgrace which caused his friends to fall away, his "well-reputed but not assertive house could claim a good-sized crowd" (*Tr.* 1.9.17–18). Given his family's comfortable circumstances and his advantageous marriage, Ovid would probably have drawn a following even if he had not gained fame as a poet. Horace, however, had only poetry to commend him, and yet he too attracted followers and would-be clients. Some of them he turns into cartoon characters in the *Satires:* the supper-guests thrown over after he receives a last-minute invitation himself (*Serm.* 2.7.36–42), the finagler who wants him to get a document stamped by Maecenas (2.6.38–39), the leech who craves an opportunity to meet Maecenas (1.9). But he also shows us some adherents we must take more seriously. Among the recipients of the *Epistles* are a series of well-connected young men with literary yearnings—Aelius Lamia, Albinovanus Celsus, Calpurnius Piso, Julius Florus, Lollius Maximus, and Titius—whom Horace addresses in a tone that varies from the avuncular to the magisterial but that is distinctly not deferential.[37] Ovid, reminiscing about his career in poetry, recalls that "as I courted my elders, so the younger generation courted me" (*Tr.* 4.10.55). The young poets of the *Epistles* must represent the clique that gathered around Horace. Success in poetry meant success in capital society, and that enabled a poet to wield influence over others even in spite of status handicaps.

Collaborators in a Cultural Marketplace

One of the bonds that poets and their friends most often had in common is that the friends too were poets. Albinovanus Pedo, Cornelius Severus, Macer, Sabinus, and Tuticanus counted among Ovid's oldest and closest friends, as did Vergil, Varius, Fundanius, and Valgius Rufus among Horace's. Ponticus, the pseudonymous "Lynceus," and perhaps Bassus were poet friends of Propertius. In some cases this mutual concern with poetry simply deepened a relationship which was already grounded in some prior association. Poets who had discovered their vocation in the school of the *grammaticus,* for example, where the study and imitation of poetry was the bedrock of the curriculum, would have known some of their fellow-practitioners first as schoolmates.[38] Or if they did not encounter each other quite so early, their scholastic activities might converge at a later stage. Serious poetry was erudite poetry. Poets called themselves "the learned" *(docti)* and termed their work their "studies" *(studia);* some were engaged in formal study long after they had finished with conventional schooling.

Even apart from school, poets were apt to become friends through having been thrown together in circumstances in which poetry was not paramount. Roman elegy obviously presupposes a situation in which young men roistered around town together in pursuit of girlfriends and boyfriends. Some were poets and no doubt many more could turn a verse, but their camaraderie grew less out of poetry than out of participation in the same diversions. Epigrammatic poetry and satire similarly reflect a kind of fraternization which must have been primarily a function of social activity.

And yet Roman poets were also conscious of belonging to another milieu in which their identity was defined specifically by their work as artists. In this realm all poets could be seen as pursuing a common interest, and intimations of professional solidarity often surface in what they say about themselves. They talk of being united in a common band, of sharing a compact or fraternal tie, and of practicing common rites by virtue of which one poet may be styled the "colleague" of another.[39] Such language is figurative, of course, and plucked for the most part straight out of Greek sources. But it nevertheless points to a genuine reality, like the equally conventional imagery of inspiration considered in Chapter 1. Metaphors of collegiality appear to be substantiated in poems whose premise is that a group of poets have gathered to celebrate a particular occasion. In the sixth poem of book 4 Propertius rehearses the proceedings of a poetic confraternity. He (or a poetic "I") begins by offering sacrifice on behalf of the assembled company and continues with a hymn recalling Apollo's intervention in the battle of Actium; the bards then repair to a feast at which others take up the recital of Augustan glories. Ovid says that the occasion of *Tristia* 5.3 is Bacchus' feast day (the *Liberalia*, March 17th), on which before his exile he used to join his fellow poets at symposia devoted to the praises of the god. Do they miss him when they gather now? he wonders.

More telling still are the vignettes which poets draw of their literary environment. In the *Eclogues* Vergil presents it as a setting in which good poets confront bad poets and newcomers measure themselves against veterans.[40] Horace, especially in his early work, paints a picture in which prima donnas, hacks, dabblers, and reactionary pundits seem to far outnumber positive forces.[41] Ovid, by contrast, who was wrenched out of literary society after long years at the height of it, remembers it as a wonderland of collegiality. Of his youth he writes:

> I cherished and courted the poets of that time and believed that every living bard was a present god. The aged (Aemilius) Macer often read to me of birds and noxious snakes and useful plants. Often Propertius used to recite his loves, by virtue of the fraternal tie which linked us. Ponticus and Bassus, renowned in epic and iambic, were dear members of my group, and melodious Horace held our ears as he struck out elegant lines to the Ausonian lyre. Vergil I barely managed to behold, nor did the jealous fates grant time for friendship with Tibullus. He was your continuator, Gallus, as Propertius was to him, while I myself was fourth in order after these. And just as I courted my elders, so younger poets courted me, and my muse was not slow to win acclaim.
>
> Ov. *Tr.* 4.10.41–56

On the evidence of this statement, the young Ovid was able to hobnob with poets whom we think of as having very disparate alignments socially, and with all the city's major poets at that.

Professional activity inevitably drew poets into a community different from the company of their intimates and different from the society in which they moved as friends of the great. It was populated not only by poetic allies and rivals, but by other virtuosi who competed with poets for public notice plus all who wielded influence over conditions of performance or publicity. The organization of this milieu is not easy to describe, however. The poets have much less to say about it than they do about their relationships with individuals, and clues available in other sources are heterogeneous, very widely scattered, and often oblique. Although the circumstances of cultural production and communication at Rome are now being studied more closely than ever before, a comprehensive account is probably not yet ready to be written. At any rate, that is not what is tendered in the following discussion, which is ultimately concerned only with poets and poetry. After emphasizing the presence at Rome of a host of performers, entrepreneurs, tradesmen, and consultants who serviced the arts, I will explore some of the ways in which Roman poets interacted with this community.

We can begin with one of the most arresting facts of Roman literary history. Although many of the 121 poets who constitute our now-familiar list came from parts of the Roman world beyond Rome and even beyond Italy (scarcely any are known to have been natives of the capital), so far as we know not one attempted to pursue a literary career from any base but Rome. Latin poetry exhibits a far different demography from that of Greek poetry, which had flourished in several cities of the Hellenic world. For that matter, the literary geography differs from the situation in Italy itself at a later time, when in the Renaissance Italy was again a congeries of ministates. At any given date, moreover, the number of Latin poets active in Rome must have been much higher than we are ordinarily in a position to know. It was pure chance that Ovid in the last of his *Letters from Pontus* chose to reminisce about the poets of his generation: he enumerates thirty-one and adds that his list is incomplete.

The influx of poets is just one manifestation of Rome's cultural density. Though formally a city-state, by the Augustan period Rome was the capital of a de facto Italian nation and of a vast Mediterranean and European empire. This double status profoundly affected the city's size and makeup. As the Roman governing class was increasingly recruited from towns all over Italy, a senator or politically active knight had no alternative but to maintain homes both in Rome and in his native place. Whatever other properties he might acquire, it became normal to have two principal dwellings. And since the capital was the main arena in which members of the elite competed with one another, more was invested in one's Roman domicile than in residences elsewhere. Rome's status as an imperial capital further swelled its population. Not only was it a major terminus for the stream of slaves and captives produced by the advance of empire, but it drew ambassadors, collaborators, petitioners, opportunists, and visitors from territories around the Mediterranean and beyond. No other city of the West (or Near East) had ever before absorbed outsiders on a comparable scale. Along with people, wealth poured in: booty from defeated enemies and tribute and imposts levied in the provinces, to say nothing of more irregular exactions. Italy was exempt from tribute, yet many of its most wealthy families spent heavily in Rome because they resided there. Among them were the newly wealthy, who were eager to spend: with Augustus came to prominence the victors and the profiteers of twenty years of civil war.

These effects of Rome's political centrality combined to make it a center of culture as well. Certain areas of the arts had long benefited from huge expenditures on public entertainment by the state and its leading citizens, whose shows included dramatic and musical productions as well as the races and gladiatorial combats for which Rome was most renowned. By the Augustan period stage performances took up a minimum of fifty-six days every year. Plays from the classic repertory of comedy and tragedy seem to have had a waning appeal, but their place was taken by new forms of spectacle staged by artists of stunning abilities, whatever might be thought of their material. Building programs also contributed to Rome's gravity as a center of culture. By Horace's death in 8 B.C. the city had acquired three permanent theaters and three public libraries. Other amenities appeared with the construction of temples, colonnades, parks and gardens, and the city's first public baths. Many of the new structures were embellished with paintings and statuary by masters new and old.

Together these public initiatives imply the presence in Rome of a sizable body of professionals who delivered or maintained the cultural services which the state and its leaders underwrote. A still larger body existed to serve the wants of private consumers. Education at this period was not publicly subsidized and did not extend to the mass of the population. Yet at Rome schools proliferated, set up by sole practitioners who offered instruction in grammar and literature or advanced training in rhetoric. Suetonius in his sketch of the teaching professions (*Gr.* 3.4) says that at times more than twenty schools of grammar were operating in the city. *Grammatici* and rhetoricians also played a role in the cultural life of adults. The former enjoyed some authority as scholars and literary critics, while rhetoricians discovered that the declamatory exercises they staged in order to attract a clientele fascinated even connoisseurs of oratory. Other tastes called for other specialists. Builders of stately homes needed architects; art collectors sought connections with artisans and dealers; book collectors depended on trained copyists, booksellers, and library expertise.

I have argued that an infrastructure of the arts developed in reaction to the pooling of wealth and power in Rome, the consumerism of an oversized elite, and the cosmopolitan mix of the city's inhabitants. All these conditions existed by the middle of the first century B.C., and they provide the surest grounds for thinking that Rome then was already the lure for practitioners of the arts that many indicators show it to be later. Representatives of the specialties I have mentioned do in fact make sporadic appearances in sources for the period. In Cicero's letters alone we catch glimpses of performers, architects, *grammatici,* scholars, art brokers, booksellers, and copyists. But their activities are documented in scant detail. Rarely were these experts the social peers of the Romans to whom they catered (more often than not, indeed, they were of servile or foreign extraction), and thus they tend to attract slight notice from Roman writers.

References to booksellers, for example, are so infrequent that some scholars consider the book trade in Rome to have been still underdeveloped at the middle of the first century. But this inference overlooks some implications of the admittedly meager evidence we have. Strabo says (13.1.54 [609]) that after Sulla shipped the remnants of Aristotle's library from Athens to Rome in 84, unidentified booksellers managed to smuggle in copyists who transcribed the books. If the details of this story are accurate, they imply not only that Rome had more than one shop interested in marketing this arcane set of texts, but that booksellers already took an aggressive role in acquiring manuscripts. Augustus believed (and Suetonius seems to concur) that a purported speech of Julius Caesar from the year 62 was not an authorized publication but originated in a careless transcription taken down on the spot by shorthand copyists.[42] Here too it is difficult not to recognize a venture organized by booksellers. They are also the parties most likely to have transcribed and disseminated the abortive oration which Cicero actually uttered in defense of Milo, as opposed to the improved version of it which Cicero later released himself (Asconius *in Mil.* p. 42.2–4 Clark). Finally, when in the 40s Caesar instructed the scholar Varro to create for Rome "the largest possible library of Greek and Latin books" (Suet. *Jul.* 44.2), he expected him to acquire the necessary stock by purchase *(comparare)*. Mass purchasing implies an organized market for books, whether the desired copies exist already or are yet to be made. While Greek books could be obtained elsewhere, there was no market but Rome in which Varro could have expected to buy Latin books.

My point is that evidence about the book trade in the first century B.C. indicates that booksellers were already functioning just as they did in the next century when information is more abundant. This argument cannot be further elaborated here, nor is there space to extend the argument to other activities in support of arts and letters. But Rome's position as a hub of Mediterranean culture can be provisionally asserted on the testimony of three Greeks who knew it at first hand. Describing how Aristotle's books got into circulation, Strabo complains that the enterprising booksellers took no pains to produce accurate copies, and he adds that the same thing happens "both here"—that is, in Rome—"and in Alexandria." To all appearances he is setting Rome on a level with the greatest book mart of antiquity. By the 30s if not before, the Sicilian Diodorus had emigrated to Rome in order to compose a history of the known world. After pointing out what formidable requirements he faced in terms of bibliography, he extols "the lavish supply at Rome of materials pertinent to my present undertaking."[43] The last comment probably dates from the earlier half of the century. Philodemus observes that Athens' prestige as a center of philosophy has caused many intellectuals to take up residence there, whereas others have come to "lordly cities and lands like Alexandria and Rome, partly from constraint and partly for their great advantages."[44]

Latin poets were one element in the infusion of talent that made Rome a literary and artistic capital. Like other purveyors of the arts, what they sought was in the first instance proximity to an elite which would support their work. The resources for which they looked to Rome's great men have been described in Chapter 1. But poets also gained something from the presence in Rome both of other poets and of that contingent of largely foreign professionals whose activities paralleled or intersected with their own. Two particular effects of this environment were that it heightened their sense of professional identity and diversified their opportunities of reaching a public.

The theater probably impinged more powerfully on the consciousness of Latin poets than any other institution. They had once had a vital association with the stage, since it was as playwrights that they first found a niche at Rome. Down to the end of the second century B.C. most poets were still known primarily as writers of comedy or tragedy. Even in the late first century as scripts became vehicles for exhibitions of music and dance, verse remained the medium in which they were composed, and poets were needed to supply them. Not many of these writers are known; what they did was viewed as hackwork. But some distinguished poets like Lucan and Statius turned out libretti along with serious verse, and poems of others, like Vergil and Ovid, were adapted to the stage by performers.[45] For the great majority of poets with no personal stake in it, the theater remained an ideological reference point as the embodiment par excellence of public poetry. Horace in his literary epistles returns again and again to the subject of drama, though he never went so far as to write one. The advantage had shifted from author to performer and literary quality now contributed little to the effect of what was played, but by every indication the theater of Horace's day was in robust health. The actors, musicians, and dancers dominating it were brilliant performers who enjoyed high visibility. And their example struck a nerve in that it posed the very issues of fame, remuneration, and artistry with which poets were preoccupied in their own right. The most prominent character in Horace's first book of *Satires* is a popular singer who serves as a foil for two of the ten pieces and is featured in three more.[46] Martial too had the example of entertainers much in mind. During a career standstill that had resulted in a temporary withdrawal from Rome, he jested that he was planning his comeback as a musical artiste instead of a poet.[47]

It has often been observed that Latin poets of the mid-first century B.C. refined their technique by the careful study of Greek and especially Hellenistic poetry. Yet they surely owed part of their new professionalism to the influence of standards which they saw realized in the arts of their own place and time. I have argued that one obvious stimulus came from the stage. Public oratory provided another. Rhetorical performances could outshine theatrical performances, and the methods of orators and rhetors were even more applicable to poetry than the methods of actors and musicians. *Grammatici,* whose expertise was not directed to performance, nevertheless possessed a knowledge of poetry that could be relevant; Horace describes them as literary gatekeepers with whom a poet had to reckon (*Epist.* 1.19.39–40). In each of these directions the poets faced seasoned practitioners whose aims overlapped with their own and against whom they tried to define themselves.

If a consciousness of professional identity develops partly as distinctions are perceived between one's own work and another's, it is consolidated as professionals of a given sort establish contact with one another. Rome contained a sufficient number of Latin poets to admit of contacts and was so laid out as to encourage them. In Chapter 1 I emphasized the social activity centered in Rome's great houses; now let me correct the balance by recalling that Romans also passed a good deal of time outdoors. In addition to the grounds of the Forum and the Field of Mars in which they had long been accustomed to circulate or loiter, the city of the Augustan period offered them a variety of more organized spaces to congregate in—arcades, baths, parks, and the new imperial plazas, for example. Summing up a relationship with one of his literary friends, Ovid writes that the two of them were always seen together in "the plazas, every portico, the High Street, and the curving theaters with serried places" (*Pont.* 2.4.19–20).[48] The literarily minded might run into one another in the city's bookshops and public libraries.[49]

Encounters between poets at Rome did not occur entirely at random. Not that we should discount the factor of chance: acquaintances belonging to the leisure class of a Mediterranean city-state had a much greater probability of meeting by accident in the city center than would middle-class acquaintances in a modern northern city. But it is clear that, just as theatrical artists were organized in professional associations, so too poets had some form of association available to them. Almost everything else about the corporation of poets is disputed, however, and I see no way a discussion of it can be made substantive and brief at the same time.

So far as internal relations are concerned, the character of the poets' association emerges most clearly in two poems of Martial. *Epigrams* 3.20 is a pen-portrait of a friend who, like Martial, is a Spaniard, a poet, and a pet of the well-to-do. The poem simply describes the friend's daily round: how he toils over various literary projects, or "relaxing in the poets' school, tells witty stories tinged with Attic grace" (lines 8–9), or dawdles at midday in the porticoes of the Field of Mars, or visits one of the baths, or takes up an invitation from a rich friend. *Schola,* the Greek word Martial uses for the poets' school, had by this period acquired a sub-sense roughly equivalent to "lounge." It indicated an area in a public place, whether under a roof or out in the open, which was physically set off from ordinary traffic so that people could collect at leisure there. Just after Martial's time the term becomes very common in inscriptions which have to do with associations or guilds *(collegia)*. It refers to the meeting place or club room in which the guild members held their sacrifices and banquets, and which were often located in public buildings. A kind of club or lounge would fit the requirements of the place to which Martial's friend repairs when he has finished writing for the day. And no other meaning can be assigned to the phrase "school of the poets" that makes any sense in terms of what we know about Roman life.

The same phrase recurs in a similar context in a piece which Martial addresses to a fictitious associate:

> Recently you boasted, Mancinus, that a friend made you a gift of two hundred thousand. Four days ago, as we were chatting in the poets' school, you said that a cloak which cost ten thousand was a present from Pompulla, and you swore that Caelia and Bassa had given you two gemstones of aquamarine and a genuine sardonyx set within a triple band. In the theater yesterday you said . . . What awful wrong have we your colleagues done to you? Have pity, sadist, and at last shut up. Or if your tongue must wag, at some point pick a subject we'd be glad to hear about.
>
> Mart. *Epigr.* 4.61

Here too, the "poets' school" is evidently a downtown spot where a poet can drop in and find colleagues *(sodales)* to chat with. It does not appear to be the center of organized literary activity, and socially the tone could not be called upscale. Mancinus and his envious colleagues clearly do not rank among the independently wealthy. All this is consistent with what is known about the ambience of *collegia*. They are formed by colleagues in occupations which lack the status of liberal professions, and they are organized more for social purposes than for the exercise of professional functions.

If Martial's poems strongly suggest that poets had a *collegium* at the end of the first century A.D., other sources indicate that a *collegium* was functioning much earlier. According to Festus' dictionary, the senate authorized poets and actors to hold meetings in a temple on the Aventine Hill at the end of the third century B.C.[50] An anecdote told by

Valerius Maximus verifies that a "college of poets" was active in the early first century B.C.[51] And to bridge the gap between that time and Martial's time, an inscription has brought to light a functionary of freedman status whose term of service as "master of the poet-scribes" (or perhaps "master of the scribes and poets") implies the existence of a *collegium* during the middle or latter half of the first century B.C.[52] This string of testimonia does not of course establish that the same institution was functioning without interruption from the third century B.C. to the late first century A.D. But it does require us to believe that at almost any period poets in Rome would have found some sort of collective in which they could associate with other poets.

If the poets' association operated like other *collegia*—and the Surus inscription appears to have brought it into a closer alignment than ever before—anyone who met the working definition of *poeta* would have been eligible for adlection.[53] The only other kinds of requirement that get mentioned in the sources are that a member had to pay his association's assessments and abide by its charter. Status within *collegia,* which were as hierarchically-minded as other Roman bodies, was typically based on seniority. Collegial activity appears to have been taken up with business meetings, sacrifices, and feasts.

It is widely believed that the poets' guild departed from this pattern in also promoting professional activity. Specifically, the guild is thought to have sponsored poetic competitions. If that is so, it might have been in a position to wield some influence over literary fashion. The possibility requires examination even if the result must be inconclusive.

Belief in collegial tourneys is based almost entirely on a passage in the *Satires* in which Horace takes a sideswipe at some fustian verses by a contemporary:

> While bloated Alpinus whacks out Memnon and demolishes the muddled well-spring of the Rhine, I amuse myself with this kind of verse, which is not meant to resound from temple walls in contests before Tarpa the judge, or to come back over and over for viewing in the theaters.
>
> Hor. Serm. 1.10.36–39

That these lines have something to do with the poets' guild has been deduced from the fact that Horace envisions organized recitations by poets in a temple. For organized activity by poets, a poets' guild would seem to be a plausible organizing body, and temples are known as apt locales for the meetings of *collegia.* The only item of extrinsic information that does anything to tie down these a priori considerations comes from Horace's ancient commentators, who suggest (among other possibilities) that the temple meant is the "Temple of the Muses." Modern scholars have in their turn equated that shrine with the Temple of Hercules of the Muses on the Field of Mars, since we know of no other temple in Rome devoted to the Muses.[54] But in fact we are dealing with a mirage. The scholiasts had no better information than we do about Horace's temple scene, and without the pseudo-intelligence which they supply, there is nothing to connect the Temple of Hercules of the Muses with a *collegium poetarum,* or with poets in any capacity.[55]

This is not to say that Horace cannot possibly be alluding to a meeting of the poets' guild, only that it would be a mistake to think that such an inference is supported by evidence outside of Horace. And his meaning here is far from transparent. Within the argument of the poem the passage forms a transition, a situation in which Horace is notorious for blurring and abruptly recombining ideas. One thing which is not clear is whether he envisions that poems of any type (the epics of "Alpinus" just mentioned, for example, or something like his own satires) could be recited in the temple, or whether he is describing tryouts organized solely to select pieces for the stage. By the end of the passage and in the lines immediately following he is definitely talking about dramatic poetry, and everything else we know about Maecius Tarpa connects him with the stage.[56] If Horace is in fact referring to auditions of dramatic pieces, that would mean that the temple competitions involved only a fraction of the poetry written at Rome, whether they were sponsored by the poets' guild or not. And the impact would be all the more limited if only scripts actually intended for production were entered in the competitions. Many more tragedies and comedies were written than were ever meant to be played.[57]

On the other hand, if what Horace envisages is not a dramatic audition but a forum open to poets of any stripe, he may not be talking about a true contest at all. While the phrase "vying before Tarpa the judge" is appropriate to describe a formal competition, the words can also signify much less. Poets repeatedly talk in terms of "vying" *(certare)* with other poets and of "winning" *(vincere* or *superare)* and of being crowned without meaning that their rivalry takes the form of an actual match. The word "judge" *(iudex)* in literary contexts often means no more than "critic" or "connoisseur."[58] Hence Horace could be referring to public recitations before a noted critic, but not to prize competitions.

That interpretation would be consistent with the witness of all other sources, which mention prizes for poetry only in connection with dramatic performances and with the festivals founded by Nero and Domitian during the latter half of the first century A.D.[59]

The one thing about the temple scene which no one disputes is that it shows us poets reciting their works before a critic in a quasi-public setting around 35 B.C. Like the shadow images of literary actuality projected in Vergil's *Eclogues* and like Ovid's celebrations of the community of all who serve the Muses, it helps articulate a corporate side of poetic activity which complemented the Augustan poets' intense awareness of their individual role. For all its ambiguities, it clearly bears on the present argument about professional consciousness. What the temple scene contributes to our knowledge of the poets' association remains entirely unclear, however.

If the poets' association did not sponsor contests of poetry, we may well wonder what function it was left to fill. As a literary phenomenon it can hardly be said to engross the attention of our sources, which yield only a half-dozen names of possible members.[60] Nothing we know about other *collegia* suggests an atmosphere of chic, and some poets who belonged to the aristocracy or who had easy entrée with the aristocracy might not have cared to do their lounging in a club chaired by a freedman like Surus. Nor have we reason to suppose that the association offered a stimulating creative environment. New poets committed to a particular ideal of poetry probably had less hope of making a dent on senior members of the guild than of swaying anyone else. What, then, was its appeal?

The pattern of activity in other *collegia* combined with the silence of the literary record makes it most unlikely that the guild concerned itself with substantive issues about poetry. To imagine it in the likeness of some Italian academy of the Renaissance or the Pléiade or the Bloomsbury group would be a gross anachronism. We must envision its aims as mainly sociable, and we must beware of assuming that its sociability was hobbled by discrepancies of status. Knights and senators mixed easily almost everywhere, and even freedmen consorted with their betters in many public situations. No doubt a gathering in the poets' *collegium* operated according to a different etiquette than a reception in a Roman salon, but if a knight like Martial felt at ease in both settings, there is no reason to think that most of his poetic confreres would not have. One anecdote about the poets' guild (Val. Max. 3.7.11) features a Roman senator in attendance. And while all members may not have been on a par socially or professionally, they had in common that poetry was their occupation and that it united them vis-à-vis practitioners of other arts. Finally, if during the Augustan period the *collegium* still retained an active connection with the theater—if, say, it was primarily members of the guild who were supplying the scripts and libretti for current productions—their club may have been one of the more lively and interesting spots in the capital. We have no way to gauge what proportion of the poets known to us belonged to it; the tendency has been to believe that the number was small. But the prospects membership held out would have included socialization, occupational solidarity, and perhaps a little glamour.

Apart from the professional tempering that contact with other poets and performers imparted, Latin poets benefited from Rome's abundant resources as a center of arts and letters. One of the main reasons they migrated to the capital in such numbers was that it offered them their best hope, indeed their only hope, of reaching an audience. They launched their reputations first of all by word of mouth through the networks of their great friends, who of course resided in the capital. But they also found in Rome a unique array of other media through which to publicize themselves and their work. I have already touched on some of these. A few poets became known to theater audiences when their works were staged or were adapted for musical or balletic performances, and poets had both formal and informal opportunities of making themselves known to one another. Beginning in Horace's time they acknowledge that they depend on booksellers to get their works into the hands of a reading public; our most copious informant about Roman bookshops, in fact, is the poet Martial, who names four of the dealers handling his oeuvre.[61] Poems circulated non-commercially as well. Cicero's correspondence shows that copies of books including books of poetry were often passed back and forth among their owners. With the opening of Rome's first public libraries in the 30s and 20s poets gained another means of reaching a public, and thereafter they are anxious to be represented in the public collections.[62] Even the competition among schools of grammar in Rome could work to their advantage if, as sometimes happened, schoolteachers took the work of contemporary poets into their curriculum. As Horace noted, the ordinary public is apt to cherish an unshakable loyalty to poets read in youth.[63]

The most effective method poets found of reaching an audience was the formal recitation, however. According to Seneca the Elder, who was close enough to events to count as a reliable informant, this practice was launched by the one-time Caesarean partisan Asinius Pollio, who after retiring from political and military activity in 39 B.C. became "the first of all Romans to recite his works to an invited general audience" (*Cont.* 4 *pr.* 2).[64] Definite as Seneca's testimony sounds, it has caused some perplexity because recitation per se was certainly not an innovation of Pollio's. The words *recitare* and *legere* cover any sort of reading aloud, and they come up in reference to a number of situations well before the 30s. In some households, slaves trained as readers were brought out during dinner to read material which the master had chosen to entertain or edify family and guests. There were writers who tried out material of their own by reciting it informally to another writer or to one or more of their confidants. Others declaimed their verse to bystanders in the Forum and other public places. The temple scene to which Horace adverts in the *Satires* evidently represents yet a different venue, and the list of situations could be extended further. But there is one form of recitation which first becomes evident in the late first century B.C. and which, though it never superseded the others, attracted far more comment than any other. This must be the fashion which Seneca traced to Pollio. These recitations were organized and staged by the poets themselves, with help as needed from socialites who acted as sponsors. (Prose writers too gave recitations, but I will not be concerned with them here.) They took place in a semi-private setting like the sponsor's mansion, but before large crowds recruited through invitations and advance publicity. The program featured the work of a single poet who also starred as the reader of his poems.[65]

The ostensible motive for any reading, formal or informal, was to test critical reaction to work in progress. But since the verse read before formal gatherings had received all but the last lacquer, it should be obvious that the true purpose of recitation was more to garner publicity than to aid composition. Viewed in this light, Pollio's innovation can be recognized as another case of adaptation to a surrounding culture. Recitations brought poets before a live audience which could bestow on them something analogous to the acclaim which musicians, dancers, and actors already enjoyed. As dramatic readers of their poems they recovered a public role they had lost when the stage fell under the sway of other artists. And there may have been a more specific stimulus behind the fashion of recitation. It arose at the same time that rhetoricians in

Rome were turning the training exercise of declamation into a bravura art form. Declaimers proved that it was possible to hold the attention of a cultured audience by the sheer display of verbal wit and dexterity. These were as much the stock in trade of poets as of rhetoricians, and it is probably no coincidence that recitations of poetry were introduced by a poet who was a connoisseur of declamation.

In the presence of an audience, Roman poets acquired a role as performers which undoubtedly had consequences for the way they conceived of and wrote poetry. But what is more relevant from the perspective of this chapter is the way the situation of performance was structured so as to couple the interests of performers and sponsors. More than either theatrical artists or rhetors, reciters of poetry needed social backing in order to draw an audience. The only segment of the populace that could be expected to attend recitations were the members of an educated leisure class who already had many other pursuits and entertainments to choose from. Sponsored readings elevated the importance of poetry by identifying it as something in which society's most important people invested their time. What sponsors gained was a new proprietary interest and a new forum for self-advertisement. By institutionalizing recitation, they finally co-opted poetry as a manifestation of Roman excellence and integrated it into existing patterns of social activity. Although there had been aristocrats who took a personal interest in poetry and poets from almost the earliest age of Latin literature, it was not until the late first century B.C. that the leaders of society came to regard poetry as a class responsibility.[66] That was when they opened their houses for public readings and in effect made attention to poets one form of attendance on themselves. Often, to be sure, and more often as time went on, the readings they sponsored were apt to be their own. But the new fashion also created literary roles which did not call for literary ability by directing the spotlight to the enthusiasts and impresarios who discovered talent.

At the same time, the poets maintained remarkable control over the circumstances of recitation. They chose what to read and decided when it was ready: at these sessions they were not called upon to perform impromptu. It was they who issued invitations to a reading.[67] While they were performing, no competing activity was permitted to distract the audience. Formal readings were not given in the course of dinner gatherings, nor, like shows in theaters, did they have to withstand attractions put on concurrently elsewhere. We never hear of a case in which one poet even had to share the dais with another poet (unless Quint. 8.3.31 implies a joint recitation).

At a public recitation, the poet's audience would not consist only of his own partisans and the friends of his host. Literary mavens of the upper class and fellow poets could also be expected to attend, as well as a variety of hustlers and hangers-on whose objectives were social rather than literary.[68] There were risks in facing an audience like this: the reading could be disrupted by wits or even sabotaged by a luminary's huffy withdrawal.[69] But the prestige of the sponsor combined with the fact that the reciter himself momentarily enjoyed the status of a public figure meant that the audience would hew to Roman norms of good behavior: at least there would be no threat from persons without social standing. Furthermore, so far as one can tell, recitations were rarely if ever followed by open criticism of the work that was presented. As often, Pliny's remarks are revealing. He makes clear that the sort of audience reaction he anticipates at his own recitations is not so much specific comment as body language expressing enjoyment or ennui (*Epist.* 5.3.9–10 and 7.17.11). And he inveighs against listeners who withhold approval from a reciter, exhorting "praise him whether he stands lower or higher or on the same level as yourself" (*Epist.* 6.17.4).[70]

No other cultural institution did as much as recitation to mobilize a community around the cause of poetry. But the partisans it mobilized have practically nothing in common with that community of professionals in the arts to whom I have tried to link poets throughout this discussion. In fact, whatever inspiration poets may have owed to the example of performers and declaimers, it is hard to resist an impression that recitations caught on in upper-class society partly because they were insulated from the conditions of vulgar performance.

This impression is strengthened by the glimpses we are given of audiences which turned out for them. Among dozens of allusions to poetic recitations, not a single one reveals a *grammaticus* present (unless the grammarian who is said by Sen. *Suas.* 2.13 to have detected a solecism by Cornelius Severus pounced during a recitation). And yet these schoolmaster-scholars frequently doubled as literary critics, and they were solidly entrenched at Rome by the time that recitations came into vogue.[71] It is just as rare to find mention of Greek literati attending recitations, though many more of them than *grammatici* can be identified at Rome, especially during the years of Augustus' rule.[72] Nor are Greeks visible among the poets who gave readings, though among declaimers performing at Rome there is no lack of Greeks.

Whether the invisibility of *grammatici* and Greek literati at recitations expresses the objective reality that they were not there or a second-order anomaly that their presence was habitually overlooked by our informants is unclear. In either case, though, we must recognize that the recitation setting as we observe it is a peculiarly bounded domain within the totality of Roman literary culture. Moreover, the same constraint (or the same filter) evidently determines another representation of the literary milieu. Latin poets in many genres invoke the names of friends, and in some genres they invoke them by the score. Yet rarely do either Greeks or *grammatici* turn up among the friends whom poets name even when they are known to have had such ties.[73]

It would surely be unwarranted to conclude that because certain personalities are missing from vignettes of recitation and are rarely complimented in Latin poetry, they played no role in literary life. We have only to turn to different sorts of evidence for them to come to light. Greek writers of the Augustan period, for example, advertise relationships with many members of the Roman elite (including in some cases the same people associated with Latin poets), and similarly Suetonius' monograph shows us *grammatici* engaged in lively intercourse with Roman magnates. What *is* true is that the evidence we have typically offers a series of isolated and limited perspectives.

This brings me to the observation with which I wish to conclude this discussion of the Roman cultural milieu. I have argued that Latin poets were conscious of belonging to a wider community in Rome consisting of other poets, performers, and specialists in the arts. At certain points the interests of the various professions overlapped or conflicted. Yet it does not appear that they were integrated into a community in any strict sense of the word. Furthermore, different poets must have had very different levels of involvement with other players. To cite but two kinds of interaction, some poets obviously had closer dealings with booksellers or with actors than others. Perhaps the milieu is best imagined as a marketplace of services and resources of which poets were always conscious but not constantly in need. In any case, the presence of other professionals is the final component we must have in mind as we proceed to consider how poets dealt with the expectations of their audience.

3

Requests and Pressure

Roman poets ate and drank and recreated with their society friends, and what they wrote they aired first in coteries over which the same friends presided. Whatever influences those luminaries might exert, the poets stood within their aura. The influence on poetry of agents other than the poets themselves is the subject of this chapter. I begin with cases in which poets and other writers received suggestions about what to write, analyzing how those suggestions were broached, what relationships they imply, and what constraints they set upon the writer. As evidence of the way poets responded to direction, I then discuss four kinds of poetry which in different ways were stimulated by the demands of friends: panegyrical epic, occasional verse, satire, and elegy.

Literary Requests

Poets were not the only recipients of literary requests. The importunity of friends was one of the working conditions to which all writers at Rome were subject, and it is best studied as a uniform phenomenon. Prefatory passages of Latin works frequently contain assertions that the author is writing at the behest of another, usually of the person to whom he presents the finished work. These claims are so common that one might be tempted to discount them as mere posturing, if they did not also turn up in contexts where it would be senseless to think that the writer is misrepresenting the situation. In private correspondence Cicero and Pliny often mention that they have been asked to write something.[1] We also have letters in which they address such requests to someone else.[2] There are even a couple of letters in which the appeals Cicero received from his correspondents are preserved just as they were made to him.³

Examples are more than adequate to illustrate the range of language that figures in requests. The vocabulary is extensive, but the words can be grouped in clusters along a line running from the deferential to the peremptory. One cluster consists of words like "ask" or "inquire" that put the request in the form of a question (*interrogare, quaerere, requirere*). Several words have a suppliant tone comparable to "entreat" in English (*agere, petere, rogare, sollicitare*), though the tone is rarely so abject as in our words "beg" and "plead." Sometimes a more insistent verb like "urge" or "wish" is chosen, emphasizing the will or desire of the person who asks. The most common members of this group are *hortari* and its compounds, but *desiderare, invitare, suadere, velle,* and *cupere* are also found. More insistent still are words which mean "suggest" and "prompt" (*monere* and its compounds). And the last group is made up of a large variety of expressions all of which usually convey some nuance of command or pressure (*cogere, exigere, (ef)flagitare, iubere, extundere, elicere, incitare, iniungere, instare, poscere, postulare, praecipere, urgere*). Of course there is nothing about any of these word groups that makes them peculiar to literary requests. Romans use exactly the same vocabulary when they solicit appointments, political support, and the like as when they solicit poems and books.

It is the last cluster of words that catches attention because they are the most forceful and because they strike the note we expect to hear in reference to work written to order. But to judge from actual usage, neither this group nor any other seems reserved to particular categories of requests. A petitioner can draw on a wide range of words, from polite to imperious, within the same request, combining and shifting terms according to the rhetorical temperature of what is at any moment being said. Cicero constantly varies his language in a letter urging that his career would make an ideal subject for a monograph by the historian Lucceius:

> I tried to raise this matter (*haec agere*) with you face to face . . . I am fired with an incredible desire that (*cupiditas ut*) my name be lit up and celebrated in your writings . . . The caliber of your work attracted and indeed inflamed me to desire (*cupere*) that my career be consigned to a book of yours . . . I could not let myself fail to suggest that (*admonere ut*) you might consider . . . I realize how shamelessly I am acting first in imposing on you (*imponere tibi*) so large a task and second in expecting you (*postulare ut*)

to display me to advantage . . . Again and again I ask *(rogare ut)* that you give full-dress treatment . . . If I induce *(adducere)* you to undertake this project . . . I am not worried about seeming to curry favor by a touch of flattery so much as making very clear that I want *(velle)* to be lauded and celebrated by you and no one else . . . If I do not prevail upon you *(a te impetrare)*, then I will have to . . . But I ask *(rogare)* that you do it . . . You may be wondering why I seek this of you *(a te petere)* so earnestly right now . . .

Cic. *Fam.* 5.12 = 22 SB

Pliny bids similarly for a featured appearance in the history of his friend Tacitus:

I foresee that your history will be immortal and so I desire *(cupere)* all the more to be included in it . . . Ought I not to wish *(optare)* that my accomplishments find a writer and herald like yourself? . . . It will be pleasant to me if *(iucundum mihi si)* you embellish my performance with your talent and your testimony . . . All this you will make more widely known, finer, grander—though I do not insist that *(exigere ut)* you stretch the dimensions of what I did.

Pliny *Epist.* 7.33

The vocabulary can be equally varied when the reference is to requests received. The elder Seneca dedicated his reminiscences of declamation to his sons and wrote in the preface that he was responding to their wishes:

You demand *(exigere)* a thing that is more pleasant for me than easy, for you bid me *(iubere)* to record my impressions of the declaimers who flourished in my lifetime . . . Since you enjoin *(iubere)* it, I will see what I can do . . . Of course, you are not questioning me about *(interrogare)* the men you yourselves have heard, but about those who did not survive to your own day. Let what you wish for *(velle)* be done . . . Hence all the more gladly will I do what you demand *(exigere)*.

Sen. *Cont.* 1 pr. 1–10

Finally, let us look at a pair of responses which not only illustrate the language in which literary requests are acknowledged, but also invite us to interpret the rhetorical motivations for it. In the course of the year 54 B.C. Cicero had two projects suggested to him by his brother. Quintus wanted him to compose an epic in honor of Caesar's British campaign, and he appears also to have asked for verse of a more descriptive sort about Britain, for which Quintus proposed to supply raw material. Writing to his brother apropos of the first project, Cicero says both "you bid me *(iubere)* to finish the poem I have begun" (3.6[8].3 = 26 SB), and "you urge me *(hortari)* to wind up the epic" (3.7[9].6 = 27 SB).[4] His brother's request for descriptive verse he acknowledged in a series of letters, as follows:

> I will send you the verses which you ask for *(rogare,* 2.16[15].4 = 20 SB) . . . I will write what you ask for *(rogare)* if I have any time (3.1.11 = 21 SB) . . . As for the verses you want *(velle)* composed by me for you, the effort is behindhand (3.4.4 = 24 SB) . . . You ask *(rogare)* me about the verse-writing: it is unbelievable how short of time I am, and to tell the truth, I don't feel drawn to the subject you want *(velle)* versified . . . Can it be that you are really appealing to *(petere)* me when you have excelled everyone at that kind of stylish description? (3.5.4 = 25 SB).

As with preceding examples, each of the two requests is expressed in more than one way. And yet even though the same person originated both, it is clear that overall the epic for Caesar is presented as something more urgent than the descriptive piece. The verbs *hortari* and *iubere* are appreciably stronger than the verbs of willing and asking that refer to the latter. Cicero's choice of language may be explained in several ways, but one fact that is relevant is that whereas he did complete the epic, he never showed much interest in Quintus' other proposal and finally begged off. His phraseology may therefore reflect more his own perception of the relative importance of the two poems than the terms in which Quintus broached them.

In any case, the Latin words used to indicate requests make a somewhat different impression in the context of particular passages than they do in the abstract. If they are considered simply as elements of a lexical set, they suggest differing degrees of urgency and might therefore be thought to correspond to different real-life situations. But in fact, the vocabulary shows a clear tendency to coalesce. A writer who makes more than one reference to a request is free to describe it in any number of ways. That is the first point that needs to be made.

On the other hand, Cicero's response to Quintus' proposals shows that the representation of one request may certainly vary from that of another. When stronger language is used, what explains it? An obvious hypothesis would be to suppose that differences of tone are related to status differences between the initiator and the recipient of a request, or between one recipient and another. But while this answer surely holds good in some cases, our sampling of passages suggests that it is not the universal or perhaps even the usual explanation. In the case of Quintus' two requests, the status ratio between the brothers obviously remains the same, yet the projects have differing degrees of urgency. Symmetry between status and tone is belied also in another pair of requests that our sample provides. Cicero's letter to Lucceius is as prostrate a solicitation as there is, yet the man who wrote it was a consular, while the man who received it had recently tried and failed to obtain the consulate. But in a comparable bid for a historian's attention, Pliny speaks almost briskly to his friend Tacitus, who had a three-year advantage in seniority over him. Not only do these letters not evince the status differences between the maker and the recipient of a request, they practically give a reverse impression of them.

For a last illustration, we may compare what Quintilian says about the promptings behind his treatise on oratory. He was originally urged to write by persons whom he describes in the proem to book I as "applying friendly insistence" *(familiariter postulare)*, "demanding" *(exigere)*, and "imposing a burden" *(onus imponere)*. One of these friends was a well-connected young senator of praetorian rank, Vitorius Marcellus, to whom the work is dedicated. Having set to work and completed a draft, Quintilian then intended to hold back from publishing until he could revise, but he was persuaded to release his manuscript to the bookseller Trypho, as he explains in a letter to Trypho that prefaces the treatise. In view of his name and occupation, the bookseller is probably a freedman. Yet Quintilian speaks of being pressured by Trypho in much the same way as he speaks of being pressured by his aristocratic friends: "With daily scolding you have importuned *(efflagitare)* me to begin releasing my books for publication."[5]

In all the passages cited, it is clear that motives other than the writer's sense of status vis-à-vis his interlocutor must govern the choice of language. A far more important consideration is whether a request is spoken of from the viewpoint of its author or of its recipient. The number of texts that present a request in its author's own words is relatively limited, but the examples we do have suggest that the initiator is rarely the party who resorts to strong language. Exceptions tend to confirm the norm. As we have seen, Cicero half apologizes for using the words *imponere* and *postulare* in his letter to Lucceius and says he realizes he is acting shamelessly. And his discomfort with forceful expression is even more apparent in an overture to Varro. After waiting fruitlessly to receive an installment of Varro's *On the Latin Language* which was supposed to carry a dedication to him, Cicero turned around and dedicated his own four books of *Academics* to Varro. He sent them on with a cover letter in which he tried to jog Varro to reciprocate:

> Even though the populace does not press for an entertainment it has been promised unless someone puts them up to it, yet I am impelled by my eagerness for what you have promised to prompt *(admonere)* though not to press *(flagitare)* you. I have however sent you four prompters *(admonitores)* somewhat deficient in tact. You know the brashness of the younger Academy: well, my emissaries are from the very thick of it. I fear perhaps they may press *(flagitare)* you, but for my part, I just told them to ask *(rogare)*.
>
> Cic. *Fam.* 9.8.1 = 254 SB

Normally it is the recipient of a request who talks of being commanded, compelled, or dunned. Furthermore, although such statements are ostensibly directed to the author of the request, they are not private utterances. They usually occur in prefatory passages incorporated into the finished work and circulated with it to the reading public. What is said must therefore be interpreted as the result of a three-cornered calculation which aims to influence the general reader as well as the particular interlocutor to whom the writer addresses himself, and which seeks to display the writer in a favorable light in the eyes of both. In this situation a writer may have several reasons to emphasize the force with which a request is pressed.

Often what he wants to project is not so much the idea that he is being constrained as that he is being pestered. That is obviously the tone of the elder Seneca, who purports to feel increasingly harassed about having to record anecdotes of declamation for his sons. Parts of his preface to book 1 of the *Controversies* have already been quoted; he opens book 7 with the words "Day after day you hound *(instare)* me," and the tenth and last book begins "You have no reason to pester me *(molesti esse)* further . . . I don't mind telling you, this project is now a bore." Horace adopts the same manner with Maecenas to whom he says, apropos of being urged to finish the *Epodes,* "You're killing me with your constant queries" ("occidis saepe rogando," *Epodes* 14.5). The note of vexation is also evident in Hirtius' letter to Balbus agreeing to supply a narrative that was needed to wrap up the account of Caesar's Gallic campaigns:

> Under pressure of unremitting appeals from you, Balbus, I have taken on a most difficult assignment, as it seemed that my daily refusals would not

get me excused on grounds of difficulty but only stuck with imputations of laziness.

BGal. 8 pr. 1

A request that must be met because it is constantly reiterated implies some intimacy between the two parties: it can be posed again and again only because they are regularly in contact. Far from weakening a writer's credit, this kind of pressure enhances it. Not only is he seen to have impressive connections, but he is revealed as someone whom it is worth the effort of coaxing.

If a writer hesitates to go so far as to talk of being nagged, he can still substitute words like "bid" *(iubere)* and "enjoin" *(exigere)* in reference to an overture that was communicated to him in terms of "asking" *(rogare)* or "entreating" *(petere).*[6] To a Roman reader, these words too imply the existence of a personal tie rather than the use of constraint. Commands belong to the sphere of personal obligations, and in upper-class society, questions of obligation arise more often in the context of relations between friends than in relationships of authority.

But the wish to draw attention to society connections is not the only motive that might lead a writer to emphasize or exaggerate the urgency of a request. If it takes a strenuous intervention to elicit the desired work, the burden imposed on the author must be formidable. The great man would not exert himself for something commonplace. In this way, the urgency of a request advertises the value of the work. Furthermore, it deepens the debt of the recipient when the finished work is presented to him. If the writer has fulfilled a charge which he was pressed to undertake, then he has a stronger claim on the good will of the recipient than if he had simply presented his work unasked. When Atticus asked Cicero for copies of some recent orations, Cicero sent him a whole year's worth, saying that if Atticus didn't enjoy reading them, "you shouldn't have called for *(poscere)* them, since *I* was not foisting myself on *you*" (*Att.* 2.1.3 = 21 SB). Any reminder of past encouragement contains a tacit assertion of privileged standing: the writer draws a line between his own service and the uninvited attentions of other men. When he flourishes words like *iubere* and *flagitare,* he draws the line more boldly. Finally, by emphasizing the role of an abettor, the author throws on to him some of the responsibility for what is written, reminding him that he has an obligation both to help promote the work and to protect the writer if it should provoke controversy. Cicero again provides an illustration. Dedicating his treatise *The Orator* to Brutus, he declares:

> I call you to witness that I made bold to write this at your request and under protest. Any criticism I want us both to share in, so that if I prove unable to meet this challenge, you will bear the blame for having laid on me an undue burden and I the blame for having accepted it.
>
> Cic. *Orat.* 35

By themselves, then, the words in which a literary request is phrased or described reveal little about its background despite the variety of nuances they seem to bear. Words with disparate connotations are so often combined that the situations to which they point become impossible to pin down. More important, a request is not usually heard in the form in which it was uttered. Instead it is reported by the writer of a work, who has many incentives to substitute wording of his own. What is significant about literary prompting is not the way it is indicated, but the fact that it occurs so often.

Literature is a pursuit that Romans shared with friends as they shared many other cultural, political, and economic activities. That Roman writers were importuned by friends was a natural result of the time they spent in one another's company. We should expect the motives behind these requests to vary, reflecting vicissitudes in the course of individual friendships as well as relationships with different sorts of friends. The motive of a literary request is mentioned in a sufficient number of cases, either by the proposer or by the writer, to show that they did vary widely.

For certain public figures the objective was self-advertisement. They sought compositions in prose or verse which would magnify their importance before contemporaries and if possible make it known to posterity. In his *Defense of Archias,* Cicero speaks as though that was the normal use a great man would find for a poet, at least a poet like Archias. But he tried to foist a similar project onto his friend Lucceius, who was a prose historian of his own social class. Pliny wanted Tacitus to write into his history of the Domitianic era an episode that highlighted Pliny. But in general a writer's friends settled for less, asking only that he contrive to mention their names in whatever work he had in hand. After Cicero began to invent contemporary settings for his dialogues, he heard from several friends who sought to be cast in speaking parts.[7] A friend of Pliny's asked to be sent a letter just to ensure that he would have a niche in the collected correspondence Pliny would one day publish (*Epist.* 9.11.1). Poets were approached by acquaintances who requested verses addressed personally to them.[8]

Writers who are so blatantly manipulated might seem to have the look of mere retainers, kept on hand for the sake of the literary services they could provide. But that does not appear to be the way in which the Romans themselves interpreted these relationships. At any rate, that is not how they spoke of them. What the tribute-seeker claims to value is not publicity per se, but the public testimonial from a friend whose judgment he prizes. Cicero wanted Lucceius to tell his story not only because Lucceius had talent, but also because he possessed "the authority of a most distinguished and respected citizen whose contributions in moments of extreme political emergency are well known and highly approved." That meant that his portrait of Cicero would stand as the "solemn witness of a great and distinguished gentleman" (*Fam.* 5.12.7 = 22 SB). Caelius asked Cicero to dedicate a philosophical work to him for a similar reason: "Among your many works I hope that one may endure to transmit the memory of our friendship even to posterity" (Cic. *Fam.* 8.3.3 = 79 SB). This habit of interpreting public gestures as effusions of esteem will be familiar from another area of Roman life. Bequests were similarly treated as testimonials which embodied the testator's ultimate and quantified evaluation of his friends. No doubt the recipients were also glad to get the cash. We are not bound to believe that it was the implicit character judgment that weighed most heavily in the case of either wills or literary favors. But both kinds of action were clearly drawn into the same interpretive scheme, and that is because both have a common origin in the sphere of personal friendship. Literary favors, like bequests, were perceived above all as transactions between friends.

Even the most self-serving suggestions, therefore, could be brought forward in the name of friendship. And literary requests were made in other circumstances which reflect even more distinctly the ethic of friendship. Sometimes a writer is called on because he has information or expertise which one of his friends happens to need. Cicero composed the *Topics* at the instance of his lawyer friend Trebatius. According to the unusually anecdotal preface of this work, Trebatius had been browsing in Cicero's library when he came across a copy of Aristotle's *Topics*. He asked what it was about, and when Cicero explained, Trebatius wanted a translation. Cicero temporized, urging him to consult more competent authorities, but finally acquiesced. The Latin treatise is not in fact a translation of Aristotle but an adaptation, slanted to the particular needs of a jurist. Cicero showed Trebatius how the topical method could be applied to legal problems of definition and distinction. Other works avowedly written in response to requests for information include the anonymous rhetorical tract known by its addressee's name as the *Ad Herennium,* Varro's manual on farming, Quintilian's *Training of the Orator,* and Tacitus' *Dialogue on Orators.*[9]

Inquiries were often conveyed by letter, and a letter was the natural vehicle for a response in those cases where a limited amount of information was sought.[10] But letters between friends also tapped emotional stores, asking for guidance and encouragment, comfort, or simply amusement and distraction. In most cases such requests will have been answered in private by a letter or a visit. That was how Atticus responded to Cicero's incessant questions about the best course to follow during the civil wars. But if the appeal was addressed to a literary man, it sometimes elicited—and may have been intended to elicit—a more self-conscious statement that was ultimately published. Seneca produced three books expounding the pathology of anger when Novatus sought counsel about mastering the emotions.

Poetry was another medium in which friends found it easy to communicate, since poetry at Rome had a particular affinity for topics of everyday life. Poets and letter-writers thus shared a common ground. When Catullus lapsed into despondency, he called on another poet, his friend Cornificius, to comfort him with "something sadder than the tears of Simonides" (38.7–8). The roles are reversed in poem 68, in which Catullus administers consolation in response to an appeal from someone else. A poet's acquaintances also expected him to keep them entertained with tidbits of his latest verse. Horace claimed to be confronted by so many conflicting preferences that he could not decide what to write:

> Not everybody is impressed with or partial to the same sort of thing. You enjoy lyric verse, this fellow is fond of iambics, and that one of black wit and colloquies in Bion's style. It is almost as though I had three ill-assorted supper guests clamoring with idiosyncratic tastes for completely different foods. What am I to serve and what not? You turn down what the first man calls for, and what you crave repels or disagrees with two others.
>
> Hor. *Epist.* 2.2.58–64

Not all requests proceeded solely from personal interests; some were made on behalf of others. When Cicero's brother hounded him for an epic about the campaign in Britain, he had uppermost in mind that such a poem would make a good impression on his commander, Julius Caesar. Atticus also instigated Cicero to take on projects aimed at third parties: Caesar, Varro, Hortensius, and Brutus.[11] Brutus himself at one point wanted Cicero to write something directed to Caesar.[12] A surviving poem of the Augustan period confesses a similar origin. In the opening of the (first) *Elegy on Maecenas,* the anonymous author explains that he writes not as a personal friend of the deceased but at the instance of another: "And yet, Maecenas, I did not have a friend's acquaintance with you, hence Lollius bespoke this piece" (lines 9–10). This disclosure sounds so gauche that one readily understands why most authors did not discuss in public the intricacies of triangular impulsion. But we have no reason to presume that it was rare. It is a short step from being asked to write for a friend to writing for the friend of a friend, though without access to letters or other confidential papers we can detect no difference in the end result. Wherever the possibility of third-party involvement remains open, it is almost pointless to try to reconstruct the web of motivation which lies behind a request.

In every situation considered to this point, literary suggestions seem to serve the ends of the proposers more obviously than those of the writers. But they could also arise from comparatively generous motives. In many cases they were initiated by people who were literary figures in their own right. Or if not writers themselves, they were leaders of fashion who prided themselves on their influence over literary opinion no less than over other areas of social life. At the least they were amateurs, whose zeal was stimulated by the literary culture imbibed in Roman schools. Advice to the writers within one's ambit therefore had a public-spirited aspect: it was a way of furthering the enterprise of Roman letters, to which all professed commitment. Cicero put a touch of this high-minded concern into his letter to Lucceius. Eager as he was in his own interest, he felt he had to point out that the monograph he proposed was the perfect subject to test Lucceius' mettle:

> Now if I induce you to take on this project, you will have, I am sure, a theme worthy of your broad background . . . You will be able to apply your knowledge of civil convulsions as you explore the causes of the upheaval and possible remedies of the impasse, passing censure on those moves that strike you as improper and making reasoned arguments for

policies you approve of . . . Furthermore my ups and downs will furnish you plenty of variety in the writing, charged with the sort of pleasure that can engross an audience's attention if the prose is yours. Nothing is more calculated to delight the reader than unstable times and vicissitudes of fortune.

Cic. Fam. 5.12.3–4 = 22 SB

Others took the interests of their writer friends to heart and exhorted them in all sincerity. The sense of responsibility to art was especially pronounced in Pliny, who made a mission of discovering younger poets. After one recitation he attended, he bore down on the reciter in a fervor he describes as follows:

> The recitation over, I swept up the young man in a long and hearty embrace. With the compliments that are a mentor's sharpest spur, I urged him to continue in the direction he had begun and to light the path for his descendants that his forefathers had lit for him. I congratulated his excellent mother and his brother too, who at that recital won no less credit for affection than the other won for eloquence, so palpable was his initial solicitude and then his joy for his brother . . . I cherish our age lest it be barren and impoverished.

Pliny Epist. 5.17.4–6[13]

An occasional Pliny does not entitle us to hypothesize a throng of enlightened and disinterested critics, poised to apply encouragement wherever they discerned talent. But in a society which generated such multifarious friendships, it would be perverse to assume that disinterested advisers appeared less frequently than they do in literary society today.

Literary requests are almost the only tangible evidence we have for efforts by the leaders of society to steer contemporary writers toward particular fashions or subjects. It is important to understand what significance this kind of evidence has, and that is why I have described it in such detail. My aim has been to show that requests to writers were common in Roman society, that they belonged to the give-and-take of friendly intercourse, and that they could be made from a variety of motives, of which I have illustrated only a few. Taken in the aggregate, literary requests certainly do not reveal the operation of concerted policies, and it would be hard to find evidence of consistent patterns even in the suggestions of particular individuals.

Furthermore, commitments to others so pervaded any Roman's life that suggestions from friends would not have been felt as intrusions on a writer's autonomy by either party. By Roman norms of social behavior, collaboration was a manifest good, in the pursuit of literature as in any other pursuit. The literary request, in fact, is but one in a series of conventions which advertise the collaboration between writers and their friends. It is related to the fiction by which poets invoke the inspiration of those for whom they write.[14] Their responsibility to supporters is also acknowledged during the gestation of a work as they issue assurances or answer inquiries about its progress—hence the motif of the "promised poem" from which this book takes its title.[15] The author again courts the favor of his friends when he presents the finished work. He may appeal to them as critics, inviting their verdict on what he has written.[16] He may commend his book to their care and ask for aid in getting it publicized.[17] He may honor them with an allocution that singles them out from the common run of readers.[18] And this interaction between writers and their friends is not simply a matter of formulaic statements. Friends do read and criticize drafts, come to recitations, and take pains to spread the writer's reputation. The suggestions they offer at the beginning are of a piece with their involvement at every later stage.

The scope of these suggestions it is in practice impossible to ascertain. In only a few instances do we know exactly what was said, and without that information we are in no position to determine how far, or indeed whether, writers were prepped about the content and treatment of the projects urged on them. Yet among the handful of requests which are directly known, it is plain that some do not circumscribe the writer's task in any significant way. Part of a request from Caelius to Cicero was quoted earlier; the whole of it runs as follows:

> If, as I hope, you expect to have any spare time, I propose that you write a treatise directed to me, so as to prove your regard for me. "You're no oddball, what put that idea into your head?" you say. Among your many works I want something to survive that will transmit the memory of our friendship even to posterity. "What sort of thing do I want?" I suppose you're asking. You will come up with the ideal subject sooner than I would, given your expertise in every discipline. But in broad terms what you write should have something to do with me, and it should be informative so that a lot of people will read it.
>
> Cic. *Fam.* 8.3.3 = 79 SB

Vague as these instructions may sound, Pliny contrives to say even less in his charge to a gentleman poet from his own home town:

In that remote and cushy retreat you have up there, why not turn over chores that are petty and mean to others (it's time) and free yourself to write? That should be your job and your pastime, your work and your relaxation. Spend your waking hours at it and invest your sleep in it as well. Fashion and bring to completion something that will be yours forever. The rest of your possessions will pass to a succession of owners after you, but this will never cease to be yours once you have made it so. I know the quality of mind and talent I am encouraging; you have but to live up to the image others will have of you if you embrace it yourself.

Pliny Epist. 1.3.3–5

Not until Caninius eventually thought of something to write about years later and had set to work did Pliny discuss specifics with him—and then only to opine that his subject was excellent in all its parts (*Epist.* 8.4). Stripped of its preciosity and politeness, the original injunction amounts to no more than what Martial claims to have been told by another friend of the arts: "Write something big: you're a shiftless sort" (*Epigr.* 1.107.2). And that in turn matches the sort of direction Cicero says he once got from Atticus: "Let's tackle something big that calls for a lot of time and thought" (*Att.* 2.14.2 = 34 SB).

Even Cicero's letter to Lucceius (*Fam.* 5.12 = 22 SB), by far the most detailed and formal literary request that is known, stops short of laying down lines which the desiderated history is to follow.[19] Cicero tells Lucceius what stretch of his career should be covered and indicates (naturally) that he would prefer to see it treated in an independent monograph rather than incorporated into a more comprehensive history. But apart from that, he does not commend any particular interpretation, though obviously he harbored one. He points to no individuals to be singled out for praise or blame, no policies to be defended, no actions to be magnified or minimized.

Direct evidence, then, so far as it goes, does not encourage us to believe that circumstantial instructions to writers were the norm. Indirect testimony—what writers report about what they were told—is on the whole unhelpful, since writers are more concerned to advertise the fact of a request than to recapitulate its terms. But the frequency of such reports raises another problem as well. If, as seems to be the case, writers were constantly showered with signals from friends, the strength of each was liable to be diluted by its concurrence with the rest. In that case, the stream of advice and comment would have done as much to complicate as to focus literary undertakings. Horace maintains in the passage quoted above that the demands of his friends had exactly this effect. And there were undoubtedly times when an author played off two or more friends, intimating to each that he was the inspiration behind the same project. In August of 45 B.C. when Atticus urged Cicero to devote his time to philosophical writing, Cicero responded that Atticus was spurring a running horse. When he dedicated the *Tusculan Disputations* that same year, he declared that it was Brutus who had impelled him to write on philosophical subjects. And in a letter to Matius a year later, he implied that he had taken his lead from Matius.[20] It does not follow from these signs of dissonance that stimuli from without were bogus or meaningless. But they were so abundant and diffuse that they may not have contributed much in the way of specific guidance.

Because literary activity was so bound up with social life, the kibitzing of friends created pressure that writers could not ignore no matter how casual, inconsistent, and profuse the suggestions they were offered. Through the scrutiny of literary requests we gain some understanding of what the pressure was like. In order to judge how writers responded to it, it will be necessary to consider what they wrote. From this point my discussion will be focused once again on poetry. In almost no case does the surviving material allow us to juxtapose a specific request with the poem which answered it and to study the relationship between the two.[21] In lieu of that approach, I will discuss four genres which can be seen as allowing for different levels of collaboration by interested parties: panegyrical epic, occasional verse, satire, and elegy. My subtext here will be that poets responded most resourcefully when guidance was least explicit.

Epic

Panegyrical epic is the genre which projects the largest image of those on whom it focuses, and the image can be adjusted without difficulty to their specifications. In fact a poet might find himself supplied with the whole recipe for an epic in the form of memoirs from the would-be protagonist. It has always been thought that when Lutatius Catulus presented his memoirs to the poet Furius of Antium, he was conveying a hint.[22]

Naevius and Ennius had established a respectable pedigree for historical epic. It was serious, had a more Roman stamp than other forms of early Latin poetry, and corresponded to what aristocratic audiences liked to hear, both about their ancestors and about themselves. From a consumer point of view, it must have seemed the perfect line in which to encourage poetic endeavor. Historical epics were produced in quantity during the late Republic and early empire (about two dozen by my count), and in some parts of the literary public the fondness for this genre never died away. Nevertheless, few of the epics which we know to have been produced were preserved, and none of those with a panegyrical slant (unless we wish to put the *Aeneid* in this category). The one contemporary who attempted to review the record of Roman literary achievement found little to praise in this area. Writing near the end of the first century A.D., Quintilian names fourteen poets in his survey of epic, which takes in all varieties of heroic verse. The authors of epics on historical themes, as opposed to mythological themes, stand fifth (Ennius), seventh (Cornelius Severus—"a better versifier than poet," says Quintilian), eleventh (Rabirius), twelfth (Albinovanus Pedo, who with Rabirius is judged "not unworthy of attention if one has the time"), thirteenth (Lucan), and fourteenth (the emperor Domitian himself, whom, along with Lucan, Quintilian indicates he has not named in order of merit).[23]

Most authors of historical epic whose names we happen to know Quintilian does not mention at all. Despite its potential appeal for aristocratic audiences, the genre evidently stayed stuck in the category of the second-rate. Its shortcomings would no doubt be fully revealed if more of this verse had survived to be examined. But even in the absence of good samples, it is possible to point out certain difficulties which changing fashion set in the way of the genre's viability.

By the Augustan period, any poet who was invited to sing of wars and heroes would have been troubled by at least three considerations that put him off. In the first place, however imposing the *Annals* of Ennius may have been, later epics were not often conceived on the same scale. Ennius had shown how the Roman people surmounted a succession of trials from the earliest days down into his own lifetime. But his successors dealt with isolated campaigns conducted by leaders who were their contemporaries. At any rate, that is the impression one gets from the titles that have been preserved: *The Istrian War* by Hostius, *The Sequanic War* by Varro of Atax, *The Gallic War* by Furius Bibaculus, *The Sicilian War* by Cornelius Severus. And to extend the list, Cicero's epic covered only the exploits of Caesar in Britain, and Albinovanus Pedo evidently confined himself to expeditions of Germanicus in which he took part.

We may fairly surmise that the scaling down of historical epic cheapened it. It fostered not only bloat in place of economy, but also servility, since a poet could hardly relate the story of contemporary feats without some regard for the opinion of the principals.

The respectability of the genre slipped still further when Greek writers invaded the field. Cicero's client Archias had composed epics in honor of Marius and the Luculli, and was expected to turn out others for one of the Metelli and for Cicero himself.[24] In the next generation Boethus of Tarsus celebrated the battle of Philippi and Polyaenus of Sardis commemorated the Parthian victory of Ventidius.[25] Toward the end of the century, Antipater of Thessalonica wrote about Lucius Calpurnius Piso's war in Thrace.[26] Greek poets had an edge in that their training and technique enabled them to outproduce their Roman competitors. Archias and Boethus, for example, are said to have dazzled audiences with their ability to reel off impromptu lines on any topic.[27] They undoubtedly made uncomfortable colleagues for Latin poets. But what was more damaging is that a scent of opportunism and hypocrisy clung to everything the Greeks purveyed to their Roman masters. This opened the way to odious comparisons. It was one thing for a writer of panegyric to seem to be following in the footsteps of Ennius, another thing to seem to be competing with Archias.

A third development which soured poets on historical epic is the most important, but since it is well known, it hardly requires elaboration. When Catullus looked around for something lumpish and foul to set as a foil beside the slowly wrought and elegant miniatures he and his friends were composing, epic is what he found: "The *Annals* of Volusius, a shit-smeared screed . . ."[28] Once the hallmarks of the genre—its martial subjects, its voluble and straight progressions, its antique accents—had been stigmatized as the quintessence of bad verse, to set one's pen to panegyric took either a very hardy or a very stolid spirit.

The taste for epic on contemporary themes persisted longer among the people around poets than among poets themselves. But even for the poet's friends, the images perceived in the mirror of epic grew duller and darker. The recitation of heroic feats can afford gratification to the hero, his family, comrades, and dependents, but it has a less certain grip on those who are neither heroes nor connected with heroes. The fact is that most of Horace's friends, and Catullus's, and Martial's—most of a poet's friends in any age—were not the stuff of which epics could be fashioned. Furthermore, the private sector was producing fewer heroes all the time. The writing of contemporary epic is stimulated by periods of expansion and conquest. In the latter half of his reign, Augustus began winding down the expansionist policy that Rome had pursued for more than a century, and by the end of his reign it was virtually over. Although provincial governors could still conduct limited military actions, in most cases they campaigned as deputies of the emperor and were not entitled to claim personal credit for any successes they achieved. After 19 B.C. no one from outside the emperor's own family was permitted to celebrate a triumph or ovation, no matter whether he campaigned as a deputy or under his own auspices. It would have been incongruous if the output of panegyrical epics continued unabated after triumphs were denied, and the incongruity was soon perceived. The last large-scale poem on the military exploits of a man unaffiliated with the imperial house was Antipater's poem for Piso in about 10 B.C.

The old-fashioned kind of subject could still be found if the poet went back to the years before the principate, or perhaps more prudently, to the years before the civil wars. But an audience of the Augustan Age could not be counted on to feel the same zest for what one may call costume epic as an audience of the Republic. Until the end of the Republic, stories about the heroes and campaigns of generations past were family matters for many who heard them told. The circles to whom poets pitched their work were filled with persons who might welcome epics that recited the deeds of grandfathers and great-uncles. But the powerful and wealthy men to whom poets of the Augustan period gravitated were the beneficiaries of a revolution, and few of them could count heroes of the Republic among their ancestors. Where the new regime had left material for panegyrical epic, it had ousted the natural audience for it.

Epic remained the genre most often commended to poets by friends and admirers, perhaps because they had clearer expectations of this than of any other genre. Yet as I have tried to show, epic did not entirely satisfy, or it gradually ceased to satisfy, the self-conception of the class which clamored for it. In addition, it had aesthetic liabilities from the writer's point of view. A poet could disembarrass himself of the genre by a graceful sidestep. Instead of an epic, he could produce a poem apologizing for his inability to do justice to deeds which beggared all powers of description. Such an apology contains the tribute to which the poet says he is unequal, but it is reduced from epic scale to a form which blends with the rest of his oeuvre as an ode, an elegy, an epigram, an epistle, or whatever. This solution simplified the literary effort required. It may even have given a certain formal interest to the task of panegyric by leading poets to confront it in a new way. And it did respond to the desire of triumphant leaders to have their deeds commemorated in verse. Nevertheless, the substitution of the refusal poem *(recusatio)* for epic did nothing to engage those members of the literary public who had no claim on famous deeds. The emperor soon engrossed the refusal poem for the same reasons that he engrossed epic.[29]

Occasional Verse

If poetry was to reflect experiences within the reach of those who formed a poet's audience, its subjects had to be drawn from civilian life. Not that poets began to write about everyday life only with the decline of epic. Topical situations and personalities already accounted for much of what Lucilius and Catullus wrote about. But both poets and their society friends became increasingly aware that the appetite for praise and public notice could be gratified by simpler genres than epic.

One variety that was enthusiastically received was what is usually termed occasional verse: poems about marriages and deaths, births and birthdays, parties and trips, artistic showpieces, favorite slaves, and so forth. Like the panegyrical epic, this kind of poetry could be adjusted to fit the specifications of the interested party. In some cases we know that particular pieces were written to order; in other cases we can deduce it because poems on the same subject by different authors are constructed according to the same pattern.[30] Occasional verse cast at least flashes of publicity onto the individuals whose activities were noticed in it. That recommendation helped to make it one of the most durable forms of Latin poetry. It is still abundantly represented in late antiquity, in the output of Ausonius and Claudian, in the *Latin Anthology,* and in the *Bobbio Epigrams.* Although literary audiences and indeed the whole composition of society changed from generation to generation, the taste for occasional verse never disappeared but was constantly reinvigorated as new men came into prominence and courted notice.

Since this kind of poetry had an abiding social function, it was always a serious business for poets, some of whom found original strategies for handling it. When Horace introduced the motifs of occasional verse into his *Odes,* he set them in a field of discourse which was essentially restricted to love and song and wine-inspired wisdom. Subjects imported

from outside this enclave were dressed in the style of their new surroundings, reducing the amount of paraphernalia that usually bolstered
them. Thus instead of being treated as poetic subjects in their own right,
events in the lives of his friends are worked into the *Odes* as strokes of
detail. For example, *Odes* 1.36 hails the return from Spain or Mauretania
of a young man belonging to the entourage of Horace's friend Lamia.
Horace says nothing about the returning traveler's adventures in the
West, where he had presumably gone on military service. Almost nothing is said about Lamia, who is the more important personage regarded
in the poem and whose family was part of the new Augustan aristocracy.
By turning the homecoming into a party, Horace moves it into home
territory. The poem describes the thanksgiving offered for the young
man's return, the glad embraces of his cronies, and the wine, the roses,
and the girl that have been waiting for him. The conventions of occasional
verse could be still more drastically reduced. In *Odes* 3.19, mention of
Murena's elevation to the augurate is slipped in as the subject of a toast. It
is not even clear that Murena is supposed to be present among the partiers.

Statius took the opposite course and tried stretching the form. He
began writing the *Silvae* about four or five years after Martial achieved
success in bringing out book-length collections of epigrams. The connection is easy to discern. Statius treats the same themes as appear in
pieces which Martial was turning out to compliment his friends; in some
cases the two poets write about the same events and the same friends.[31]
Statius moreover acknowledged the influence of Martial when he characterized some of his own poems as "light works written more or less
on the level of epigram" (*Silvae* 2 pr. p. 31.15–16 Courtney). The great
difference is that the *Silvae* are much longer than epigrams. Statius evidently set out to make the genre more grandiose by laying on elements
of high poetic style (the studied diction and erudite epithets of the Alex-
andrian tradition, the miracles and divinities that embellished epic, and
a scattering of lyric verse forms, for example). Ornamented and enlarged,
the *Silvae* could be presented as a superior form of occasional verse,
containing a more ponderous tribute to the friends honored in them
than ephemera like Martial's pieces.

But despite continuing pressure from interested parties and despite
some original experiments on the part of poets, occasional verse did not
attain the status of a major genre. Many of its themes were slight to
begin with, and they were worked to death by writer after writer. In a
way this sort of verse must have come off poorly in comparison with

panegyrical epic. It was more hermetic, since it sometimes alluded to details of private life that were intelligible (let alone interesting) only to the honorand and his immediate associates. And poets who embroidered the doings of private persons could make no pretense, as the authors of epic could, that they were setting before their readers actions of national significance.

Both epic and occasional verse could be more directly controlled than any other genre by the individuals who were the subjects of them. Even if the poet did not depend for information on the person he was writing about, or was not pressed to transmit the latter's interpretation of events, the whole content of the poem was based on what that person had done or suffered. Yet this monopoly of content offered no guarantee that the principal would be satisfied with the result. Quality and dictation were if anything inversely related.

Not all of a poet's cronies insisted on getting poems whose content they were in a position to prescribe. I have said that most had no personal stake in having the poet produce epic. Occasional verse too, at least from the standpoint of the individual recipient, must have been a comparatively infrequent demand. There were not that many moments in a single lifetime which invited poetic commentary—certainly very few in comparison with the number of times that friend and poet crossed paths. In any case, no matter what part the calculation of private advantage may have played in the suggestions made by friends, egoism did not ride rampant over taste. A poet owed many of his connections to the knowledge and passion for poetry that already existed among elements of the upper class. It was not possible to satisfy them simply by producing hackwork.

Satire

The pressure to provide pleasing images of upper-class life was real enough, but we have seen that literary solicitations did not necessarily comprise specific instructions. The friends who wanted samples of a poet's work were sometimes content to let him choose the subject. If the choice was left open, something slanted toward the vagaries of human behavior—the behavior of individuals in private life, or the foibles of collective behavior under the sway of tradition or fashion—could be expected to have broad appeal. This was the realm of "life and manners" *(vita et mores),* which is perhaps the most deeply rooted preoccupation of

Roman literature from its origins to its latest age. In comedy it appears in those broadsides against current practices which have been recognized as characteristically Plautine interpolations into his Greek models.[32] It underlies the Roman taste for biography, and for the particular style of biography popularized by Suetonius, and it helps explain the greater importance of memoirs and epistolary collections at Rome than in Greece. The faithful representation of human experience was the purpose by which Phaedrus justified the writing of fables and Martial justified his epigrams.[33]

It was also an impulse behind satire. Satire came into its own as comedy withered away, its roots having failed to spread out in the Italian soil in which it had been put down. From the fragments of Lucilius it is clear that the new genre immediately took into its repertoire material about Roman pursuits and stereotypes which comedy never managed to appropriate. More than any other kind of poetry, satire regaled its readers with the spectacle of a world they knew, and that gave it a popularity which it held to the end of antiquity.[34]

It was not in those terms, however, that Horace commended the first satires that have descended to us intact. In the opening pieces of book 1, he takes up an exaggerated didactic pose, borrowing clichés and gaudy turns from the preachers of diatribes and aligning his activity with that of the schoolteacher, the social reformer, and the scholarly bore.[35] The explanation for this performance is not yet clear. Although Lucilius was given to moralizing pronouncements on human conduct, decked out occasionally with streamers plucked from his philosophical reading, we cannot tell whether his satires had the homogeneous, flattened, impersonal appearance that Horace cultivated in the first satires of book 1. If Horace was not following a Lucilian precedent here, perhaps he thought that the eccentric mannerisms of the diatribe tradition would help to firm up the contours of a genre which in its early stages was defined only negatively by the lack of a distinctive meter, style, or subject. Or perhaps the use of broad methods was meant to diffuse the punch of satire and make it impossible for any individual to feel that he was struck.

But whatever may have induced Horace to essay the didactic mode, his material defied him. Already in book 1 he abandons argument for narrative in several pieces, three of which can be seen to share a relationship. The *Fifth Satire* relates anecdotes of a journey from Rome to Brundisium on which Horace was joined en route by fellow-travelers who included his friends Maecenas, Plotius, Varius, and Vergil. The *Seventh*

Satire describes, for the sake of the concluding *mot,* a legal wrangle which Horace had witnessed when he was traveling in Asia with the entourage of his old commander Brutus. The *Ninth* is the celebrated sketch of his run-in with an unnamed social climber who wanted to be taken along to Maecenas' house. These three poems contain vignettes of individuals, especially outsiders, observed from a vantage point inside a group. The relationships within the group either come in for comment as other persons impinge on it, or they provide an implicit reference point for appreciating what is noticed about outsiders. If these satires serve the ostensible end of attacking folly and vice, it is by momentary ambuscades at best. What they really illustrate is how the poet's ties with friends frame the material he chooses to treat.

By the time Horace published his second book of satires five or six years after the first, he had modified his didactic posture considerably. Book 2 contains no formal diatribes in which the moralist harangues a faceless interlocutor. All but one of the satires of this book are conceived as dialogues or discourses by characters with distinct personalities, whether real or fictitious. Even the *Sixth Satire,* spoken in Horace's own voice at the beginning, ends with his report of a long speech by someone else. In contrast to the satire against avarice which heads book 1, the poems of book 2 all have distinctly Roman locales—sets are provided for the dialogues, in other words—and they concern behavior which is depicted as contemporary rather than simply universal. In two poems which take aim at obnoxious practices (the *Fourth* and *Fifth* satires), Horace does not preach against but just describes the target vices. When the diatribe style of book 1 does crop up again in stretches of the *Third* and *Seventh* satires, the effect of it is different and rather puzzling. The sermons against greed, adultery, and foolishness which Horace himself had delivered in book 1 are here turned back against him by characters who seek him out—his slave in the *Seventh Satire,* a bankrupt speculator converted to radical Stoicism in the *Third Satire.* Both lambaste personal shortcomings which Horace has taken care we should know he admits to. But these indictments are flung out amid a hail of others, some demonstrably off target, and all enunciated with such dogmatism and hectic rhetoric that one has to wonder whether Horace is not mocking his interlocutors here, and by implication his own performances in book 1.[36] At least it is true that his aim as a moralist is more ambiguous than it seemed in the first collection of satires. By adding details and dramatizing his themes, Horace has shifted attention from the underpinnings to the surface of his material. The reader can savor Davus' or Damasippus' tirade as a deadly imitation of what was heard in the streets, without knowing how it applies to Horace.

In the eighth and final poem of book 2, the study of manners for their intrinsic interest has altogether displaced the search for salutary lessons. This satire involves no preaching and no vice. On meeting his friend Fundanius, Horace asks how he and the rest of Maecenas' party enjoyed dining with the rich gourmet who had recently entertained them. Fundanius then describes the evening's progress: the host's inept and tedious annotations on the food, the sallies by his restive guests, the collapse of the dining-room canopy in the middle of dinner, and the host's discomfiture as his guests decamped. Like the three pieces from book 1, the *Eighth Satire* offers portraits to be relished by the insiders for whom the poet wrote. But more than anywhere else in his work, Horace has exploited imbalances of status, sophistication, and manners to create the dynamism of his narrative. It is no accident that he lets it be told by a man whom he elsewhere singles out as the best living author of comedy (*Serm.* 1.10.40–42). The literary production which stands next in succession to the *Eighth Satire* is *Trimalchio's Dinner*. But the line has been prolific and is still recognizable in modern (especially British) drama and fiction.

Satire took form under the osmotic pressure of friends for poems which had the astringency of real life and some trace of acts in which they themselves had taken part. The satires of Horace stand out as the most collectively oriented portion of his oeuvre. He contrives to name and compliment far more friends in them than in either his *Odes* or his *Epistles,* and in the last satire of book 1 (which contains two separate catalogs of comrades, in lines 40–45 and 81–88) he expressly directs his work to a collective audience rather than to any one reader.

Elegy

That a collective orientation should be evident in a genre which was concerned above all with social behavior is not surprising. But it is also noticeable in that other literary invention of the Romans, the elegiac poetry which celebrates the love between a poet and his mistress. Two passages from elegy point up the connection between love poetry and social life in the most striking way. In the *Fifth Elegy* of book 1, Tibullus urges his beloved Delia to take into consideration certain merits which make up for lack of money:

> It is the poor man you will always have handy, the poor man who will step up first and hedge your gentle person. As your faithful companion in the narrow, crowded street, the poor man will thrust out his arms and clear a path for you. The poor man will discreetly conduct you to shady friends, and with his own hands will undo the straps from your snowy feet.
>
> Tib. 1.5.61–66

Except for the mention of snowy feet, this promise of zealous and constant attendance could as easily have been addressed to one of the great men of Rome by a would-be companion as to Delia by her lover. The direction which Tibullus essays here is subsequently pursued by Propertius in a poem to a woman whose husband or keeper has just gone abroad. Into his place glides the poet with these words:

> Your beauty is overpowering. You have mastered the arts of chaste Minerva. You have a bright name lit by the literary reputation of your grandfather—a house favored by fortune, if only you were to have a trusty friend. I will be that trusty friend: quick, come to my bed.
>
> Prop. 3.20.7–10

Until the surprise ending, this is practically the opposite of what one might expect a seducer to say. Propertius does not intimate that he is drawn to the lady by sentiments too profound to be bounded by any of the conventional roles of social life. Instead of trying to make her forget her public standing, he plays it up. Her distinctions, he says, give her the right to take a prominent role in society—a role in which he is ready to support her by becoming her faithful attendant. The closest parallels to this approach are found outside love poetry, in encomiastic pieces like the *Panegyric of Messalla* and the *Encomium of Piso* in which the poet praises a distinguished public figure and begs to be taken into his entourage.

If these passages remind us of the way poets speak to their great society friends and of situations enountered in other sorts of poetry (satire, epigram, and occasional verse of various kinds), the resemblance is not fortuitous. In several ways the attachment of the elegist to his mistress resembles the relationship by which poets and others were tied to the leaders of society. In the first place, the lover and the friend, both of whom are wont to declare their feelings of affection repeatedly, use similar language in describing them. Words like "friendship" (amicitia), "love" (amor), and "care" (cura), "dear" (carus), and "courting" (colere) are basic to the discourse of both. Poets pray to be allowed to spend their lives in the company of the friend and benefactor, and the elegists say the same kind of thing to their girlfriends. Both society friends and mistresses receive assurances of the poet's fidelity (fides).

Moreover, the setting of elegy exhibits one feature which is prominent also in poetry about relations with the aristocracy. Episodes of the elegist's story are often set at the house of his beloved. The lament of the excluded lover is sung before the unreceptive door, or in a variation on that theme, the lover may enlist the door's complicity to slip inside. Beyond the door stand members of the household whose cooperation the lover must secure before he can be sure of enjoying his lady's favor: the porter, the maid, the mother or duenna or warder, and the husband or the woman's current keeper. As we saw in Chapter 1, the house of the great man looms equally large in the eyes of his dependents. His accessibility is symbolized by the threshold or the door, which either opens to or is shut upon aspirants to his friendship. The desired intimacy is expressed in activities carried on within the house: receptions, recitations and entertainments, dinners, and household celebrations for births, marriages, and holidays. The satirists allow us to glimpse a ring of characters inside (freedmen, Greeks, parasites, old cronies) past whom the new friend must learn to make his way.

Even some situations or occasions on which elegiac poems are based have parallels in occasional verse. Elegies too are written about parties, journeys shared with the beloved in fact or imagination, and celebrations or troubles in her life.[37] There are similarities in the conceits which poets contrive in both contexts. To the mistress as to the society friend, a poem may be offered as a gift (munus or donum) or as a service (officium) superior in value to the gifts and services ordinarily exchanged in society.[38] The mistress may be proclaimed the source of the poet's inspiration or be assured of lasting fame through being celebrated in verse.[39] On one occasion Propertius declares that Cynthia is his ideal reader, the only critic whom he cares to please (2.13a.11–14); this kind of statement has an ample background in occasional verse. Both kinds of poetry feature advisers who step forward to offer instruction in the techniques of ingratiation.[40] What Horace's Teiresias says about courting rich old men in Satires 2.5 needs surprisingly few adjustments to fit Ovid's purposes in the Art of Love. Finally, elegists and society poets express the negative aspect of their respective attachments in the same metaphor: they see both situations as a form of slavery.[41]

The resemblance between conventions of elegiac verse and those which arise in the courtship of great men is to be explained by a combination of reasons. To begin with, a woman in Roman society (unlike Greek society) did have the opportunity to play a role something like that of a Roman magnate. Ladies of high status could receive throngs of friends and favor-seekers without compromising their reputation. Augustus' wife, his sister, his daughter, and his niece all drew followers over whom they held court.[42] Women of the demimonde had fewer restrictions than high-born ladies on their movements in public, and if they acquired complaisant husbands, that gave them the greatest freedom of all. The independent and autocratic mistress of the elegists is far from being a literary figment unrelated to life.

Second, if elegy was to imitate plausibly the experiences of a young man in love, it was inevitable that it would borrow many of the conventions we associate with occasional verse and other varieties of society poetry. When the subjects of Roman poetry are drawn from life, they are drawn from upper-class life. The wealth and leisure which are such salient features of this milieu were largely spent in parties and jaunts, amusements and celebrations. Such pursuits necessarily turn up in any sort of poetry that proposes to deal with life.

Furthermore, the subjects of elegiac poetry are selected not so much to exercise the private sensibility of the poet-lover as to exhibit the common experience of a class. The elegists always have in mind a double audience: their ladies, and at the same time the members of their set who are engaged in like pursuits—hence their frequent references to a circle of onlookers. Erotic adventures were as much a diversion for Rome's gilded youth as the writing of poetry, and one reason for the popularity of love poetry is that it managed to combine these two avocations of the well-to-do.

That love elegy was consciously directed toward the poets' upper-class comrades may be seen first of all in the fact that many of the poems are formally addressed to socially prominent persons. No one except Augustus himself held a more distinguished position in Roman society than Messalla Corvinus, the friend of Tibullus and Ovid. Several of Propertius' poems are addressed to Tullus, the nephew and protégé of a consular governor of Asia. Ovid in one of his poems (*Am.* 2.10) claims to have confuted an erotic maxim he learned from Pomponius Graecinus, whose career was to take him to the consulate and beyond. Moreover, some of the pieces which the elegists wrote are not about their own loves but about the affairs of their friends. In three poems of the *Monobiblos* (1.10, 1.13, and 1.20), for example, Propertius adopts the posture of an observer and reports on the love life of his friend Gallus. In the Tibullan Corpus there is a set of poems about the romance between Sulpicia and Cerinthus written from the viewpoint of an unknown third party (3.8 = 4.2, 3.10 = 4.4, 3.12 = 4.6). The elegists also give the impression at times that they are competing with senators and knights, who are in some cases their own friends, for the same women (as for example Propertius 1.5.23–24, 2.16, and 2.34b). And finally, the books of Tibullus and Propertius include a number of pieces which are not about love at all but about their relations with society friends.

This convergence of elegy with other forms of society-oriented poetry can be partly explained on the hypothesis that elegy evolved as a specialized type of occasional verse. For the most part it did not address specific events in the lives of specific friends, and therefore it did not invite direction from interested parties. But elegy did idealize a way of life that had many devotees in that stratum of society where young poets found a footing. In that sense it took its orientation from those on whom the poets depended. It may even have been their ties to wealthy young aristocrats that led the elegists to imagine the dominance of a mistress in terms which so often suggest the vicissitudes of friendship with the great.

ELEGY, SATIRE, occasional verse, and epic each have features which help us to interpret the testimony gathered at the beginning of this chapter about the bidding of friends. Taken by itself, that testimony is apt to leave a false impression of the extent to which an author's friends intruded on his work. There may have been cases (though none we know of) in which uncommonly articulate dilettanti prescribed the design and tendency of poems composed for them. But on the whole, it seems more fruitful to think of the pressure to which poets responded as something more diffuse: the educated taste of a well-defined social class which would recognize but could not stipulate the sort of literature it desired.

Whether poets received more clear-sighted direction from the emperor than from ordinary friends is the question we will begin to consider in the following chapter.

PART TWO

Poets and Augustus

4

The Political Perception
of Augustan Poetry

To interpret the behavior, let alone the motives, of Augustus has never been simple. He acted both to conserve and to innovate, with results that often seem ambiguous, and our understanding of his actions is further limited by the duplicity which the exercise of power encourages, by the lack of openness in imperial decision-making, and by the impossibility of disentangling the leader's public and his private roles. Certainty about Augustus' relations with poets is no more attainable than it is for any other riddle of his reign. But in the next three chapters I will argue that it is convenient to believe that they fit the dynamic described in the chapters which precede. Augustus approached poetry and poets in the same benign and patronizing spirit as did other Roman aristocrats, and poets in their turn experimented to devise overtures which would please him.

This bland pronouncement contains a polemical subtext. For the better part of the twentieth century, most though not all scholars have believed that Augustan poetry directly reproduces (or in exceptional cases contests) the viewpoint of the regime. What these critics have in common is less a precise position than an approach, which can be recognized by the common assumptions on which they draw. Not every assumption enters into every interpretation, but the set is approximately as follows: Augustus has a program which he seeks to communicate to the public; the program turns as much on issues of policy or government as on the projection of a personal image; poetry in Roman society is at least potentially a medium of mass communication; certain poets receive advisories of some sort directly from Augustus or members of his government; the advisories come systematically, and they concern specific messages to be broadcast by the poets. These are the main components of what I will call the political interpretation of Augustan poetry.

Since this habit of thought effectively precludes the viewpoint I propose, it has to be combated head-on. In subsequent chapters I will show that it fits poorly both the poems and the known record of Augustus' dealings with poets. Here the argument I will make is that it is a poor model because the historical situation from which it was extrapolated was defined by institutions very different from those of the early principate. Put simply, the political interpretation is anachronistic.

This interpretation is sometimes conflated with another view of Augustan poetry that will require little discussion here beyond noting that the two conceptions do in fact differ. The second is older, having been prevalent for almost as long as there have been princely courts in Europe, and it holds that the verse produced by Horace and Vergil and some of their contemporaries is a species of court poetry. Like the political interpretation, it is anachronistic, though not to the same degree. A structure of roles and practices that can fairly be termed a court did spring up around the Julio-Claudian emperors. Their personal routines evolved into ceremonies, family celebrations became public holidays, the palace grew to be a prime focus of capital intrigue and social life, and a series of marriages and births articulated a princely house in which pedigree could be exactly quantified and came more and more to define nobility in the eyes of society at large. Little more than a hundred years after the founding of the principate, the Romans themselves equated the society of the palace with the kind of court milieu *(aula)* they had encountered in Hellenistic kingdoms of the East.[1]

For two reasons, however, it seems questionable whether we should classify poetry of the Augustan period under the rubric of court poetry. First, both Augustus and his immediate successor strenuously renounced the trappings of monarchy, which meant that there was no official etiquette in place from which poets might take their cue. Poets were free to improvise a courtly idiom of their own, of course, and even found models to turn to. Latin traditions of historical epic and of house poetry for important men had treated themes that were applicable also to emperors, and the corpus of Greek poetry offered models of discourse with monarchs and their courts. But any poet of the early principate (as opposed, say, to Statius or Martial a century later) had to work out his own synthesis of these materials, and each was thus in the position of a pioneer. If in the concept of court poetry it is implicit that familiar conventions govern poetic subject matter, treatment, and tone, that is a second reason for doubting its relevance to poetry of the Augustan period.

But in the context of the present argument, the peril of anachronism is a side issue. The main thing to be said about court poetry here is that the concept need not concern us because it is too vague to be seriously misleading. Historically, it has been used to designate poetry which represents a wide range of recipients, subjects, and purposes. Court poetry may be addressed to the monarch, to his immediate family, to more distant kinsmen, or to court eminences who are not related to him. Its subject matter may be drawn not only from the great deeds of war and statecraft but also from the celebrations, pastimes and amusements, and even scandals that occur at court. As for intention, court poets may write to instruct the monarch as well as to praise or advertise him; they may write for cliques contending with other cliques; or they may write for no other end but to amuse a smart society which craves entertainment. Finally, since the lines tossed off by the monarch and his nobles must be considered court poetry just as much as the verse produced by lowly scriveners, the term "court poetry" does not even have the value of specifying a particular class of writers or a single point of view. It is a nearly formless notion that will cover anything written at, for, by, or sometimes even against a monarch's court. As such, I see no reason to quarrel further with it.

The political interpretation, by contrast, imports ideas about Augustan poetry and Augustan politics that do mislead. In order to fix as a reference point the perceptions which were current in antiquity, let us begin with several comments on the relation between literature and government by authors of the imperial period. The first text actually skips over the subject of literature, though it has quite a lot to say about government. In Cassius Dio's history of Rome, Maecenas is given a long and famous speech (52.14–40) in which he tells Augustus what must be done to establish the principate on a safe and solid basis. Although the measures Maecenas advocates are often commended in terms of their effect on public opinion, and although at one point (chap. 26) he even urges a system of public education for service in the new state, he never adverts to the propaganda value of either poetry or literature in general. To be sure, the words that Dio puts in Maecenas' mouth are not and could not be a transcript of words really uttered on a real occasion. Most scholars consider the speech not only fictitious but anachronistic, expressing Dio's own sentiments as an imperial subject of the early third century

A.D. But this vantage only makes his silence about poetry the more re-markable. The imperial regime had grown much more bureaucratic and authoritarian by the Severan period than it had been under Augustus, yet even at that date it did not occur to a reasonably well informed observer that poetry might be exploited as a tool of government.

Tacitus, writing a century earlier, does perceive a direct link between government and literature, though the kind of literature which concerns him is history rather than poetry. In the initial chapters of both the *Histories* and the *Annals* he contends that the principate witnessed a decline in historical writing. But the reason is not that the emperors tried to manipulate their historians. As one-man rule began to encroach on "eloquence and liberty," he says in the *Histories,* there was a falling off in literary talent: "At the same time truth was distorted in several ways, at first because of people's disinvolvement with politics as the prerogative of others and later by frenzied adulation or alternately by hatred against autocrats" (*Hist.* 1.1.1). In the *Annals* too he stresses the biases of the writers themselves, and as in the *Histories* the principal corrupting influence he identifies is flattery, which thrust itself forward without needing to be solicited. Furthermore, in the *Annals* he concedes something he had not granted in the earlier account, that "there was no shortage of admirable talents to relate the age of Augustus" (*Ann.* 1.1.2). Over this branch of literature, at any rate, Tacitus does not encourage us to think that Augustus exerted open or clandestine control.

Of all observers of the principate, ancient or modern, Tacitus' contemporary Suetonius had perhaps the best opportunity to know how the emperors used their literary men. He was himself a literary man whose talent had won him preferment in the form of palace secretariats under Trajan and Hadrian. He may even have had the opportunity to learn something about the literary policies of earlier emperors if these posts gave him access to palace archives, as has often been thought. Yet he like Tacitus failed to perceive any sign of official pressure on the poets. In his biography of Augustus he discusses the emperor's attitude toward literary matters in a series of chapters which he organizes under the head of "eloquence and liberal studies" (*Aug.* 84.1). The last chapter of this section appears to raise the very issue of literary propaganda, because in it Suetonius mentions some of Augustus' efforts to promote right thinking among his subjects:

> As he browsed among writers in either language there was nothing he sought so keenly as precepts and examples with sound applications to indi-

vidual or public life. These he often copied out word for word and sent to members of his household, to heads of armies and provinces, or to the city's magistrates as each had need of admonition. He even read entire books to the senate and often brought them to the notice of the citizenry through edicts. So, for example, with Quintus Metellus' oration *On Increasing Family Size* and Rutilius' speech *On the Proper Scale of Buildings:* he wanted it understood that he was not the first to address these two issues but that they had already worried men of former days.

The creative minds of his age he fostered in every way. With patience and generosity he listened to recitations not only of poems and histories but also of orations and dialogues. Yet he objected to the composition of any piece about himself that was not a serious contribution by a major writer, and he instructed the praetors not to let his name be trivialized by competition pieces.

Suet. *Aug.* 89.2–3

However it may seem at first glance, this passage is decisive testimony against an official literary policy of the sort commonly assumed. Editors rightly paragraph it in the middle, recognizing that by a typically Suetonian arrangement its content has been subdivided into "attitudes toward ancient authors" and "attitudes toward contemporary authors." Only in his treatment of ancient authors does Suetonius impute anything like a propagandistic intent to the emperor, and even there, what Augustus is said to do amounts to nothing more than the traditional practice of culling inspirational examples from the treasury of literature. Augustus' interest in contemporary writers, on the other hand, is described with no reference to their value in molding opinion. It is hardly conceivable that, having just raised that issue in the preceding paragraph, Suetonius would here have let it drop if he were aware that the moderns had been taken under government tutelage. The relationship he notices is just the opposite. It is the writers themselves who crowd forward with panegyrics, a situation parallel to that which Tacitus discerned among writers of imperial history.

So far as I am aware, no writer of antiquity expressed a view of relations between writers and emperors that differed significantly from the view implicit in these passages from Dio, Tacitus, and Suetonius. While there may yet be evidence which will bear the interpretation that Augustus groomed poets to be publicists for his regime, it must be conceded that no such interpretation had been formulated by the end of the classical period.

This interpretation first emerged in post-Renaissance Europe, and some of the conditions which incubated it are readily identifiable. The growth and rapid alteration of political regimes in Italy and elsewhere had renewed debate about the mechanics of government, adding a host of examples observable at close hand to the systems which humanists knew from books. In Spain and France large, centralized, absolutist states perfected methods of control which suggested explanations for the success of the Roman emperors in controlling the population they had ruled. During the sixteenth and seventeenth centuries the joint ascendancy of Machiavelli and Tacitus predisposed political thinkers to find the fingerprints of the ruling power on the phenomena of every age. Not least important, writers of all sorts had grown accustomed to raiding antiquity for materials with which to construct the present. Whether they came for empirical data or proof texts or allegories, haste and pragmatism often desensitized them to differences between the past and the present. One of their favorite stamping grounds was the half-century in which the Roman Republic devolved into a monarchy.

For the most part, however, both apologists and detractors of the Augustan principate were content to retail anecdotes and information that ancient sources supplied. What is curious about their interpretation of the poets' role is that it went well beyond anything they found in classical sources. In this case, they were beholden to a later work which wore a semblance of classical authority. In 1675 the French abbé René Le Bossu published a six-book disquisition which sought to apply Aristotelian principles to every aspect of the criticism of epic poetry.[2] For approximately the next hundred years, his *Treatise of the Epic Poem* was to enjoy unrivaled authority in France and Britain. Since Le Bossu's theory was given its ultimate twist in Britain, I will quote him in the version in which he eventually circulated there: *Monsieur Bossu's Treatise of the Epick Poem, Containing Many Curious Reflexions, Very Useful and Necessary for the Right Understanding and Judging of the Excellencies of Homer and Virgil,* first published at London in 1695 by a translator who identified himself as "W. J."[3]

Le Bossu started from a premise that would nonplus Aristotelians of today: epic has a primarily moral purpose, "to form the Manners by such Instructions as are disguis'd under the Allegories of some one important Action" (book 1, chap. 3, p. 10 Le Bossu = vol. 1, p. 11 W. J.). For the instruction purveyed by the *Aeneid* he identified a twofold audience. Vergil's first object was "to instruct *Augustus* as the Founder of a great Empire, and to inspire into him as well as his Successors, the same Spirit and Conduct which had rais'd this *Empire* to such a Grandour" (book I, chap. II, p. 44 Le Bossu = vol. I, p. 52 W. J.). This lesson was inculcated through the contrast between Aeneas and Mezentius, the one representing the advantages of a "mild and moderate Government," the other signaling "the Misfortunes which attend a Tyrannical and Violent Reign" (pp. 44–45 Le Bossu = vol. I, p. 53 W. J.). On a second level, Le Bossu held, the *Aeneid* was addressed to the subjects of Augustus, and here Vergil's purpose was "to make them lay aside the old Antipathy they had to *Monarchy*, to convince them of the Justice, and the legal Prerogative of *Augustus*, to divert them from so much as desiring to oppose his Designs, and to raise in them a Love and Veneration for this Prince" (p. 46 Le Bossu = vol. I, pp. 54–55 W. J.).

There can be no question but that from this perspective the *Aeneid* looked like a more political poem than it had seemed even to the allegorical interpreters of late antiquity. Early in the fifth century, Servius had maintained that Vergil wrote in order to praise and honor Augustus and to proclaim his glory, and in roughly a score of notes out of a commentary covering twelve books he claimed to detect implicit parallels or transferences between events in the *Aeneid* story and incidents in the career of Augustus.[4] But the eulogistic purpose that Servius ascribed to Vergil was conventional and apolitical by comparison with the purpose articulated by Le Bossu, who held that Vergil wrote in order to justify a change of government. Furthermore, the double meanings which Servius found in the *Aeneid* were not systematically or exclusively indexed to Augustus. In some lines he thought he glimpsed foreshadowings of Pompey's death and of Marius' concealment in the marshes of Minturnae, and he also detected allusions to the career of Romulus, Servius Tullius, Scipio Africanus, and even Plato.[5] For him the Augustan allegory was only part of a voluminous patchwork. The allegory which Le Bossu identified, on the other hand, was firmly centered on Augustus and was the whole key to Vergil's meaning. As he imagined the process of poetic composition, the message dictated the story line:

> The first Thing we are to begin with for Composing a *Fable*, is to chuse the Instruction, and the point of Morality, which is to serve as its Foundation, according to the Design and End we propose to our selves. I would, for Instance, exhort two Brothers, or any other Persons, who hold an Estate in Common, to agree well together, the better to preserve it: And this is the *End* of the *Fable*, and the first Thing I thought on. For this purpose I endeavour to imprint upon their Minds this Maxim: *That a*

Misunderstanding between Friends is the Ruin of Families, and of all sorts of Socie-
ties. This Maxim which I make choice of, is the Point of Morality, and
the *Truth* which serves as a Foundation to the *Fable* I would compose. In
the next Place this *Moral Truth* must be reduc'd into Action, and a general
Action must be feign'd in Imitation of the true and singular Actions of
those who have been ruin'd by a Misunderstanding that has happen'd
among them . . . This is the first *Platform* of a *Fable.*

book 1, chap. 7, pp. 25–26 Le Bossu = vol. 1, pp. 28–29 W. J.

More than once in the *Treatise,* epic poetry is said to concern itself
with "la politique" or "instruction politique," expressions which the
British translator duly renders as "politicks," "policy," or "political instruction."[6] Yet Le Bossu's interpretation was political in a rather restricted sense. Latin writers of the Renaissance and earlier had employed
the words *politicus* and *civilis* as Greek and Latin alternatives for the same
set of ideas, and the words remained in some measure synonomous as
they were naturalized in Italian and French. Le Bossu uses the word
politique when he talks about the constitution of the state, political philosophy, the role of the statesman, or the role of citizens; in the last-
named context he often varies the adjective *politique* with *moral* or *civil.*
He never uses the word with reference to political programs or to practical issues of government.

The abstractness of his ideas about the political content of the *Aeneid*
comes out especially clearly when they are seen in relation to his theory
of poetry. Le Bossu held that the epic poet performs almost the same
social function as the moral philosopher, but that the poet "has a nearer
Regard to his own Country, and the Necessities he sees his own Nation
lie under. 'Tis upon this account that he makes choice of some piece
of Morality . . . accommodating himself to the particular Customs and
Inclinations of his Audience, and to those which in the general ought
to be commended in them" (book 1, chap. 8, p. 29 Le Bossu = vol. 1,
p. 34 W. J.). On this showing, the epics of Homer and every other poet
have as strong a political or civic tendency as the *Aeneid.* The situation
of each audience and therefore the "morality" of each poem will differ
from nation to nation, but the protreptic intent is always the same. The
twofold message which Le Bossu elicited from the *Aeneid* was likewise
the consequence of a schema which he brought to the interpretation of
every epic: "A State is compos'd of two Parts; the *Head* which commands
is the first, and the *Members* which obey make up the other. There
are Instructions requisite for the *Governour,* and some likewise neces-

sary for the *Subjects*" (book 1, chap. 10, p. 37 Le Bossu = vol. 1, p. 44 W. J.).

The *Treatise* appeared at the height of Louis XIV's reign, when the French government energetically recruited and subsidized writers who were willing to put their talent at its disposal.[7] But suspicion that Le Bossu's poetic theory owed anything to familiarity or complicity with this effort would be misplaced. The tone of the *Treatise* is disengaged and academic throughout; Le Bossu scarcely takes note of his own times, let alone hinting at applications to them. Nor does his theory replicate the salient feature of the contemporary relationship between literature and government, which is that the writer collaborates with the regime. The atemporality and schematism of the *Treatise* make it all but certain that its inspiration came from reading rather than observation.

Le Bossu himself admitted allegiance to no masters but Aristotle and Horace. But an obvious direction in which to look for influences on a French Aristotelian of the seventeenth century is to the treatises that poured forth in Italy after translation and dissemination of Aristotle's *Poetics* in the previous century; Le Bossu's contemporaries made no secret of their debt to Italian predecessors.[8] As Italian critics had debated whether pleasure or utility was the end of poetry, one position which a number of them adopted was that insofar as poetry had a public dimension, it was subordinate to the authority of the state.[9] The most radical exponent of the statist approach was Giason Denores (his name also appears in the form de Nores), who assessed every feature of poetry by its suitability to promote the public weal. His theory contains the germ of Le Bossu's political interpretation. In times past, Denores wrote, "legislators and governors" of cities in Greece had ordained that

> for their fellow citizens several different forms of poetry be presented through song or representation, arranged and composed in such manner as to deter them from vice, instil in them virtue, and motivate them to the preservation of that well-constituted form of state to whose government and laws they owed obedience. By this means they intended to guide their minds toward the love and desire of the republic whether it was administered by one man or by a few or by the many, but overwhelmingly to this last form, by which in those times the greatest part of Greece was ruled . . . Hence they determined that three sorts of poetry be proposed to their citizens: the heroic poem, recounting an action of some legitimate prince who struggles to liberate from distress and to render happy his companions and subjects, by contrast with the tyrant who is

accustomed to bring upon them every sort of ruin and destruction for the sake of gain and self-interest [as well as tragedy and comedy]. All three of these genres cause them to respect and embrace the legitimate ruler and to abhor the domination of tyrants and the most powerful.[10]

The summation of this doxography is that, whatever the message of the *Aeneid,* Le Bossu's own message was oddly muffled. On the one hand, he was crucial in transmitting to French and English readers the suggestion that Vergil's poem had a profound relation to the prevailing regime. Yet he took no interest in any practical implications of this position, to which he had evidently been led by philosophical considerations rather than by observation of either ancient or contemporary practice. Perhaps it would be fair to say that what Le Bossu contributed was less a developed interpretation than a then-novel perspective on the *Aeneid.*

Once the *Treatise of the Epic Poem* crossed the Channel, however, it encountered readers whose point of view differed drastically from Le Bossu's. Three recent developments in England colored reaction to his work there. First, whereas the French intelligentsia under Louis XIV was, at least on the surface, comfortably royalist, their British counterparts had become much less persuaded of the right of kings (and were more than a little scornful of the regime in France). In the seventeenth century England twice chastened the crown, beheading one king in 1649 and deposing another in 1688. Readers with these events in mind were apt to balk at being told that the *Aeneid* was a vehicle by which the subjects of Augustus were indoctrinated "to divert them from so much as desiring to oppose his designs."

A second development which conditioned reception of Le Bossu, and proximately of Vergil, was the birth of English political parties. The struggle that culminated in the "Glorious Revolution" of 1688 polarized the governing class, producing an ideological opposition between Whigs and Tories that persisted for decades afterward.[11] What was important about parties is that they steered political discourse toward issues that seemed to transcend personalities and to have more substance than the short-term or arbitrary calculations that motivated most acts of government from day to day. Whigs and Tories, for example, split over the role of the national church, the prerogatives of the king vis-à-vis Parliament, and the line of succession. The tendency to conceive of politics in terms of issues was further aggravated as the British king lost authority to his parliamentary ministers, and as his ministers came to be drawn entirely from one parliamentary faction or the other. Once the Ministry was perceived to represent a particular party, it was inevitable that it would be opposed at least partly on ideological grounds no matter how innocuous the measures it introduced.

Finally, experience of the London press also led English readers to take Le Bossu's remarks about Vergil's political moral in a different sense than he intended. After official licensing requirements lapsed in 1695, the writers of newspapers, magazines, and pamphlets became increasingly bold, echoing and amplifying and sometimes even fomenting political controversies. The press was thus institutionalized as a medium of mass communication operating in parallel with government. Much of the London press, moreover, had a vehemently partisan slant. Tory and Whig administrations of the eighteenth century were under constant attack from opposition papers, and they in their turn published or subsidized newspapers of their own in order to counterattack. And though this was the era when the "Grub Street hack" came into his own, it was by no means only scribblers who produced copy for party newspapers. Party writers and for that matter government propagandists included some of the preeminent names in eighteenth-century literature: Swift, Defoe, Steele, and even Fielding. An Englishman of this era would not find the least reason to question that literary talents of the highest order might collaborate directly in the efforts of a government to promote its policies.

The effect of these developments was that in early eighteenth-century England, "political" came to mean something very different from what it had meant to Le Bossu. A predominant sense now was *"party-political"* or "partisan," and since parties rallied themselves around causes, the word tended to imply as well that politics turned on competing ideologies. When someone was termed a "political writer," what was meant was not that he was a philosopher or student of government, but a propagandist, committed (as one contemporary put it) "to write for a Faction in the Name of the Community."[12]

This environment substituted a provocative new context for the idea that the *Aeneid* carried a political message, and English critics tacitly adapted Le Bossu in a way that made the message more obtrusive. What happened can be illustrated from the dedicatory essay Dryden wrote to accompany his translation of the *Aeneid* in 1697. Le Bossu is one of several Continental authorities touted in the essay, and it was clearly he who inspired Dryden's account of Vergil's purpose. Although Vergil regretted the need for Augustus to assume monarchic power, Dryden wrote, "he concluded it to be the Interest of his Country to be so Govern'd: To infuse an awful Respect into the People, towards such a Prince: By that respect to confirm their Obedience to him; and by that Obedience to make them Happy. This was the Moral of his Divine Poem."[13] But this paraphrase reproduces only half of Le Bossu's position. Dryden has dropped that part of the moral which pertained to Augustus, whom Le Bossu had considered the primary target of Vergil's instruction. And even though two pages later Dryden acknowledged the point that the *Aeneid* also taught Augustus "how to behave himself in his new Monarchy," it no longer counted as an equally important part of Vergil's message.[14]

From then on, Le Bossu was regularly credited with the view that Vergil wrote simply in order to foster allegiance to Augustus—so, for example, in the once influential but now forgotten tome *Polymetis* by Joseph Spence, Professor of Poetry at Oxford between 1728 and 1738. Summarizing Vergil's literary career, Spence wrote that he "last of all, undertook a political poem, in support of the new establishment. I have thought this to be the intent of the Aeneid, ever since I first read Bossu: and the more one considers it, the more I think one is confirmed in that opinion."[15] In this way Vergil came to resemble more the kind of propagandist English readers knew from journals and pamphlets than the moral philosopher Le Bossu had fancied him to be. It was anything but a flattering likeness. Spence quoted his friend Alexander Pope as saying in 1739 that "the *Aeneid* was evidently a party piece, as much as *Absalom and Achitophel*. Virgil [was] as slavish a writer as any of the gazetteers."[16]

In origin, then, the political reading of Augustan poetry appears doubly misbegotten. It arose when Le Bossu put into circulation a pseudo-Aristotelian doctrine that his English readers misunderstood, relating it to political institutions which had no place in Le Bossu's or Aristotle's thought, much less the world of Augustan Rome. And the perception of Vergil as a propagandist that imposed itself on criticism of the *Aeneid* was carried a step forward by an English contribution in another area of Vergilian criticism. In the proem to the third book of the *Georgics* Vergil had claimed to be writing in compliance with Maecenas' "far from easy commands" ("haud mollia iussa," G. 3.41). Neither Vergil nor his ancient commentators elaborated on this charge, and in fact it hardly called for comment. As we have seen, no overture is more common in Latin prefaces than the claim to be writing at another's behest.

But English critics looked deeper and concluded that Maecenas was acting as the intermediary of Augustus. They argued that Vergil wrote the
Georgics in order to help implement the emperor's project of reviving
Italian agriculture after the civil wars. When Heyne combated what he
called this "opinion of several Englishmen" in 1767, he identified its
proponents as Joseph Warton, John Martyn, and Lewis Crusius.[17] But it
goes back a generation earlier than those writers, to the biography of
Vergil that Knightly Chetwood supplied for Dryden's monumental edition of 1697:

> The continu'd Civil Wars had laid *Italy* almost waste; the Ground was
> Uncultivated and Unstock'd; upon which ensu'd such a Famine, and In-
> surrection, that *Caesar* hardly scap'd being Ston'd at *Rome;* his Ambition
> being look'd upon by all Parties as the principal occasion of it. He set
> himself therefore with great Industry to promote *Country-Improvements;*
> and *Virgil* was serviceable to his Design . . . That Emperour afterwards
> thought it matter worthy a publick Inscription, *Rediit cultus Agris:* Which
> seems to be the Motive that Induced *Maecenas,* to put him upon Writing
> his *Georgicks.*[18]

The merits of this interpretation need not concern us here. What is
more important is its significance in the evolution of a line of criticism.
So far as I know, this was the first time that an Augustan poem was
interpreted as propagating a government-inspired message about a practical issue of policy. For a poet to concern himself with policy at this
level of particularity implied an even more intimate collaboration with
government than Le Bossu's theory about the *Aeneid* had been thought
to suggest. The approach had only to be generalized to other poems and
poets for the political interpretation of Augustan poetry to be complete.

This argument can be telescoped and terminated with the help of one
last text. By the second half of the eighteenth century, the tide of intellectual influence had reversed itself and begun to flow from England to
France, and at the close of the century France weathered her own great
political upheaval. The emergent Gallo-British strain of criticism, having
in the meantime been borne back to France, thrived anew in the post-
Revolutionary ambience. It found the following expression in the intro-
ductory lecture of a course which the Professor of Latin Poetry, Henri
Patin, conducted at the Sorbonne in 1836:

> When the sovereign power seized possession of a literature which had
> reached its highest point of perfection, and therefore its highest point of
> credit and authority, the thing was done quite naturally, so that it did not

appear that the condition of poets had changed, any more than the nature of poetry itself. Only like everything else it was recognized, regularized, put in order: it seemed to take its place among the establishments of empire . . . The Roman poets passed easily from the patronage of men like Livius Salinator, Fulvius Nobilior, the Scipios . . . and so many others to what was exactly the same thing: the patronage of Pollio, Messalla, and of Maecenas above all. Augustus received them from Maecenas and through his ministrations that skillful politician made them work for the moral rehabilitation of his authority, for the popularity of his acts, for the present brilliance and the future glory of his reign. This protection of letters . . . seemed in the case of Maecenas to take on the character of an official ministry. Maecenas appeared to have the charge, not simply of supporting and encouraging men of talent, but of recruiting them, enrolling them, disciplining them, giving them the word of command from that virtual Department of National Genius of which he was the head . . . It is really curious to see how, under the government of Augustus and the administration of Maecenas, literature comes in a short time to be organized, to coalesce, to form a society apart within the bosom of society, a state within a state, something which has been called in later times and elsewhere the Republic of Letters, but in this case a thoroughly monarchical republic, entirely in the hands of the emperor.[19]

After several more lines in this vein, Patin invites his auditors to recall the reason of state which inspired the founding of the Académie Française at a certain juncture in their own history:

You are well aware how, during the first years of the seventeenth century, certain intellectuals who cultivated literature or who simply loved it conceived the idea of gathering together on certain days of the week . . . in order to share their productions and to exchange ideas on language, style, taste, eloquence, poetry, and the arts . . . You also know how Richelieu, when apprized of these gatherings, formed the notion of transforming them by a stroke of his power into an assembly that would be permanent, regular, emanating from the authority of the State, and charged by it with representing developments in literature, and even with directing them in the interests of good taste and also, of course, in the interest of the policies and the glory of the minister. Well then: it seems that there took place in Rome something very similar.[20]

Patin's lecture provides a good point at which to break off. With the endorsement of a Professor of Latin Poetry, the political interpretation had crossed the threshold of modern mainstream opinion if not of orthodoxy. In just another fifty years it would be accepted into Teuffel's history of Roman literature and the *Encyclopedia Britannica*.[21] And Patin leaves us with a particularly vivid statement of the view that Augustus co-opted the poets. It is still one of the boldest formulated. Its power lies not in details of argument, however (Patin appeals to no details), but in a kind of ruthless simplicity of vision. In the first place, the generalization that had not been carried out in eighteenth-century British criticism has been accomplished here. Patin is not talking about isolated works like the *Aeneid* or the *Georgics* or about some poets only, but about all poetry written under Augustus. He has also screened out every shading of behavior that is not political. In interpreting relationships between Maecenas and the poets, he takes no account of seemingly casual intercourse between them nor of the language of friendship they use toward each other. He has also discarded the once common assumption that relations between Augustus and the poets can be understood in terms of conventions familiar from later European court poetry. Finally and once again, what he sees in Augustan poetry depends on something he has seen much closer to home. It is the analogy with Richelieu and the Academy that seems to clinch the interpretation for him.

The political interpretation of Augustan poetry cannot be invalidated by showing that it represents a modern point of view, or even by showing that it developed partly on mistaken premises. But its intuitions have manifestly owed much of their power to the fact that the interpreters were extrapolating from their own experiences of politics, and that should put us on our guard. Intuitions stand no less in need of verification for being powerful. In the next chapter I will examine the classical evidence which has been adduced to support them.

5

Literary Initiatives from Augustus' Side

The founding of the principate reoriented political and social life in Rome and complicated the vocations of the upper class, altering the scope and style of oratory, the framework of military service, the practice of jurisprudence, and the bias of philosophical study. It is unthinkable that it could have had no impact on poetry produced in the same milieu. Taking the fact of the emperor's influence as beyond question, I will begin to investigate in this chapter what sort of influence it was. Because it was attached first of all to the position which he occupied, literary influence can be said to belong to any emperor, at least to any of the Julio-Claudian emperors. Beyond that, their involvement with arts and letters varied according to each one's temperament and interests and according to his conception of his public role. The emperor with whom I am particularly concerned is Augustus, for whose activities our information is most copious and whose influence on the literary environment has long been controversial. He is almost uniquely controversial. If one may judge by the volume of past discussion, the issue of imperial guidance which springs to life with him all but disappears with him as well.

The ascendancy which the emperors held over literary life is illustrated by a quip which the elder Seneca reports (*Cont.* 10.5.21). A showman and professor of oratory from the eastern provinces came in his travels to Rome, where he impressed Augustus and began to benefit from his good will. But when Augustus offered to introduce him to another leader of fashion, the rhetor brushed aside the suggestion with the comment, "While the sun is shining, I do not light a lamp."

The emperor blazed above the heads of poets too. From very early on, the Caesars held a monopoly over all new subjects that could be worked up in the venerable tradition of martial poetry. Even in the civil sphere their comings and goings overshadowed the movements of lesser notables, which meant that the palace was preeminent in the many forms of occasional verse as well as in epic. The birthdays, marriages, and funerals of the imperial family were more splendidly observed and their acts in public were grander than those of private citizens. They made better subjects of verse because they were more colorful and because their doings were better known to a wider audience.

The emperor's influence was not simply a matter of capturing certain themes. Poets looked to him no matter what their subjects because his favor was the consummation of literary success. Insofar as success took the form of material benefits, the emperors had richer resources for bestowing them than anyone else. As we have seen, with the exception of testamentary bequests, most of the great money gifts we hear of poets receiving were given by the emperors (see Chapter 1, n. 22). Imperial favor also brought nonmaterial benefits. Because an emperor was not just the head of state but also the leader of society, his tastes set up a resonance throughout the network of orders and individuals of which he was the center. A writer who was taken up by him could be virtually certain of gaining public acclaim. Martial maintained that Domitian had "given fame, which is to say life" to all his books (*Epigr.* 8 *pr.*). In addition the emperor controlled certain media. He could authorize shelf space and a portrait bust in the state libraries. He might underwrite performance of a writer's work as part of a festival program. He bestowed the crown for poetry at the quadrennial competitions that began to be celebrated in Rome during the latter half of the first century A.D.[1] Last of all, the emperor's friendship opened the door to fruitful relationships between poets and his other friends, the great and wealthy personages who frequented the palace. The benefits conferred by the emperor were then reproduced and multiplied in each new circle in which the poet gained a footing.

From the very beginning of the principate the outlook of literary men upon their audience was transformed by their consciousness of the emperor's presence. The preoccupation continued to grow as time passed. A century after the comment of Seneca's rhetor, Juvenal espoused the even more radical position that there was "hope and reason for writing in Caesar alone" (*Sat.* 7.1).

The effect which the principate had on literary life was to some degree an automatic, institutional pull. Even an emperor without any known predilection for literature would have been evangelized by contemporary writers because his presence was so conspicuous and because the potential return was so great. The emperors of the first century, however, were anything but unlettered men. Anecdotes about their early years indicate that most of them had been exposed to the universal curriculum of literary and rhetorical studies. Those who had grown up in the palace had been tutored by the best teachers in Rome. As a result most emperors took an active interest in literature. Claudius wrote history, and Augustus, Tiberius, Nero, Titus, Domitian, and Nerva all tried their hand at poetry—as did many private citizens of the same class and cultural background. And again like private citizens, the emperors often took an interest in the full-time practitioners of literature. It is reasonable to start from the assumption that their treatment of poets and other writers may reflect a class outlook as much as calculations of state, and that their attitudes will be broadly comparable to those which have been discussed in Chapters 1 and 3.

Augustus' Literary Leanings

Something of Augustus' outlook is evident in his relationship with Titus Pomponius Atticus, with whom, according to Atticus' biographer, he kept up a correspondence lasting through most of the 30s. While on the move in Italy or abroad, the triumvir and future emperor wrote his impressions of the places where he paused and of the reading he dipped into. He continued to write, often daily, even when he and Atticus were both in Rome. "He would seek some information on the subject of antiquities or put to him a question relating to poetry or sometimes try with bantering remarks to pry long letters out of him" (Nep. *Att.* 20.2). As Nepos describes them—incessant, good-humored, filled with chat about books and peregrinations and erudite interests—the letters from the triumvir sound as unofficious and unstudied as the extant letters from Cicero. The queries and entreaties are if anything more disinterested than those made by some of Atticus' other friends.[2] And the tenor of the correspondence as a whole sounds apolitical. The only matter of public policy which it is said to have touched on—the rebuilding of an ancient temple on the Capitoline (Nep. *Att.* 20.3)—was raised by Atticus with Augustus, not the other way around.

The letters are important because they reveal a side of Augustus that has nothing to do with his function as a leader of the state. When he consulted Atticus about points of history or tried to coax long letters out of him, he was engaging in the same courtesies which aristocrats who were private citizens practiced toward their literary friends. The literary orientation of the correspondence with Atticus is not unique. Augustus repeatedly performed those offices by which the Roman elite went about integrating literary pursuits and practitioners into Roman social life. Fragments of his letters show him discoursing about literary standards to various people in his orbit: to Livia, to his grandson and granddaughter, and to Antony.[3] In one letter he pokes fun at the preciosity of a poem Maecenas had written to Horace.[4] His own literary enterprises went forward under the scrutiny of friends. When he began composing a tragedy, his fellow literati (including the most prominent contemporary writer of tragedy) wanted to hear how it was coming along.[5] He wrote an autobiography which opened with an allocution honoring Agrippa and Maecenas, the two friends who were most closely acquainted with his career and had done the most to further it.[6] He launched his autobiography and some of his other writings by reading them before audiences recruited from friends and family (Suet. *Aug.* 85.1). In his turn he helped prepare a favorable reception for works written by others. "With charity and patience he listened to recitations not only of poems and histories, but also of orations and dialogues" (Suet. *Aug.* 89.3). The elder Seneca reports two occasions on which Augustus attended recitations by orators (or more precisely declaimers), and he was also present for a reading by the historian Cremutius Cordus. Vergil was invited to read the *Georgics* and parts of the *Aeneid* before the sort of semi-private audience which attended readings of Augustus' own works.[7]

Since Augustus' behavior so often exhibits that chivalry toward letters which is characteristic of his class, that is the natural context in which to consider his connections with Vergil and Horace. We have a fair amount of information about those connections, most of it in the form of extracts from Augustus' correspondence which preserve the spirit as well as some particulars of his dealings with the two poets. That they communicated so often by letter is in itself significant.[8] When Augustus' cultural proclivities come into play, Vergil and Horace stand on the same footing with him as Atticus or Maecenas: they are intimates whom he teases, cajoles, consults, and strives to envelop. Suetonius' whole purpose in quoting from the correspondence between Augustus and Horace is to show what a warm relationship the two men had, and the samples he gives are replete with the language of friendship. In a letter about Horace, Augustus uses the affectionate possessive, calling him *noster Horatius*.

To Horace himself he writes, "Please allow yourself a little liberty with me, as though you were a regular messmate here. You will not be acting out of line, since that is the kind of relationship I have wanted with you" (p. 297.25–28 Roth). And he remonstrates when Horace is loath to flaunt the friendship which has been thrust upon him (pp. 297.31–32 and 298.3–6 Roth).

Several incidents in which Augustus appears to be pressuring Vergil or Horace to write something for him belong to the period of about a decade and a half when he and they enjoyed personal contact as friends. The evidence comes, again, from correspondence, though only twice are Augustus' solicitations directly quoted. The background is clearest in the case of Horace's *Letter to Augustus*, which was written after Augustus had read some of the poet's *Epistles* and asked for a comparable poem directed to him. Suetonius first paraphrases the emperor's letter, then quotes from it:

> After reading some of the discourses he complained that Horace had not mentioned *his* name, saying, "You should know that I am angry with you because out of all the pieces you have written in that vein you do not reserve a single one for me—are you afraid that you will be disgraced in the eyes of future generations if you leave the impression that you were a friend of mine?" And so he forced out of him the piece which begins "Cum tot sustineas et tanta negotia solus."
>
> Suet. *Vita Hor.* p. 298.2–8 Roth

Although Augustus certainly asked for a poem, the circumstances of this request make it unlikely that he also prescribed the theme or direction of the poem. He was reacting to the success of a literary initiative by Horace, whose *Epistles* established a new direction in poetry and at the same time were uniquely suited to put his friends on display. Augustus wanted to be identified with that success, just as Caelius and other friends had wanted to be identified with fashionable new work by Cicero, and as friends of Martial and Pliny later sought to ride on the popularity of their works. Other attitudes behind the request are also familiar from the requests of private citizens. Augustus is anxious to have his name mentioned in verse which will keep it alive, and from a personal friend like Horace he feels entitled to a public avowal of the bond which unites them.

According to the Suetonian life, the *Letter to Augustus* was not the only poem written at the emperor's instance:

He thought so well of Horace's works, and held that they would endure forever, that he set him to write *(iniunxerit)* not only the *Secular Hymn* but also the *Vindelician Victory* of his stepsons Tiberius and Drusus. And this was the reason he obliged *(coegerit)* him to add a fourth book of *Odes* to the three which had come out a long time before.

Suet. *Vita Hor.* pp. 297.35–298.1 Roth

Although no letters are formally adduced, phrases from the correspondence are almost certainly embedded in this statement. Suetonius is at bottom an antiquarian, who shakes out his oddments in a pastiche of quotation, paraphrase, and exemplification. His account of Augustus' requests to Horace contains two of the formulas *(iniungere* and *cogere)* in which friends converse about the suggestions they have advanced or received. This language is likely to have been lifted either from Augustus' letters to Horace or from cover letters in which Horace conveyed the finished poems to Augustus. The judgment that Horace's poems would endure forever is another echo of actual discourse. It is introduced by the verb *opinari,* which in Suetonian usage generally points to recorded statements.[9] And it has a perfect counterpart in the gambit with which Pliny leads up to a request to Tacitus: "I foresee that your history will be immortal and so I desire all the more to be included in it" *(Epist.* 7.33.1). In at least one of the letters Suetonius saw, Augustus must have slipped into a refrain which literary people were used to hearing from publicity-seeking friends.

Of the letters to Vergil only two scraps survive, neither of which happens to contain the suggestion which allegedly induced Vergil to write the *Aeneid.*[10] Not that the suggestion is intrinsically improbable. Epic was in the literary mainstream at Rome, and by the time Vergil was ready to contemplate a new project, his friendship with Augustus was close enough that offers of advice would have been natural. The important question is not whether the emperor did or did not propose the *Aeneid* to Vergil, but, if a suggestion was made, in what terms it was presented. Did Augustus content himself with the direction later given to Martial, "Write something big"? Or did he point Vergil specifically to the Aeneas story and spell out certain ramifications touching the Julian house and the mystique appropriate to portraits of founding fathers?

What he said is irrecoverable, but a subsequent letter at least provides a clue to what he did *not* say. According to Donatus' life, "when Augustus was away on the Spanish campaign, he used to write insisting *(efflagitaret)* with pleas and even jocular threats that he be sent—to use his own words—'just the preliminary sketch *(prima carminis hypographe)* or just a chunk of the *Aeneid*'" (*Vita Verg.* 31 Hardie). If he had specified the subject in any detail at the beginning, he would not have needed to ask Vergil for an outline later on. In fact Vergil did have an outline by which he worked, and it was one which he had composed himself.[11] It seems clear that the emperor's advice, if he offered any, did not extend to the design of the *Aeneid*. He must have expressed himself in general terms, as he did when he asked for a letter in verse from Horace, and as other gentlemen are known to have done in their requests. The badgering that Augustus does in the letter from Spain is also part of a style of discourse one encounters in other literary relationships. Pliny writes in a similar vein to Suetonius, begging him to publish a work whose imminent appearance Pliny had announced in one of his poems:

> Either put an end to your delays, or face the prospect of having me force out of you by scurrilous satires the books which I cannot get by means of complimentary lyrics . . . Let me see your title, let me hear that the volumes of my dear Suetonius are being copied, read, and put on sale.
>
> Pliny *Epist.* 5.10

In all outward appearances, Augustus' association with Atticus, Horace, and Vergil resembles forms of literary and social intercourse which are familiar from the first part of this book. His interventions with these people reflect above all the consciousness that he is dealing with respected friends. This was by no means true of every writer with whom he came in contact, as two examples will illustrate. Macrobius (*Sat.* 2.4.31) tells the story of a Greek who used to take his stand outside the palace, waiting for a chance some morning to present a complimentary poem as the emperor emerged. For several days Augustus ignored him, until he was struck by an idea for a practical joke. He jotted a few verses of his own and the next morning passed them to the loitering bard. But his joke was trumped. With that nimbleness for which the Romans so envied Greeks, the poet read out the lines he had been given, exclaimed at their felicity, plucked some coins from his purse, and pressed them on the emperor. Augustus took the hint about princely deportment and produced a generous gratuity. Every detail of this encounter reveals a poet in very different circumstances from the poets described in Chapter 1. He is not Roman, but Greek; no gentleman, but poor. He waits outside the palace because he knows no one who could introduce him or even slip him in the door. He barters his poem openly for a reward and the money is paid on the spot, in the full view of bystanders. The end of the transaction is the end of the relationship. The incident is not thinkable with Horace or Vergil or one of the elegists as protagonist: it would have been humiliating.[12]

Augustus acted almost as coolly toward another writer who was Greek. For information about the eastern lands in which his son Gaius was to campaign, he called upon a scholar who was a native of the lower Tigris region and a distinguished geographer. The man was sent out in advance of the expedition and instructed to draw up a comprehensive memorandum for Gaius. Friends often received invitations to share a great man's company on tour or campaign, but this was something different: the geographer was assigned the status not of a companion but an agent. When a later emperor wished to procure similar information, he dispatched centurions.[13]

Many of the individuals with whom Augustus dealt in his long career were writers, and his responses to them doubtless ranged through all the nuances between his behavior toward Atticus and his treatment of the poet at the palace door. He had different sorts of relationships with the dilettante and sybarite Maecenas; with the historian Asinius Pollio, once an unfriendly power in the Caesarean camp and afterward a mogul on the cultural scene; with the poet Gallus, another Caesarean partisan, who rose to a position as commander and administrator under Augustus; with the scholar Hyginus, who was his freedman and his librarian; with the rhetor Apollodorus, who had been his teacher; and with the Damascan diplomat Nicolaus, who became his Greek biographer. If the full spectrum of these relationships were visible, we would find it more complicated to talk about the emperor's literary policy because so many more variables than literary activity could be seen to be in play. Despite the wealth of anecdotal material about Augustus, it still illuminates only a few of the situations in which he was in direct contact with contemporary writers.

In one sense, therefore, the glimpses that we get of Augustus' dealings with Atticus, Horace, and Vergil can be considered fortuitous, yet at the same time there is an apparent consistency to them. Our evidence in all three cases comes largely from correspondence, and that is purely a matter of chance. The significant thing these relationships have in common is that Atticus, Horace, and Vergil were the sort of friends with whom Augustus cared to correspond. The epistolary relationship both helps to define the level of intimacy and makes it possible to draw comparisons with other friendships known through the evidence of correspondence. When we see that Augustus' manner conforms to patterns of interaction one observes in the correspondence of Cicero or Pliny, it is reasonable to infer that in at least these cases his actions were prompted by sentiments and standards shared with his peers rather than by his narrower agenda as head of state.

Propaganda Resources of the Regime

Augustus' correspondence represents only a segment of his activities along the literary front. Even in the letters, his posture could be deceptive. He may have lavished the traditional courtesies in pursuit of a new objective, hoping to enlist talents who would create publicity on behalf, not simply of him, but of the political order he had imposed. The view that such considerations regularly underlie his treatment of writers and their work will be examined in the remainder of this chapter. Having argued that this is a modern and not an ancient perception of Augustus' practice, I cannot pretend to impartiality as I proceed: I find the political interpretation unsatisfactory. But I will try to acknowledge all the evidence that seems to commend that interpretation, and so at least to leave in place a framework for continuing discussion if I cannot explain the evidence in other terms.

The enormous power of Augustus is the fact from which every discussion must begin. If he wanted to control what his contemporaries were writing, he was unquestionably in a position to make his desires felt. He communicated directly with the public through edicts in which he promulgated his opinions and issued regulations. He controlled publication of the gazette which carried news and gossip of the city. He could require the senate to take legislative action on matters which concerned him. Through his prefects he directed the security and police forces which operated in the capital. He had broad opportunities to inject himself into the administration of justice. He established the lists of jurors who were allotted to the public courts, and he could sit alongside the magistrates in charge of them. He voted in and could even preside at trials in the senate, or he could remove any case he chose to his personal jurisdiction.

Extensive as these constitutional powers were, Augustus rarely needed to invoke them. He had so many servitors in public life who were willing to make his agenda their own that he could achieve his purposes indirectly, without expending his authority. The attitude that covert manipulation can always be assumed comes out occasionally in comments by writers of the imperial period. Suetonius at one point declines to quote from senatorial resolutions honoring Augustus because "they might seem to have been elicited by pressure or a sense of fealty" (*Aug.* 57.1). In Dio's account of the institution of the principate in 27 B.C., the famous speech in which the consul and erstwhile triumvir restored governance to the senate is an imposture. Loyalists had been instructed to clamor against his resignation and thus stampede their colleagues into a vote normalizing Augustus' extraordinary mandate.[14] No ancient observer noted signs that Augustus was making a parallel use of operatives in literary circles, but given his leverage over all public institutions and his reputation for subtle management, one is bound to entertain the possibility that he pressed writers also into service.

That possibility is strengthened by the fact that he cultivated so many other media for influencing the minds of his fellow citizens. Their attention was stirred by a drumbeat of holidays and thanksgivings which filled the calendar with imperial rhythms. Year after year new aspects of Augustus were found to celebrate. By the end of his reign the calendar had been enriched with some fifteen new holidays which called on citizens to put work aside and devote themselves to sacrifices, feasts, and public entertainments. A number of other anniversaries touching the life of the emperor or members of his family were marked by lesser observances. Even the sorrows of the imperial house invited yearly rites of condolence. An inscription from one Italian town shows not only that the townspeople mourned Augustus' heir-apparent when he died in A.D. 4 but that they memorialized the day:

> No public sacrifice or thanksgiving or nuptials or public banquets are henceforward to be proclaimed, organized, or consummated on the twenty-first day of February, nor are circus or stage performances to be held or witnessed, and on that day every year offerings are to be made to the spirit of the departed . . . by the magistrates or persons charged with the administration of justice.
>
> *ILS* 140.28–34

Those holidays on which Augustus had not actually stamped his name he could commandeer at will by prodigious expenditures for circuses and games.

Building was another way of stimulating public sentiment. Augustus and his associates raised or refurbished scores of imposing structures which gathered in much of the sacral and civil business of the city. Roman buildings made more than architectural statements, and many Augustan buildings bore witness for the emperor. They carried his name, commemorated his victories, and displayed his trophies. They were decorated inside and out with images and inscriptions which expressed his ideology. Although none of these structures has survived intact, the kind of message they preached is to some extent still preserved on the coinage, which was another medium of public suggestion. Coins kept the likeness of the leader before the people's eyes and introduced the faces of intended successors as dynastic plans matured. The portraits were juxtaposed with emblems of divine and popular approbation and with tokens of the peace, plenty, and supremacy which Augustus had conferred upon the Roman state. The design of the coins was constantly changing, especially the legends, which disseminated the titles by which the emperor set most store ("Son of the Deified Julius," "Augustus," "Holder of the Tribunician Power," "Chief Priest," "Father of the Nation") and proclaimed his latest feats at home and abroad.

The iteration of prayers was another means he found to catechize his people. Libations were poured to the Genius of Augustus at public banquets, and dutiful citizens offered a libation during private dinners as well. Midway through his reign, when he revived an old spirit-cult centering on crossroads shrines, he installed images identifying the spirits of the shrines with his personal and household tutelaries and organized neighborhood ministries to maintain the cult with prayer and sacrifice.

Finally, after rituals, slogans, images, and festivals had inculcated the values of the new order, the emperor drafted a last manifesto on the subject of himself. It resembled the kind of inscription which traditionally accompanied the statues of generals and statesmen, and which Augustus himself had solicitously inscribed to the memory of those leaders whose statues ornamented his new forum. But his own *Res Gestae* far outstripped the record of any Roman before him. The inscription was so long it covered two pylons set up before his riverside mausoleum, and copies were inscribed in other parts of the empire as well.

Augustus had a keen eye for any medium that could serve as a sounding board for official verities. Would he have failed to think of poetry, in a society gone mad for the Muses?

Precedent for a policy of literary management existed, and close to home. Less than a generation earlier, Julius Caesar confessed the power of poetry to shape opinion, saying that he had been branded for all time by Catullus' scurrilous Mamurra poems (Suet. *Jul.* 73). He also took steps to domesticate or neutralize fashionable writers. As soon as Catullus and Calvus gave signs of backing away from the abusive verses they had published, he began to court their good will (ibid.). As he gained power his methods became less amiable. During the civil war one of his antagonists scored a verbal hit against him with a widely circulated lampoon or tract. When the author later surrendered in North Africa, Caesar spared his life but refused to let him come home to Italy. Cicero tried to intercede and after months of unavailing negotiations he observed that the unforgivable mistake had been to satirize the Dictator rather than to fight him: "You would not have spent a single moment in your present plight if Caesar did not have the sense of being injured by the gift you have, which is something he prizes" (*Fam.* 6.5.3 = 239 SB). He further suggested that the way back into the Dictator's good graces was to redeploy the literary talent which had given offense. At about the same time another writer was subjected to a different sort of constraint. During Caesar's victory games a popular actor of farces challenged his rivals to compete with him in putting on a performance that was wholly improvised. Laberius, the most eminent practitioner of mime, was then an old man of sixty, but Caesar insisted not merely that he contribute to the contest, but that he perform in person. For the first time in his career, Laberius had to take the stage, which meant the forfeiture of his standing as a Roman knight (Macr. *Sat.* 2.7.1–9).

The only firsthand report of literary duress during the Caesarean era comes from Cicero, whose report also gives us our best picture of the way pressure was likely to be applied under any regime. In May of 45 B.C. he told Atticus about a memorandum on government which he had been trying to draft for Caesar's benefit—something along the lines of the letters to Alexander by Aristotle and Theopompus, he implied.[15] It is clear from the context and from subsequent references to the project (especially *Att.* 13.26.2 = 286 SB) that Atticus was the proximate instigator. For months he had been urging his disconsolate friend to come to terms with the political results of the civil war and to resume his role as an elder statesman. From Atticus' point of view the letter to Caesar evidently offered itself as a suitable vehicle for Cicero's comeback. Behind Atticus stood unnamed confidants of Caesar with whom he was consulting.[16] And behind them stood Caesar himself, eager for some gesture which would signify that the leading spokesman of the senate

was cooperating with the new regime.[17] At no point did the two principals deal directly with each other. Caesar seems to have given no positive
indication of what Cicero's discourse should say, and Cicero for his part
did not want Caesar to see what he had written until it had been vetted
by the nameless intermediaries. In the event, the letter may never have
been shown to Caesar. The indirection with which all parties proceeded
led to a fiasco. Though in one sense Cicero was free to write as he
pleased, having received no guidelines, he found the task practically impossible. He could not afford to give offense by uttering his true opinions, and from outright flattery he recoiled.[18] The only course left was
for him to try to divine the drift of Caesar's projects, and then to concoct
advice about them—as he put it in an outburst to Atticus, "What guide-
line was I supposed to follow, except my understanding of Caesar's purposes?" (*Att.* 13.27.1 = 298 SB). Though he more than once despaired
of finding anything to say, he managed to complete a draft, which was
passed along to Atticus' contacts. It turned out to be not what was
wanted. For one thing, Cicero's advice about the timing of Caesar's projected expedition to Parthia was judged inapposite. For another, some
high-minded statements about the conduct of policy were (rightly) construed as a criticism of actual policies.[19] Cicero abandoned the project
because "they want so many things changed there is no point in rewriting" (*Att.* 13.27.1 = 298 SB), and he rejected all of Atticus' efforts to
set him to work again.

Although the attempt to co-opt Cicero miscarried, it is a valuable
paradigm of pressure tactics translated into Roman forms of behavior.
What is sought from the writer is more the gesture of allegiance than
anything specific he has to say, and for that reason little effort is made to
dictate the content of his work. Pressure is applied, not directly through
institutional means, but through a concatenation of friends, each of
whom has some stake in the outcome. Although the author has liberty
to shape his work as he thinks best, he is constantly preoccupied with
fitting it to idiosyncrasies and interests of which he has at best a murky
understanding. He skirts hollowness, misunderstanding, offense, and
failure at every step.

The scheming by which Cicero was induced to compose his memorandum is not apparent in any of the stories about Augustus' relations
with literary men. But even if it could not be proved in a single instance
that Augustan writers were being mobilized for political ends, one
would continue to suspect it. The time was ripe for government en-

croachment. Augustus possessed the right resources to monitor literary activity. He effectively exploited other channels of communication. And he could build on foundations which Caesar had laid down. The fact that circumstances encouraged a policy of literary management is the most seductive part of the argument that Augustus did put such a policy into practice.

His known dealings with writers, however, furnish scant evidence of policy. The record consists first of all of those literary requests by Augustus which have already been mentioned, together with requests by others who had close ties with him. A number of poets offer promises or excuses which have been taken as responses to further initiatives from the emperor. There are a few cases in which his intervention came later, in the form of comments on material not yet published. And he rewarded or chastised several authors after publication.

Overtures from Augustus and His Partisans

The only works of literary character which Augustus undoubtedly instigated are all by Horace: the *Secular Hymn,* which was performed at the games of 17 B.C., the lyrics on the Alpine campaign fought by Augustus' stepsons Tiberius and Drusus two years later, and the *Letter to Augustus,* which evidently belongs to the same decade though it is not precisely datable.

The genesis of the *Secular Hymn* sets it apart from every other poem that Horace wrote. For that matter, it is unique in ancient literature. Though there are other songs and hymns which originated as performances at public ceremonies, this is the only one connected with a ceremony of which the full details are also known. Augustus celebrated the Secular Games in 17 B.C. By his reckoning it was the fifth time they had been celebrated since the founding of Rome, but the early history of the Games was a snarl of fabrications. Romans of the late first century would have owed such information as they had about the Secular Games to the descriptions which historians and antiquarians provided of the last official celebrations. An educated man would have known that the Games had gained a place in the state cult when harm seemed to threaten the nation; that they had been enjoined by the Sibyl, whose prophecies, treasured in sacred books, were consulted by Roman priests at times of crisis; that the celebration honored the divine rulers of the underworld, and was to take place periodically at a site holy to them in the Field of Mars; and that the Games had been held in the middle of the third century, again in the middle of the second century, but not since. The *saeculum* which divided performances was not a precisely defined span like a day or a year, but a variable measure, the length of time needed to ensure that no person alive at the commencement of one cycle lived to see the start of the next. But in practice it was counted as about a century. (We would do better to speak of the Century Games and the Century Hymn, if the term "Secular" had not become canonical in this context.)

Elastic as the measure might be, however, there was no known base or formula by which a *saeculum* could be computed to expire in the year 17 B.C. To celebrate the Games at that point, Augustus required a new chronology. Under his presidency the priests responsible for the Sibylline books discovered a hitherto unnoticed prophecy which specified the length of a *saeculum* as 110 years.[20] A search of the priestly archives established that previous performances had taken place in 456, 346, 236, and 126. Apart from her tip about the date, the Sibyl prescribed an order of ceremonies which transformed the entire ritual. The infernal powers to whom the games had been dedicated were ousted in favor of more constructive deities, with precedence given to the bright Olympians Jupiter, Juno, Apollo, and Diana. The Sibyl also stipulated that a hymn was to be sung by a chorus of girls and a chorus of boys, and that provided the impetus for Horace's *Secular Hymn*.[21] It would be difficult to think of an occasion on which a Latin poet had to cope with a more audacious official line. Add that the the poem was solicited by the man who was to be the chief officiant in all the ceremonies, and Horace's guidelines would seem to have been strait indeed.

The *Secular Hymn* does touch on matters with which Augustus was directly concerned. It alludes to the marriage legislation which he had initiated in the previous year (lines 17–20), to the Temple of Apollo which he had raised on the Palatine (65), to the legend of his ancestor Aeneas, freshly retold in the the epic which he was credited with salvaging after Vergil's death (37–44), to his controversial computation of the *saeculum* (4–8 and 21), and to all the deities honored in the new order of ceremonies. Three quatrains in the middle of the poem carry reminders of Augustus' achievements at home and abroad (49–60). But to filter and amplify these segments by introducing data extraneous to the poem gives a false impression of its effect. The only point at which it invites the hearer or reader to focus his attention on Augustus is in the middle quatrains. Otherwise, though many details have implications which could lead to Augustus, that is not the direction in which Horace takes them. Apart from drawing on the same myth, the lines on Aeneas do not allude to Vergil's poem, much less evoke Augustus' special relationship to it. They are a prayer, asking continuance of the care with which the gods have sustained their people from the wreck of Troy to the realization of a greater destiny in Italy. Apollo's sanctuary is brought in not to publicize the builder, but because the *Secular Hymn* was sung there, just after sacrifice to Apollo at the altar. The poem alludes to the recent regulations concerning marriage without noting that Augustus was behind them: "Goddess, bring forth a new generation, and bless the decrees of the Fathers for giving partners to our women, and for a rule of marriage that will bear new fruit of children" (17–20). Though in other poems (as in the opening lines of the *Letter to Augustus* and in *Odes* 4.15.9–12) Horace praises the emperor as the author of social reform, that would be alien to his purpose here. Exploiting both the literal sense of the word "fathers" and its value as an appellation meaning "senators," he has contrived a stanza which defines the makeup of the citizen body as it relates to procreation: the children, the women who marry and give birth, and the fathers who preside over household and community. At the same time he juxtaposes the two generations of young and old, as he does at other points when speaking about the gods' blessings.[22] This linking of generations is fundamental to the scheme of the *Secular Hymn* in two ways. The *Hymn* is conceived as a prayer by the youth of the community, framed in terms appropriate to their station, but offered on behalf of the whole community. Horace sets their prayer beside the supplications offered by spokesmen from the adult population (Augustus and the priests), who similarly have their claims on the gods' attention and who likewise pray on behalf of all.[23] He wants it to be remembered that in these rites young and old cooperate. He could not have intruded praise of Augustus into the lines quoted without detracting from the civic theme he was trying to develop.

The linking of generations is in its turn only a manifestation of a larger theme. At least as Horace understood them, the Secular Games celebrated continuity, in nature, society, and history. That theme is announced at the outset in the invocation to the gods who "will be worshiped always as you always have been" (2–3), in the image of the sun born each day different and the same (10), in the "sure cycle" which is to bring back hymns and games (21–22), in the utterance of destiny pronounced once forever and kept in place by the unbudgeable end-marker of time (26–27), and so on throughout the poem. It is sometimes said that Augustus staged the Secular Games to signal either the burial of bad times or the opening of a golden age. If that was the message he had in mind, it barely carried over into Horace's conception of the steadiness of Rome's course through the centuries.[24]

Where Augustus stands in that perspective is made clear in the last third of the *Hymn:*

> And may the bright scion of Anchises and Venus, as overpowering to the belligerent enemy as he is merciful to the prostrate, obtain the things he asks of you with sacrifices of white cattle.
>
> Already now the Parthians dread the hands which have won mastery on land and sea, and the insignia of Alban rule; now hitherto proud Scythians and Indians solicit words of counsel.
>
> Now Trust and Peace and Honor and pristine Purity and disregarded Virtue venture to return, and blessed Plenty appears with her copious horn.
>
> Hor. Saec. 49–60

Augustus is introduced as the principal celebrant and sacrificer. Apart from that, his lineage links him with Aeneas, whose relationship with the gods the young singers had made the basis of their immediately preceding prayer. They do not say what Augustus' prayer is for, but they suggest by the way they characterize him that it involves national interests graver than their own concerns with nature and family. And in fact their next words address the functioning of Rome as a state, first in relation to foreign powers and then internally.[25] These lines strike notes often heard in hosannas to Augustus, making it easy to associate him with Rome's ascendancy over other nations and with the stability that had returned to civic life.[26] No doubt Horace counted on his audience to respond subliminally to those associations, but they are not part of his overt strategy at this point. As with the nuptial laws, he alludes to activities which are as much collective as individual. It is left open whether the hands dreaded by the Parthians are those of Roman legionaries or of Augustus, and the word "Alban" can be understood equally as meaning "Roman" or "Julian." Horace keeps the human actors indistinct because they are less important than the proof observed in one event after another ("now . . . now . . . now") that the gods have resumed their watch over the fortunes of the Roman state. The two stanzas are transitional.

They suggest the focus of Augustus' prayer, and at the same time they point to evidence that the gods are already answering that prayer. They thus provide a basis for the affirmation which forms the coda of the children's hymn, that because Apollo "is adding another happy *saeculum*" and "Diana is heeding the prayers of the priests and the children, we come away with well-founded hope that Jupiter and all the gods are in accord with our desires" (65–74).

It would be perverse to read the *Secular Hymn* as a composition written to glorify Augustus, to articulate his ideology, or to summarize his administrative program. He and his works have only a small part in Horace's design. Lines of development which might have led to him instead veer away, and other subjects which a panegyrist would have been hard put to ignore do not come up at all. The most noticeably missing subject is the succession, which could easily have been worked into a poem on the turning of the *saeculum* and which was then topical. One year previously Augustus had conferred a greater share in his power on Agrippa, and during the year 17, perhaps in one of the months preceding the Secular Games, he adopted Agrippa's two sons and began preparing them for the succession.[27] Also missing from the poem, for all the prominence Apollo has in it, is any reminiscence of the god's miraculous intervention at Actium.[28] The little which Horace does say about Augustus is muted in comparison with effusions in other poems and strictly accommodated to the situation of the children and their prayer.

Suetonius does not quote the invitation which Horace received to write the *Hymn,* and so we cannot know in what light the project was presented to him. But what he made of it is evident from the text. Drawing his inspiration from the content of the exotic ritual, he tried to illuminate for his fellow citizens meanings not conveyed by the brittle formulas of official prayer.[29] His consciousness of stepping into a spokesman's role comes out also in references he makes to the *Secular Hymn* in other poems. In *Odes* 4.3.13–15 he speaks as though he owed the distinction of being chosen to the young singers, suggesting that it is they for whom he speaks. In the *Letter to Augustus,* on the other hand, the role he envisions is that of spokesman for the entire community. The *Secular Hymn* is a prime exhibit in his argument that a poet benefits the city by mediating communication between gods and men (lines 118–138). He never insinuates that he spoke or was encouraged to speak on behalf of Augustus.

It is more difficult to interpret how Horace handled the injunction to celebrate the victory of Augustus' stepsons. The Alpine campaign is less well documented than the Secular Games, but the main difficulty is that Suetonius' report of the request does not exactly correspond with what we read in Horace. What the life says (that Augustus set him to write about the Vindelician victory of his stepsons Tiberius and Drusus and obliged him in consequence to add a fourth book of *Odes* to the three published some years earlier) suggests a single request for a poem or a pair of poems focusing on Drusus and Tiberius. What we have are two poems (*Carm.* 4.4 and 4.14) written at different times, one focusing on Drusus and the other focusing on Augustus though it compliments both Drusus and Tiberius. Were both poems generated by the emperor's request? In the absence of direct evidence, the only way to answer this question is to try to relate the poems to the known determinants of the situation they address. Though I hope my answer will seem to fit the facts, it appears that a perfect fit is not to be achieved.

The campaign took place during Augustus' long sojourn in Gaul, where he went in 16 B.C. after German tribes had crossed the Rhine and trounced the governor Lollius and his legions. Although the Germans promptly patched things up, Augustus stayed on and stepped up operations against the tribes who controlled the Alpine passes leading from Italy toward Gaul and Germany. On the grounds that the tribesmen persisted in raiding the settled communities of north Italy, he dispatched Drusus to bring relief to subjects and terror to the mountains. In the summer of 15 Drusus and his force went up the valleys of the eastern Alps and over the passes of the Tirol, dislodging the natives from their strongholds. For having quelled the threat to Italy, he was awarded honorary standing as a praetor. But then on the northern side of the mountains a second phase of the campaign was opened along a much wider front. Drusus continued to take part, but now the ranking officer was his brother Tiberius, who had marched from the west into Switzerland. This time the Romans were involved in sieges of major strongholds and in pitched battles against massed forces as far north as the Danube. By August they had achieved their objectives.[30]

In the first of the two poems, Horace speaks solely of Drusus' expedition in the Tirol and not of Tiberius' activities, though at one point (line 28) he adverts to Tiberius as being Drusus' brother. This poem must therefore have been written before commencement of the second and more extensive phase of operations. It is the only poem in the Horatian corpus which treats a martial subject primarily in order to glorify the protagonist.[31] It is Horace's equivalent of one of Pindar's victory odes, a fact emphasized by Pindaric trademarks posted throughout the poem. After two long similes describing an eagle and a lion (both of which neatly establish a locale in high altitudes), Horace comes to Drusus in the Alps:

> As upon a lion, the Vindelicians looked on Drusus as he waged battle below the Rhaetian Alps. Whence derives the usage that during all their history has armed them with the Amazon's battle-axe, I have foreborne to seek. It is forbidden to know all things. But those hordes which had so long ranged victorious were dealt a check by the lad's strategy. They felt the effects of talent and character which had been properly nourished in Augustus' home.
>
> Hor. *Carm.* 4.4.17–27[32]

Horace continues with praise for the upbringing which Drusus and Tiberius had received from their stepfather, and praises also the heritage of the Claudian family into which they were born. A great victory won by an earlier Claudius is the node around which the second half of the poem takes shape. Horace thinks of the Battle of Sena and of Hannibal brooding on the indomitability of the Romans.

Drusus' own campaign is told in the passage quoted, essentially by way of a preterition that is Horace's most egregious rendering of Pindar's manner. Instead of detailing events of the war or the nature of the adversary, he lets us see the murderous heirloom which links the Vindelicians to the age of heroes. The exact provenance of the battle-axe is beside the point: what is emphasized (in the phrases "has armed through all their history," "long ranged victorious") is that the Vindelicians have made formidable adversaries since legendary times. Having implanted that idea, Horace dispenses with further comment on the fighting. The poem as he conceives it is not about the war but about the first test of a young aristocrat's capacities; hence he dwells on themes like nature, inheritance, and education which are tied up with youth. The action of the similes is presented from the same angle: the eagle chick quits the nest, learns to fly, preys first on sheep and then with increasing boldness on more combative victims; the lion cub has been driven from its mother's teat and is stalking its first kill.

This approach would not have worked if the poem had also had to accommodate Tiberius, who was by that time a seasoned leader.[33] But it was perfectly adapted to the situation of Drusus, who was being showcased for his first performance in the field. In the summer before, Augustus had taken care to have resistance in the Alps softened up by a veteran officer. Then at the age of twenty-three, after Drusus had been rotated through a couple of magistracies which displayed his dexterity in the conduct of civil affairs and after he had presided at a gladiatorial show which introduced him to the populace, he received his first field command. His brother had been accorded similar treatment a few years earlier, when at the age of twenty-one he was sent with an army to install a Roman protégé on the Armenian throne. (In its time that expedition too had elicited Horatian flowerets, in *Epist.* 1.3.1–5 and 1.12.26–28.) At the close of Drusus' first assignment, his services were hailed with a decree of praetorian honors. The *Fourth Ode* appeared at about the same time. Its individualistic focus and frank panegyrical intent give it a very different tone from Horace's other poems, and the difference is best explained if the poem is related to Augustus' arrangements for his stepson's debut. What Horace has written is compatible with the report of a request. But if Augustus supplied the motive and the subject, he did not impose himself on the design. Horace compliments Augustus by name in one stanza (lines 25–28), and his presence is felt in two others (1–4 and 33–36). But otherwise the poem regards only Drusus and his Claudian antecedents.[34] As with the *Secular Hymn,* one must conclude either that Augustus' instructions about content were singularly self-effacing or that he left the execution of his request to Horace's discretion.

The *Fourteenth Ode* is often described as the companion piece to the *Fourth,* the poem for Tiberius to complement the poem for Drusus. But that description gives a poor idea of what it says. It opens with this worshipful salute:

> Augustus, greatest of leaders as far as the sun brightens populated coasts, what ingenuity in the full outpouring of honors by senators and citizens could perpetuate your heroic acts in accolades and enduring registers? Latest to have learned what puissance you have in war are the Vindelicians who stood outside the laws of Rome.
>
> Hor. *Carm.* 4.14.1–9

The next stanza quickly sketches Drusus' march through the Alps, then five stanzas enlarge on Tiberius' more arduous campaign, from which the poem leads back to Augustus: "Cutting a swathe from first to last, Tiberius heaped the battlefield and conquered without casualties, borrowing from you manpower and counsel and your patron gods" (lines

31–34). Once Horace returns to Augustus, he remains with him throughout the last five stanzas. He observes that the decisive victory in the Alpine war took place on the anniversary of his entry into Alexandria fifteen years before, sustaining a tide of successes that has daunted nations around the world.

It should be apparent that *Odes* 4.14 cannot be called a Tiberius ode in the same sense in which 4.4 is a Drusus ode. A radical shift of thought stands out in turns of phrase. In 4.4 Horace had said that the enemy were conquered by the strategy of Drusus ("consiliis iuvenis," 24); here he says that Tiberius conquered through the strategy of Augustus ("te praebente consilium," 4.14.33–34). In 4.4 it was Drusus whose puissance the enemy came to know ("sensere quid mens rite, quid indoles nutrita . . . posset," 25–26); here it is Augustus ("didicere nuper quid Marte posses," 4.14.8–9). And the whole orientation of the poem is different. An integral but subordinate figure in the *Drusus Ode,* Augustus here engrosses more attention than Drusus and Tiberius combined. It will be noticed that the occasion of the poem is not precisely the culmination of the war; that would have thrown too much emphasis on the leaders in the field. Instead Horace takes his start from the honors decreed after the good news has broken in Rome: reaction in the senate naturally centered more on the emperor than on his stepsons. The stanzas in which the poet treats the stepsons' exploits are punctuated with reminders that Augustus was the mastermind behind them ("with your soldiery," 9; "under your favoring auspices," 16; "borrowing from you manpower and counsel and your patron gods," 33–34). Finally by the end of the poem it is made clear that the Alpine victory is only the token of a broader assurance. Having traced a line from the victory in Egypt fifteen years earlier to the victory just accomplished, Horace extols Augustus as the safeguard of Italy and Rome (lines 43–44). He lists the surrounding nations who in the interval have learned to acknowledge the emperor's might: Cantabrians of Spain, Parthians, Indians, Scythians, peoples of the Nile, Danube, and Tigris, the Britons on their island in the ocean (this catalog fills two stanzas, lines 41–48), then in the last stanza Gaul, Spain, and the Sugambri. Spain figures twice, which is a clue that the list is divided into two parts. The first consists of nations with whom Augustus had dealings some years previously. The last stanza lists those regions to which he has devoted attention since establishing himself in Gaul in 16 B.C. Between these two phases of foreign policy came the Lollian catastrophe, which snapped the web of Roman success abroad.

The chief perpetrators of that affront were the Sugambri, with whom Augustus had to postpone a reckoning and settle for a truce. Two years later his stepsons handed him a victory which restored his credit, and Horace in the *Fourteenth Ode* spun the threads which patched the tear.[35]

That he wrote this poem at Augustus' urging, however, is doubtful for two reasons. First, the natural reading of the Suetonian life is that Augustus made one request for commemorative verse. A single request would not ordinarily result in two poems written at different times from such different angles. If one poem appears to respond straightforwardly to the request, it is reasonable to seek a different explanation for the other piece. Second, Suetonius says that Augustus called for a poem about his stepsons' victory, which ought to mean a poem in honor of his stepsons. The *Fourteenth Ode* does speak of both stepsons, unlike the *Fourth*, but it is only incidentally about them and their victory. All its dynamism is concentrated on Augustus himself. Rather than suppose that Augustus maneuvered to obtain a poem about himself which would be disguised as a poem about his stepsons, it seems preferable to think that Horace proffered 4.14 on his own initiative, some weeks after he had completed the *Drusus Ode* in response to a request.[36] To appeal once more to Suetonius' testimony, Horace was urged not only to write a victory ode, but to bring out a book which featured it. That meant marshaling enough material to fill a book. As two odes (*Carm.* 4.3 and 4.6) may be considered spin-offs of the *Secular Hymn,* so *Odes* 4.14 may be considered a spin-off of the *Drusus Ode.*

The only other poems expressly said to have been prompted by Augustus are Horace's *Letter to Augustus* and Vergil's *Aeneid.*[37] The scope of the request in each case has been discussed earlier, and little needs to be added here. Augustus solicited the *Letter* after Horace turned to writing verse epistles. What he received was not a letter about himself but a letter about poetry, framed in terms which Horace imagined would appeal to him. (In general it is not so much the subjects as the effort to play them against the mentality of specific recipients that makes the *Epistles* personal.) For his colloquy with the leading citizen Horace chose to reflect on the public dimensions of his profession: the clash between popular taste and professional standards, the place of the moderns in the evolution of poetry at Rome, the utility of the poets to the state and their relationship to the leader of the state. Because at some points Horace is so vehemently arguing personal convictions, there has been little temptation to read the *Letter* as the exposition of an official viewpoint. One last observation may be made about the *Letter* here for the sake of a problem which will be considered later. A critic relying on purely internal evidence, if he detected any sign of pressure at all, would surely have guessed that Horace had been invited to write a panegyrical epic. Toward the end of the poem the poet apologizes for being unable to chronicle Augustus' wars, in a passage (lines 250–259) which is as full-blown a *recusatio* as any we have. Thanks to a fragment of correspondence quoted by Suetonius, however, we know that Augustus asked not for an epic but for a letter in verse. The case is worth remembering when inferences are teased from other refusal poems.

As already indicated, the evidence that Augustus prompted Vergil to write the *Aeneid* is considerably weaker than evidence of his interventions with Horace. While an extract from one of Augustus' letters to Vergil clearly demonstrates his interest in the *Aeneid,* we have only the authority of two late Vergilian lives for the assertion that Augustus instigated the poem. But even if this report should be true, I have argued earlier that Augustus could not have prescribed the content of Vergil's poem in any detail.

If the emperor strove to propagate his views through the medium of poetry, the touchstone of his policy should be those poems which he is known to have encouraged. The less certain his involvement, the less certain it must be that a given poem bears his imprint. The four poems with which he can be most directly linked show little sign of having been tailored to a common pattern. As a group, they are appreciably less fulsome than the norm for Augustan panegyric. The facets which they hold up for public appreciation vary from poem to poem. Both the heterogeneity of the poems and the clues we have about Augustus' requests make it unlikely that his intervention extended to instruction about the way subjects were to be treated. The projects he proposed to Horace all kept to lines marked out by the poet's earlier work. The requests for the *Secular Hymn* and the *Drusus Ode* followed publication of three books of lyrics; the request for a letter in verse followed the first book of the *Epistles* (or perhaps the first fruits of them). Augustus did not, so far as we know, solicit an epic about his wars.

The idea that poets were pressed into service by the regime could not have established itself solely on the basis of these initiatives by Augustus. Historically, it has been argued more in terms of Maecenas' activity than of Augustus'. The confidant and deputy of the emperor was the doyen of Rome's most admired literary cenacle. One has only to conflate those functions in order to make him into a kind of literary commissar. This interpretation of his role has more than logical simplicity to commend it. Literary relationships at Rome often fall into triangular configurations whereby one person asks a writer to produce something for a third party. It would have been perfectly normal if Maecenas had sometimes suggested projects which he thought would please his friend Augustus. Even a program of scouting out and domesticating talent would not have been unprecedented: Oppius and Balbus had blazed that trail in Cicero's time.

Cogent examples of Maecenas' ministerial operations are hard to pin down, however. Cicero's letters to Atticus give us our bearings for understanding the role of Atticus, of Caesar's agents, and of Caesar himself in relation to Cicero, and the scraps of Augustus' correspondence allow glimpses of his intercourse with Horace and Vergil. But not even scraps remain of Maecenas' correspondence. The only testimony about the kind of work he encouraged consists of remarks in poems written by his protégés. To have no more circumstantial information than this is a great handicap to understanding his role. Literary requests can be made from a variety of motives, and the possibilities are doubly complicated if one person happens to be acting on behalf of someone else. Nothing entitles us to paint in the background to such a request when we have no clues about it.

The testimony of poets is sparse as well as vague. There are only four poems which allude to Maecenas' prodding. In 3.9 Propertius protests at being urged out onto the high seas of poetry when Maecenas himself shuns the glory to which he is called by his relationship with Augustus. The poet identifies the high seas with epic themes from the Theban and Trojan cycles, which he renounces for the slighter themes of love elegy. At that point he makes a confusing lurch and affirms that with Maecenas to guide him, he will essay even poems about Jupiter's battle with the Titans and about Rome's primeval history. As his abilities "measure up to your commands" ("crescet . . . ingenium sub tua iussa meum," 3.9.52), he will write of Augustus' triumph and Antony's fall.

The implication that Maecenas encouraged Propertius to write something grander than love poems is clear. He may have recommended an epic on Augustus' victory over Antony, but that is not so clear. In the last part of the poem Propertius contemplates a series of epics, each more ambitious than the one before (the first is sketched in two lines, the second in three, the last in four). He seems to be proposing a bargain: if he continues to enjoy Maecenas' favor, by degrees he will gird himself to write the kind of poetry Maecenas expects.[38] As for the subjects, a literal reading of Propertius' words "at your guidance I will sing" in line 47 would seem to entail either that Maecenas urged all three of the epics then enumerated, which critics have been loath to assert, or that Propertius was simply volunteering three examples of what he might try. It forces the text to isolate the last as the only poem specifically asked for.

If Propertius is imagining possibilities rather than fielding requests, what he says in 3.9 is roughly compatible with what he says in 2.1, his one other poem to Maecenas. Pressed for an explanation of why he always writes love poems, he answers by extolling the fertile invention which the thought of his mistress inspires in him. But if fate had endowed him with a talent for epic, he continues, he would choose as his theme, not the battle of the gods and Titans, or Thebes or Troy or remote events in the sagas of Greece and Rome, but Augustus' successes in the civil wars. Here it is clear that none of the subjects, including the last, has been suggested by Maecenas. The poem on the civil wars would have been a spontaneous offering, if only the poet felt equal to it.

Our information about Maecenas' most celebrated request comes from Vergil's prelude to the third book of *Georgics*. The poet begins by evoking the deities and setting appropriate to a book which will treat of herds and farm animals. He tells how he longs to create an original poem, and he imagines his triumphant return to his home region, where he will erect a temple in Augustus' honor. The evidently allegorical temple is limned in some detail. Then Vergil breaks away: "In the meantime, let us keep to the woods of the Dryads and the virgin ranges—your far from easy commands ["haud mollia iussa" again], Maecenas. Without you my wit conceives nothing sublime" (G. 3.40–42). He scolds himself for procrastinating, promises a future work on Augustus' battles, and tackles the subject of oxen.

Every reader finds that it takes a powerful blast of exegesis to shake useful data from these wisps. To begin with, the simplest interpretation is probably in this case false. Despite Vergil's words, Maecenas' charge must have embraced something more than just animal husbandry (which is what the woodlands and ranges represent). Since he is saluted at the beginning of all four books of the *Georgics* and since he is invited to collaborate in spirit as Vergil expounds the art of arboriculture in book 2 (line 39), it has always been assumed that Maecenas gave the stimulus to the whole poem.

Contention over the precise nuance of "far from easy commands," however, seems misdirected. The word *iussa* is conventional language in literary requests. And Vergil appears to have supplied his own gloss on *haud mollia* in the following line. Maecenas' bidding is hard to carry out because it requires the poet to conceive a lofty theme. And by that, Vergil means an original theme: something, as lines 8–9 say, by which "I can lift myself above the ground."[39] But if Maecenas' command is understood as an exhortation to strive for something lofty, one must question whether it stipulated any particular subject.

Finally, if the evidence of Maecenas' involvement with the subject of the *Georgics* is ambiguous, the evidence of Augustus' concern with it is subperceptible. Vergil appeals to him for inspiration in the invocation of book 1; he brings the names of both Augustus and Maecenas into the preludes of books 1 and 3; and in book 4 he dates the end of his work on the *Georgics* to the period of Augustus' campaigns in the East. Those are the piers on which critics have raised the theory that Maecenas solicited the *Georgics* for the emperor in order to promote the agricultural policy of the regime. Vergil himself gives no indication of the motives behind Maecenas' request, or of possible interest on the part of Augustus, or of any way in which the *Georgics* might be related to policy.

Though it is far from apparent that Maecenas had political reasons for wanting Propertius to write epic or for welcoming Vergil's poem on agriculture, both projects are such that political overtones are at least imaginable. They are more difficult to imagine in the case of the other two works which Maecenas is credited with encouraging. In the *Fourteenth Epode* Horace says that Maecenas is "pestering him to death" ("occidis saepe rogando," line 5) to finish up a collection of iambic poems begun several years earlier. As usual, the circumstances of this intervention are left unexplained, but it cannot have been the political utility of the *Epodes* which led Maecenas to press for publication. These poems are modeled on the outspoken verse of early Greek iambists who reacted hotly to contemporary events and personalities. In Horace's adaptations, however, invective is reserved for nonentities and political comment is circumscribed. Only four of the seventeen pieces in the collection address political themes. Two which deplore the folly of civil war (the *Seventh* and the *Sixteenth*) adopt a nonpartisan stance and spotlight neither heroes nor villains. Two other pieces have to do with the battle of Actium. In the *First Epode*, Horace asks leave to stay by Maecenas' side as his friend prepares to embark with the Caesarean fleet. This poem preserves a scrupulously personal focus, without adverting to any of the issues which were bruited in the war against Antony. After Antony's defeat and flight from Actium, Horace composed the *Ninth Epode,* which exalts the victor and vilifies the enemy. This is the only poem in the book which can be described as a pro-Caesarean piece.[40] Since it is also the latest datable poem of the book, it probably did not not exist at the time when Maecenas was urging Horace to hurry up.

About a decade after publication of the *Epodes,* Maecenas was again coaxing Horace to produce. The opening lines of the first book of *Epistles* fix the situation. Likening himself to a gladiator who has earned retirement after a successful career, Horace protests that Maecenas is trying to put him back in the old arena. He says that his age and outlook have changed and that he is now committed to the task of bettering himself through philosophical discipline. It is clear that *Epistles* 1.1 is a species of refusal poem which introduces a series of ethically oriented verse epistles in place of some other kind of poetry Maecenas had asked for. But what was it that Maecenas asked for? Since Horace's last pub-lished poems were the *Odes* of books 1 through 3, the most obvious reference of the phrase "the old arena" (line 3) is to lyric poetry. It is because love poetry is at issue that he can beg off on grounds of age. This interpretation is consistent with a passage in the *Seventh Epistle* which responds to Maecenas' nostalgia for the boon companionship he used to enjoy with Horace. That phase of their friendship they have outgrown, Horace argues. He recollects it as a time when he had stam-ina, a handsome head of hair, and readiness for sweet words and mirth, wine and romance (lines 25–28). The reminiscence, half literary and half factual, is meant to conjure an erotic mood. Life in Maecenas' circle may not have been given over entirely to amorous adventures, but they were a real and important pastime of upper-class society, and for Horace they symbolized better than any other pursuit that period of his career which was associated with the writing of the *Odes.* Although his lyrics include a variety of pieces which have nothing to do with love, neither Maecenas nor Horace would have identified the genre overall with any other theme.[41] What Maecenas sought, then, was evidently more of the same—more of Horace's genial company, and more of his winy love poems. If that is so, his efforts in this instance would seem to have been working at cross-purposes to Augustus' reform of morals rather than in furtherance of it.[42]

We have only the statements of Propertius, Vergil, and Horace to define Maecenas' influence on contemporary poetry. They never hint that he was acting in anyone's interest but his own when he offered them suggestions. And it is at least not obvious that the projects he is on record as having encouraged had a political tendency. Admittedly the poets do not tell us very much about his role, and what they do say may not be entirely candid. If we knew on other grounds that Maecenas tried to harness the writers he befriended to the Augustan bandwagon, we would have no trouble imagining that it was so in these cases too. For purposes of argument, however, the point to be made is this: although the passages from Propertius, Vergil, and Horace could be reconciled with the hypothesis that Maecenas was acting for Augustus, they are not themselves evidence for that hypothesis. He might have been acting for himself.

Another figure who has been pinpointed as an emissary between Augustus and the poets is Trebatius Testa, a well-connected jurist of the period. This interpretation of his role is based on his presentation by Horace in *Satires* 2.1, a dialogue in which the poet asks the lawyer what he should do about the hostile reception his satires have encountered. When Horace cannot bring himself to accept Trebatius' initial advice, which is to quit writing altogether, Trebatius suggests a change of direction: "Venture to relate the deeds of invincible Caesar and you will be amply rewarded for your pains" (lines 10–12). Horace rejects this advice too, saying that he lacks a gift for martial poetry. Trebatius replies that he might do a pen portrait in the manner of Lucilius, depicting the leader in civilian repose. Horace agrees that something of the sort would go over well if launched at the right moment, but he still has his heart set on writing satire. With that he flies off into a pugnacious defense of his art. Trebatius points out that he risks offending the bigwigs on whose good will he depends, and adds that it is his professional duty to caution him about the laws against libel. Horace turns the warning aside with a joke that brings the dialogue to a close.

Although Horace's interlocutor is a bona fide contemporary, one may doubt whether this poem can be read as the report of an actual conversation. It may be governed by the same convention which allowed Cicero to put unhistorical utterances into the mouths of the true-life characters who speak his dialogues.[43] But let us suppose that Trebatius in the satire is made to say, if not things he actually did say to Horace, at least things that it was in character for him to say, or that he was known to have said to other writers. Even in that case his advice need not be seen as expressing his zeal for Augustus' greater glory. In the dialogues which make up the second book of *Satires* Horace introduces speakers whose personalities are bound up with the subjects they discuss. Trebatius' professional background creates an occasion for Horace to approach him as a layman consulting an expert, and it also comes out in their discussion of libel at the end.

But Trebatius' character has a still more important bearing on their conversation. When Horace talks in his own person, the only issue he can recognize is his integrity as a writer. All of Trebatius' interjections, on the other hand, emphasize the importance of getting along with people, at which he was one of the greatest adepts the age had seen. When he was first trying to establish his reputation as a specialist in legal science, he attached himself to Cicero, who then enjoyed preeminence in the courts and public life. Through Cicero he obtained a sinecure at Caesar's headquarters in Gaul, where he befriended Matius, who emerged during the civil war as one of Caesar's political caretakers in Italy. Trebatius often collaborated on missions with Matius, and by the end of the war he belonged to Caesar's inner circle, while still maintaining his ties to Cicero. After Caesar's assassination, he managed to align himself with the faction which was to triumph in the next round of civil war. During the closing decades of the century he was ensconced as a respected legal adviser of Augustus. It was the instinct for self-alignment as much as his legal expertise that qualified Trebatius to dispense advice. One may not wish to call the attitude he expresses in the poem opportunistic, but it is pragmatic. He tries to steer Horace toward panegyrical verse only when he cannot persuade him to give up poetry altogether. He suggests an epic on the victor of Actium because that is the most lucrative undertaking that occurs to him. But he is ready to drop the idea when Horace makes it clear that intends to stick to satire. Trebatius talks more like the careerist he was than the bearer of a serious proposition from Augustus' inner circle.[44]

All these contacts between poets and the masters of the new order have promoted a belief that Augustan poetry was entrammeled in politics. But taken one by one, they show less influence of political imperatives than of long-established tendencies which anchored literary activity in aristocratic social life. In all known overtures by Augustus or persons close to him, the suggestions that are made resemble overtures by other Roman aristocrats past and present. They seem for the most part just as loose and offhand, and they evince no sign of an overall strategy. What has magnified them in spite of their intrinsic conventionality is the sense a reader of Augustan poetry gets that they were endless—that demands from Augustus and his satellites far outnumbered those that poets encountered in private circles. This impression would plainly be erroneous if our evidence consisted only of the passages already discussed, in which some sort of request is explicit. Four requests by Augustus and four by Maecenas hardly match the amount of haggling we can detect in the correspondence of Cicero or Pliny. But there is another group of texts, perhaps as many as a dozen more, in which poets either refuse or defer themes having some connection with Augustus.[45] If these are added to the rest, it does begin to look as though Augustus asserted his literary wishes on an unprecedented scale.[46]

The two categories of poems need to be kept distinct: texts which do not unambiguously testify to outside pressure have less authority than those which do. In addition to their elusiveness on this point, poetic promises and refusals have also an air of stylization that makes them unconvincing witnesses. In all but two cases (Hor. *Carm.* 3.25 and *Culex* 8–10) the projects contemplated or declined are epics rehearsing Augustus' feats of arms. If this remarkable coincidence really reflects a series of initiatives from his side, it would appear that he was consumed with a desire for panegyrical verse. That conclusion is hard to reconcile with the details Suetonius gives about his taste in poetry (*Vita Hor.* pp. 297.35–298.11 Roth) or with his report that Augustus discouraged the indiscriminate manufacture of verse in his honor (*Aug.* 89.3). Suspicion that the poets are striking attitudes and not parrying suggestions is strengthened by two situations in which the inference from poem to request can be rejected. The first has already been mentioned. Toward the end of the *Letter to Augustus* Horace confesses his inability to treat the emperor's wars in worthy verse. But Augustus did not ask for an epic. We know from Suetonius that what he wanted was one of Horace's letters in verse.

An argument for a spontaneous disavowal can also be made out in the case of the ode to Agrippa (*Carm.* 1.6), where Horace says that he would only botch the great exploits of Agrippa and Augustus if he tried to celebrate them. Agrippa's career is documented in unusual detail, yet he scarcely figures in any anecdote or incident of Augustan literary life, from which he evidently kept aloof.[47] In Roman society requests normally emanate from friends and fellow travelers in the world of letters, not from outsiders. Furthermore, all through his career Agrippa made a point of downplaying his military contributions. Every triumph that was offered to him he turned down.[48] An epic glorifying his victories is the last sort of poem one would expect him to have pressed for.

For most poems in the group, the possibility of a prior request can no more be excluded than it can be verified. But it is not the only etiology which would account for them. The poet who promises or declines to write epic may be presuming on conventional attitudes, either of the aristocracy, for whom epic had always been the most congenial form of poetry, or within the literary confraternity, which had ordained epic as the highest test of genius. Or he may be using the device of a promise or apology in order to adapt grand themes to a form more compatible with the rest of his oeuvre, as lyric, elegy, or epistle. Poems of this type admit of too many other explanations to be considered good evidence of pressure from without.

So far as one can infer from the poems and other texts available, Augustus looked to literary men for much the same services as did his peers, and he broached his suggestions in the same way. But there are three anecdotes about his interference at later points in the literary process which suggest a more aggressive role. The first concerns his arrangements for publication of the *Aeneid*. According to Donatus' life of Vergil, at the time the poet died, he possessed a draft of his epic which he had planned to spend three years revising in seclusion overseas. During a stop at Athens on the outbound journey, he met Augustus, who was returning from an inspection of the eastern provinces. For reasons unexplained, he decided to accompany Augustus back to Rome, but on the way he fell sick and ultimately died. During his last days he did his best to suppress the manuscript, which he considered not yet fit for publication. Even before leaving Italy, he had asked his friend Varius to burn the poem in the event of his death, but Varius refused. When Vergil was lying ill, he wanted to burn the manuscript himself, but it was kept out of his hands. And so he willed it to Varius and another friend along with the rest of his papers, stipulating that they not publish any material which he had not already published himself. After Vergil's death, however, Augustus stepped in and insisted that the legatees put the manuscript into readable form and publish it despite the will.[49]

The coolness with which Augustus contravened a friend's testamentary request is by no means alien to his principles of behavior in politics.[50] That he was pursuing a political objective in this case is unlikely, however. One's judgment will depend very much on how one interprets the *Aeneid:* the more of an Augustan bias that work is thought to embody, the more self-serving Augustus' insistence on publication will seem. But self-serving or not, his action did not affect the content of Vergil's poem. The Donatan life reports that Varius published the manuscript essentially in the form in which Vergil had left it, with minimal corrections. Furthermore, there were unusual personal reasons for Augustus to take charge on this occasion. Vergil had been traveling with him, and he and his manuscript were evidently still with the imperial entourage at the time he died. Augustus was named as one of the principal heirs in Vergil's will. He may therefore have felt that circumstances justified his having something to say about the final arrangements. Finally, his behavior was at least partly determined by that sense of collective responsibility to claims of art which is so marked a feature of Roman literary society. Because writers worked to a great extent under the eyes of friends, they did not fully control what they wrote. Unpublished work circulated freely, with or without an author's consent during his lifetime, and after his death it passed as a trust to his colleagues in the enterprise of letters. When Augustus rescued the *Aeneid,* he was acting on the same kind of impulse that later led Ovid's friends to put private copies of the *Metamorphoses* into circulation when the author burned the original.[51]

The other two stories about Augustus are more significant because in both, his actions lead to substantive rewriting. The first is from a prose writer, the historian Livy, who relates how a discovery by the emperor prompted him to alter a section of his narrative. In book 4, chapters 17–20, he describes a long-ago battle between Romans and Veientines in which a mere military tribune performed the most outstanding deed of valor. Cornelius Cossus confronted, killed, and stripped the enemy king, thus taking what were known as the "prime spoils" *(spolia opima)* and eclipsing the performance even of his own commander. He deposited the armor of the slain king in the temple of Jupiter Feretrius, where Romulus had deposited the only comparable prize ever taken previously. At the end of his narrative, Livy abruptly corrects himself as follows:

> Following all previous authorities, I have recorded that Aulus Cornelius Cossus was military tribune when he set up in the temple of Jupiter Feretrius the second dedication of prime spoils. Yet strictly speaking only those spoils which a commander strips from his opposite number are considered "prime," and "commander" can only be understood as the man under whose auspices a war is waged. Over and above that fact, the very inscrip-

tion on the spoils argues against me and my predecessors that Cossus was consul when he took them. As I had heard that Augustus Caesar, the founder or restorer of all our temples, personally read this on the linen breastplate inside the dilapidated shrine of Jupiter Feretrius which he rebuilt, I thought it little less than sacrilege to dispossess Cossus of a witness to his trophy who is none other than Caesar, the establisher of that temple.

Livy 4.20.5–7

Livy adds that he cannot account for the later date to which his sources have assigned Cossus' consulate, and insists that in any case there can be no question of redating the dedication of spoils to that year. He acknowledges another battle in which Cossus was involved later on and which might have confused the issue, but he finally takes refuge in the now certified fact that on the inscription which Cossus set up at the time he took the spoils, he called himself consul.

This passage is generally and perhaps rightly thought to have been inserted after Livy had written the rest of the book, or at least this portion of it. It does form a most peculiar excrescence. Not only is it appended after the Cossus story has already been told another way, but a few chapters later (at 4.30) Livy presents the conventional account of Cossus' consulate as though there were no question about it. Worse, at 4.32.4 he wants his readers to remember Cossus as being only a military tribune when he took the spoils. From several points of view, this is one of the most perplexing passages in Livy.

What makes it relevant to a discussion of manipulation by Augustus is an incident which took place not long before Livy was writing. In 29 B.C. Crassus, the governor of Macedonia, engaged and killed the king of a tribe which had invaded allied territory. Whereupon, according to the historian who records Crassus' activity (Cass. Dio 51.24.4), "he would have dedicated the king's armor as prime spoils in the temple of Jupiter Feretrius if he had been commander in his own right." In this supererogatory note modern critics have caught the reverberation of a quarrel: Crassus did claim the right to dedicate the prime spoils, but his bid was thwarted by the newly returned victor of the civil wars, who feared that Crassus' distinction might overshadow his own.[52] The tradition about Cossus provided the one precedent which Crassus could invoke to support his claim: if Cossus could dedicate the spoils without holding the position of commander-in-chief, then so could Crassus. Augustus' discovery in the temple of Jupiter Feretrius voided that precedent.

Many have doubted that a linen breastplate could have been preserved for four centuries in a roofless, tumbledown shrine, or that an authentic inscription of the early Republic would have registered the donor's cognomen, or have applied the anachronistic name of consul to an occupant of Rome's highest magistracy. And one cannot but marvel at Augustus' serendipity in stumbling upon antiquities—the inscription of Cossus on this occasion and the Sibyl's oracle some years later.[53] But for the present purpose we can set aside the question of authenticity and all other questions related to the Livian text except for two: what sort of pressure did Augustus put on Livy to publicize his find, and how did Livy respond?

Modern writers who discuss Livy's excursus often speak as though he received a personal communication from the emperor. That assumption is not contradicted by his words, and it is compatible with the witness of the generation after Livy that he enjoyed the friendship of Augustus (Tac. *Ann.* 4.34.3). But the sentence about Augustus' discovery does not actually say from whom or how Livy heard about it. Considerations of chronology suggest that the information did not come directly from Augustus. Livy was writing at least a year and a half after Crassus had established a claim to dedicate the prime spoils in Jupiter's temple. The forum in which the claim would have been heard was the senate, to which proconsuls in the field traditionally addressed their dispatches, and which had the power to approve or deny triumphal celebrations. Augustus could control but he could not easily bypass debate about Crassus' claim, and for debating purposes he had to allege some grounds for refusing Crassus. If it was at that time that he announced his discovery of the Cossus inscription, then the inscription was a matter of record and Livy had no need of a tip in order to have heard about it. Do we have any means of determining when Augustus made his announcement? By 32 B.C. he had rebuilt the temple of Jupiter Feretrius and so put himself in an excellent position to have found or feigned the inscription.[54] The announcement, however, did not necessarily coincide with the discovery. A mere antique would not have warranted a proclamation, least of all a proclamation by the head of government. The inscription did not become newsworthy until the year 29, when it acquired contemporary relevance. On the other hand, it is difficult to imagine why Augustus would have refrained from playing the card he held until after that date, when the debate about Crassus' request was over. One cannot rule out the possibility that the sequence of events was different and that Livy was the privileged recipient of private information. But nothing he says implies that he was.

If Livy was not responding to an overture from Augustus, the Cossus passage has no place in a discussion of efforts by the emperor to influence writers. But since the details have now been set out, let us consider what Livy made of Augustus' discovery nevertheless. In the first place, the focus of the excursus is on the inscription rather than on the person of Augustus; Livy's purpose here is not panegyrical.[55] It is also not propagandistic. Livy embraces the inscription (though not very resolutely, since he allows his subsequent narrative to contradict it at 4.32.4). But he severs its link to the episode in which it played such a decisive role. If we had only the Livian passage to rely on, we would never guess that Augustus used the Cossus inscription to strike down a rival's claim. (In fact, not until this century did scholars think to connect Dio with Livy, and bring the events of 29 into the interpretation.) Contemporary readers might have recalled the circumstances of the discovery, but Livy has fed them nothing that would consolidate a partisan interpretation, beyond restating the general principles to which Augustus appealed.[56] His response to the situation is best described in the diplomats' parlance as "correct." As a historian he was bound to take note of evidence which threw new light upon the events he was recording. And a prudent writer could not afford to close his eyes to what the reigning strongman said and did.

The most flagrant intervention charged against Augustus is his demand that Vergil rewrite part of the *Georgics*. This allegation comes from Servius, who begins his commentary on the *Tenth Eclogue* with a note about Cornelius Gallus, the dedicatee. After recapitulating Gallus' accomplishments in poetry, Servius proceeds:

> At first he enjoyed the friendship of Augustus Caesar; afterwards, when he had come under suspicion of conspiring against him, he was killed. He was moreover a friend of Vergil, to such an extent that the fourth book of *Georgics* contained his praises from the middle to the end. These Vergil later changed into the Aristaeus tale at the bidding of Augustus.

At the beginning of his commentary on book 4 of the *Georgics,* Servius sets out the chronology he has in mind a little more succinctly:

> It must be understood, as we said above, that the final portion of this book was changed, for the praises of Gallus used to occupy that place which now contains the Orpheus tale, which was inserted after Gallus was killed owing to the anger of Augustus.

As it happens, we know the dates which fix the range of Servius' "after-wards" and "later." The coda of the *Georgics* (4.559–566) indicates that the poem was finished in late 30 or early 29 B.C., and the vanquisher of Antony heard a complete recitation of it in the summer of 29, when he returned to Italy to celebrate his victory (Don. *Vita Verg.* 27 Hardie). The death of Gallus, which is the other terminus, occurred in 27 or 26 B.C.[57]

Servius' story that a long passage about Gallus was excised from the *Georgics* has run up against critical misgivings of two sorts. There is first the question of its intrinsic probability. Servius himself noticed the most salient anomaly: if Vergil was obliged to write Gallus out of the *Georgics* some two years after he finished the poem, why did the parts of the *Eclogues* devoted to Gallus (lines 64–73 of the *Sixth* and all of the *Tenth*) remain intact?[58] Some years after Gallus' disgrace, Propertius and Ovid referred to him sympathetically, so at least there was not an official silencing.[59] Moreover, is it credible in the first place that Vergil would have dedicated half a book to Gallus, honoring him with more than twice the number of lines which Augustus and Maecenas together get in all the rest of the *Georgics?*[60] And how could the praises of Gallus in any capacity, as poet, lover, soldier, or administrator, have been integrated into a disquisition on bee-keeping?

Critics could probably reconcile themselves to these difficulties, however, if the credit of the source were higher. As it is, the report of the excision comes not from the Donatan life, but from Servius, whose commentary is often a wallow of half-truth, confusion, and error. He is guilty of one manifest inaccuracy in his statement about Gallus, who was not executed but committed suicide. And he is capable of far greater distortions than that. He posits a conquest of Germany and Persia by Julius Caesar and a conquest of Britain by Augustus (on *Ecl.* 1.61 and *G.* 3.25); he thinks that Cicero lived long enough to attend a dramatization of one of Vergil's *Eclogues* (on 6.11); and he dates the *Eclogues* to about the same time as the battle of Actium (on *Ecl.* 1.70). Nevertheless, his testimony about the end of the *Georgics* cannot simply be brushed aside. He is honest in the sense that he does not willfully fabricate the lore he transmits. At this point in his commentary he cannot be accused of drawing mistaken inferences from Vergil's text, because he gives details which demonstrate awareness of more than just the text. If his story that Vergil rewrote the last book is based on a false combination of facts true in themselves, at least it was not Servius who made that combination. He presents his information as though it raises questions. He may well have garbled something that he picked up, but from a fair reading of his words one must conclude that he picked up something.

A clue to the kind of material he could have found is provided by a miscellany of literary and antiquarian jottings published two centuries before him. Gellius writes that according to a commentary he had seen, *Georgics* 2.225 originally contained a compliment to the town of Nola, but Vergil expunged it after a tiff with the townspeople.[61] If Servius' report about the fourth book derives from a similarly undatable and unidentifiable commentator, we cannot evaluate it by the standards we would apply to pronouncements we felt sure were typically Servian. We must acknowledge it as a singularity which we are not in a position to explain, though we may think of reasons either to reject or to accept it.[62] In any event, out of all our evidence about Augustus' dealings with literary men, this is the only case in which we are clearly told that he prescribed what a work should or should not say.

Rewards and Punishments

Although with this possible exception it does not appear that Augustus tried to meddle in the creative process, he had opportunities to act later, when writers began to circulate their works. If by the judicious allocation of rewards and penalties he encouraged certain forms of literature and discouraged others, his method of control would have been more indirect but still potentially effective.

Augustus did upon occasion make lavish gifts to poets. But by and large he followed the practice of other men of wealth and standing, who did not coordinate their benefactions with the literary output of their protégés. There is no evidence that recompense was ever negotiated in advance, with writers working on commission. Only rarely do we hear of rewards bestowed at the moment when a writer presented his work, and the few cases we do hear of have features which mark them as atypical. The Greek poet who collected 100,000 sesterces from Augustus for an honorific epigram (Macr. *Sat.* 2.4.31) had no personal connection with him. The shallowness of the relationship was what made it possible for Augustus to discharge the man's claim on the spot, by a direct and open payment. Varius, who was a personal friend, received one million sesterces for a tragedy produced at the games which feted the emperor's Actian victory.[63] But drama had an institutional function which set it apart from other kinds of poetry. It had long been customary for magistrates and other producers of public shows to pay for the scripts which playwrights provided. The only remaining case in which presentation of a poem resulted immediately in a reward is somewhat dubious. According to Donatus' life (sec. 32 Hardie), when Vergil read the sixth book of the *Aeneid* at the palace, his lines on Marcellus had such a powerful effect on Marcellus' mother Octavia that she fainted. Servius, on the other hand, offers a version of the incident in which Octavia does not swoon and Vergil receives a present of unstamped bullion.[64] What makes this version suspect is not so much that it comes from Servius as the fact that a more reliable source reports the recitation without mentioning a reward. But even if Servius' account were trustworthy, Octavia's response could not be taken to represent the usual etiquette. Since she had cut herself off from society after the death of Marcellus (Sen. *Dial.* 6.2.3), there was no likelihood that her contact with Vergil would be renewed. If she was to show her gratitude for the lines on Marcellus, she had to respond when Vergil read them.

In general, Augustus seems not to have exchanged rewards for poems. For him as for other Roman gentlemen, liberality reflected ideas of friendship. It was ungracious of a man who had received a favor to counter too hastily with a gift of his own: that extinguished the sentiments of gratitude and obligation which the other party had a right to expect from him. Nor would Augustus have wished it to be thought that the great gifts he did bestow simply paid back prior courtesies. They were dramatic flourishes, testifying in the eyes of all to the worthiness of the recipients and the discernment of the donor (as Horace noted in his *Letter to Augustus,* lines 245–247). There is no sign that Augustus distributed his largesse in order to recruit new talent or to promote specific directions in poetry.

Subornation has been thought to be the aim behind one other sort of offer which came to an Augustan writer. Suetonius says that Augustus wanted Horace to help him with his personal correspondence, and he quotes from a letter in which the emperor outlines his proposal to Maecenas:

> In days past I could handle letter-writing to friends by myself. Now, since I am tremendously busy and my health is poor, I want to requisition our friend Horace from you. So then: from that parasitic table you keep, he shall come hither to the royal board and give us a hand with the correspondence.
>
> Suet. *Vita Hor.* p. 297.19–22 Roth

It is possible to interpret this proposal as a mere pretext for detaching Horace from Maecenas' orbit and bringing him directly under Augustus' own influence. But the lines quoted contain nothing which invites that interpretation. We can draw no inferences from the circumstances surrounding Augustus' proposal because, as generally happens in the case of fragments, we do not know the circumstances, not even the approximate date.[65] If it could be shown that the position which Augustus invited Horace to fill was irregular by Roman standards, there might be some grounds for probing into the issue of motive. But in fact the secretaryship is typical of the positions which Roman aristocrats used to find or create for lesser friends.[66] We have no reason to think that either Augustus or Horace would have considered it anything but a gracious invitation.

The sanctions which Augustus meted out were no less staggering than the rewards. There is no doubt that he intensified the kind of persecution which Roman writers had to fear from government. But only in a very loose sense of the term did this persecution take the form of literary censorship. Augustus' measures against books and writers arose from a variety of limited and uncoordinated aims rather than from a comprehensive policy.

Some actions should be seen as latter-day sallies in the long counter-reformation which the state had waged in fits and starts against un-Roman influences. The only books known to have been publicly burned at Rome up until Augustus' time were the scriptures of exotic cults which had gained a foothold in Italy.[67] Considering what a profound distrust the authorities felt toward foreign cults (which set at nought the worship of the ancestral gods, encouraged unregulated assembly, and lured women from the confines of the house), it is remarkable that the response was so often to compromise with rather than to extirpate them. As for book burnings, the principle involved was closer to modern attitudes about the circulation of currency than the circulation of ideas. The incinerated books were subliterary documents. They did not contain teachings to be studied in private, like the Judeo-Christian scriptures, but prophecies and rituals which threatened to disrupt the state religion on which Rome's welfare was thought to depend. And not only did they run contrary to existing institutions, they also represented a repugnant standard of access to sacred lore. Not even Roman sacred books were allowed to circulate. When Augustus reviewed the canon of Sibylline literature and burned those prophecies which failed to satisfy his criteria of authenticity (Suet. *Aug.* 31.1), he was following a centuries-old method of dealing with pseudo-religious paraphernalia.

Punishment was sometimes visited on an author rather than his books: in about 28 B.C. Augustus banned a Pythagorean philosopher named Anaxilaos from Italy.[68] This action too had ample precedent in the history of the Republic, whose magistrates had on numerous occasions ordered the expulsion of philosophers, rhetors, or astrologers.[69] Although many if not all of these offenders would have been writers, no effort was made to ban their books as well. It was not so much what they wrote that made them objectionable as the insidious influence they acquired, chiefly over members of the upper class who craved their services. In the first place, then, the ban periodically invoked against undesirable elements was not exercised primarily as an instrument of literary control. In the second place, it did not amount to systematic control. The authorities generally tolerated the presence of philosophers and astrologers alike until some incident, often scandalous, provoked them to crack down again.

The worst scourge ever to be used against Roman writers was devised by Augustus himself during the last decade of his reign when he set out to curb defamatory literature by applying legislation which punished injuries to the majesty of the state. After the repeated eruption of ditties and broadsides impugning many respectable citizens including himself, Augustus announced that such outrages could not continue to go unpunished. The courts and the senate were charged to seek out the authors and bring them to trial on capital charges under the Julian *maiestas* law. According to Tacitus, the first victim was the reckless and vitriolic Cassius Severus, who was deported to Crete. His books were burned on the Forum in a ritual reenacted more than half a dozen times over the next century.[70]

Virtually every other fact about the *maiestas* trials of the early principate is so obscure that there is no point in trying to present a more elaborate background.[71] Besides, the charge quickly engulfed such a range of actions that fuller discussion of it would inevitably lead away from the question which is relevant here: did it serve to regulate what Augustan authors wrote about? The kind of writing that triggered prosecution during Augustus' reign meets a fairly narrow description. It consisted of or contained abusive remarks about living persons of high degree, and it was circulated under a false name or no name.[72] But most Roman poetry was not open to censure under either head. Even vituperative genres like satire and epigram had lost their bite long before Augustus unlimbered the *maiestas* charge. The only prose form in which personal abuse had a major place was oratory. History often contained attacks on individuals, but historians with a censorious bent tended either to focus on persons no longer living or to reserve publication until after their own demise. If therefore the purpose of the defamation trials was to establish machinery for a general inquisition into literary affairs, the writing which Augustus chose to prosecute seems oddly marginal.

On the other hand, the trials are perfectly intelligible if we suppose that Augustus was in earnest about suppressing the pasquinades which were their ostensible target. He was extraordinarily sensitive to the importance of appearances and to the enormity of public humiliation. Suetonius quotes a revealing passage from a letter to Livia in which Augustus considers what is to be done with her awkward grandson, the future emperor Claudius:

> If we think he is *non compos* . . . people should not be given the opportunity of laughing at both him and us . . . To deal with the case at hand, I have no objection to his presiding at the priests' banquet during the Games of Mars provided he will follow advice from Silvanus' son (the fellow is related to him) so that he doesn't do anything that will attract attention and be derided. I do not want him watching the circus games from the state box: he is bound to be noticed if he is seated way out front at the show. I do not want him going to the Alban Mount or staying in Rome during the Latin Festival.
>
> Suet. *Claud.* 4.2–3

But it was not just his own dignity that Augustus protected. He showed the same consideration for the public image of his peers. He banished an actor for pointing his finger at a heckler (Suet. *Aug.* 45.4). After a senator failed to find a seat at a local festival performance, he moved legislation which guaranteed senators reserved seats at all future shows (Suet. *Aug.* 44.1). When he trimmed the senatorial roster, he allowed those members who were being cut to go on wearing the senatorial garb and to participate as before in ceremonial functions (Suet. *Aug.* 35.2 and Cass. Dio 54.14.4). When he revived the annual dress parade and inspection of the knights, he took care to issue reprimands for minor infractions in such a way that those concerned were not publicly embarrassed (Suet. *Aug.* 39). Deference to rank and worth was a priority of the restored Republic. Augustus cherished no nostalgia for the unbridled speech of the Republic that had foundered. He found the style of personal invective which orators of the late Republic had cultivated just as obnoxious as the malicious wit of pamphleteers. Two of his associates once assisted in the defense of a man who was being tried in the adultery court, and so, by the ground rules of forensic confrontation, they came under fire from the prosecutor along with the defendant. At the next session Augustus appeared in court, took the judge's seat, forbade the prosecutor to insult his relatives or his friends, and walked out.[73] An orator of the Ciceronian age would have been dumbfounded at such a ruling, had there been anyone to issue it.

To look for subtlety behind the *maiestas* trials of Augustus' reign is unnecessary and probably mistaken. They make sense if taken for what they seem to be, efforts by a conservative reformer to suppress traces of Republican license. But after Augustus' death, the scope of the *maiestas* charge expanded so much that it could be brought to bear on any form of literature. By the time Augustus' successor died, it had been used to bring down both a poet and a historian. The potential for a broad program of censorship did eventually exist therefore; whether the successors of Augustus recognized and cultivated that potential is another question, which does not need to be discussed here. But as far as the policy of Augustus himself is concerned, the *maiestas* trials had no significant effect on the literary environment. They came at the end of his reign, long after most Augustan poetry and prose had been produced, and they turned on issues which were not pertinent to most writing of the time.

Another writer's collision with Augustus also dates from late in the reign and is surrounded by as deep a controversy as the defamation trials. Yet this case is even more difficult to assess because, so far as we can tell, it both lacked a precedent and failed to set one. The treatment of Ovid was *sui generis*. In the year A.D. 8 he was relegated to the Black Sea outpost of Tomis for a transgression which he consistently describes as twofold. The more serious offense (according to his own assessment at *Pont.* 3.3.72) he says is too sensitive to be made public, though he skitters around it constantly, throwing out dozens of dark allusions. In the course of his movements among people of dazzling and mighty rank (*Tr.* 3.4.4–8), he was drawn into a compromising situation in which he witnessed a "grievous wrong" (*Tr.* 3.6.27–28). His action at that time, which he variously attributes to stupidity (*Tr.* 3.6.35), lunacy (*Pont.* 2.3.46), naiveté (*Tr.* 1.5.42), and lack of nerve (*Tr.* 4.4.39), offended Augustus and brought down his wrath.[74] The other action held against him was the writing of the *Art of Love,* a primer on seduction for the man about town which he had published some years earlier. It allegedly advocated adultery and thus flouted the marital legislation which Augustus had been at such pains to promulgate (*Tr.* 2.211–212). The emperor assumed jurisdiction and passed sentence on Ovid personally (*Tr.* 2.131–134).

Ovid's links to the high nobility, the emperor's touchiness on the subject of adultery, and his harsh adjudication of the case have long caused scholars to suspect some connection with another scandal. In the same year Augustus' granddaughter Julia was convicted of adultery and banished.[75] At the least it is evident that, however much the poem contributed to Augustus' displeasure, Ovid was already vulnerable because of complicity in some other misdeed. That involvement overshadows the indictment against the *Art of Love* and diminishes its force as an expression of policy. Taken by itself, the charge of promoting immorality was something radically new in relations between Roman writers and the state. It may well represent a censorial standard which Augustus would have liked to apply more widely. But we do not know whether it could have stood by itself without the carrying power of the graver charge against Ovid. The poet himself, who was not given to bravado and who conceded some culpability for his part in the mysterious contretemps, insisted throughout book 2 of the *Tristia* that the attack on his poem was arbitrary. And for quite a long time after Augustus, no emperor renewed the effort to regulate the moral tone of literature. But what best illustrates the ad hoc nature of the immorality charge is that it was not raised during the eight or more years between publication of the *Art of Love* and Ovid's entanglement with glittering friends.[76] Augustus either had not yet begun to subject literary work to a morals test before A.D. 8, or he was not yet using the courts and the law to implement it.

Finally, there is an odd disproportion between the treatment of the author and the treatment of his books, if the aim of the prosecution was to purge a corrupting influence. Unlike the proceedings against the pamphleteers, it did not result in an auto-da-fé upon the Forum. Ovid indicates that, except for the *Art of Love,* all his books remained available to the general reader, though they may have been barred from the three public libraries which were under Augustus' control.[77] The incriminated poem did fall under some sort of interdiction, but how stringent or how broad it was is not clear. In his most specific allusion to what happened Ovid says that the *Art of Love* was "ordered removed," by which he evidently means that it was banned from the public libraries.[78] He assumes that his friends will have gotten rid of their copies (*Tr.* 3.14.5–6 and *Pont.* 1.1.12), but it does not follow that their copies were impounded. Loyal citizens would have acted voluntarily in sympathy with the emperor, or so one must pretend. For Ovid to have written any differently would have compromised his friends, who he well knew were not the bravest of the brave. But if a search and seizure had been ordered, Ovid could not have described how his own copy continued to skulk in disgrace on the bookshelf of his house in Rome (*Tr.* 1.1.111). The fact that the *Art of Love* was quoted in antiquity and transmitted along with the rest of the Ovidian corpus also tells against the supposition that Augustus exerted himself to suppress it. We have no evidence to show that he did more than order its removal from the three libraries which were under imperial administration. Given that he was capable of dealing much more ruthlessly with writings which offended him, puritanical ardor was probably not the keenest impulse behind his prosecution of Ovid. As Ovid himself reminded the emperor when the *Art of Love* was banned, the classics of ancient pornography still remained in place on the shelves of public libraries in the capital (*Tr.* 2.409–420). It looks rather as though Augustus plucked the charge of immorality out of thin air in order to exorcise a personal embarrassment.

In this long survey of interactions between Augustan writers and the emperor or his surrogates, I hope to have shown that they are not all of a piece. The issue (in my opinion) is not usually that the value of the sources varies. It is true that our most explicit testimony that Augustus dictated literary content (in the *Georgics*) stands on somewhat shaky authority, but in general the sources seem credible enough. Often indeed it is the Augustan writers themselves who comment on their relations with Augustus or Maecenas. When these contacts are scrutinized one by one, however, behavior on Augustus' side does not reveal the political tendency it can seem to have if all his literary interventions are lumped together. The sources simply do not bear out the conclusions which have often been drawn from them.

Two tendencies that Augustus' behavior does show have been noted several times in the preceding discussion. One is that his literary initiatives are for the most part conventional: they either continue public policies of the Republican era or express a traditional ethos of the Roman elite toward literature and its acolytes. And second, they give the impression of being random acts without a consistent purpose behind them. This is true even in those cases in which Augustus most clearly departed from tradition, as in the trials of Ovid and the pamphleteers.

It appears, then, that Augustan poetry did not acquire its Augustan stamp as the result of a conscious and concerted effort on Augustus' part. If much of the poetry nevertheless bears a very strong partisan character, the explanation must be sought in initiatives proceeding from the poets' side.

6

Poetic Approaches to Political Themes

The evidence of direct interaction between Augustus and contemporary poets is so meager that by itself it would not have encouraged anyone to think that he made a systematic effort to cultivate them as publicists. That belief is at bottom a reaction to the effusive testimony poets offer about him, and in practice it is from the evidence of the poems that the case for imperial guidance has to be argued.

This kind of argument is more difficult to make or to rebut than is generally acknowledged, however. It comes down to a question of proving systematic correlations between two sets of data, the corpus of Augustan poetry on the one hand, and on the other, all those images, utterances, gestures, deeds, and documents which we take as manifesting aspects of Augustan ideology. Major uncertainties beset both sides of the comparison.

The problem with making Augustus' political program one of the terms of argument is that there is no detailed and generally accepted formulation of it to which we can refer. For various reasons, the ancient sources available to us give only intermittent glimpses of policy. Augustus' own remarks in the *Res Gestae* conform to patterns which are traditional for honorific inscriptions; he speaks of his successes and honors and munificence in public life, but not of his continuing role as head of state. His coins draw largely on the same themes and treat them even more allusively. In the area of public law, the extant documents deal mostly with issues of low-level importance. We have no record of the legislation by which Augustus reformed the currency, restructured the judicial system, broadened the definition of treason, and regulated marriage, sexual conduct, manumission, and the consumption of luxuries,

nor any record of the enabling acts which accompanied his constitutional innovations. A mere fraction of the public art and architecture
which gave a face to the new regime has survived in its original state,
and none of it is accompanied by literary or epigraphic comment expli-
cating what is represented; even the visual aspect of Augustan buildings
is better known from schematic representations on Roman coins than
from on-site remains. Among narrative accounts of the period, Dio
downplays administrative history, dwelling by preference on foreign
affairs and on dynastic and constitutional conflicts. (The speech in book
52 in which Dio has Maecenas outline a government agenda is generally
considered to be a free invention based on Dio's impressions of the later
principate.) Suetonius, although he devotes several chapters to Augustus'
administrative and legislative actions, merely catalogs them, giving no
dates and few details, under simplistic rubrics like "measures affecting
senators," "measures affecting knights," and "measures affecting ordinary
citizens." Velleius' epitome of Roman history communicates little more
about Augustus' policies than Velleius' global enthusiasm for them. Dis-
jointed as the record is, it is nevertheless ample enough that we could
probably deduce from it most of the concerns which Augustus might
have listed as forming his political agenda. But the fact remains that at
the present time no such summation of his program exists, and even if
it did, we would still lack a firm chronology for it.

The poems are the other term of reference. What hinders comparison
on this side is, first, that here too our knowledge of dates is often vague.
Donatus reports that Vergil worked on the *Aeneid* for about a decade,
and that he did not compose books or even parts of books in the order
in which they were ultimately assembled. For most passages of the poem,
therefore, the date of composition could fall at any point along a ten-
year span. Horace's first three books of *Odes* are generally believed to
have been written over a period of eight years or more and to have
been published all together in 23 B.C.; fewer than a dozen pieces in the
collection admit of a more exact dating within that period. The range
for the elegies constituting Propertius' fourth book is at least six years
long. We have also to reckon with the possibility that some works were
revised or reissued years after they were initially composed. The six
books of Ovid's calendar poem were substantially completed during the
decade preceding his exile in A.D. 8, but he reworked at least parts of
the poem after the death of Augustus six years later. The three-book

edition of his love poems which has descended to us replaced an earlier five-book edition. In general, Augustan poems cannot be precisely plotted along a time line.

Another difficulty is that we rarely have an opportunity to see the Augustan poets reacting to the same occurrences at the same time. The degree of resemblance between different poems on the same subject would be one way to measure whether the authors were working in concert or independently. Unfortunately, the nature of Augustan poetry is such as to make convergences between authors exceptional. Vergil's epic, Propertius' love poems, and Horace's moral epistles, for example, may all allude to contemporary events, but they are primarily about other subjects. They are not occasional poems which respond immediately and directly to events in the realm of politics. Consequently, each poet's ruminations on Augustus and his works tend to occur in isolation from what other poets were writing.

But the many difficulties of assessing the political element in Augustan poetry are offset by one great advantage. For this period—unlike any other period of classical literature—we possess almost the complete oeuvre of the major poets. We lack Ovid's *Medea* and some of his occasional pieces, but we have every reason to think that we possess the full corpus of poems by Horace, Vergil, Tibullus, and Propertius. If Augustus did try to exert an influence on contemporary poetry, the evidence should certainly be discernible in the texts known to us. There is nothing missing which could significantly affect the argument on either side.

A thorough investigation of the topic would take account of all echoes of politics in Augustan poetry, as well as of those aspects of Augustus' program about which the poets are mute. It would fill much more than the space reserved for it in this book. What I attempt here is only a foray, directed at four themes which can reasonably be termed political: the greatness of the empire, the quasi-divine stature of Augustus, the contrast of primeval and modern Rome, and the dynastic role of Augustus' family. Among many other themes which merit discussion, I have selected these four because they interested me, because they can be set into at least a rough chronological framework, and because in each case they allow for comparisons among several poets. They also serve the argument I want to make about the independence of poetry from political constraints, since they show the poets taking various positions in relation to publicly sanctioned ideas about Augustus.

The Grandeur of Empire

One motif whose appearance in poetry was predictable no matter what kind of political order imposed itself after the civil wars was the celebration of Roman supremacy in the Mediterranean. Though more or less dormant while the Romans battled one another, pride in empire had thrust up a new peak in the range of national consciousness in the middle of the second century B.C. After Roman victories over the Hellenistic kingdoms of Syria and Macedon, the Greek historian Polybius declared that Rome had supplanted and eclipsed all previous world empires. That conception became a commonplace in both Greek and Roman writing.[1] By the end of the 70s, Roman coins featured an array of emblems signifying domination: winged victories, the triumphal chariot, the scepter and the diadem, and the terrestrial globe, sometimes shown beneath the foot of a figure personifying Rome.[2] Cicero and his contemporaries habitually spoke as though Rome's power encompassed the entire "ring of lands" *(orbis terrarum)* which made up the inhabited world, though that pretension never inhibited magniloquence when it came to speaking about fresh conquests.[3] Pompey marked the climax of his progress through eastern lands with an inscription asserting that he had "advanced the boundaries of the empire to the boundaries of the earth" (Diod. Sic. 40.4), a formulation on which Cicero improved by saying that Pompey had carried the empire to the ends "not of the land but of the sky" (*Catil.* 3.26). The triumph voted for these achievements was the third of Pompey's career, after triumphs for earlier campaigns in Africa and Spain. Panegyrists were led to meditate upon the symbolism of triumphs won on the three continents of their world.[4] It is probably fortuitous that the imperial theme is rare in Republican poetry, since few poems and no historical epics of that period survive.[5] But whether Republican versifiers took the lead in celebrating the glories of empire or not, it is clear that an idiom for handling that subject had been developed well before the Augustan period.

When the subject does get taken up in poems of the civil war period, it is not initially connected with the person of Augustus. The first Augustan poet who invites reflection on the breadth of Rome's dominion finds such a dark meaning in the theme that it is scarcely recognizable.[6] The shepherds of Vergil's *First Eclogue* converse in dialogue which is composed to emphasize responses in what they say. Thanks to the intervention of a godlike youth in Rome, Tityrus has been confirmed in possession of his little holding, while Meliboeus, who has been expelled, is setting out on a trek that will take him far from home. Toward the close of the conversation, Tityrus says he will never be able to forget his benefactor:

> Sooner will skittish deer graze in the sky or the seas leave fish destitute on the shore; sooner will the Parthians and Germans rove over each others' frontiers and come as exiles to drink the Saône and the Tigris.

To which Meliboeus replies:

> *We,* though, shall go from this place. Some of us will fetch up among waterless Africans; some in Scythia and by the chalk-roiled Oaxes and in Britain which is sundered from the whole world . . . A black-hearted soldier will occupy these well-tended acres, a barbarian these fields of grain. That is where strife has brought hapless citizens.

Verg. Ecl. 1.59–72

All of the figures by which Tityrus symbolizes the impossible are taken beyond conventional limits and given touches of the desolate feeling that pervades this section of the poem. But the most original and striking image is the cross-migration of Germans and Parthians. A Roman reader would instantly understand what Vergil leaves unsaid: the hindrance that will keep the peoples of East and West from migrating in opposite directions must be the empire that lies between them. Tityrus, to whom the established order has after all brought security, is able to take assurance in patriotic verities. Meliboeus' reply is more explicitly political: his references to soldiers and barbarians, to citizens, and to strife disclose for the first time that the background of the poem is civil war in Rome. Without challenging Tityrus' confidence about the immobility of Parthians and Germans, he fixes on a paradox: a displacement really is in progress, not on the borders but in the heart of the empire. The emphatic "we" (*nos,* line 64) must stand in contrast to the Parthians and Germans just mentioned rather than to Tityrus; the following "some of us" *(alii)* and "others" *(pars)* further indicate that Meliboeus is not using an editorial "we" but has in mind a true plural. The identity of this collective he finally discloses in line 71: not barbarian nomads but Roman citizens *(cives)* are being driven off their lands. The word "citizens" is astonishing to encounter in a bucolic context; in fact, this is Vergil's only use of it outside the *Aeneid.*[7] Meliboeus suggests that

Rome's native sons might as well be dwelling on the marches of the empire, for all the security it has brought them.

Though Vergil's poem evidently dates from the time of his first contact with the future Augustus, the theme of empire is introduced for reasons which are unrelated to him. It is similarly autonomous in another poem of the civil war era, Horace's *Seventh Epode,* which excoriates his fellow citizens for spilling so much blood,

> not in order that Romans may burn the proud citadel of jealous Carthage, or that unscathed Britons may walk in chains down the Sacred Way, but so that this city may perish by its own hand, in answer to the Parthians' prayer.
>
> Hor. *Epodi* 7.3–10[8]

Horace's use of the theme is primitive, both in the sense that the sentiment is cruder than Vergil's and that it echoes a very old idea—at least as old as Isocrates.[9] He holds up the empire as a cause to which Romans should rally, turning their swords away from one another and against their enemies abroad. But the poem predates Horace's association with Augustus, perhaps even with Maecenas, and therefore points out no leader around whom to rally.

As it happens, the first person to be glorified as a world conqueror in extant poetry was not one of the triumvirs but a lesser figure of the age. Marcus Valerius Messalla, a scion of the Republican nobility, was the subject of a panegyric by an unknown author who versified the high points of his career in war and public life, interlarding these with digressions on more exotic themes.[10] Though at one point the Illyrian campaign of 35–34 B.C. is described, during which Messalla operated under the command of Octavian, there is no acknowledgment of Octavian's participation.[11] Having recapitulated Messalla's past career, the poet announces that omens presage even more glorious successes to come, and with that he steals into his most extravagant set-piece. Messalla is not to contemplate the sort of triumph that beckons ordinary warriors, for exploits in Gaul, Spain, Africa, Egypt, Parthia, India, or Scythia. Over all the land mass surrounded by the Ocean there is no nation which will dare resist him. He must therefore look past the known world, first to Britain, then to the antipodes, that belt of habitable lands, imagined but not actually verified, which was thought to lie beyond the tropics. After sketching the position and climate of this new land in relation to the rest of the globe, the poet winds up his digression with the assurance, "and so when your deeds establish your claim to splendid triumphs, you alone will be hailed as 'Great' in both worlds alike" (lines 175–176).

Readers are often taken aback by the author's obliviousness of the commander in whose enterprise Messalla had only a supporting role. Diplomatic finesse the *Panegyric* certainly lacks, but it would be going too far to conclude that the silence about Octavian was intended as a snub. What drives him out of the picture is partly intensity of focus. Having served with Messalla during the Illyrian campaign (lines 106–107), the author is bent on using that connection to improve their acquaintance. That is the target at which he unloads all his ammunition. He is also writing at a time before the image of one man has superimposed itself on visions of world conquest. The ideology of imperial Rome was formed more than a century before the emperors assumed control of the state, and despite increasing linkage with the emperors, it retained a certain vitality of its own. For a time even after Actium, poets could praise the feats of army leaders without reference to Augustus, and they often celebrate Roman conquests and dominion without bringing in the name of any leader at all.[12]

Apart from illustrating the autonomy of the empire theme, the *Panegyric of Messalla* also helps us to understand some of the magnetism which attracted poets to it. There can be no question but that Messalla's blitz of the two anti-worlds is a conceit which the author dreamed up himself. He could not have been writing to order because he was not personally acquainted with Messalla at the time of the poem.[13] No doubt he hoped that the honorand would be pleased to be given a role on such a grand stage, but the poet was at least as taken with the mise-en-scène as he expected anyone else to be. The catalog with which he begins, of regions already daunted by Messalla's reputation, covers the four points of the compass, as logic and convention require. But it contains more than a medley of place names. Many of the locales have been culled from Herodotus and ornamented with bits of lore which he retailed about them. Here as in many other passages which deal with the spread of Roman power, romance has infiltrated the patriotic theme and invested faraway places with associations inspired largely by literature. The ethnographic tradition, which stretched back beyond Herodotus into the sixth century B.C., was one influence on Roman writers, as the *Panegyric* demonstrates. They were even more powerfully affected by the literature which had sprung up about Alexander the Great, both because Romans identified with the precursor who had opened up the East, and because they had imbibed their first knowledge of Alexander at school, where his adventures furnished grist for literary exercises.[14] The poets would have warmed to the march of empire in any case, but part of the thrill it gave them was that it crystallized their reading.

Having brought Messalla to the edge of the known world in line 149, the author draws back the curtain on a second terrain available for conquest, and the reader senses a spike in the emotional temperature of the poem. Twenty-four lines of pure description are lavished on the globe and its five zones; Messalla is forgotten until he is haled back at the very end. This passage illustrates the excitement a taste of philosophy could inspire after the narrow education dispensed in Roman schools. For a poet trying to imagine the vastness of Rome's territory, the field of ideas which offered the readiest scale of comparison was natural philosophy or cosmology (in ancient times, still part of philosophy rather than a separate discipline). Clearly our poet gets somewhat carried away. The cosmological comparison which occurs to him becomes more than a comparison, as he begins to envision the extension of the empire through the cosmos. But although this particular literary experiment may fail to impress us as being anything but eccentric, the enrichment of the empire theme with cosmic imagery was to take a firm hold in the literature of the imperial period.[15]

The response of poets to Roman domination of the Mediterranean cannot be summed up by three selections from Vergil, Horace, and the *Panegyric of Messalla*. But the examples do show that during the 30s the theme of empire lent itself to multiple associations, and that its currency owed nothing to initiatives from Roman strongmen. As far as we can judge from extant texts, it was not linked with Augustus before Actium.

A linkage was effected almost immediately afterward, however.[16] No doubt Augustus was pleased: that he prided himself on his aggrandizement of Roman power is evident from both his actions and his words. In the year 29 B.C. he celebrated a triple triumph, for victories in Illyricum and other parts of Europe, for vanquishing the eastern forces arrayed against him at Actium, and for capturing Egypt (Cass. Dio 51.21.5–7). The three-day pageant appropriated the global symbolism which had invested the triumphs of Pompey and of Caesar a generation earlier.[17] Two decades later, Augustus' co-regent Agrippa planned a portico with panels outlining the world and the empire along its inside wall. When Agrippa died before carrying out the project, it was Augustus who completed the portico and erected the first world map displayed in

Rome.[18] In the *Res Gestae* he calls attention to shows of strength which he has projected into every corner of the world, and to all the territories which he has brought under Roman domination (sections 3.1–2, 4.2–3, 13, and 26–33). Poets who acclaimed him as the nation's champion against enemies abroad were therefore very much in line with Augustus' own perspective on himself.

We have no way of telling whether that image was commended to their attention or whether it was an illumination they experienced in the quiet after Actium. But if we look at the way the empire theme evolves, Augustus seems not so much to seize possession of it as to be absorbed into it. Poets often express their pride in Roman supremacy as before, without referring to him. During his principate new variations of the idea appear which are not linked with him. For example, poets begin to surmise that the geographic range of Roman influence will help to propagate their fame.[19] Taking a different tack in other poems, they point to campaigns in distant lands as proof of the greed that pervades Roman society.[20]

When the empire theme is integrated into discourse about the principate, it does not always require much adjustment. Thus Horace picks up his old refrain that Romans ought to be fighting foreign enemies instead of one another, but now he identifies Augustus as the leader who will unite them in a common cause. Having recycled that motif in a couple of *Odes* of book 1 (1.2.21–52 and 1.35.29–40), he discards it. Since Horace alone among Augustan poets makes use of it, and since it appears in his work both before and after Actium, he rather than any external agent must be responsible for it.

The simplest and most common way of seeing Augustus in relation to the empire was as a military leader whose campaigns were bringing about the Roman dream of worldwide rule. Others had been cast in this role before him, and so there was bound to be an element of convention in the literary presentation of his wars. One sign of it is the tendency of poets to retreat from the particular events of a campaign, and to dwell instead upon the imperial teleology which guides their history overall. This penchant for the visionary over the narrative mode underlies certain oddities which have long been noted in poets' approach to Augustan foreign policy. Many passages which speak of territorial gains are framed as predictions of conquest rather than as proclamations of it, the prediction usually issuing from the mouth of a god or other prescient being.[21] Regions to which Augustan armies were never sent are listed alongside those to which they were as though both alike were being overrun.[22]

Yet despite the swell on which the imperial theme is played, it is thin in topical content. The poets pay surprisingly little attention to campaigns, battles, and victories as they occur. During the four and a half decades between Actium and the end of the reign there was hardly a stretch of as many as three years when Roman armies were not campaigning in some corner of the world. But except for Actium, only a handful of martial episodes receive extended treatment. I count seven. Augustus' Cantabrian expedition of 26–24 B.C. was the occasion of *Odes* 3.14, in which Horace exults over Augustus' homecoming but does not mention any detail of the fighting.[23] Horace devoted two poems (*Carm.* 4.4 and 4.14) to the the Alpine war fought in 15 B.C. by Drusus and Tiberius, at least one of which was reportedly prompted by an explicit request from Augustus. In 1 B.C. Gaius set out on his eastern campaign amid fanfare to which Ovid contributed in book 1 of the *Art of Love*.[24] Tiberius' suppression of the Pannonian revolt in A.D. 12 earned him a triumph which is described in *Letters from Pontus* 2.1.[25] And finally, Ovid wrote up brief treatments of two skirmishes on the lower Danube in order to compliment persons in the district where he was interned.[26] Otherwise the poets do not draw their subjects from Augustus' wars. Their poems do contain plenteous references to clashes with hostile nations, but these are mostly brief tangents, and abundant as they are, they do not add up to anything like a bulletin on Augustus' military enterprises. Some engagements are noted at the time of their occurrence, others years afterward; the poets do not strive to furnish up-to-date publicity. Furthermore, their allusions to martial enterprises tend to cluster around fantasies of conquest rather than around actual events (except for Actium). Many campaigns of the Augustan era they disregard entirely; many of those they notice are mentioned only once or twice. The military targets evoked over and over again, however—Parthians, Indians, Scythians, and Britons—lie in outlands which had excited the Roman imagination for at least a generation, but which Augustan armies never penetrated. These features which recur in so much of the poetry written under Augustus—the fatidic intonation, the jumbling of real and unreal designs, the perfunctory attention to actual operations—are already present in the *Panegyric of Messalla* and evidently represent conventions which poets of his day took over from their predecessors. Although Augustus revolutionized the state, the wars he waged abroad still lent themselves to treatment along traditional lines.

The empire theme did contribute to the creation of an ideology for the new regime in three important ways, however. As head of the army, Augustus took responsibility for guarding the territorial integrity of the empire, and it was mainly (though not only) on that basis that the poets extolled him as the savior and protector of Romans and of all mankind.[27] A second direction in which the idea of empire carried them is best illustrated by the close of one of Horace's *Odes,* in which the poet prays to Jupiter:

> Offspring of Saturn, father and guardian of the human race, the fates have entrusted to you the care of great Caesar: let his sway be second to your own.

> Whether he shall beat down and lead in rightful triumph the Parthians who threaten Latium, or the Chinese and Indians apportioned to the Orient,

> his sober rule of the broad earth will not level him with you. You will rumble over Olympus in your heavy chariot; you will hurl fatal lightning bolts on desecrated ground.

> Hor. *Carm.* 1.12.49–60

Establishment of the principate produced a refinement in the long-standing comparison between the empire and the earth or the cosmos. Once the administration of Rome's armies and provinces became virtually one man's preserve, it was inevitable that his function would be likened to that of the god who ruled the universe. The equation of Augustus with Jupiter was soon entrenched as one of the clichés of imperial verse.[28] In this way the empire theme helped to thicken the atmosphere out of which the formalities of the emperor cult condensed.

The third and most important effect of the empire theme's use in poetry was to change people's perceptions of the level at which they were governed. As Augustus' position was defined within a Republican framework, he was (at one time or another) consul, ranking member of the senate, holder of proconsular power and tribunician authority, and head priest in several colleges which regulated the state religion. To these capacities the poets rarely or never refer, and they seldom speak of Augustus in relation to the two pillars of the Republican state, the Senate and the Roman People.[29] Rather than bring him into relation with traditional offices and institutions, they resort to emotionally charged but nonpolitical conceptions like "Rome" and "country." Furthermore, as the regime settles in, grand universals like "world" and "empire" begin to be more prominent in poetry than strictly national watchwords. Not only does the number of references to empire steadily increase, but certain images traditionally associated with citizen government are metamorphosed into imperial images. The body politic, one of the oldest metaphors in Western literature, now appears in the guise of "the body of the empire" (*corpus imperii,* Ov. *Tr.* 2.232, with 3.5.46). The title "Father of the Country" *(pater patriae),* which the senate conferred in order to signalize extraordinary service, was amplified in poetry to "Father of Mankind" *(pater hominum)* or "Father of the World" *(pater orbis).*[30] The emphasis on empire had the effect of suggesting that Augustus' political mandate was defined not at the level where power was regulated by established institutions, but at a level above and beyond the state, where it was not regulated at all. If internally Augustus' position was something of a riddle, in relation to the empire he could be unambiguously acclaimed as ruler and lord.[31]

The empire theme added touches which proved to be important in the rhetoric which festooned the principate. That the poets were consciously constructing a new ideology, however, is improbable. Individually, the motifs I have discussed were not new. In the Greek world it had long been customary to praise leaders (often Roman leaders) as saviors, and that tradition left an even stronger imprint on Greek testimonials to Augustus than on Roman ones. Similarly, there were precedents in Hellenistic literature for the identification of an earthly ruler with Zeus, a motif which persists in Greek poems of the Augustan period.[32] Much of the phraseology emphasizing sovereignty over the nations was pre-Augustan. The difference is that prior to Actium expressions like "head of the world" and "ruler of the empire" were applied to Rome and the Roman people, whereas afterward they began to be transferred to Augustus.[33] In every instance, therefore, Augustan poets found ready-formed conventions on which to draw. That Augustus guided them to these selections cannot be disproved, but it is by no means a necessary assumption. In a speech given during the dictatorship of Sulla a half-century earlier, Cicero previewed the idiom which was to be standardized under the principate. When one of Sulla's freedmen had the property of Cicero's client confiscated and then auctioned off to himself,

Cicero was obliged to argue that Sulla was unaware of what his freedman was doing:

> Almighty and perfect Jupiter, at whose nod and will the heavens, the earth, and the seas are ruled, often brings harm to men, wrecking cities and destroying crops with raging winds or violent storms or oppressive heat or unbearable cold, yet we consider that such things happen not of divine purpose for our ruination, but through the sheer potency and scale of nature. But the blessings from which we benefit and the light which we enjoy and the breath we draw—these we consider that Jupiter bestows and confers upon us. That being so, gentlemen of the jury, why do we marvel that Lucius Sulla failed to notice something, while unaided he was ruling the state and governing the world and strengthening by laws the majestic empire which he had recovered by force of arms?
>
> Cic. *Rosc. Am.* 131[34]

Analogies like these were within the grasp of every rhetorically competent writer. We have no more reason to suppose that poets had to be led to them by Augustus than that Cicero took his cue from Sulla.

The fact that motifs used by one poet are often disregarded by others, or differently applied, also tells against the operation of a coordinating influence. And if Augustus was responsible for encouraging the line that the empire was uniquely represented in him, it is paradoxical that it should be most fully articulated by Ovid, whose relationship with him was least intimate—and articulated mainly in the poems from exile at that.

Finally, there was one argument about empire which apologists of the principate put forward, but which found no echo in contemporary poetry. During a senate meeting after Augustus' death, when the senators sought to overcome Tiberius' apparent unwillingness to step into Augustus' place, both sides appealed to considerations of empire. Tiberius had Augustus' inventory of imperial assets and encumbrances read out, and said that he was unequal to so massive a burden but willing to undertake some part of it. The spokesman on the other side insisted that the parts constituted one body, which needed to be governed by one mind.[35] Here is a slogan known to have been invoked, and compatible with imagery cultivated in Augustan verse. If the poets had been drafted as spokesmen for the regime, one would expect at least one of them to have taken it up. But such is not the case. Even Ovid, who knew the episode of Tiberius' refusal (*Fasti* 1.533–534 and *Pont.* 4.13.27–28), does not advert to the argument which brought him around.

The Transfiguration of Augustus

When Augustus died in A.D. 14, the senate decreed that he was to be recognized and honored as a god just as it had consecrated his father Julius Caesar before him. But that decree was only the last word in a spiral of magniloquence which had carried him heavenward since the start of his career. Augustus' metamorphosis into a god was subtler and more gradual than Caesar's.

Among many other agents, the Augustan poets played a part in the process, and it is their contribution I will examine here. So far as we know, Augustus is the first political figure who in his own lifetime was celebrated as a god in Roman poetry.[36] In that sense the divinity theme is new, but the statement is obviously hedged with qualifications. When the poets proclaimed Augustus' divinity, they were not advancing an idea which was totally unheard of. Language equating men with gods had become familiar in several connections. It was a forceful way of acknowledging the aid of benefactors: thus Cicero salutes the consul who had espoused his recall from exile as "father and god."[37] Dependent friends often resort to religious imagery when speaking of their relations with the rich and lordly.[38] In elegiac verse, the lover's mistress is called a goddess, and even in fairly colloquial contexts, it is not uncommon for the wielder of influence or the outstanding achiever in any field to be dubbed a god among men.[39] For disciples of the Stoics, a man could be a god in more than just a figurative sense. They held that after life on earth exceptional individuals took up their station as immortal beings in the heavens.[40]

That such habits of speech and the attitudes behind them would also affect political discourse should not be surprising. Even before the ascendancy of Augustus or Caesar, there had been occasions when public figures at Rome received honors which were normally reserved for the gods. After the Gracchi were killed, sympathizers set up images of them at which they prayed and sacrificed (Plut. *C. Gracch.* 18.3). When news reached Rome that Marius had crushed a German invasion of Italy, householders celebrated by offering libations to him "as though to the immortal gods" (Val. Max. 8.15.7). People throughout the city erected statues and lit candles and incense to honor a praetor who did no more than announce plans for stabilizing the currency (Cic. *Off.* 3.80–81). Furthermore, apart from these irregular manifestations at home, many Romans were acquainted with foreign lands in which rulers were formally accorded divine honors. Kings throughout the eastern Mediterranean took the appellation of "savior and god" into their titulature and had temples, festivals, and sacrifices dedicated to themselves and their families. Indeed, as the Roman presence in the East increased, Roman officials found that they were courted with the very same honors themselves.

By the time of Augustus' debut, therefore, divinizing language was a rich idiom which could be understood in various ways. The range of possible connotations is part of what makes pronouncements by poets difficult to assess, since one cannot in every case decide what a passage is meant to suggest. But what complicates the situation more than anything else is the fact that the state as well as the poets took a position on the divinity of Augustus, enacting a series of honors which gradually coalesced into an official cult. The involvement of the state not only places Augustus' cult on an entirely different level from the impromptu rites paid to forerunners like Marius and the Gracchi; it also calls in question the spontaneity and independence of the poets who hailed him as a god. Were they perhaps acting in concert with the government and attempting to strengthen a quasi-religious regard for the new ruler? I would argue that neither part of this supposition has much to recommend it. Down to the mid-20s, at any rate, the poets do not seem to be acting in concert with the government or to be concerned with political uses of the divine imagery they elaborate in their poems. After that, they simply lose interest in the theme.

We may begin to explore this issue by trying to track the echoes in poetry of official measures associating Augustus with the gods. When the senate reaffirmed the divinity of Julius Caesar in 42 B.C., his inheritor took advantage of the decree to add the title "Son of the Divinity" *(Divi filius)* to his own name. Since Caesar's new position was not just honorary, but substantiated with a temple, priest, and public ceremonies, it conferred a visible new glory on the son as well. Yet Augustus' status as the son of a god drew no attention from the poets either when the issue first arose in the 40s or when the temple of Julius was dedicated in 29 B.C. For that matter, it received little attention thereafter.[41] No poet reacted during the 30s to the enlargement of cult that took place when the war with Sextus Pompey ended in 36 B.C. and statues of Augustus were set up in the temples of many towns throughout Italy (App. *BCiv.* 5.546). The allegorical temple on the banks of the Mincius that Vergil imagines in the proem of the *Third Georgic* may be a muted later reaction; I will return to this passage below. After Augustus' victory at Alexandria in 30 B.C., the senate decreed that he was to be honored with a libation whenever citizens came together for a common meal; that observance is alluded to twice in Augustan poetry, years after it was instituted.[42] There is no echo in poetry of a subsequent decree, that Augustus' name be inserted into the hymn of the Salian priests, and that he be invoked along with the gods (Cass. Dio 51.20.1 and Aug. *Anc.* 10.1).

When Augustus came home in the summer of 29 B.C., the surge of official adulation subsided for about a decade, leaving us with no obvious landmarks to which to refer poetry written during these years. But then the construction of a cult began to go forward again more boldly than ever. In 19 B.C. an altar of Fortune Returning *(Fortuna Redux)* was set up to commemorate Augustus' return from a second tour of the East. Another altar, in honor of the Augustan Peace *(Pax Augusta),* was vowed in 13, and in subsequent years the old spirit cult of the Lares Compitales was resuscitated with a new focus on the leader's own guardian spirits.[43] Thus by the beginning of the last decade of the first century B.C., the rudiments of a cult were in place. Citizens paid homage to aspects of Augustus, if not to the man himself, in a series of annual celebrations.

Augustus' response to the growth of the cult just described can be interpreted in a number of different ways, as covert encouragement, acquiescence, resistance, or plain inconsistency. But however he may have viewed the efforts to initiate a cult on his behalf, it is clear that for a long time poets did not follow the leads that were laid down in public discourse. We find instead that down to about the mid-20s they take an entirely independent line. Although these were the years in which Vergil and Horace made their most impressive contributions to the literature of the emperor cult, they imagine Augustus' divinity in private, poetic terms rather than as an idea with civic implications.

VERGIL'S FIRST ECLOGUE

The premier text on the divinity of Augustus is Vergil's *First Eclogue,* the dramatized conversation between a herdsman who has been forced off his land and a neighbor who has been spared which briefly occupied us in the previous section of this chapter. The dialogue begins as the herdsman voices his surprise that Tityrus seems untroubled by the turmoil evident everywhere else, and his friend responds:

O Meliboeus, a god has given me this ease and peace. For in my eyes that man will always be a god, and the blood of many a little lamb from my

sheepfold will run down his altar. He permitted my cows to browse as
you see, and let me play to my content upon my rustic pipe.

Verg. Ecl. 1.6–10

Talk between the shepherds then veers off on a tangent before Tityrus
gets back to his benefactor and identifies him as a young man *(iuvenis)*
to whom he brought a petition, making a long journey into Rome. The
suit was granted and now, says Tityrus, "on twelve days in every year
smoke rises from my altars in his honor" (lines 42–43).

Interpreters are nearly unanimous and probably correct in thinking
that Tityrus' god is supposed to be the young Octavian, who in the late
40s was directing from Rome the expropriations that supplied land for
veterans of the Caesarean army. That makes Vergil's testimony to his
divinity so early as to be prophetic: it is a decade earlier than the next
allusion in poetry and some five years earlier than any mention of divine
honors in the historical sources.[44] More than that, the assertion of divinity seems as complete and unqualified here as any in later poems. It
is no wonder that this passage has long preoccupied students of the
emperor cult.

Nevertheless, it would be unhistorical to think that the forms of homage surrounding the future Augustus had crystallized by the beginning
of the triumviral period or that Vergil could have somehow foreseen
them then. Tityrus' statement is in fact qualified by its context: the *First
Eclogue* is a dramatic dialogue, and what Tityrus says reflects his character
and circumstances. He is first of all a rustic, as Vergil reminds us by
painting his awed reaction to the size of Rome in lines 19–25. A readiness to discern the presence of gods in human form is one of the traits
conventionally ascribed to simple folk.[45] Another trait dissociating Tityrus from Vergil and Vergil's readers is that he is Greek, like the Theo-
critean shepherds on whom he is modeled. He is thus able to utter sentiments at variance with accepted Roman ideas. It has often been pointed
out that his monthly sacrifices in honor of the *iuvenis* have their closest
parallel in ceremonies honoring Hellenistic rulers.[46] Many within the
Roman elite were acquainted with that milieu, and Vergil could assume
that they would recognize the Hellenistic affinities of Tityrus' new god.
Finally, throughout the poem Tityrus offers his testimony as a private
interpretation of private experience. That the divinity of his benefactor
is not a truth of the natural order he concedes by explaining "for in my
eyes that man will always be a god" (line 7), and as the dialogue contin-

ues, he talks more of "that one," "that youth," than of a god. Octavian's divinity is not a revelation which Tityrus' interlocutor or anyone else is expected to embrace.

These facets of characterization may not be perfectly integrated—a bona-fide rustic would probably not report a divine epiphany quite as self-consciously as Tityrus does, for example—but each throws some light on his assertion that "a god has given me this ease." That kind of language would still have seemed bizarre in the late 40s, and Vergil does not introduce it without at the same time trying to create a dramatically plausible context for it.

Tityrus' benefactor is neither the only nor the most remarkable version of a god-man presented in the *Eclogues.* The *Ninth Eclogue* contains a snatch of song in praise of the comet which had been hailed as the soul of the deified Julius Caesar. It is celebrated as a new sign in the heavens, radiating fruitfulness and stability for all who work the land (lines 46–50). The *Fifth Eclogue* traces the death and apotheosis of Daphnis, paragon of shepherds: all living things and even the rocks and hills are stricken when he dies, only to flourish more exuberantly than ever when he takes his place on Olympus. And last there is the mystical child of the *Fourth Eclogue,* who has so little to do with bucolic conventions that they are virtually absent from the poem. The child has been sent down from heaven, and is destined one day to live among the gods; during the time he dwells on earth, his growth from infancy to maturity draws nature and mankind back in stages to a primeval state of perfection. His field of influence is cosmic, covering "the universe, the lands, the expanse of sea, and the vast sky" (lines 50–52). These conceptions are all far more apocalyptic than that of the *iuvenis* in the *First Eclogue,* and I do not believe that Vergil was led to them by meditation on Augustus.[47] But they did undoubtedly color his thinking about Augustus by the time he was finishing the *Georgics* a decade later.[48]

VERGIL'S FIRST GEORGIC

In the proem of the *First Georgic,* Vergil entreats the favor of a host of divinities with ties to the land, and then addresses himself to Augustus in an invocation (lines 24–42) as long as the whole preceding litany. Augustus too is ultimately to join the celestial ranks, though exactly where remains uncertain: whether he will take charge of the great earth as "potent source of crops and weathers" (27); or become god of the vast sea, "sole cult of sailors" (29–30); or ascend to the zodiac where

Scorpio retracts from Virgo to make way for a new sign; or dally with the prospect of becoming king of the underworld. Whatever he is to become, the poet asks, "bless my bold endeavor and give me a smooth course. Taking pity on rustics ignorant of the way, set forth along with me, and even now become familiar with the prayers of suppliants" (40–42).

Doctrinally, this passage conforms to what became the official line about apotheosis: the emperors attain their divine status only after death. That Vergil anticipated this nicety is not surprising. One might have deduced that the treatment of Augustus would resemble the treatment already given to Julius Caesar. But even with the qualification that it takes effect after death, the proclamation of Augustus' divinity is more radical in the *Georgics* than in the *First Eclogue*. Vergil no longer cultivates the dramatic viewpoint of a rustic but speaks directly, and he has installed Augustus in a pantheon which raises him above the level of Tityrus' purely personal god. He minimizes the distinction between Augustus' present and his future status by already praying to him for guidance.

But what is most striking is the sort of divinity that Vergil prognosticates. Augustus will not simply join the heavenly company of other great men who have been heroized, like Scipio Africanus and Aemilius Paulus in Cicero's *Dream of Scipio*. Even the admission of Hercules among the Olympian gods provides no true parallel, though Vergil at one point borrows the conventional picture of the "councils of the gods" (24–25).[49] What distinguishes Augustus is that he will supplant established powers in whatever sphere he decides to make his own. If for earth he is to be the source of crops and weathers, he will have charge of functions traditionally associated with deities like Ceres and Jupiter. If as god of the sea he engrosses the veneration of sailors, he will have ousted Neptune and Castor and Pollux. If he takes his place in the zodiac, he will set his sign in a tract hitherto occupied by Scorpio.[50] If he should inhabit the underworld, it would be to rule there as king, replacing Pluto. Another atypical feature which Vergil emphasizes is the magnitude of the provinces reserved for the god-to-be: cities and lands of the great earth, the vast sea, the astral belt which governs both the seasons and human destinies, or the underworld kingdom.

The whole conception of apotheosis in the proem is based on these two ideas of supremacy and cosmic efficacy, which can only be projections from present facts.[51] Augustus' future role as god mirrors his eclipse of all rivals and his terrestrial conquests during the years down to 30

B.C.[52] And if these worldwide exertions have inspired speculation about his role at higher levels of the cosmos, the cosmic role in turn explains why his guidance can be invoked for a poem on agriculture. When at the end of the proem Vergil asks Augustus to take pity on rustics ignorant of the way, he is certainly not suggesting that Augustus has any particular expertise about farming. And he probably does not mean to imply that Augustus has a philosopher's understanding of man and nature, although that is the context in which the way-of-life metaphor would have been most familiar to his readers.[53] Vergil has given the metaphor a new application. Rather than the passive understanding of philosophers, Augustus shares the intimate knowledge of the gods who direct natural processes.

VERGIL'S *THIRD GEORGIC*

The *Third Georgic* presents the more-than-mortal Augustus in yet a different aspect. The subject of the book is no sooner broached than Vergil cuts loose from it, avowing his deep desire to excel other poets and "sweep in victory over the lips of men." He then launches into this remarkable hariolation:

> I will be the first (should life sustain me) to escort the Muses with me to my homeland, returning from Mount Helicon; I first will bring back to you, Mantua, Palestinian palmsprays, and will build a temple of marble on a green meadow by the water, where the broad Mincius lines its banks with pliant reeds as it meanders in slow loops. In the center I will have Caesar. He will occupy the temple, while I as victor, resplendent in Tyrian purple, will field a hundred chariots on the riverbank before him. All Greece will abandon Olympia's stream and the groves of Nemea and come to me to vie at running and with boxing gear. Crowned with my own chaplet of olive leaves, I will bestow gifts.
>
> Verg. G. 3.10–22

The imagined festival accrues events for a couple of more lines. Then, coming back to the temple, Vergil describes its portals, which depict the conquests of "victorious Quirinus" in Egypt and Asia and beyond, and its sculptures, which represent figures from the earliest history of Troy (26–36).

So much about this proem is enigmatic that probably no two readers share the same line-by-line understanding of it. One of the enigmas is precisely the status of the temple's occupant. In the other passages we have examined, Vergil conveys fairly definite ideas about the kind of divinity he imagines for Augustus. Those ideas evidently do not carry over here: Augustus is not presented as the object of a peasant's veneration, nor of musings about cosmic order. Yet the context offers little that would help readers conceive a different image of his divinity. In fact, the image of Augustus begins to fade from the moment he is installed in the temple in line 16. He is forgotten as Vergil gets caught up in details of the festival program, and even when the temple is described in lines 26–36 he does not come in directly. Although some at least of the victories represented on the portals are his victories, they are not identified as his; by speaking instead of the "arms of victorious Quirinus," Vergil makes them national accomplishments.[54] It is also noticeable that he recounts them with passive verbs which bypass the naming of a particular agent: "the *conquered* cities of Asia and *vanquished* Niphates" (30), "two trophies *wrested* from enemies at the ends of the earth and nations twice *led* in triumph from East and West" (32–33). In the following lines about the temple statues, he puts the spotlight not on the divine ancestress of the Julian line but on Jupiter, and on heroes and protectors belonging to the whole Trojan people: Tros, Assaracus, and Apollo.[55] Only at the very end of the proem, in lines 46–48, does he reintroduce Augustus, and not as a god, but as a warrior.

Since the sole indication of Augustus' divinity in this passage is his enthronement in the temple, his status as a god evidently depends on the status of the temple. In Vergil's description of it there are possible points of contact with contemporary manifestations of emperor worship. It is a fact, for example, that in Italy temples and festivals were dedicated to Augustus from a fairly early date.[56] Vergil may well have known of such foundations. He may also have been aware that the divine honors lavished on Augustus elsewhere were not countenanced in the capital, and that may have been one reason he located his temple at Mantua rather than at Rome. But whatever it owes to historical realities, no one has ever mistaken it for a real-life temple. It exists in an imaginary future of which Vergil transmits impressions with the self-absorption of a seer or dreamer; he makes far more references to himself than to Augustus.[57] The scene described does not even have the potential to become reality, since poets do not build temples, much less temples of marble and gold and ivory, or establish festivals. In real life, all these actions—the parade of illustrious captives, the ceremonial presentation of a palm, the building of a new temple, the inauguration of victory games—would be performed by a general at the end of a victorious campaign. As acts by

Vergil, they serve to elaborate the picture of a poetic triumph, but they are purely symbolic. Furthermore, as several critics have pointed out, the victory symbolism of the temple is complicated by influence from another source. Since at the end of the proem Vergil vows to treat the victories of Augustus in a future work, and since the visionary temple seems to imply a narrative program in its portals and sculptures, it may itself be a metaphor for the poem he plans to write. Vergil's inspiration here would be Pindar, who was fond of drawing comparisons between a poet and the builder of an edifice (as for example in *Ol.* 6.1–5 and *Pyth.* 6.5–9). But if the temple is metaphorical, Augustus' enshrinement in the temple must function on the same level. The essential point should be, not that he is divine, but that he stands at the center of Vergil's projected poem. If that is what Vergil means, the religious overtones of his image have less to do with ruler cult than with the literary conventions that poetry is sacred, and that it confers immortality on those it celebrates.[58]

HORACE ODES 1.2

One of Horace's early lyrics ascribes to Augustus a status which is as exalted as any he has in Vergil's poems, but different. The *Second Ode* of book 1 starts gloomily, describing storms which have filled "the City and the nations" with fear of a new world deluge. The Tiber itself has risen up to avenge the old wrong done to Rhea Silvia, who was ordered drowned after giving birth to Romulus and Remus. It leaves its banks and hurls its waters against the sanctuary which holds the sacred fire and the ancient image guaranteeing continuance of Roman rule.[59] The next generation of Romans will be depleted because their parents have used against one another swords that ought to have been turned against the Parthians. Having traced the cause of his gloom to the recently concluded civil wars, Horace continues thus:

> On which of the gods should the nation call to aid its perishing domain? With what prayer should the Sacred Virgins assail Vesta, who does not heed their hymns?

> To whom will Jupiter assign the charge of expiating crime? Prophet Apollo, whose bright shoulders are mantled in cloud, we pray that you may come at last,

> Or you instead, smiling Venus of Eryx, round whom Mirth and Desire hover, or you Mars, our progenitor, if you care about the race and the descendants you have abandoned

—Fond as you are of battle shouts and smooth helmets and the grim look
of a Marsian soldier facing his bloodsoaked enemy, you should be glutted
with a sport that has lasted too, too long—

Or you Mercury, winged son of kindly Maia, if you have transformed
yourself into the likeness of a youth and deign to be called Caesar's
avenger,

Put off the return to heaven, and be pleased to linger among the people
of Quirinus. Let not the whirlwind sweep you away too soon because you
are offended by our faults.

Here instead enjoy great triumphs, and savor your acclaim here as father
and leader, and do not allow the Medes to ride unpunished when you
hold command, Caesar.

Hor. Carm. 1.2.25–52

The ode is unique as being the only contemporary poem which intimates that Augustus is not who he seems to be but an Olympian god
disguised as a man. Not only is the idea unparalleled; the poem stands
isolated in the Horatian corpus from all others which contemplate the
divinity of Augustus. It is the earliest piece in which Horace takes up
this theme, and it is the only time he does so in the first two books of
Odes. (The next pieces that take it up are in book 3, poems 3, 4, 5, and
25.) The exceptional content of *Odes* 1.2 has always stimulated attempts
to reconstruct a context for it.

For many critics, it is important testimony about the beginnings of
the emperor cult. Either Horace is expounding an official myth which
Augustus wished to have put out in the early 20s, or he is echoing a
belief that had arisen spontaneously among the people. The main
difficulty with this interpretation is that there is virtually no sign, apart
from the poem itself, that Augustus was formally identified with Mercury.[60] The truth is that any one of the other deities Horace invokes,
Apollo, Venus, or Mars, could be fitted into official ideology more easily
than Mercury can be.

The concern to detect echoes of policy has also encouraged a myopic
reading of the poem. Whatever the exact point of the stanzas about
Mercury, they are based on the often-met idea that gods sometimes drop
down into the world of men. Familiar as this fantasy is, however, and
despite the Roman application Horace has given it in *Odes* 1.2, it does
not accord with traditional Roman beliefs about divine behavior. As
Cicero reminds us, it is a literary import: "Do not suppose that what

you often see happening in plays is really possible: that some god drops down from heaven to visit human gatherings, dwells here on earth, and holds converse with men."[61]

For Horace too, the epiphany of Mercury-Augustus presupposes a literary frame of reference, which he has been at some pains to construct in the earlier part of the poem. The premonitions with which the ode begins are meant to draw contemporary events into line with the enormities of Greek mythology. The great flood in the story of Deucalion and Pyrrha was sent to punish human iniquity, and that is the only eschatology which Horace finds adequate to Rome's civil wars. His image of Jupiter sending hail and snow and torrents upon the earth originates in Greek epic (Hom. *Il.* 10.5–8 and 16.384–392 being two early exemplars). He had a Homeric warrant for appearances by precisely those gods whom he first invites to manifest themselves at Rome. According to the *Iliad,* Apollo, Venus, and Mars had come down from Olympus to fight alongside the Trojan ancestors of the Romans. Horace has even worked several epic floscules into his description of the gods. Venus' smile and her hovering attendants and Apollo's cloud-wrapped shoulders are direct borrowings.[62] In the lines on Mars Horace has varied traditional formulas: the god whose appetite for war he prays has been quenched is the god whom Homer calls "insatiate of battle" (*Il.* 5.388, 6.203). The catalog of things which Mars delights in conforms to a pattern often found in the *Homeric Hymns.*[63] Horace supposes that Jupiter must send a god to earth because no human agent can administer purification for crimes in which all men have been involved. This notion of moral purification is alien to Roman religion, which possessed no rites that could cleanse a man of willful wrongdoing, and which certainly did not envision the possibility of absolution by divine agents. Here again, Horace has mythic precedents in mind: how Apollo, in obedience to the will of Zeus, purified Orestes after he had killed his mother; how Athena and Hermes were sent by Zeus to purify the Danaids after they had killed their husbands; how Zeus himself purified the first murderer, Ixion.[64] But perhaps the most telling clue to the conceptual background of the ode is the passage about the Tiber in the middle. Horace's picture of an outraged river god surging into the midst of a human melee is surely meant to evoke the bizarre scene in book 21 of the *Iliad* in which the Trojan river Scamander assaults Achilles.[65] The point of these odd stanzas is to invest the civil wars with the same monumental, surreal aspect that Homer gave the final battles of his poem.

Mercury's descent in the form of Augustus belongs to the same realm of ideas as the epic transmogrification of the Tiber. Horace has imagined Augustus' effect on events in terms which fit the mythological perspective of his poem; the Homerization of *Odes* 1.2 is similar to Horace's Pindarization of *Odes* 4.4. But it is only within the fiction of this poem that the conceit is meant to be understood. The reason parallels are so hard to discover inside or outside the corpus of Horace is that the equation between Mercury and Augustus is unrelated to public opinion, or even to any abiding belief on the part of Horace himself. What suggested it was first of all the conventional image of Mercury in Greek mythology: he usually figures as a young man (see Hom. *Il.* 24.347–348 and *Od.* 10.278–279), like Augustus, who was in his mid-thirties when Horace's poem was written. But Mercury's character in myth is probably even more significant than his looks. Of all the Olympians it is he who consorts most frequently with men, and he is recognized as "the god who most loves humanity."[66] If a higher power was to be discerned behind the beneficent activity of Augustus, Mercury was therefore a reasonable guess.

Among the scores of lines in which contemporary poets acclaim Augustus' godlike glory, these four passages stand out as both the earliest and most complex. Each presents an image of transcendence which is integrated into a distinct and carefully developed context (this holds good even for the proem of the *Third Georgic,* although as we have seen its imagery does not focus primarily on Augustus' divinity). Yet it seems clear that they are improvisations. Vergil and Horace do not pick up on the same ideas, nor do they even repeat their own ideas elsewhere. The four passages coexist with a variety of others in their works where Augustus is imagined as a different sort of god or as not a god at all. Nor do these passages match the expressions of homage broadcast through public and official channels. What makes them so intense, in fact, is that they precede the institution of a cult. Vergil and Horace were not echoing formulas, but reacting to the political shocks which brought the imagery of the superman to life.

After the early 20s, however, poets handle the theme less creatively. Not that they cease to vary it: during the period of Augustus' Spanish campaign, Horace explores analogies with the demigod Hercules, who accomplished one of his last toils in Spain.[67] Ovid too contributed, with the glibness that allowed him to twist almost any cliché into some new shape; he more often than any other poet identifies Augustus with Jupiter. But on the whole, the images are less bold and the space devoted to them is briefer. In the *Aeneid* there are no more than half a dozen lines which touch on the divinity of Augustus.[68] Poets begin to treat it as an idea that can be taken for granted. Propertius abruptly launches a poem of the late 20s with the line, "The god Caesar ponders a campaign against the rich Indies" (3.4.1). But the poem contains nothing more about the god, except for an allusion to his descent from Venus at the end. The imperial divinity is just as perfunctorily treated in the elegy for Cornelia, where Propertius brings Augustus into a catalog of grieving relatives: "We have seen tears issue from a god" (4.11.60).[69]

These bare statements presuppose an audience for whom such transfigurations of Augustus were already commonplace—so commonplace, in fact, that wags as well as flatterers had picked up on them.[70] Their conventionality is further evident in a different way in the later poems of Horace, whose expressions of homage are always most sonorous when he associates himself with public sentiments. In *Odes* 4.5, for example, Horace does not proclaim the divinity of Augustus in his own voice, but makes a peasant Everyman his spokesman:

> The close of day finds each man at home on the hillside where he trains his vines on solitary trees. From work he heads back happily to a drink of wine, and hails you as a god at the clearing of the tables.

> You he honors in litanies and with libations from his cup, and your sacred name he links with his family gods, as men of Greece remember Castor and great Hercules.

> Hor. *Carm.* 4.5.29–36

In the *Letter to Augustus* Horace submerges himself in a throng of reverential citizens:

> Here and now we bestow on you honors in season, and we set up altars where men take oaths in your sacred name, confessing that your like has never yet been seen, or will be seen again. But only in this do your people act wise and just . . .

> Hor. *Epist.* 2.1.15–18[71]

Unlike the Mercury ode, which explored Augustus' providential role in terms of an original conceit, these passages voice attitudes in which all humanity is assumed to share.

If it is true that the divinity theme in Augustan poetry flowered early and then went into greenery, the reason is not difficult to understand.

What poets could offer in this line was soon overshadowed by the extravagance of official and unofficial public discourse, which poets were increasingly content to reproduce. Horace in his later poems alludes to ceremonies and altars established by senate decree. The influence of public cult on Ovid is even stronger. In his calendar poem he undertakes to celebrate "the altars and new holydays of Caesar" (*Fasti* 1.13–14), and it is Ovid in whose verse we hear the first echoes of the new theology of apotheosis.[72] There is no reason to think that the poets were pressured to take note of Augustus' quasi-religious status, which after the 20s became so obtrusive that one could hardly help but register some aspect of it. A more significant indication of relations between poets and the regime is that the importance of the divinity theme diminished even as echoes of the official cult increased. When Vergil and Horace first cast Augustus in the image of a god, they were working with material that was "rare, fresh, as yet unvoiced by any other tongue," as Horace put it (*Carm.* 3.25.7–8). Then it was a poetically exciting theme. That changed as the cult of Augustus was institutionalized. Poets left the development of the idea to official spokesmen, and looked for fresh material elsewhere.

Primeval Rome

Toward the end of the 20s, Vergil, Tibullus, and Propertius each produced vignettes depicting the site of Rome as it looked before a city had risen there.[73] The Tibullan passage makes a good example because it is short and self-contained. It comes from a poem celebrating the induction of a new priest into the college which had charge of the Sibylline books. The poem opens with a prayer asking the god Apollo to guide his priest; then Tibullus begins to reflect on the involvement of Sibylline prophecies in Rome's history, starting from the time of Aeneas' encounter with the Sibyl. After describing Aeneas' despair over the burning of Troy, and just before relating the Sibyl's prophecy, the poet inserts these lines:

> Romulus had not yet laid out the walls of the eternal city, which were not to be the habitation of his partner Remus. At that time cows grazed on the grassy Palatine, and lowly huts stood upon the citadel of Jupiter. A Pan drenched with offerings of milk had his place there in the shade of a holm-oak, and there was a wooden Pales made by a peasant's crook-knife. On a tree was hung the offering of a roving shepherd, a trilling pan-pipe

consecrated to the woodland god; its reeds were arrayed in a sinking curve, for each length bound in with wax was shorter than the one before. And little boats used to ply over what is now the area of the Velabrum, sculling through water. By that route on holidays a girl would travel over to the rich herd owner whom she meant to captivate, and with her came back gifts of the bounteous country-side, cheese and the white lamb of a snowy sheep.

Tib. 2.5.23–38

After this digression comes the Sibyl's prophecy to Aeneas, telling him of the new foundation he is to plant in Italy. Her revelation soars to an ecstatic close:

Now, you bulls, crop the grass of the seven hills while there is time; soon this will be the site of a great city. Rome, your name is destined for the mastery of the world, wherever Ceres looks down from heaven on cultivated ground, from the distant rising of the Sun to the ocean stream which bathes his panting horses in its waters.

Tib. 2.5.55–60

Some elements in this picture are thoroughly Tibullan. The dedication fastened to a tree, the rough carvings venerated by ingenuous country folk, and the imagining of the game of love in rustic surroundings all recur in some of his purely elegiac pieces. But beneath the individual touches is a vision of Rome which Tibullus has in common with other poets writing at the time. It is focused on a series of specific localities and landmarks running from the deep eastern bend of the Tiber past the Capitoline, Palatine, and Aventine hills to the area of the Forum. Rarely does the panorama take in the heights on the east (Caelian, Esquiline, Viminal, and Quirinal) or the Field of Mars which opens out to the north. The spots described belong to the most ancient part of the city, and the poets like to emphasize the sacred aura which hangs over them or their connections with the adventures of gods and heroes.

Another common feature of these passages is that they pointedly contrast the undeveloped look of early Rome with its present aspect. In Tibullus the contrast lies in the interplay between past and present tenses, and in the construction of discords (a shepherd community introduced as "the eternal city," and images like cows upon the fashionable Palatine). Other poets often refer to monuments (chiefly temples and holy precincts) that occupy the ancient sites. The contrast is not simply visual. The poets almost always draw out a symbolic correlation between the lowliness of the original settlement and the worldwide reach of the modern city.

As in Tibullus, the theme of primeval Rome may also acquire overtones which are particular to a given poet. It lends itself to multiple interpretations. Nevertheless, at its core is a recognizable combination of elements (topographical focus, with particular attention to hallowed places; paradoxical juxtapositions of past and present; pride in empire) which comes up in similar form time after time, making it one of the most well-defined commonplaces in Augustan literature. One has to ask what is behind the sudden efflorescence of this theme in the late 20s.

In terms of literary history, the genetic background of these sketches is not difficult to unravel. They are first of all examples of ecphrasis, that technique of word-painting taught by rhetoricians and imported into poetry, where it generated many a set-piece on groves and mountains and caves and pools. Poetic pictures of early Rome also owe something to Lucretius, who had clothed in verse Epicurus' postulates about the life of primitive man, and something to the conventions of pastoral poetry.[74]

But the most critical influence undoubtedly came from the writings of Roman antiquarians, foremost among them Varro, who devoted more than a half-dozen works comprising over fifty books to the elucidation of Roman antiquities.[75] The great difference between these works and the treatment of early Rome by conventional historians was that the antiquarians concentrated on describing environment, customs, and institutions rather than on narrating events. They treated exactly the kind of detail which the poets worked into their vignettes of early Rome. Topography, for example, was a major preoccupation of Varro, in whose writings "places" was one of the rubrics under which material was regularly collected and set out.[76] This wealth of information about their surroundings impressed contemporaries. Cicero claimed that until Varro enlightened them, Romans were as ignorant of their city as tourists: "We were like outsiders, abroad and astray in our own city, until your books led us home, enabling us to recognize who and where we were" (*Acad.* 1.9). Sacred sites loomed large in Varro's tour of Rome (three books of the *Antiquities* were devoted to shrines, sacred buildings, and holy places), and like the poets, he was fond of contrasting ancient simplicity and modern opulence.[77] And finally, it is clear that the etymological deductions on which Varro and other antiquarians based parts of their reconstruction of the past lurk beneath the more vivid pictures painted by the poets. The Tibullan passage, for example, reproduces a Varronian etymology which connected the place name *Velabrum* with the verb *vehi*, meaning "ride" or "travel."[78] Though it would be naive to think in every case that the poets had studied the works of Varro and his fellow scholars, it is impossible to deny that their vignettes of early Rome are related in some way to the antiquarian tradition.

Awareness of these literary antecedents does not help us understand what made the motif so popular around 20 B.C., however. The influences which we can identify in idylls like the Tibullan passage go back to material which was current at least two decades earlier. The question remains, What was the catalyst that finally activated them?

Between 27 and 24 B.C. Livy brought out the first installment of a monumental new history of Rome.[79] Book 1, on the city's beginnings, dealt with the same period as the sketches which the poets began to compose soon afterward. But Livy's influence on those sketches seems to be tenuous at best. He does not incorporate some legends, and many details of legends, which do appear in the poems. And most important, he does not try to visualize the primitive city in the way the poets do. His narrative is almost bare of scenic and topographical detail. (Livy's neglect of antiquarian sources in book 1 is well known, but it is best appreciated if one reads his account beside book 1 of Dionysius' history, which brings in lore about sites and shrines at every turn.)

In recent years there has been a certain predisposition to believe that Vergil himself might have been the catalyst. His description of the site of Rome in *Aeneid* 8 is certainly the most original and powerful rendering of the theme, and one would expect other poets to have been influenced by it. But the hypothesis has difficulties which make it questionable. Chronology is the first problem. The passages from Vergil, Tibullus, and Propertius are so nearly contemporaneous that it is by no means clear which came first. It is ordinarily supposed, on the basis of an epigram saying that Death sent Tibullus to accompany Vergil to the underworld, that they died within a short time of each other in the year 19 B.C.[80] If that is so, Tibullus could not have read the *Aeneid*, which was not published until after Vergil's death. He could have been acquainted with its contents only if he had heard recitations or seen preliminary drafts in Vergil's lifetime.[81] Even Propertius did not have much time to read and be influenced by the *Aeneid* before he wrote his own poems on early Rome. He was at work on his last book from about 22 to 16 B.C. Half of the poems (five out of eleven) deal with Rome's ancient past, and these are the pieces to which the poet gives pride of place. For Vergil to have been his inspiration here, we would have to suppose that Propertius did not hit upon the major emphasis of book 4 until he was more than halfway done.

Furthermore, there is little sign that the elegists borrowed anything from Vergil's picture of early Rome. Opinions differ as to whether or not their verses contain verbal echoes of the Vergilian passage.[82] It is clear, however, that they sometimes went their own way in regard to story and setting. According to Vergil, the peculiarity of the cattle-rustler Cacus was that he could belch fire (*Aen.* 8.194–267); Propertius gives him three heads but no ignition (4.9.10 and 15). According to Vergil, when Aeneas saw the Capitoline, it was a numinous spot where relics of a long-extinct settlement were visible (*Aen.* 8.347–358); Tibullus holds that in Aeneas' time it was inhabited by shepherds (2.5.26–30). Vergil has Aeneas walk from the Tiber bank to Evander's dwelling on the Palatine by way of the Velabrum (*Aen.* 8.306–362); for both Tibullus (2.5.33–36) and Propertius (4.2.7–10, 4.9.5–6), the Velabrum in those days was an arm of the Tiber, negotiable only by boat. On the whole, the two elegists seem more akin to each other than to Vergil in the way they handle the theme of primeval Rome. It is not just that their vignettes are much briefer than Vergil's, but that they seem more superficial as well. The interrelationships could be explained by supposing either that Vergil invented a theme which Propertius and Tibullus quickly stereotyped, or that Vergil deepened a theme which all three poets took up independently. The evidence of the respective texts gives no more support to the first than to the second interpretation.

There is one bit of evidence suggesting that the theme was topical even before Vergil wrote. In a poem written between about 25 and 22 B.C., Propertius says that he might someday feel emboldened to write epic, and he instances as one possibility a work about "the Palatine heights when they pastured Roman bulls, and the walls that held firm after Remus was slain, and the twin kings suckled by a wild teat" (3.9.49–51). This epic on early Rome is evidently something keyed to conventional expectations. Propertius is casting about for projects that will be more readily received than his love poems. Unlike the old-time epics, which followed a narrative line from the remote past down to the present, the poem Propertius envisions would be devoted entirely to early Rome and would feature descriptive embellishments as well as saga. In the midst of one scene that he evokes stand the Palatine kine which are the central cliché of all later set-pieces on primeval Rome.

If neither Livy nor Vergil established the vogue for this motif, there is no other contemporary author we can trace it to. But the influence we are looking for did not have to come from literature at this point. The literary picture of early Rome had been created a generation before by Varro and others; what was needed in the 20s was not someone to originate it but something to draw attention to it.

I suggest that the catalyst in this case was Augustus himself, and that he influenced the poets not by any direct approach to them, but by a campaign of public works which was steadily transforming the appearance of the city. In the year 29 B.C., he dedicated two new buildings which dominated and redefined the Forum area. The Julian Senate-house closed in the angle to west and north, while the Temple of the Deified Julius formed a new boundary across the eastern end.[83] In that year also a triumphal arch in honor of Augustus was raised over the processional avenue leading into the Forum from the east.[84] Many of the other great buildings surrounding the Forum were under construction at roughly the same time. Augustus was responsible for completing the Julian Basilica, which enclosed the south side, and also the colonnade and temple complex which Caesar had laid out behind the Senate-house (*Anc.* 20.3). At his instigation, lesser leaders undertook the rebuilding of the Regia or Pontiff's House, the Aemilian Basilica, and the Temple of Saturn.[85]

Augustus built aggressively in other areas of the city as well. In the year 28 B.C. he carried out a crash program to restore every dilapidated temple in Rome, repairing or rebuilding a total of eighty-two structures (*Anc.* 20.4 and Suet. *Aug.* 30.2). The sacred area on top of the Capitoline benefited from several improvements. One of the first shrines Augustus restored was the ancient Temple of Jupiter Feretrius, founded according to tradition by Romulus.[86] In 22 B.C. he erected a major new temple on the site, in honor of Jupiter the Thunderer.[87] And he deposited a princely offering of gold and jewels worth fifty million sesterces in Jupiter's third and largest temple on the Capitoline.[88]

Across from the Capitoline, he put up a complex of buildings which commanded the brow of the Palatine hill above the Circus Maximus. The anchor building was a temple of Apollo dedicated in 28 B.C. (Cass. Dio 53.1.3). The area immediately east of and below the temple was opened up for public use through construction of a portico, a public library, and reception rooms; hitherto the Palatine had been covered mostly by private residences. West of the temple stood Augustus' mansion, accommodating both public and private functions.[89]

According to Suetonius, the edifices which sprang up throughout the city during these years bore witness to Augustus' concern that Rome was ill-attired for its role as capital of an empire (*Aug.* 28.3). Even the emperor's own contemporaries must have been conscious of the nationalism in his building program. Certainly it was apparent to Vitruvius, who says that he was led to dedicate a treatise on architecture to Augustus after observing his "alertness to the vital function of public buildings, that the state might not only be enlarged with provinces, but possess in its public buildings outstanding symbols of the majesty of its empire."[90] This imperial symbolism carried over into the poets' vignettes of Rome, and helps to explain why they focused on the political and religious center, without taking in the Field of Mars where so many other buildings were being erected at the same time.[91]

Another tendency which spotlighted the ancient heart of the city was Augustus' systematic resuscitation of ancestral rites and practices. Priestly confraternities which had been inactive for years, like the Arval Brethren, the Fetials, and the Titian Sodality, were revived.[92] As they resumed their archaic rituals, they necessarily heightened public consciousness of the sites at which those rituals were performed. On two occasions during the 20s Augustus proclaimed that the world was at peace by closing the gates of Janus' precinct on the Forum (Cass. Dio 51.20.4 and 53.26.5). That ceremony had been last performed two centuries earlier. He revived the annual dress parade of the knights, which culminated in solemnities at the Temple of Castor on the Forum and at Jupiter's great temple on the Capitoline.[93] He made a shrine at the cave beneath the Palatine where legend held that Romulus and Remus were nursed by a wolf, and he revived the race around the hill which was associated with it (*Anc.* 19.1 and Suet. *Aug.* 31.4).

As builder and conserver, Augustus lent visible expression to ideas which the antiquarians had put in circulation about Rome's past. If his exertions were what chiefly reawakened curiosity about the city in the 20s, then the early-Rome topos of the poets can be considered a theme which, at least proximately, he inspired. From that angle what is most interesting about this theme is that it was not turned into a vehicle for the glorification of Augustus. The poets realized the source of the wealth

that was flooding their city and knew that Augustus had built many of
the edifices which met their gaze.[94] Yet he is not brought directly into
any of the passages we have been considering. (At best his presence may
in some cases be implicit, as in *Aeneid* 8, where critics have noted that
Aeneas arrives at the site of Rome on the day of the year on which
Augustus began his triple triumph in 29 B.C., and that Aeneas is given a
night's lodging on the spot where Augustus' mansion later stood.) Nor
do the poets try to glorify Augustus at a remove, by substituting a recital
of his works for an encomium of the man himself. Not only do they
touch on sites and structures on which he left no mark, but they disregard many of his most impressive contributions to the city's redevelop-
ment. The new buildings which they do mention receive no more emphasis than other topographical features they describe. The Augustan
renascence seems to have heightened consciousness of the city more than
the man. The city was clearly the object of Propertius' feeling when he
vowed to rededicate his poetry:

> Wolf of Mars, best nurse of Roman strength, how big our walls have
> grown upon your milk! I pray that I may trace the measure of those walls
> in patriotic verse, but oh how small is the range of my eloquence. Yet
> whatever trickle of talent flows from within me, all of it will serve my
> country.
>
> Prop. 4.1.55–60

This patriotic repositioning may have been partly based on calculations of expediency. The celebration of primeval Rome offered poets a
ground of rapport with a wider public than did the etiolated themes of
coteries. Furthermore, it suited the political climate of the 20s: though
not slanted toward Augustus personally, it was consonant with attitudes
which he sought to foster. Insofar as it was actually a double image (of
the modern city superimposed upon a pristine site), it dangled the flattering suggestion that Rome in the age of Augustus had somehow managed to unite old-fashioned values with unprecedented dominion. But
the more artistic values which attracted poets to the theme should not
be overlooked. In contrast to the idea of wars and conquest, for example,
it was fresh, and capable of stretching the imagination. It invited poets
to project themselves into the past, in the same way that the idea of the
cosmos held out regions beyond the "ring of the lands" for them to
visualize. Another important asset was that the lore of early Rome com-
prised an abundance of poetic materials. It opened a new vein for Prop-

ertius and later for Ovid to work when they found that they had depleted the primary resources of elegy.

The Founding of a Dynasty

Let us now consider a theme which had no background in Roman literature before the principate but which originated in the political environment that Augustus created. The dynastic theme has both a broader and a narrower focus. The first concerns the imperial house as a whole. Attention lavished on the leader and first citizen *(princeps)* begins to be diffused among living members of his family—his wife, sister, children, and other relations by blood and marriage. The poets celebrate Augustus' ancestors too, but that is a traditional perspective. What is new and important is the emphasis on the *domus,* his household as it exists in the present. The narrower focus of the dynastic theme is on the idea of succession. It is gradually acknowledged that Augustus occupies a position to which someone else will eventually succeed and that, contrary to the procedures which rotate new incumbents through other public offices, his successor will be taken from within his house. Both these ideas were foreign to Roman civic discourse when Augustus first entered on the scene, yet by his death they were naturalized in forms which persisted for the rest of the imperial period. In the following pages I will trace how they became established in Roman poetry. But first it is necessary to consider what Augustus himself did to fix attention on the dynastic tableau.

The exploitation of family connections was part of the political art at Rome long before the middle of the first century B.C., but there had been little to parallel the degree of nepotism which gave Augustus his start. In the period when he was only Octavius, son of a small-town, small-time senator who had the added liability of dying prematurely, his great-uncle Caesar introduced him into public life with commendations which gave him precedence over most sons of the aristocracy. He was installed in the college of pontiffs, elevated to the patriciate, and given a turn in the honorific position of city administrator during the Latin Festival.[95] He was decorated and placed at the head of a victory parade for a campaign at which he had not been present, and he officiated as master of ceremonies at one of Caesar's theatrical entertainments in Rome.[96] For the last ten years of Caesar's life, the family pride which motivated so many of his actions had no one on whom to focus except his sister's grandson, and those were the years in which Octavius made his debut. The exposure which Caesar gave him set the pattern for the honors with which he later introduced princes of his own house to public life.

Octavius received a powerful boost from his great-uncle even after the assassination. In the will he was adopted as Caesar's son and named as his principal heir.[97] Not only did he gain title to Caesar's fortune and claims over his freedmen and clients, he also acquired a charismatic name, which he immediately took up in place of his own. Beginning even within his lifetime, there were writers who went so far as to say that Caesar's will invested him with the late Dictator's power and political position.[98] An interpretation so foreign to Republican principles could not have been publicly enunciated in the first years after the Ides of March. But the adoption and inheritance did furnish another pretext on which Caesar's heir was able to capitalize immediately: "Those who murdered my father I drove into exile, having punished their crime through lawfully established tribunals, and afterwards when they made war upon the state, I conquered them twice in battle" (*Anc.* 2).

The domestic maneuvering continued after Octavian had gained a toehold in Rome. Both of the major partners in the triumvirate used matrimonial alliances to cement relationships among themselves and with other dynasts. Child-poor by comparison with Antony, Octavian began by bartering himself. He negotiated and broke off three matches before he married Livia. Even after that, according to his enemy, he toyed with the idea of contracting marriage with the daughter of the Getic king.[99] He also brought his sister, his daughter, and his nephew into play: Octavia was married off to Antony, her son Marcellus was briefly promised to a daughter of Sextus Pompey, and Julia was promised to one of Antony's sons.[100] This continuous recycling of himself and his kinsmen was another lesson Octavian had learned from his great-uncle. When the daughter of Caesar whom Pompey had married died, Caesar offered to replace her with his grand-niece (Octavian's sister) who was already married to someone else. Caesar further undertook to divorce his own wife in order to marry Pompey's daughter (Suet. *Jul.* 27.1).

Octavian also had the good fortune to have dumped in his lap a marital issue that could be exploited to Antony's disadvantage. When Antony married Octavian's sister, soldiers and the civilian population celebrated the union as a guarantee that the two leaders would cooperate to restore peace (App. *BCiv.* 5.272–273 and Cass. Dio 48.31). Yet within two and half years, Antony abandoned his wife and returned to the Egyptian seductress Cleopatra. He conferred grandiose titles on her and her children, and even turned over to her territories of the Roman people. When Antony resumed this liaison, Octavian began to turn the spotlight on his own chaste and old-fashioned ménage. At the end of the Sicilian War in 36 he obtained the right to commemorate his victory by holding an annual banquet with his wife and children in Jupiter's Capitoline temple (Cass. Dio 49.15.1). And later in the same year he instigated a cynical decree which invited Antony to celebrate a temple banquet with *his* wife and children (Cass. Dio 49.18.6). He took the occasion of his first successes in the Dalmatian War a year later to have statues raised to his wife and to Octavia; at the same time it was decreed that their persons should be sacrosanct (Cass. Dio 49.38.1).

Even spontaneous events involving family members lent themselves to exploitation. During the year after Caesar's assassination, when the senate was attempting to reassert its authority, it glorified the senatorial cause and rallied support by elevating the funerals of its defenders into national observances.[101] Chance gave Octavian an early opportunity to mobilize the spectacle of a public funeral for his own purposes. Shortly after he extorted the consulship from the senate, his mother died, and he took advantage of his position to have her buried with official honors (Cass. Dio 47.17.6 and Suet. *Aug.* 61.2). But the most flagrant appropriation of public institutions for family concerns occurred a couple of years later, when he organized a state funeral for the ex-slave who had attended him as a schoolboy.[102] It is not easy to say what caused him to summon the city fathers to a ceremony which they were bound to find repugnant.[103] They had had their noses twisted more than once during the period after the triumvirs took over, and that may have been the point of the funeral given to Sphaerus. But it could also have been a step in Octavian's self-rehabilitation after the proscriptions. The triumvirs had stigmatized themselves by their wholesale violation of personal ties. One of Octavian's victims was his former guardian; perhaps with Sphaerus he wished to be seen tilting the other way.[104]

The proscriptions are relevant to another factor in the politicization of family ties, which is that the civil wars drew wives and mothers into more visible roles than they had ever taken before. As families were broken or set at odds, influence gravitated to the women in them. Only Antony's first wife, Fulvia, went to the length of becoming a combatant, but many figure as intercessors and mediators between the combatants.[105]

Finally, mass psychology had already begun to play an important part in magnifying the families of political leaders before the civil wars began. One of the plainest manifestations of the new mood occurred when Julia, the daughter of Caesar and wife of Pompey, died in 54 B.C. Since she was the embodiment of people's hopes that their leaders would remain at peace (just as Octavia was two decades later), they reacted extravagantly. Though Pompey wanted to have her buried at one of his villas, the citizenry turned out in force and buried her with full solemnities on the Field of Mars.[106]

Long before Actium, therefore, an environment had been created in which not only dynasts but also the women and children around them were seen as public figures. As a first family was installed alongside the first citizen in post-Actian society, the process accelerated. Marital alliances were designed and executed as carefully as they had been during the triumvirate, and the senate continued to patent honors for Augustus which drew attention to other members of the household as well. Public consciousness of the emperor's family was also heightened in ways which were new. A year after his return from Egypt, Augustus built a gigantic mausoleum in which the members of his house were henceforward to be buried. It was a monument which he wanted his fellow-citizens to frequent: he appropriated a site for it on the Field of Mars and laid out a public park around it (Suet. *Aug.* 100.4 and Strabo 5.3.8 [236]). He spent years of his reign in an effort to propagate old-fashioned family virtues, which he believed he had caused to flourish in the palace, and it is on an Augustan monument, the Altar of Peace, that mothers and children are shown participating in a public ceremony for the first time in the history of Roman art.

Even when Augustus was not propounding examples from his domestic life, domestic affairs were constantly on view. Births and birthdays and weddings and funerals in Rome's great houses had always stirred flurries of courtesy and curiosity in the rest of society. After the civil wars, the palace was the apex of the social hierarchy, and its news overshadowed everything else that happened in the capital. As the anonymous author of a condolence to Livia expressed it some years later, "You draw our eyes and ears to you, we register your doings, nor can any utterance emanating from princely lips be concealed."[107]

Curiosity about the succession, however, was undoubtedly what caused people to scrutinize the palace family most closely. One would like to know when the question first raised itself in the minds of contem-

poraries, and for that matter, in the mind of Augustus himself. But unambiguous contemporary evidence is hard to come by. Augustus could
not speak openly of transferring his power, both because his official position was something constructed for him personally and not part of the
state's constitutional structure, and because, according to traditional
practice, no man had the right to name his own successor. Hence no
public utterance is recorded in which Augustus speaks in his own words
about who would succeed him. The closest he ever came to such a
statement was his avowal in A.D. 4 that he was adopting Tiberius "for
the sake of the state" (Suet. *Tib.* 21.3).

In a private letter written three years earlier, however, Augustus does
confess the expectation he cherished at that time of having his adopted
sons Gaius and Lucius succeed him.[108] His hopes were no secret from
the public. When Gaius died, the citizens of Pisa mourned him as one
"marked out to be first citizen, perfect in justice and resemblance to his
father's virtues" (*ILS* 140.12–13). Popular awareness of Augustus' dynastic plans can be documented by texts which are somewhat earlier,
though less explicit. In 3 B.C. the inhabitants of Paphlagonia in the eastern half of the empire took an oath in which they swore their allegiance
"to Caesar Augustus and to his children and descendants." They do not
say that the sons and descendants will come in turn to hold the position
Augustus holds now, but if that is not the understanding, it is difficult to
see the point of including them in the oath. More surprising is a recently
discovered inscription showing that Spanish subjects of the emperor also
swore allegiance to Augustus and his children, though nothing like the
monarchic institutions of the Hellenistic East had ever existed in the
western half of the empire.[109]

The evidence of contemporary documents makes the closing decade
of the century the very latest point at which anyone could suppose that
Augustus began planning the succession of Gaius and Lucius. But according to narrative accounts of the reign, preparations were under way
long before then. Dio (54.18.1) reports that in 17 B.C., right after Lucius
was born, Augustus adopted both boys, "not waiting for them to grow
to manhood, but appointing them successors to his rule right away, so
that he might be the object of fewer conspiracies." The implication that
Augustus publicly designated two infants as the nation's future rulers is
unsupported by any other source and is questionable on several grounds.
It may be no more than an inference drawn by Dio himself, reasoning
that the first adoption in the imperial house already possessed the sig-

nificance which attached to subsequent adoptions. However, it is also possible that he is echoing inferences drawn by Augustus' contemporaries. In subsequent chapters as well (especially 54.27.1, 55.9, and 55.10.17), Dio gives the impression that Gaius and Lucius were popularly perceived as heirs apparent. If this representation is correct—and the sudden appearance of their images on Roman coins of the year 13 B.C. suggests that it may be—then the succession issue was in the air all through the last two decades of the century.[110]

But the point at which our sources first report speculation about the question is earlier still. In the year 23, Augustus became so sick that he put his affairs in order and prepared to hand over the government. Velleius and Dio say that it was generally assumed he would designate Marcellus, his nephew and son-in-law, to take his place.[111] But to everyone's surprise, he left Marcellus completely out of his arrangements. And when rumors about his intentions persisted even after his recovery, he insisted that he had made no provision for a successor, and backed up the assertion by producing his will (Cass. Dio 53.30–31).

As Dio presents it, the crisis of 23 brought into the open discrepant understandings about Augustus' arrangements. The Roman public expected an announcement that Marcellus was to succeed, while Augustus insisted that no such announcement would be forthcoming. These contrary standpoints do not necessarily imply that the succession itself was in dispute, however. Augustus created successors by irradiating them with powers and publicity so that they would have a monopoly on public attention when he died. But what gave them their ascendancy were the powers which they exercised during his lifetime. It would have been superfluous—perhaps even dangerously premature—to bestow titles like "successor," "crown prince," or "heir apparent," indicating arrangements not meant to take effect until after his death. Augustus gradually disclosed his plans for the succession by gestures toward his favorites. At no time in his reign was it necessary for him to resort to proclamations that they would take his place.

We have now at least a rough chronology to apply as we consider how poets dealt with the subject. We know that the earliest documents which advert to the succession date from the turn of the century, in the years from 3 B.C. to A.D. 4. According to narratives of the reign, however, speculation had already sprung up two decades earlier, in the lifetime of Marcellus. And if we believe that Augustus' method of grooming a successor was to isolate him upon a pedestal of honors, we must believe

that the process began as soon as Augustus returned to Italy in 29, when
he distributed money to the citizens in Marcellus' name as well as his
own, and had his nephew ride one of the horses that drew his triumphal
chariot (Cass. Dio 51.21.3 and Suet. *Tib.* 6.4).

In view of the care Augustus bestowed on his nephew's advancement,
it is remarkable that none of the Roman poets makes any mention of
Marcellus during his lifetime. His role in Augustus' triumph, his military
debut in Spain, his marriage to Augustus' daughter, and his early induction into public life all pass without remark.[112] Only after his death do
the poets begin to celebrate him, and even then, his involvement in
Augustus' dynastic plans is not what they look back on. Consider the
way in which Propertius characterizes him in 3.18:

> What help to him was his lineage or merit or his excellent mother and
> connection with the house of Caesar? Or the canopy which a little while
> ago fluttered above an overflowing theater, and all the enterprises in his
> mother's hands? He died, poor lad, and found his term in the twentieth
> year. One day rounded off those many talents in a little sum. Go on, lift
> your thoughts and fantasize of triumphs, enjoy the theaterfuls of people
> rising to applaud, outclass the fabrics of Asia, and deck everything with
> jewels for the grand games: it will all be fuel for your funeral pyre.
>
> Prop. 3.18.11–20

Propertius keeps to observable and public facts: Marcellus' Claudian ancestry, his relationship to the Julian house, and his mother; his age, endowments, martial aspirations, and popularity; and above all, the lavish
outlays for his aedilician games. Some facts he downplays or disregards.
He barely acknowledges that Marcellus was married to Augustus' daughter, who has all but vanished beside the figure of Marcellus' mother.[113]
Propertius says nothing of the extraordinary privileges showered on
Marcellus in the years between 29 and 24, and about his prospects as
heir and successor there is not even a hint.

In the famous lines at the end of *Aeneid* 6, Vergil does reflect on
Marcellus' prospects; the thought of prospects thwarted is the whole
burden of the passage. As Anchises walks with Aeneas in the underworld, he points out the great consular Marcellus. Aeneas notices behind
Marcellus a distinguished but downcast youth whom he takes to be a
son or descendant. Impressed by the young man's stature and the size of
his entourage, he asks for information. Anchises confirms that he too is

a Marcellus, and pronounces a eulogy. The young Marcellus is so capable that the gods begrudge Rome the full enjoyment of him, but while he lives, he will be the nation's pride and hope, as the outcry at his death will testify. Anchises extols his devotion to gods and kin *(pietas),* his old-fashioned reliability *(fides),* and his military prowess, dilates on the last attribute, and concludes his speech.

Like Propertius, and like the sources, Vergil draws attention to Marcellus' popularity. And he makes much of Marcellus' soldierly bent, on which Propertius also touched. But otherwise he pursues an independent line. What is most remarkable about his treatment of Marcellus, if it is studied for its bearing on the succession theme, is the absence of all reference to Augustus. Vergil introduces Marcellus as a descendant of the Claudii Marcelli and then eulogizes him without mentioning any of his relationships to Augustus, as nephew, son-in-law, or coadjutor. Vergil also refrains from forecasts about the dynastic role Marcellus would have played if he had lived. Although the three virtues he singles out are not incompatible with an image of the ideal ruler, his emphasis suggests that Marcellus is being given the more conventional lineaments of a military hero. In any case, he is certainly not described as standing next in line to Augustus.

For the next decade and a half, Augustan poetry offers little that impinges on the succession theme. Both Horace in his late works and Ovid in his early ones let the birth, adoption, and early upbringing of Gaius and Lucius pass without comment. Propertius has a single line about them. After first declaring that the surrender of Crassus' standards by the Parthian king foreshadows the complete conquest of Parthia, he adds, "Or if Augustus shall still allow Eastern arrowcases a little peace, let him reserve that triumph for his sons" (4.6.81–82). Since Augustus had deployed a stepson and an army some years earlier when he wanted Crassus' standards back, it was not difficult to foresee a military role for Gaius and Lucius in any future operation. Propertius does not speculate about a political role.

In two poems purportedly written a year apart, in 9 and 8 B.C., the attitude taken toward the princes varies.[114] They are not even mentioned in the *Lament for Drusus,* although the poet brings in more than a half-dozen other palace personalities, and although Augustus is known to have concluded his own eulogy of Drusus with a prayer that his sons would follow in the footsteps of the deceased.[115] The other poem does take note of Gaius and Lucius. The second of the *Elegies for Maecenas* is conceived as a monologue in which the dying Maecenas takes leave of Augustus. Near the end he is made to say:

> Live long, dear friend, put off the journey to the stars till you are old. That is what earth needs and you should accept. May your boys grow up worthy of Caesar two times over and carry on the line of Caesar. May your wife Livia be soon relieved of grief and may your son-in-law complete the foiled mission of his brother.
>
> *Eleg. Maec.* 171–176

These lines come very close to declaring the hope expressed in some later poems, that after a long life Augustus will be followed by a worthy successor. If the first two distichs (from "Live long" to "carry on the line of Caesar") form an unbroken sequence of thought, the author *is* probably thinking about the succession of Gaius and Lucius. The *Elegy* moves jerkily, however, its thought often stopping and starting between couplets, and so it is possible that the princes are no more connected in the poet's mind with the eventual departure of Augustus than are Livia and Tiberius in the next distich. Taken by themselves, the lines about Gaius and Lucius put them in the context of the family rather than the state. Maecenas prays that they will grow up and carry on the family name, which is no more than could be said to any other aristocrat.[116]

Only at the close of the last decade of the century do the poets' forecasts become unambiguous. In 2 or 1 B.C. Gaius' embarkation for the East prompted a digression in (or an addition to) Ovid's *Art of Love* which rings the changes on Roman chauvinism and Parthophobia. At one point Ovid exhorts the prince:

> You will take up arms with the benefit of your father's auspices and experience, and with your father's auspices and experience you will be victorious. That is the debut we expect from you with your great name, first man among the younger generation today, and one day to be first among the elder.
>
> Ov. *Ars* 1.191–194

What is noteworthy about these lines is that Ovid does not just coast safely along the edge of facts. He makes a prediction, saying that Gaius will one day hold a rank comparable to the rank Augustus holds in the present. Nevertheless, it is a carefully grounded prediction; Ovid is not giving rein to his imagination on the subject of the succession. Some three years earlier Gaius had acquired the freshly minted title Chief of the Youth *(princeps iuventutis)*. Ovid now suggests that the status of "first man among the elder generation" is nothing more than an extrapolation from Gaius' present status. His primacy will mature as he and his generation mature.[117]

Far more direct is a verse inscription honoring the sons of Augustus which must date to within three or four years of Ovid's lines, if the prevailing view of it is right. The last four verses deal with the succession:

> When time shall claim you as a god, Caesar, and you return to the domicile in heaven from which you shall rule the world, let it be these who govern this earth in your place and rule over us, with successes answering to hopes.
>
> *ILS* 137.4–7

For the first time in Latin verse, in these lines written or bespoken by a centurion from Campania, every note of the succession theme is distinctly played: Augustus, retiring to the astral plane, will pass on the government of the world to a designated successor.

The theme does not emerge in literature proper, however, for another decade, by which time Gaius and Lucius were dead and Augustus had a new successor biding in the wings. Ovid, writing now from exile, reacts to the approaching change with a jittery fixation on palace relationships. His late works rain benedictions not only on Augustus but on the whole imperial family, down to the youngest princes and princesses. Sometimes his anxiety about the post-Augustan alignment surfaces in the form of explicit references to the succession. After victories won by Tiberius in Germany, Ovid imagines a celebration put on in the capital, and in his mind's eye he catches sight of Tiberius' sons Germanicus and Drusus, "young men maturing under Caesar's name, in order that that house may rule the lands forever" (*Tr.* 4.2.9–10). He prays that the earth may remain under a Caesar's care, "passed on from hand to hand within this family" (*Pont.* 1.2.99–100). On one occasion, when Augustus' death is still a year or so away, Ovid even voices a prayer for the accession of Germanicus.[118] But though in the late poems the subject is at last out in the open, it is still not a major motif. Rather than peer rudely into the future, Ovid prefers to avert his eyes, offering instead prayers for the protraction of Augustus' reign.[119] A good example of a passage in which the idea of succession is bruited and then quickly sidestepped are these lines from the *Metamorphoses,* on Augustus' relationship to his stepson Tiberius:

> Gazing forward into the age of future time and of descendants yet to be, he will tell the son born of his holy wife to take up his name and cares together. Yet not until he has reached a Nestor's age years hence will he pass up to the heavenly abode and his kindred stars.
>
> Ov. Met. 15.834–839

The striking fact about the succession theme in Augustan poetry is that it is so faint. For the most part, the poets disregard Augustus' efforts to propel his heirs into public life until the last third of the reign, and references to the succession do not proliferate until shortly before his death. What accounts for this reticence? The answer cannot be that poets were unaware of Augustus' dynastic schemes. From the moment he returned to Italy in 29 B.C., he practiced such blatant favoritism toward the princes who were to take his place that to many other observers in Roman society his plans seemed clear-cut. Nor can the issue of the succession have been too sensitive to raise in public, or officials and public bodies would not have flirted with it. Gaius and Lucius would not have been portrayed on coins, or included in the oath of allegiance sworn in the provinces, or invested by the Roman knights with the title Chief of the Youth; Gaius would not have been mourned in Pisa as *princeps designatus.*

The near-total silence of Vergil and Horace might suggest that those closest to Augustus downplayed the succession theme on purpose, knowing that he did not want the matter aired prematurely, however titillating it might be to the population at large. It is certainly true that Augustus evinced ambivalence about some of the attention shown to Gaius and Lucius.[120] And as we have seen, he always stopped short of openly naming a successor. But even if one were to suppose that the poets followed his lead in avoiding mention of the succession, that would not explain why they say so little about the princes. Augustus did everything in his power to entrench and commend his heirs during his lifetime. Saturation publicity was his alternative to proclaiming their status as successors. If the poets were part of that effort, they ought to have reacted at least to those episodes in the lives of Marcellus, Gaius, and Lucius which were made into public events—Marcellus' military debut in Spain, his marriage to Julia, and his first magistracy; the births of Gaius and Lucius, their adoption by Augustus, and so on. But this is one area

of Augustan public relations which finds almost no reverberation in contemporary poetry until late in the reign.

The comparative silence about the princes is difficult if not impossible
to explain as a response to palace guidance. However, it is probably not
a sign of criticism either, given the poets' generally favorable orientation
to the regime. I suggest that what it indicates is the uncertainty of writers
who were responding to a new phenomenon as onlookers rather than
accomplices. The founding of a dynasty was the most radical part of
Augustus' political reconstruction. Other aspects of the emperor's position—even intimations of his divinity—could be presented in terms of
Republican precedent and idiom. But Republican tradition could not
accommodate the notion of dynastic succession, and so the poets had
no style of discourse to fall back on in speaking of it. In fact, the subject
may have been most difficult to address for those poets who were most
politically engaged. Not only did it not fit the teleology which they
were prepared to discover in Roman history, but in that first age when
the figure of the *princeps* entirely possessed their imagination, the
thought of successors would have simply been distracting.

To a certain extent, the diffidence poets felt about addressing the subject of the succession seems to have carried over into their attitude toward Augustus' family generally. Augustus had drawn his wife and
his sister into positions of prominence beside him even before Actium,
and the palace family accumulated children, grandchildren, and affines
throughout his reign. Yet initially the poets were as hesitant to register
the presence of any of them as they were to confront the phenomenon
of heirs apparent. From the beginning of the triumviral period to the
end of the 20s, living relatives of Augustus are introduced rarely and
cautiously into Latin poetry. Antony, who was his brother-in-law during
the 30s, scarcely counts in this connection; in any case, it was not this
tie that earned Antony what notice he received, and the notice was
almost never favorable.[121] Agrippa too, though he entered Augustus'
family by marrying one of his nieces in 28 and then married his daughter
Julia seven years later, is never presented as a kinsman by poets of the
20s. What they emphasize is his public role as a builder or general.[122]

If an insistence on Agrippa's public role is unsurprising, it was hardly
to be expected that the same sort of frame would be contrived for the
first reference in Latin poetry to women of the palace. Horace wrote
Odes 3.14 late in 25 or early in 24 B.C., when Augustus was reported to
be heading home from his campaign in Spain. The prospect of his re-

entry points to a celebration, and Horace accordingly envisions a thanks-giving procession of Roman matrons which will include "the wife re-joicing in her one and only husband" (line 5) and "the sister of the illustrious leader" (7). This treatment of Augustus' wife and sister con-forms to the line Horace adopts in all his poems, which is to emphasize Augustus' role as warrior and statesman, while ignoring all palace affairs that do not directly impinge on public life. Hence the one and only time he introduces Livia or Octavia into his verse, they are shown participat-ing in a traditional ceremony performed under state auspices.

By the end of the 20s when Horace begins to introduce Augustus' stepson into his verse *Epistles,* the focus he chooses is similar.[123] Tiberius at that time had been invested with his first independent command and was leading an expedition to Armenia; this mission is the context of every reference Horace makes to him. Most of these references have another motivation as well, in that they are either directed to or impli-cate young friends of Horace who were currently serving on Tiberius' staff. In this way Horace gives himself both public and personal grounds for bringing Tiberius into his poems, while alluding only once to the fact of his relationship with Augustus.[124]

The one remaining member of Augustus' family to be treated in Latin poetry of this period is Marcellus, whose death in 23 elicited tributes from Propertius and Vergil. Both these passages were discussed earlier, apropos of poetic approaches, or non-approaches, to the subject of the succession. As noted there, Vergil does not connect Marcellus with Au-gustus or any other member of Augustus' family. Marcellus is given his own claim to distinction as a natural leader cut off in his prime. Prop-ertius' elegy for Marcellus, however, does show signs of a shift away from the civic perspective on the first family that is otherwise maintained in Latin poems of the 20s. It too is anchored in public life, in that Marcellus was given a state funeral to which the elegy is a response. Still, Propertius treats him more as a relation of Augustus than as a public figure in his own right. He notes Marcellus' "attachment to the hearth of Caesar," attributes his accomplishments partly to the generosity of his mother Octavia, and envisages his reception in heaven by the soul of the dei-fied Julius.

Propertius' elegy forecasts attitudes that would be the norm in poetry in little more than a decade. During this time Augustus' family came to be perceived as an ever-present adjunct of Augustus himself, with the result that its members were invoked more freely and with less motivation than before. What occasioned the shift is not entirely certain. Augustus' three-year absence in the East between 21 and 19 B.C. evidently intensified feelings of dependency and anxiety in the Roman public—his return was precisely the point at which the elaboration of an official cult resumed—and his adoption of Gaius and Lucius in 17 undoubtedly drew increased attention to the palace family. But whatever the causes, the results are plain. Horace, who had kept his distance in earlier poems, brings several of the emperor's relations into the last book of *Odes:* Drusus in 4.4, Drusus and his brother Tiberius in 4.14, and Iullus Antonius, who had just married Octavia's daughter Marcella, in 4.2. The poem heading the collection is dedicated to Paullus Fabius Maximus, who was soon to marry Augustus' cousin Marcia. These pieces do not quite qualify as court poems, since Horace still avoids themes like palace marriages, births, and anniversaries, and never again alludes to any of the palace women. The situations to which he attaches his poems usually have something to do with public life, as before. But there is no question that the fourth book of *Odes* is more palace-oriented than any previous book.

Propertius, who had highlighted the court background in his elegy for Marcellus, went another step in his last book and introduced the court in order to play its light onto another family. The elegy for Cornelia (4.11) is a funeral piece, and as one would expect, its primary focus is on Cornelia and her kin. Propertius extols the fame of her Scipionic ancestors, the nobility of her husband, and the promise of her children. But he also contrives to link her with Augustus, to whom she was not in fact related, by recalling her mother Scribonia's brief marriage to Augustus two decades earlier. In lines 57–60 the deceased Cornelia is made to say:

> A mother's tears and the lamentations of the city declare my praise, and the grief of Caesar vindicates my name in death. He cries out that I was a worthy sister of his daughter: we have seen tears come to a god's eyes.
>
> Prop. 4.11.57–60

The evident premise of these lines is that a connection to the sovereign house is now the ultimate warrant of nobility.

By far the most court-oriented poem of this period is the anonymous *Lament for Drusus*. Augustus' younger stepson had died while campaigning in Germany in 9 B.C., and like Marcellus fourteen years earlier, he was honored with a public funeral. But the *Lament* reads very differently from the elegy Propertius composed for Marcellus. Propertius had maintained the standpoint of a commentator and did not address himself to any member of the court, whereas the *Lament* is frankly directed to Drusus' mother Livia, on whom it releases a barrage of condolence. Propertius had noted Marcellus' attachment to the house of Augustus without defining it. The author of the *Lament* does everything he can to assimilate Drusus into the Julian family: he is called the "creation of Caesar" (line 39) and the "highest glory of the house in which he was born" (366), and toward the end of the poem, where the ghost of Drusus is made to address his mother, it refers to the "house of high Caesar, which is my house through you" (453). The poem makes no mention of Drusus' father, and pays only the briefest glance to his Claudian ancestors (330–333 and 451–452). Yet it abounds with references to palace figures: not only Drusus' mother and his brother, but also Octavia, Marcellus, Antonia, and Agrippa. Finally, as the author pursues his doleful commentary on the death of Drusus, he finds repeated opportunities to offer homage to the Augustan house. He opines, for example, that the sacred house of Caesar ought to have been exempt from human sorrows (59–74); that Livia deserved better of fortune because she has used her eminent position so temperately (41–56); that as first lady and wife of the first citizen, she must set an example of fortitude in distress (342–356). But nowhere is the un-Republican spirit of this piece more egregiously manifested than in line 64, where the author (a Roman knight, according to line 202) declares that he and his fellow citizens are a mere rabble *(vulgus)* by comparison with the imperial family.

From the time of the *Lament* on, the motif of the Augustan house is solidly established in Augustan poetry. It recurs in the anonymous *Elegies on Maecenas* written after Maecenas' death in 8 B.C., and it is ubiquitous in Ovid's late works. But what is noteworthy is that it took three decades to emerge. The cult of the family was not obviously fraught with delicate political consequences like the succession issue, and Augustus never tried to dissemble his relentless favoritism toward relatives. It is therefore something of a mystery why Latin poets shied away from this theme for as long as they did.

It is so mysterious, in fact, that we should perhaps entertain the possibility that despite appearances they did not forgo the theme. In Greek epigrammatic verse of the Augustan period, the imperial family receives proportionally greater attention and earlier attention than it does in Latin poetry. Epigrammatic verse differs from other poetry in that it is more directly responsive to topical happenings of private and public life. It is an ideal medium for poetry about palace society. Few epigrams or any other sort of occasional poems in Latin survive from this period, but there must have been some such output by Latin writers. Not only is it unlikely in the abstract that they would have ceded this terrain to Greeklings, but in one instance we have testimony about lost productions.[125] If the poetic exaltation of the Augustan house began with writers of occasional verse, it might well have taken time to infiltrate into more serious poetry for two reasons. First, in forms like lyric, elegy, and epic, genre restricted the topics that could be treated. But more important, for the Augustan poets serious poetry meant civic-minded poetry, which was by no means interchangeable with occasional verse. As with the succession theme, the new conventions evidently took some getting used to.

7

Conclusion

From a limited inquiry into the political element in Augustan poetry only tentative conclusions can reasonably be drawn. But with the exception of one doubtful anecdote about the *Georgics,* the information we have about Augustus' relations with literary friends does not suggest that he intruded on their work any more than did other members of the elite. Nor do the poetic themes examined in the previous chapter appear to carry the trademarks of direction from without. Some elements of the official mystique the poets echo, others they anticipate or outstrip, and others they disregard. Moreover, their treatment of particular motifs varies from poet to poet, and even within the oeuvre of any single poet. Yet in their different ways they all contribute to the chorus of Augustan panegyric. If Augustus did not lay down the lines to be followed, how did these and other motifs related to him come to engross such an important place in contemporary poetry?

The answer seems to be that the poets elaborated an Augustan thematic by themselves, independently both of Augustus and of one another. Some poets, like Vergil and Horace, had personal contacts with Augustus that would have disposed them to write about him positively. Even Ovid's catastrophic encounter stimulated an obsession with Augustus in the late poems that was not without creative consequences.

But purely personal motivations made up only a part of the poets' response to Augustus. As citizens, they shared convictions that led many elements of Roman society to welcome the new order, and they prided themselves on having a distinctive medium in which to express civic sentiment. Their pride as citizens was the public counterpart of their claim in private life to a place in the friendship of the well-to-do. Both were rooted in the self-assurance that came of belonging to an upper class. But Augustus also did much to absorb poets, like all parts of the population, into the political culture he was creating. It is a truism that as he contracted the power of the senatorial class he opened opportunities for many others—knights, the elite in the provinces, freedmen, and even slaves—to involve themselves in the public pageantry of state and empire. The civic note that differentiates so much Augustan poetry from the poetry of Catullus and Lucretius should be recognized as one effect of his effort to broaden the franchise symbolically.

All poets, however, had in addition two professional reasons for favoring themes related to Augustus. One was pragmatic. Poets in Roman society had always attached themselves to great houses in order to gain visibility, legitimation, and support. When the palace began to eclipse other centers of social life, the poets gravitated toward Augustus as their luminary of choice. As Horace wrote in his *Letter to Augustus,* it was their fantasy that "as soon as you learn we are involved with poetry, you will oblige with an invitation and say 'be poor no longer' and set us to work" (lines 226–228). They trumpeted Augustus' greatness in order to attract his favor and then to seal it.

Yet there was more than opportunism behind their overtures. It is clear from the poems that Augustus was a poetically exciting idea. He shook out the canopy of empire and revived the dream of world dominion. He rebuilt the capital, anchoring the new in a series of monuments to the past. He set the terms of political discussion and he dominated social life. Just at the moment when Roman poets had become masters of their craft, Augustus laid bare a wealth of material which no poet had mined before, and it was irresistible. The worst consequence of reading Augustan poetry as propaganda is that it hinders us from studying this material critically. If we think that the poets had their subjects handed to them, we will not be prepared to see what they invented themselves, where they experimented with the resources they found at hand, or how their Augustan thematic connects with the rest of their oeuvre. Nor will we appreciate the poignancy of the next part of the story, in which Roman writers began to shed their illusions about the principate they had done so much to glorify.

Augustus did not assume the role of literary arbiter that some of his successors took up. Unlike Caligula, for example, he did not pronounce on the merits of books in the state libraries. Unlike Nero, he did not hold literary suppers at the palace or institute festivals at which new poets could display their talents. His few initiatives toward poets outside the circle of his friends came at the very end of his reign, and all are negative. He tried to silence writers who offended him, but he did not cultivate new laureates. For the greater part of his life, his relationships reflect the kind of sensibility one meets in cultured aristocrats of the late Republic.

I do not mean to minimize Augustus' impact on Roman literary society. If the role he played was not new in conception, it was certainly new in its effects, since he outdrew all possible competitors for the attention of poets and also inspired verse which was superior to any that competitors received. More important, the discourse that poets carried on with him reached further into the realm of public life than the discourse of any poet with any magnate during the Republic. In part this entanglement with public themes reflects the reality that there was no clear boundary between Augustus' public and his domestic life. A poet could not treat his birthday or his return from abroad, for example, simply as a day of rejoicing in one of Rome's great houses. Yet the defining quality of Augustus' impact was not so much that themes related to him almost inevitably became public themes as that they supplanted all other public themes. The political culture which he established in place of the one that had been swept away in the civil wars was to a large degree based on what would now be called a cult of personality.

In the last analysis, however, Augustus dominated poetry by dominating public opinion, not by cultivating a literary policy. Poets, like the rest of society, responded to him as a phenomenon without parallel, and the image they created of him was very much a response to him personally. Although the regime he founded outlasted him and even grew stronger after his death, no later emperor remotely equaled his hold over the imagination of poets. And if we are to understand what fascinated them, we have no choice but to try to surrender our imagination to him in the way they did. To the extent that we succeed, it can be a disconcerting exercise.

Appendixes
Bibliographical Note
Notes
Indexes

The Social Status of Latin Poets

This appendix registers those Latin poets (in the broadest sense) from the third century B.C. to approximately A.D. 140 of whose verse any portion is extant in a manuscript tradition. If a given oeuvre is normally printed by itself under the poet's own name, no edition is specified. For poets represented in collections of fragmentary authors, reference is made to *TRF* = O. Ribbeck, *Tragicorum Romanorum Fragmenta,* 2nd ed. (Leipzig, 1871); *CRF* = Ribbeck, *Comicorum Romanorum praeter Plautum et Terentium Fragmenta,* 2nd ed. (Leipzig, 1873); and *FPL* = W. Morel, *Fragmenta Poetarum Latinorum epicorum et lyricorum praeter Ennium et Lucilium,* 2nd ed. (Leipzig, 1927). The revised and expanded edition of *FPL* by K. Büchner (Leipzig, 1982) adds no new names (except to split Furius Bibaculus in two or possibly three).

An indication of date and of social status is given for each poet listed. The dates are as specific as they can be short of excursions into conjecture or controversy, though no sources are cited. A source attesting status is cited if any is known, since status is the focus of this inquiry. If the data available do not make clear what a poet's status was, it is marked "unknown." Where there is no biographical information at all, that is noted.

Certain names included in the standard corpora have been omitted here: (1) the Cassius listed in *TRF* as the alleged author of a *praetexta* entitled *Brutus* is of dubious historicity; (2) the authorship of the fragment attributed to Sextius Paconianus in *FPL* is conjectural; (3) the identification of Dorcatius *(FPL)* as a poet of the Augustan period is equally conjectural; (4) Acilius Glabrio, (5) Atilius Calatinus, and (6) M. Aemilius (all in *FPL*) are not to be understood as the actual composers of the verses which celebrate their deeds.

?	Abronius Silo *(FPL)*
	Late 1st century B.C. Status unknown.
subequestrian	L. Accius *(TRF, FPL)*
	Born in 170 B.C. "Natus . . . parentibus libertinis," Hieron. *Chron.* p. 144 h Helm.

senatorial	P. Aelius Hadrianus *(FPL)*
	A.D. 76–138. Hadrian's senatorial cursus is summarized in *Hist. Aug. Vita Hadr.* 2.2–4.6.
?	Aemilius Macer *(FPL)*
	Died in 16 B.C. Status unknown.
?	L. Afranius *(CRF)*
	Latter half of the 2nd century B.C. Status unknown.
equestrian?	Albinovanus Pedo *(FPL)*
	End of the 1st century B.C., beginning of the 1st century A.D. Tac. *Ann.* 1.60.2 mentions a *praefectus equitum* who bears the same rare cognomen as the poet and participates in a campaign of which the poet is known to have described one episode.
equestrian	Albius Tibullus
	Died in 19 B.C. The appellation *eques regalis* applied to Tibullus in the *Vita Tib.* (p. 171 Lenz-Galinsky = 112 Luck) is thought to be a corruption of *eques Romanus,* a supposition partly confirmed by the further information in the life that Tibullus was Messalla's *contubernalis* during the Aquitanian campaign and that he "militaribus donis donatus est."
senatorial	M. Annaeus Lucanus
	39–65 A.D. "A Nerone . . . quaestura honoratus," Suet. *Vita Luc.* p. 299.22–23 Roth.
senatorial	L. Annaeus Seneca
	Died in 65 A.D. "Agrippina . . . pro Annaeo Seneca . . . praeturam impetrat," Tac. *Ann.* 12.8.2.
?	Aprissius *(CRF;* the name may be corrupt)
	Cited in Varro's *Lingua Latina,* therefore prior to 45 B.C. No biographical information.
?	Aquilius *(CRF)*
	2nd century B.C. No biographical information.
senatorial	C. Asinius Gallus *(FPL)*
	40 B.C.–A.D. 33. Gallus' interventions in senatorial debate are mentioned by Tacitus at *Ann.* 1.8.3 and elsewhere in books 1 through 4.
senatorial	C. Asinius Pollio *(FPL)*
	76 B.C.–A.D. 4 "C. Asinius Cn. f. Pollio proco(n)s(ul) ex Parthineis [triumphavit]," *Fasti Tr. Cap.*

?	Atilius *(CRF)* Cited in Varro's *Lingua Latina*, therefore prior to 45 B.C. No biographical information.
?	Attius Labeo *(FPL)* Middle of the 1st century A.D. No biographical information.
senatorial	Caecilius Metellus *(FPL)* End of the 3rd century B.C. "[Naevio] Metellus consul iratus versu responderat senario hypercatalecto qui et Saturnius dicitur," Pseudo-Asconius on Cic. 1 *Verr.* 29 (p. 215.19–20 Stangl); Metellus is often identified as the Q. Caecilius Metellus who was consul in 206 B.C.
freedman	Caecilius Statius *(CRF)* Died in 168 B.C. "Caecilius . . . ille comoediarum poeta inclutus servus fuit et propterea nomen habuit 'Statius.' sed postea versum est quasi in cognomentum," Gell. *NA* 4.20.13.
?	Caesius Bassus *(FPL)* Middle of the 1st century A.D. Status unknown.
?	Calpurnius Siculus Conventionally dated to the middle of the 1st century A.D., but a date in the 3rd century has strong advocates. Status unknown.
senatorial	Appius Claudius Caecus *(FPL)* Censor in 312 B.C., consul in 307 and 296. "Appius Claudius C. f. Caecus, censor, co(n)s(ul) bis, dict(ator), interrex III, pr(aetor) II, aed(ilis) cur(ulis) II, q(uaestor)," *ILS* 54.
equestrian	C. Cornelius Gallus *(FPL)* Died in 27 or 26 B.C. "C. Cornelius Cn. f. Gallus eques Romanus . . . praefectus Alexandreae et Aegypti primus," *ILS* 8995.
senatorial	Cn. Cornelius Lentulus Gaetulicus *(FPL)* Consul in A.D. 26, died in 39. "Gaetulicus . . . superioris Germaniae legiones curabat," Tac. *Ann.* 6.30.2.
?	Cornelius Severus *(FPL)* Late 1st century B.C. Status unknown.
senatorial	Q. Cornificius *(FPL)* Died in 41 B.C. "Q. Cornificius Q. f. praetor augur," *ILLRP* 439.

?	Cornificius Gallus *(FPL)* Latter half of the 1st century B.C. No biographical information.
?	Domitius Marsus *(FPL)* Latter half of the 1st century B.C. Status unknown.
?	Egnatius *(FPL)* Cited as a predecessor of Vergil, therefore prior to 19 B.C. No biographical information.
subequestrian	Q. Ennius 239–169 B.C. "[Q. Nobilior] Q. Ennium . . . civitate donavit cum triumvir coloniam deduxisset," Cic. *Brut.* 79.
subequestrian?	(P. Annius?) Florus *(FPL)* End of the 1st century A.D., beginning of the 2nd century. *Vergilius orator an poeta* establishes Florus' status as a *grammaticus* without independent income, if he is the poet represented in *FPL*.
?	A. Furius Antias *(FPL)* Latter half of the 2nd century B.C. Status unknown.
?	M. Furius Bibaculus *(FPL)* (The fragments collected in *FPL* consist of epigrammatic fragments attributed to (Furius) Bibaculus and annalistic fragments most of which are attributed simply to Furius. Several scholars, including Büchner, distinguish them as the work of separate poets. If Furius is distinct from Bibaculus, he may be the poet mocked by Horace at *Serm.* 1.10.36–37 and 2.5.40–41, but nothing else is known about him.) Born in 103 B.C. Status unknown.
?	Gannius *(FPL)* Date unknown. No biographical information.
senatorial	Germanicus Iulius Caesar 15 B.C.–A.D. 19. "Germanico Caesari Ti. Augusti f. . . . auguri, flamini Augustali, co(n)s(uli) iterum, imp(eratori) iterum," *ILS* 176.
senatorial?	(Sempronius?) Gracchus *(TRF)* Died in A.D. 14. The senatorial status of Gracchus is contingent on his being the Sempronius Gracchus of Vell. Pat. 2.100.5 and Tac. *Ann.* 1.53.3–6.

?	Grattius End of the 1st century B.C., beginning of the 1st century A.D. Status unknown.
senatorial	C. Helvius Cinna *(FPL)* Died in 44 B.C. Cinna is identified as a tribune at the time of his death by Dio 44.50.4 and Plut. *Brut.* 20.4.
equestrian	Q. Horatius Flaccus 65–8 B.C. "Me . . . rodunt omnes libertino patre natum . . . olim quod mihi pareret legio Romana tribuno," Hor. *Serm.* 1.6.46–48.
senatorial	Q. Hortensius Hortalus *(FPL)* 114–50 B.C. Cicero compares Hortensius' career in the senate and at the bar with his own at *Brut.* 317–329.
?	Hostius *(FPL)* Latter half of the second century B.C. No biographical infor- mation.
senatorial	C. Iulius Caesar *(FPL)* 100–44 B.C. Caesar's senatorial career is recounted in Suet. *Iul.* 6–30.1
senatorial	C. Iulius Caesar Augustus *(FPL)* 63 B.C.–A.D. 14. "Princeps senatus fui usque ad eum diem quo scripseram haec per annos quadraginta," Aug. *Anc.* 7.2.
senatorial	C. Iulius Caesar Strabo *(TRF)* Aedile in 90 B.C., died in 87. "C. Iulius L. f. Caesar Strabo, aed(ilis) cur(ulis), q(uaestor) . . . pontif(ex)," *ILS* 48.
?	C. Iulius Montanus *(FPL)* First half of the 1st century A.D. Status unknown.
equestrian	D. Iunius Iuvenalis Late 1st century and early 2nd century A.D. The equestrian status of Juvenal is contingent on his being the ". . . nius Iu- venalis" identified as a *tribunus cohortis* in *ILS* 2926. The oldest of the *vitae* transmitted in manuscripts of Juvenal identifies him as the "filius an alumnus" of a rich freedman, and says that late in life he was posted as *praefectus cohortis* to Egypt.
equestrian	L. Iunius Moderatus Columella Middle of the 1st century A.D. "L. Iunio L. f. Gal. Moderato Columellae trib(uno) mil(itum) leg(ionis) VI Ferratae," *ILS* 2923; compare Col. 2.10.8.

?	Iuventius *(CRF)* Cited in Varro's *Lingua Latina,* therefore prior to 45 B.C. No biographical information.
equestrian	Laberius *(CRF)* 106–43 B.C. "Laberium divus Iulius ludis suis mimum produxit, deinde equestri illum ordini reddidit," Sen. *Cont.* 7.3.9.
?	Laevius *(FPL)* Date uncertain, but if he is contemporary with the *lex Licinia* of which he speaks in frag. 23, he belongs to the mid-2nd century B.C. No biographical information.
?	Licinius Imbrex *(CRF)* Date uncertain, but probably 3rd century or 2nd century B.C. No biographical information, unless Licinius Imbrex is identical with the poet P. Licinius Tegula who is mentioned in Livy's narrative of the year 200 B.C. (31.12.9); there is nothing to fix his status in either case.
senatorial	C. Licinius Macer Calvus *(FPL)* Middle of the 1st century B.C. Calvus' father is identified as a *vir praetorius* at Val. Max. 9.12.7.
freedman	Livius Andronicus *(TRF, CRF, FPL)* Latter half of the 3rd century B.C., beginning of the 2nd century. "Titus Livius tragoediarum scriptor . . . a Livio Salinatore cuius liberos erudiebat libertate donatus est," Hieron. *Chron.* 137 c Helm.
equestrian	C. Lucilius Died in 102 B.C. "Celebre et Lucili nomen fuit, qui sub P. Africano Numantino bello eques militaverat," Vell. Pat. 2.9.3.
equestrian	Lucilius Iunior *(FPL)* Middle of the 1st century A.D. "Eques Romanus es, et ad hunc ordinem tua te perduxit industria," Sen. *Epist.* 44.2 (i.e., Lucilius did not have equestrian status from birth).
?	T. Lucretius Carus 94–54 (or 50) B.C. Status unknown.
?	Luscius Lanuvinus *(CRF)* First half of the 2nd century B.C. Status unknown.
senatorial	Q. Lutatius Catulus *(FPL)* Consul in 102 B.C., died in 87. "[Archias] Romam venit Mario consule et Catulo. nactus est primum consules eos quorum

alter res ad scribendum maximas, alter cum res gestas tum etiam studium atque auris adhibere posset," Cic. *Arch.* 5.

subequestrian	T. Maccus Plautus Died in 184 B.C. "In pistrino [Plautum quasdam fabulas] scripsisse Varro et plerique alii memoriae tradiderunt, cum pecunia omni, quam in operis artificum scaenicorum pepererat, in mercatibus perdita inops Romam redisset et ob quaerendum victum ad circumagendas molas . . . operam pistori locasset," Gell. *NA* 3.3.14.
equestrian	C. Maecenas *(FPL)* Died in 8 B.C. "Maecenas, eques Etrusco de sanguine regum," Prop. 3.9.1.
?	M. Manilius Early 1st century A.D. No biographical information.
?	Manilius *(FPL)* Cited in Varro's *Lingua Latina,* therefore prior to 45 B.C. No biographical information, but the poet is often identified with a senatorial savant of the same name known to have been writing in the year 97 B.C. (Pliny *HNat.* 10.4–5).
senatorial	Cn. Marcius *(FPL)* (Some sources attribute the *carmina Marciana* to a pair of brothers rather than to one *vates.*) Before 213 B.C. "[Hoc] in genere [divinationis] Marcios quosdam fratres nobili loco natos apud maiores nostros fuisse scriptum videmus," Cic. *Div.* 1.89.
?	Cn. Matius *(FPL)* Cited in Varro's *Lingua Latina,* therefore prior to 45 B.C. No biographical information.
senatorial	C. Memmius *(FPL)* Praetor in 58 B.C. "Praetores habemus amicissimos et acerrimos civis, Domitium, Nigidium, Memmium, Lentulum," Cic. *QFr.* 1.2.16 = 2 SB.
senatorial	Q. Mucius Scaevola *(FPL)* Tribune in 54 B.C. "[Pomptino] obviam Cato et Servilius praetores ad portam et Q. Mucius tribunus," Cic. *Att.* 4.18.4 = 92 SB.
?	Mummius *(CRF)* 1st century B.C. No biographical information.

subequestrian?	Cn. Naevius *(TRF, CRF, FPL)* Died in 201 B.C. Status unattested, but Naevius' Campanian origin and the fact that he was jailed for opprobrious comments in his plays (Gell. *NA* 3.3.15) make it virtually impossible to ascribe to him the status of an *eques Romanus.*
?	Naevius *(FPL)* Date unknown. No biographical information.
senatorial	Nero (Claudius Caesar Augustus) *(FPL)* A.D. 37–68. Nero's consulates are listed at Suet. *Nero* 14.
?	Ninnius Crassus *(FPL)* Date unknown. No biographical information.
?	Novius *(CRF)* 1st century B.C. No biographical information.
?	Numitorius *(FPL)* Latter half of the 1st century B.C. No biographical information.
equestrian	P. Ovidius Naso 43 B.C.–A.D. 17. "Seu genus excutias, equites ab origine prima / usque per innumeros inveniemur avos," Ov. *Pont.* 4.8.17–18.
?	M. Pacuvius *(TRF, FPL)* 220–ca. 130 B.C. Status unknown.
?	Papinius *(FPL)* Cited in Varro's *Lingua Latina,* therefore prior to 45 B.C. No biographical information.
?	P. Papinius Statius Latter half of the 1st century A.D. Status unknown (mention of the golden *bulla* at *Silvae* 5.3.116–120 is not sufficient to establish that Statius' father was equestrian).
equestrian	A. Persius Flaccus A.D. 34–62. "Eques Romanus," Probus *Vita Pers.* p. 37.4 Clausen.
?	Petronius Middle of the 1st century A.D. No biographical information, but attribution of the *Satyricon* to "Petronius Arbiter" in manuscripts of the work and in late sources has suggested that the author may be the consular Petronius whom Tacitus dubs Nero's "elegantiae arbiter" at *Ann.* 16.18.2.

freedman	Phaedrus First half of the 1st century A.D. "Libertus Augusti," according to the *tituli* in manuscripts of Phaedrus' work.
senatorial	C. Plinius Caecilius Secundus *(FPL)* Ca. A.D. 61–ca. 110. "C. Plinius L. f. Ouf. Caecilius . . . augur, legat(us) pro pr(aetore) provinciae . . . consulari potestat(e)," *ILS* 2927.
?	Pompilius *(TRF, FPL)* Quoted in Varro's *Menippean Satires,* therefore prior to ca. 65 B.C. Status unknown.
?	L. Pomponius *(CRF)* First half of the 1st century B.C. Status unknown.
senatorial	P. Pomponius Secundus *(TRF)* Consul in A.D. 44. "Decretus . . . Pomponio triumphalis honos, modica pars famae eius apud posteros, in quis carminum gloria praecellit," Tac. *Ann.* 12.28.2.
?	Porcius Licinus *(FPL)* Latter half of the 2nd century B.C. or beginning of the 1st century. No biographical information, but other known Porcii Licini are senatorial.
?	Sex. Propertius Latter half of the 1st century B.C. Status unknown. (Mention of the golden *bulla* at 4.1.131 is not sufficient to establish that Propertius was equestrian.)
freedman	Publilius Syrus *(CRF)* Middle of the 1st century B.C. "Publilius natione Syrus cum puer ad patronum domini esset adductus, praemeruit eum non minus salibus et ingenio eius quam forma . . . . ob haec et alia manu missus [est]," Macr. *Sat.* 2.7.6–7.
?	Pupius *(FPL)* 1st century B.C. No biographical information.
?	T. Quinctius Atta *(CRF, FPL)* Died in 77 B.C. Status unknown.
?	Rabirius *(FPL)* Latter half of the 1st century B.C., beginning of the 1st century A.D. No biographical information.
?	Santra *(TRF)* 1st century B.C. No biographical information.

?	Scaevus Memor *(TRF)*
	Latter half of the 1st century A.D. Status unknown, but Scaevus' brother Turnus was "libertini generis" according to the Vallan scholia on Juv. *Sat.* 1.20.
senatorial?	Sentius Augurinus *(FPL)*
	Early 2nd century A.D. Pliny's poet friend is probably the Hadrianic proconsul Q. Gellius Sentius Augurinus of *ILS* 5947a.
freedman	Sevius Nicanor *(FPL)*
	Late 2nd century B.C. or early 1st century. "Sevius Nicanor . . . libertinum se . . . indicat," Suet. *Gr.* 5.1.
?	Sextilius Ena *(FPL)*
	Latter half of the 1st century B.C. Status unknown.
?	Sueius *(FPL)*
	(The name is uncertainly transmitted in most citations of this poet's work.) Cited as a predecessor of Vergil, therefore prior to 19 B.C.; probably also cited in Varro's *Lingua Latina* ca. 45 B.C. No biographical information.
senatorial	(Ti. Catius Asconius) Silius Italicus
	Consul in A.D. 68, died ca. 101. "Silius Italicus . . . ex proconsulatu Asiae gloriam reportaverat," Pliny *Epist.* 3.7.3.
senatorial	Sulpicia I ([Tib.] 3.13–18)
	Late 1st century B.C. Sulpicia proclaims her dignity as the daughter of the consular Servius Sulpicius Rufus at [Tib.] 3.16.4; compare [Tib.] 3.14.5.
?	Sulpicia II *(FPL)*
	End of the 1st century A.D. Status unknown.
freedman	P. Terentius Afer
	194 (or 184)–159 B.C. "Publius Terentius Afer, Carthagine natus, serviit Romae Terentio Lucano senatori, a quo ob ingenium et formam non institutus modo liberaliter sed et mature manumissus est," Suet. *Vita Ter.* p. 292.1–4 Roth.
senatorial	M. Terentius Varro
	116–27 B.C. "Tribunus cum essem, vocari neminem iussi nec vocatum a conlega parere invitum," Varro apud Gell. *NA* 13.12.6.
?	P. Terentius Varro Atacinus *(FPL)*
	Born in 82 B.C. Status unknown.

equestrian?	Ticida(s) *(FPL)* Middle of the 1st century B.C. Given the rarity of the name, the poet is almost certainly the *eques* of [Caes.] *BAfr.* 44.1.
?	Titinius *(CRF)* Predates Varro. No biographical information.
?	Trabea *(CRF)* Quoted by Cicero in a letter of 51 B.C. No biographical information.
senatorial	M. Tullius Cicero *(FPL)* 106–43 B.C. Cicero's senatorial career is most comprehensively presented in Plutarch's biography of Cicero.
senatorial	Q. Tullius Cicero *(FPL)* Ca. 102–43 B.C. (Cicero to Quintus) "praeclarum est . . . [te] summo cum imperio fuisse in Asia triennium," Cic. *QFr.* 1.1.8 = 1 SB.
freedman	Tullius Laurea *(FPL)* Middle of the 1st century B.C. Laurea is identified as Cicero's *libertus* at Pliny *HNat* 31.7.
at least equestrian	Turnus *(FPL)* Latter half of the 1st century B.C. "Turnus hic libertini generis ad honores ambitione provectus est, potens in aula Vespasianorum Titi et Domitiani," Valla's scholia on Juv. 1.20.
?	Sextus Turpilius *(CRF)* Died in 104 B.C. Status unknown.
senatorial?	Vagellius *(FPL)* Middle of the 1st century A.D. Seneca's poet friend is probably the Claudian consul L. Vagellius attested by *ILS* 6043.
?	Valerius *(CRF)* Date unknown. No biographical information, but this comic author is often identified with a mime-writer of the same name who was a friend of Cicero (Cic. *Fam.* 7.11.2 = 34 SB) and who may in turn be his friend the jurisconsult L. Valerius (*Fam.* 1.10 = 21 SB, 3.1.3 = 64 SB).
?	Valerius Aedituus *(FPL)* 2nd century or 1st century B.C. No biographical information.
?	C. Valerius Catullus First half of the 1st century B.C. Status unknown.

senatorial   C. Valerius Flaccus Setinus Balbus
Latter half of the 1st century A.D. Valerius alludes to his membership in the priestly college of *quindecimviri* at *Arg.* 1.5–7.

equestrian   M. Valerius Martialis
Died ca. A.D. 103. "Sum . . . pauper sed non obscurus nec male notus eques," Mart. *Epigr.* 5.13.1–2.

senatorial   Q. Valerius Soranus *(FPL)*
End of the 2nd century B.C., beginning of the 1st century. "Tribunus plebei quidam Valerius Soranus, ut ait Varro et multi alii, hoc nomen [Romae] ausus enuntiare . . . in crucem levatus est," Servius Auctus on Verg. *Aen.* 1.277.

senatorial   C. Valgius Rufus *(FPL)*
Consul in 12 B.C. Valgius' consulship is attested by *ILS* 8150.

?   L. Varius Rufus *(TRF, FPL)*
Latter half of the 1st century B.C. Status unknown.

?   P. Vergilius Maro
70–19 B.C. Status unknown. (Vergil is described as being "dignitate eques Romanus" in the *Vita Bernensis*, p. 66.4 Brummer = 248.1–2 Bayer, but the credit of this source is low.)

senatorial   L. Verginius Rufus *(FPL)*
Ca. A.D. 14–97. "Perfunctus est tertio consulatu, ut summum fastigium privati hominis impleret," Pliny *Epist.* 2.1.2.

?   Volcacius Sedigitus *(FPL)*
Date uncertain, but probably first half of the 1st century B.C. No biographical information, but other known Volcatii are mainly equestrian or senatorial.

?   Volumnius *(FPL)*
Date unknown. No biographical information, but other known Volumnii are overwhelmingly senatorial and equestrian.

APPENDIX 2

Connections of the Augustan Poets

The five registers which follow complement the argument of Chapters 1 and 2, charting the social milieu of the Augustan poets by identifying their friends. The entries in each register first specify the ancient sources that connect the person lemmatized with a given poet and then briefly indicate who these persons were and how they were connected with the poet. If a person can (or cannot) be identified with someone listed in another register, that is also indicated by cross-references in full capitals. Taken together, the five registers thus offer one means of measuring the cohesiveness of the Augustan literary milieu. The entries in each register should not be mistaken for prosopographical sketches, however. The ancient sources cited concern only a given person's relationship with a poet, not his or her life in its own right. But references have been provided to full modern discussions of everyone lemmatized (usually to *PIR* = *Prosopographia Imperii Romani,* 1st ed. by E. Klebs, H. Dessau, and P. von Rohden [Berlin, 1897–1898], 2nd ed. by E. Groag, A. Stein, and L. Petersen [Berlin, 1933—] and to *RE* = *Paulys Realencyclopädie der classischen Altertumswissenschaft,* ed. G. Wissowa [Stuttgart, 1893—Munich, 1980]; it is always prudent to consult in addition the well-indexed books and collected papers of Ronald Syme).

With the exception of slaves, I have tried to identify all persons known by their real names who came into amicable personal contact with a given poet during his working years. Often the evidence is adequate to document such contacts. But sometimes our only clue to a relationship is a poet's positive mention of a contemporary in his poems, though that need not always point to personal acquaintance. (In the case of references to Augustus, it is no criterion at all, and it is not much stronger where references to members of his family are concerned; in the absence of other indications, I have generally not relied on it.) Wherever a compliment does not seem enough of a basis on which to postulate a connection, the entries carry question marks. Italicized lemmata, on the other hand, indicate entries for which a source other than the poet testifies to a connection and the authority of that source (in my judgment) is insufficient. Square brackets represent cases in which I think presumed relationships can be ruled out.

Because so little is known about the lives of the Augustan poets, there can be no disguising that these registers are but a crude tool for examining social relations. It will also be apparent that the registers are not fully comparable with one another, since we are not informed either to the same degree or in the same way about the friends of each poet. The information is offered simply as what we happen to know. *Caveat lector.*

Year dates to the end of the first century B.C. are set down without the qualification "B.C."; dates from A.D. I on are always qualified as "A.D."

Appendix 2A: Connections of Horace

Horatian prosopography preoccupied ancient scholars (see Porphyrio on *Serm.* 1.3.21 and 91); hence in addition to what Horace says about his friends we often have details about them supplied by the scholiasts Porphyrio and Pseudo-Acro. Some of this information is corroborated by other sources, some of it is manifestly wrong, and much of it is problematic.

The sheer abundance of persons mentioned in the Horatian corpus poses several problems of which readers should be aware. (1) It is not always clear (as with Cascellius and Paulus, for example) which names belong to living contemporaries and which do not. (2) Certain names (such as Murena, Varus, Vergilius, and Viscus) clearly belong to more than just one of Horace's connections, and the distinctions are not always easily made. One must also reckon with the possibility that some of the following entries represent an undetected conflation of two or more persons. (3) Conversely, some names listed as belonging to different persons may actually be alternate names for the same person (as possibly in the case of Quintilius and Varus, or Quinctius and Quinctius Hirpinus). (4) Pseudonyms are more of a riddle in Horace than in his contemporaries. I have excluded some Greek names which seemed to be obvious pseudonyms or type names; yet Greek names do sometimes form a bona-fide part of the nomenclature of Roman gentlemen. And on the other side, Horace may not have restricted himself to Greek when he was inventing pseudonyms. Some scholars believe that certain names listed below (like Bullatius, Mulvius, Ofellus, Postumus, and Scaeva) are not the names of real people.

1. Aelius Lamia: *Carm.* 1.26, 1.36, 3.17, and *Epist.* 1.14.6–8.

   PIR² A 203, compare A 199; *RE* 1:523 no. 79, compare Suppl. 6:1 and 14.1 no. 75a; K. Kraft, *JNG* 16 (1966): 23–31; senator. A well-born young friend with literary interests whose villa or town house Horace frequented. He is probably the moneyer Q. Aelius Lamia, brother of the Lucius who governed Tarraconensis in 24 (and whose death is mentioned at *Epist.* 1.14.7). He may also be the author of *praetextae* and *togatae* named by Pseudo-Acro at Hor. *Ars* 288 (a notice partly corroborated by Festus' note on *ocissume*, p. 192.22–23 Lindsay).

2. Albinovanus Celsus: *Epist.* 1.3.15–20 and 1.8.

PIR² A 478; *RE* 1:1314 no. 4. A young poet friend of Horace traveling as the *scriba* of Tiberius on a military expedition to Armenia in 20. The nomen Albinovanus is rare enough to suggest that he should be related in some way to Ovid's friend and fellow poet Albinovanus Pedo (OVID 2). But the cognomen Celsus is too common for him to be plausibly identified with Ovid's friend Celsus (OVID 13).

3. Albius: *Carm.* 1.33 and *Epist.* 1.4.

PIR² A 484; *RE* 1:1319–1329 no. 12. A well-to-do writer of *elegi* who appreciated Horace's verse and received avuncular advice from him. He is identified as the elegist Albius Tibullus by the scholiasts and by a majority of modern scholars. But certain comments Horace makes about Albius do not parallel, though they do not quite contradict, what Tibullus says about himself in his poems, and so the identification remains not completely secure. (OVID 53, VERGIL 47)

4. *Amicius: Epodi* 13.

At *Epodi* 13.3–4 Horace writes "rapiamus, amici, / occasionem de die." In order to obtain a specific addressee to whom the singular imperatives in the following lines can refer, some editors capitalize the vocative *amici,* creating a reference to an Amicius rather than to generic "friends." But the imperative in line 6 at least is surely addressed to a slave; in any case, Amicius is otherwise unknown.

5. Iullus Antonius: *Carm.* 4.2.

PIR² A 800; *RE* 1:2584–2585 no. 22; *cos.* 10. Mark Antony's younger son and husband of Augustus' niece (the younger) Marcella. Horace presents him as a fellow poet from whom he anticipated a grand piece celebrating Augustus' expected return from Gaul.

6. ?Antonius Musa: *Epist.* 1.15.2–5.

PIR² A 853; *RE* 1:2633–2634 no. 79; *eques.* A Greek physician to whose fashionable cold therapy Horace alluded, apparently as though Musa were his own physician. In 23 Musa cured Augustus of a near-fatal illness, though he failed to cure Marcellus some months later.

7. Aristius Fuscus: *Serm.* 1.9.60–74, 1.10.83, *Carm.* 1.22, and *Epist.* 1.10.

PIR² A 1048; *RE* 2:906 no. 2. A long-time friend whom Horace claimed in the mid-30s as one of his preferred readers. The scholiasts identify him as a *grammaticus* and writer of comedies; a corrupt text at *GL* 7:35.2 Keil may contain a reference to a grammatical work addressed by Fuscus to Asinius Pollio. (VERGIL 3)

8. (C. Asinius) Pollio: *Serm.* 1.10.42–43 and 85 and *Carm.* 2.1.

PIR² A 1241; *RE* 2:1589–1602 no. 25; *cos.* 40. A magnate whose literary sympathy Horace claimed to enjoy and whom he celebrated as a *triumphator,* historian, tragedian, and orator. Pollio turned from military to civilian activities in 39. He founded the first public library in Rome and launched the fashion of public recitations. His other literary connections include Catullus, Cinna, Cornelius Gallus, Vergil (VERGIL 6), Messalla Corvinus, Ateius Philologus, Timagenes, and perhaps Parthenius and Aristius Fuscus.

9. ?Bassus: *Carm.* 1.36.14.

PIR² B 81; *RE:* no entry. An otherwise unknown crony of Aelius Lamia whom Horace mentioned in a poem about the homecoming of a friend of Lamia. There is nothing to suggest a connection with the like-named friend of Propertius (PROPERTIUS 4) and Ovid (OVID 7).

10. Bullatius: *Epist.* 1.11.

No entry in *PIR* or *RE*. A much-traveled friend who received a verse letter from Horace counseling him to seek within for contentment; he is otherwise unknown.

11. Butra: *Epist.* 1.5.26.

PIR² B 178; *RE* Suppl. 6:18. A supper guest of Horace and perhaps a mutual friend of Horace and Manlius Torquatus; he is otherwise unknown.

12. (L. Calpurnius) Bibulus: *Serm.* 1.10.86.

RE 3:1367–1368 no. 27; senator. One of a group of prominent contemporaries whom Horace claimed as sympathetic readers in the mid-30s. Bibulus had studied at Athens in the mid-40s when Horace was there, and like Horace he had fought on the side of Brutus and Cassius at Philippi. He was a partisan of Antony when Horace complimented him.

13. (Calpurnius) Piso I: *Ars.*

PIR² C 280; senator. The undatable *Ars Poetica,* which contains advice about poetry for gentleman poets, is addressed to an aristocratic father and two youthful sons who cannot be certainly identified. Three views are current. (1) According to Porphyrio and a majority of modern scholars, the father is L. Calpurnius Piso, *cos.* 15 (*PIR²* C 289; *RE* 3:1396–1399 no. 99), son of the Graecophile Piso Caesoninus and a poet and friend of poets in his own right; he cultivated the epigrammatist Antipater of Thessalonica and possibly Apollonides of Nicaea. But none among the numerous Pisones on record can be sons of his. Even if the two missing sons were to be postulated for him, they would be too young to fit the *iuvenes* described in the *Ars* unless that poem is dated to the closing years of Horace's life. A late date is complicated by the fact that the father was occupied in service far from Rome for at least four continuous years between 15 and 10. (2) The father is Cn. Piso, *cos.* 23 (*PIR²* C 286; *RE* 3:1391–1392 no. 95). Gnaeus has the requisite two sons, Gnaeus (*cos.* 7) and Lucius (*cos.* 1), though for them to be the *iuvenes* of the *Ars* the poem would have to be dated in the mid to late 20s, which is earlier than most critics place it. Neither Gnaeus nor his sons are on record as having any interest in poetry, but Gnaeus did fight on the same side as Horace at Philippi. (3) The father is the Graecophile Piso Caesoninus, *cos.* 58 (*RE* 3:1387–1390 no. 90); for the argument see B. Frischer, *Shifting Paradigms: New Approaches to Horace's Ars Poetica* (Atlanta, 1991), pp. 52–68. This hypothesis also requires the *Ars* to be dated to the 20s, and it accounts for only one of the two sons. The elder is identified with the consul of 15, making him a young man of more than 20 and perhaps already a senator when Horace describes him as still being molded by fatherly words (*Ars* 366–367). Hypothesis (2) appears to have the least against it.

14. Calpurnius Piso II: see 13 above.

15. Calpurnius Piso III: see 13 above.

16. ?Aulus Cascellius: *Ars* 371.

PIR¹ C 389; *RE* 3:1634–1637 no. 4; senator. Instanced by Horace as a distinguished jurist.

17. Catius: *Serm.* 2.4.

PIR: no entry; *RE* 3:1792 no. 2. A devotee of culinary science whom Horace satirized though he purports to be a friend. Despite Porphyrio's note, Catius is probably not the Epicurean philosopher Titus Catius, dead at least a decade before Horace wrote.

18. Cervius: *Serm.* 2.6.77–79.

PIR: no entry, but compare *PIR²* C 682; *RE* 3:1994 no. 2. An otherwise unknown Sabine country neighbor of Horace into whose mouth he put the fable of the city mouse and the country mouse.

19. *M. Claudius Marcellus:* *Carm.* 1.12.45–46.

PIR² C 925; *RE* 3:2764–2770 no. 230; *aed.* 23. In a catalog of heroes Horace includes a Marcellus who must be the third-century M. Claudius Marcellus, five times consul and winner of the *spolia opima* (as in catalogs at Verg. *Aen.* 6.855–859 and Man. 1.788). But the scholiasts and most modern scholars interpret the reference as a compliment to Augustus' teenage nephew. (PROPERTIUS 5, VERGIL 9)

20. ?Nero Claudius Drusus: *Carm.* 4.4, 4.14.9–13, Suet. *Vita Hor.* pp. 297.35–298.1 Roth, scholia on Hor. *Carm.* 4.1.1 and 4.4.1.

PIR² C 857; *RE* 3:2703–2719 no. 139; *cos.* 9. Augustus' younger stepson was featured in two odes celebrating his campaign against the Vindelici in 15. But since Augustus is said to have requested verse in Drusus' honor, the poems need not imply a personal connection between Horace and Drusus.

21. (Ti.) Claudius Nero: *Epist.* 1.3.1–5, 1.8.2, 1.9, 1.12.26–28, 2.2.1, *Carm.* 4.4.28, 4.14.14–34, Suet. *Vita Hor.* pp. 297.35–298.1 Roth.

PIR² C 941; *RE* 10:478–536 no. 154; *cos.* 13. Augustus' older stepson, whose expedition to Armenia in 20 and Rhaetian campaign in 15 Horace celebrated; in *Epist.* 1.9 Horace commended one of his friends to Tiberius. Despite the military exertions of his early and middle years, Tiberius had sophisticated literary interests. He wrote verse in both Latin and Greek and cultivated the company of literary men.

22. ?(L.) Cocceius (Nerva): *Serm.* 1.5.28, 32, and 50–51.

PIR² C 1223; *RE* 4:130–131 and Suppl. 7:90 no. 12. Member of a diplomatic party which Horace, Vergil, and other friends of Maecenas accompanied in the early 30s; Cocceius entertained the group at his villa in Caudium. (VERGIL 10)

23. ?Damasippus: *Serm.* 2.3.

PIR: no entry; *RE* 10:1034 no. 72. A bankrupt connoisseur and speculator who after a conversion to radical Stoicism attempted to proselytize Horace in turn. He is probably related to the senator L. Iunius Brutus Damasippus, and he may be the connoisseur who appears in Cicero's letters.

24. (Q.) Dellius: *Carm.* 2.3.

PIR¹ D 29; *RE* 4:2447–2448; senator. A prosperous landowner who entertained Horace and received an ode counseling that prosperity and poverty all come to the same end. Dellius had been a partisan of Antony until the eve of Actium, when he deserted to Augustus. Thereafter he enjoyed Augustus' friendship although he took no role in public life.

25. Paullus (Fabius) Maximus: *Carm.* 4.1.

PIR² F 47; *RE* 6:1780–1789 no. 102; *cos.* 11. Recipient of the opening piece in Horace's last collection of lyrics, which paints him as a noble, an orator, and an ideal candidate for the pursuit of romance. He married Augustus' first cousin Marcia, possibly soon after Horace wrote; later he was a protector of Ovid (OVID 18). Juvenal cited him as a model of generosity toward literary men (*Sat.* 7.95).

26. ?(C.) Fonteius Capito: *Serm.* 1.5.32 and 38.

PIR² F 469; *RE* 6:2847 and Suppl. 3:528 no. 20; *cos.* 33. Antony's man in a diplomatic party which Horace, Vergil, and other friends of Maecenas accompanied in the early 30s. (VERGIL 18)

27. Fundanius: *Serm.* 1.10.40–42 and 2.8.

PIR¹ F 394; *RE* 7:292 no. 2. A friend whom Horace lauded as the greatest living writer of *palliatae*. Porphyrio identifies him as Gaius Fundanius, a name which is borne by several first-century *equites* and senators.

28. (C.) Furnius: *Serm.* 1.10.86.

PIR[2] F 591, compare F 590; *RE* 7:377 no. 4, compare 7:375–377 no. 3; senator. One of a group of prominent contemporaries whom Horace claimed as sympathetic readers in the mid-30s. It is uncertain whether he is the elder C. Furnius, a partisan of Antony at the time, or his Caesarean son, the consul of 17.

29. ?Heliodorus: *Serm.* 1.5.2–3.

No entry in *PIR* or *RE*. An otherwise unknown Greek *rhetor* traveling in the early 30s with a diplomatic mission which Horace, Vergil, and other friends of Maecenas accompanied. (VERGIL 19)

30. Iccius: *Carm.* 1.29 and *Epist.* 1.12.

PIR[2] I 15; *RE* 9:819–820 no. 2. A young, well-educated friend who received an ode marking his departure for military service early in the 20s and later received a verse epistle when he was managing Agrippa's affairs in Sicily; he is otherwise unknown.

31. (C. Iulius) Caesar Augustus: (selected references only) *Serm.* 1.3.4–6, 1.5.29, 2.1.16–20 and 83–86, 2.6.50–58, *Epist.* 1.13, 1.19.41–45, 1.20.23, 2.1, 2.2.46–52, *Carm.* 4.4, 4.14, *Saec.*, Suet. *Vita Hor.* pp. 297.9–298.33 Roth, and *ILS* 5050.149.

PIR[2] I 215; *RE* 10:275–381 no. 132. In 42 Horace fought on the losing side against Augustus' forces at Philippi, after which he was pardoned and allowed to return home, but with diminished resources. Friendship with Maecenas seems not at first to have extended to Augustus, toward whom Horace's poems of the 30s maintain a distinct reserve. Augustus is absent from the list of literary admirers he claims at *Serm.* 1.10.81–90. But Horace does claim to enjoy the approbation of Augustus shortly after Actium, when he begins pouring out lyrics which celebrate him in various aspects as leader and savior of the nation. Fragments of letters from Augustus to Horace are also extant; in one from about the year 20 he entreats Horace to direct one of his verse epistles to him. He commissioned Horace to write the hymn for the Secular Games of 17. In 15 he asked him to commemorate the Alpine campaign of his stepsons Drusus and Tiberius. He is said to have bestowed large sums of money on Horace at least twice, and he sought unsuccessfully to appoint him to a secretarial position at the palace. When Maecenas died in 8, he left a will commending Horace to Augustus' especial care, and when Horace himself died two months later, he named Augustus his sole heir. (VERGIL 22)

32. Iulius Florus: *Epist.* 1.3 and 2.2.

PIR[2] I 316; *RE* 10.589 no. 237. A young poet friend traveling with Tiberius' entourage in the East to whom Horace addressed verse letters on literary topics in about 20. Porphyrio identifies Florus as an otherwise unknown writer of satires.

33. (M. Iunius) Brutus: *Serm.* 1.7 and *Carm.* 2.7.2, compare *Epist.* 1.20.23.

RE 10:973–1020 no. 53; *pr.* 44. Horace's commander in the civil war, remembered after his death in an anecdotal satire of the early 30s and in an ode written a decade later.

34. Licinius: *Carm.* 2.10.

*PIR*² L 218; *RE* 5A:706–710 no. 92. Recipient of an ode on moderation who cannot be confidently identified. Some ancient scholars and many modern ones have equated him with the brother-in-law of Maecenas, who was soon to be involved in a conspiracy against Augustus and whose name is given in various sources as "Licinius Murena," "Varro Murena," "Murena," or "Varro." The nomen Licinius is common, however, and there is nothing else to link Horace's addressee with the conspirator.

35. ?Livia: *Carm.* 3.14.5–6.

*PIR*² L 301; *RE* 13:900–924 no. 37. Augustus' wife: in a poem written in 25 or 24 Horace envisions that she will join Octavia and other matrons in ceremonies welcoming Augustus home from Spain, but he suggests no personal acquaintance with her.

36. (M.) Lollius: *Carm.* 4.9.

*PIR*² L 311; *RE* 13:1377–1387 no. 11; *cos.* 21. Praised for his incorruptibility and public service in an ode whose implicit context may be a military embarrassment Lollius had suffered as governor of Gaul in 17. He was a friend of Maecenas and had other literary connections.

37. Lollius Maximus: *Epist.* 1.2 and 1.18.

*PIR*² L 317; *RE* 13:1389–1390 no. 19. A well-to-do young orator and poet whom Horace advised on the wisdom to be found in Homer and on the art of cultivating the great; possibly but not probably a son of M. Lollius (36 above).

38. ?Lollius III: *Epist.* 1.18.60–64.

Horace describes a mock sea-battle which Lollius Maximus (37 above) and his brother staged on a lake on their father's estate; he may have been a friend of both brothers.

39. ?Lollius IV: *Epist.* 1.18.60.

Horace witnessed a mock sea-battle staged on the paternal estate of Lollius Maximus (37 above), where he may have been the father's guest as well as the son's. The father is possibly but not probably M. Lollius (36 above).

40. (C.) Maecenas: Hor. (selected references only) *Serm.* 1.3.38–75, 1.5, 1.6, 1.9, 1.10.81, 2.3.312–313, 2.6, 2.7.32–35, *Epodi* 1 with Porph. on 1.31, *Carm.* 2.18.12–14 with schol., *Epist.* 1.1, 1.7, Maecenas frags. 2–3 *FPL* pp. 101–102 Morel = 132 Büchner, *Laus Pis.* 236–242, Mart. *Epigr.* 1.107.4, 12.3, Suet. *Vita Hor.* pp. 296–298 Roth, Fronto *Ad M. Caes.* 1.9.5 p. 19 van den Hout, Servius Auctus on Verg. *Aen.* 8.310.

*PIR*² M 37; *RE* 14:207–229 no. 6; *eques*. In 38 Augustus' counselor invited Horace into his entourage at the instance of Vergil and Varius. In that year or the next he took Horace along on a diplomatic mission, and they may have been together at Actium in 31. Horace's poems, some two dozen of which are directed to or make mention of Maecenas, give glimpses of him in Maecenas' company on numerous other occasions through the 30s and 20s; the fragmentary remains of Maecenas' writings in turn make much of Horace. By Horace's own testimony, Maecenas enriched him and (apparently) gave him property in the Sabine country. In his will Maecenas commended Horace to the care of Augustus, though Horace died two months later in 8. (PROPERTIUS 13, VERGIL 25)

41. ?(Sp.) Maecius Tarpa: *Serm.* 1.10.38 and *Ars* 386–387.

*PIR*² M 63; *RE* 14:238 no. 24. A *iudex* of dramatic poetry whose opinion Horace says is worth hearing. He must be the Sp. Maecius who selected the classic plays which were revived for the dedication of Pompey's theater in 55 (Cic. *Fam.* 7.1.1 = 24 SB).

42. (Manlius) Torquatus: *Epist.* 1.5 and *Carm.* 4.7.

*PIR*² M 162; *RE* 14:1193 no. 72a. An orator of distinguished lineage to whom Horace sent a versified supper invitation in the late 20s and an ode on springtime and mortality in the following decade. He may be one of the Torquati who Pliny says wrote verse (*Epist.* 5.5.3); he may also be the (Manlius) Acidinus who was studying in Athens at the same time Horace was studying there (Cic. *Att.* 12.32.2 = 271 SB).

43. (C. Marcius) Censorinus: *Carm.* 4.8.

*PIR*² M 222; *RE* 14:1551–1552 no. 44; *cos.* 8. Recipient of an ode tendered in lieu of a material gift, of which Horace pointedly observes Censorinus has no need.

44. ?Messius Cicirrus: *Serm.* 1.5.51–70.

*PIR*² M 517; *RE* 15:1244 no. 6. An uncouth character of Oscan stock whose behavior provided amusement for a diplomatic party which Horace, Vergil, and other friends of Maecenas accompanied in the early 30s. Despite Porphyrio's assertion that Messius was an *eques,* he was probably a rustic encountered at Caudium rather than a member of the party. (VERGIL 28)

45. Mulvius: *Serm.* 2.7.36.

*PIR*² M 698; *RE* 16:516 no. 2. An otherwise unknown supper guest whom Horace describes as a *scurra*.

46. Munatius: *Epist.* 1.3.30–35.

*PIR*² M 718; *RE* 16:535 no. 3. A young friend traveling with Tiberius' entourage in 20 for whom Horace asked of news in a verse letter to another member of the entourage (Julius Florus, 32 above). Munatius may be related to L. Munatius Plancus (47 below) and to Titius (84 below).

47. (L. Munatius) Plancus: *Carm.* 1.7 and 3.14.28.

PIR² M 728; RE 16:545–551 no. 30; *cos.* 42, *cens.* 22. Horace's host at Tibur, who received an ode counseling him to assuage distress with wine. Plancus was a prominent careerist of the civil wars and a successful orator thereafter.

48. ?Murena I: *Serm.* 1.5.38.

PIR¹ T 74; RE 5A:707 no. 92; senator. Host at Formiae of a diplomatic party which Horace, Vergil, and other friends of Maecenas accompanied in the early 30s. Murena surely belonged to one of the senatorial families of that name, though the Murenae of this period have not yet been successfully disentangled. Horace's host may be the A. Terentius Varro Murena who supported first Pompey and then Antony in the civil wars (RE 5A:705–706 no. 91), but he is probably too old to be (as usually thought) the man who conspired against Augustus in 22 (or 23). Most identify him with Murena II (49 below) and many with Licinius (34 above). (VERGIL 29)

49. Murena II: *Carm.* 3.19.11.

PIR¹ T 74; RE 5A:708 no. 92; senator. Recipient of a compliment from Horace on the occasion of his adlection into the augurate in the mid-20s. Horace's friend may be the A. Terentius Varro Murena who died before taking up a consulate in 23. Most identify him with the Varro who was Maecenas' brother-in-law and who conspired against Augustus in 22 (or 23), whom they in turn identify with Licinius (34 above) and Murena I (48 above).

50. Numicius: *Epist.* 1.6.

PIR² N 203; RE: no entry, but compare 17:1342 no. 5. Recipient of a verse epistle on the vanity of worldly goods. The uncommon nomen has suggested identification with the senator P. Numicius Pica Caesianus known from *ILS* 911, possibly of Augustan date.

51. ?Numida: *Carm.* 1.36.

PIR¹ P 556; RE: no entry, but compare 21:19 no. 25. An otherwise unknown young friend of Aelius Lamia to whose homecoming from *ultima Hesperia* Horace devoted an ode. Manuscript superscriptions identify him as Plotius Numida (attested as a senator's name at Val. Max. 4.6.2); the scholiasts identify him as Pomponius Numida.

52. (Numonius) Vala: *Epist.* 1.15.

PIR² N 244; RE: no entry, but compare 17:1460–1461 no. 1; M. G. Granino Cecere, *Epigraphica* 49 (1987): 219–227; senator. A wealthy friend whom Horace consulted about the climate of Paestum and environs before visiting. The cognomen is so rare that he must be a Numonius Vala (as identified in manuscript superscriptions and by Pseudo-Acro); a Q. Numonius Vala is known as *patronus* at Paestum (*CIL* 10.481). But Horace's friend should be the C. Numonius Vala who was a moneyer in 41 and praetor later.

53. ?Octavia: *Carm.* 3.14.7–8.

*PIR*² O 66; *RE* 17:1859–1868 no. 96. Augustus' sister: in a poem written in 25 or 24 Horace envisions that she will join Livia and other matrons in ceremonies welcoming Augustus home from Spain, but he suggests no personal acquaintance with her. (PROPERTIUS 14, VERGIL 31)

54. Octavius: *Serm.* 1.10.82.

*PIR*² O 18; *RE* 17:1851–1852 no. 73. One of several discerning readers (all possibly associated with Maecenas) whose approbation Horace claimed to enjoy in the mid-30s. Octavius may but need not be the Octavius of [Verg.] *Cat.* 11.1 (VERGIL 33); he can hardly be the surveyor Octavius Musa (VERGIL 30).

55. Ofellus: *Serm.* 2.2.

*PIR*² O 82; *RE* 17:2043. A Venusine farmer reduced to tenancy (compare App. *BCiv.* 4.11) whom Horace claims to quote as a source of precepts on the simple life.

56. "Onysius": Suet. *Vita Horati* p. 298.14 Roth.

*PIR*² O 105; *RE:* no entry. An otherwise unknown messenger from whom Augustus told Horace that he had received a *libellus* of Horace's work; the name has often been thought to be corrupt.

57. ?(L.) Orbilius (Pupillus): *Epist.* 2.1.70–71 with the scholia, Suet. *Gr.* 9.3, compare *Serm.* 1.10.★4-★8.

*PIR*² O 131; *RE* 18:876–877. Horace's erstwhile schoolmaster, remembered for his rough tutelage. Though Orbilius was still alive when Horace mentioned him, there is no hint of a continuing acquaintance.

58. P. Ovidius Naso: Ov. *Tr.* 4.10.49–50.

*PIR*² O 180; *RE* 18:1910–1986 no. 3; *eques.* The leading second-generation Augustan poet attended recitations of Horace's lyric poems in his youth. (PROPERTIUS 15, TIBULLUS 5, VERGIL 34)

59. ?Paulus: *Serm.* 1.6.41.

No entry in *PIR* or *RE.* One of two men instanced as (presumably contemporary) examples of noble birth (the other is Messalla). Paulus should be one of the Aemilii Lepidi, but his identity cannot be more precisely determined.

60. ?Pedius Poplicola: *Serm.* 1.10.28. (N.B.: it is possible that the cognomen *Poplicola* should be taken with *Corvinus* in line 29 rather than with *Pedius* in 28, which would yield a Poplicola Corvinus as unknown as Pedius Poplicola.)

*PIR*¹ P 147, compare V 90; *RE* 19:40–41 no. 2. Cited (with Corvinus) as a good example of an effective forensic orator. He is often taken to be Q. Pedius, *quaest.* 41, who is not known to have borne the cognomen *Poplicola* but might have derived it from his mother Valeria.

61. Pettius: *Epodi* 11.

PIR: no entry; *RE* 19:1381 no. 1. Recipient of a poem in which Horace ventilated the sorrows of unrequited love; Pettius is otherwise unknown.

62. *Philodemus*: *Serm.* 1.2.120–122.

RE 19:2444–2482 no. 5; T. Dorandi, *ANRW* 2.36.4:2328–2368. The contemporary Epicurean philosopher and epigrammatist, whom Horace once quotes approvingly. Horace's friends Vergil, Varius Rufus, Quintilius, and Plotius Tucca all had personal connections with Philodemus, but there is presently no evidence that Horace did. His name cannot be restored in the fragmentary papyrus (*PHerc.* 253, *Vol. Herc. Coll. Altera* 7:196, frag. 12, line 4) that contains Philodemus' allocution to Varius, Quintilius, and a third friend whose name ends in "-tius," since a papyrus deciphered by M. Gigante and M. Capasso (*SIFC,* 3 ser., 7 [1989]: 4) has shown that the friend addressed was *Plotius* Tucca. (VERGIL 36)

63. Plotius (Tucca): *Serm.* 1.5.40, 1.10.81, and Hieron. *Chron.* 166 e Helm.

PIR[1] P 394; *RE* 21:1266–1267 no. 17a. A companion on a trip through Italy which Horace made with Maecenas and others in the early 30s, and one of a group whom Horace claims as his preferred readers. Plotius is best known as a long-time associate of Vergil (VERGIL 38).

64. Pompeius: *Carm.* 2.7.

PIR[1] P 498; *RE* 21:2262–2263 no. 50. A fellow partisan of Brutus in the civil war whose restoration to Rome Horace celebrated in an ode. He is identified as Pompeius Varus or Pompilius by the scholiasts (the nomen Pompilius originates in a corruption in line 5 of the poem). The displaced comrade-in-arms should probably not be identified with Horace's prosperous friend Pompeius Grosphus (65 below), and there is nothing but a common cognomen and the authority of the scholia to connect him with Varus (90 below).

65. Pompeius Grosphus: *Carm.* 2.16 and *Epist.* 1.12.22–23.

PIR[1] P 464; *RE* 21:2273 no. 84. A Sicilian rancher to whom Horace addressed an ode on the futility of wealth, and whom he commended to his friend Iccius (30 above) when Iccius acquired influence in Sicily. Grosphus was an *eques* according to Porphyrio; the name Pompeius Grosphus is later borne by two *duoviri* at Pompeii (*CIL* 4 Suppl. p. 389, no. cxliii, lines 1–2). The name and the domicile of Grosphus suggest Greek origins. He is probably not to be identified with Horace's civil war comrade Pompeius (64 above).

66. Postumus: *Carm.* 2.14.

PIR[1] P 673; *RE* 22:987 no. 6. A wealthy coeval who received an ode on the inevitability of death. Postumus cannot be certainly identified, but he should be older than the friend of Propertius (PROPERTIUS 18).

67. ?(C.) Proculeius: *Carm.* 2.2.5–6.

*PIR*¹ no. 736; *RE* 23:72–74 no. 2; *eques*. Complimented for his exemplary generosity and loyalty to his brothers. Proculeius was one of Augustus' most trusted friends in the 30s and 20s; he was also a brother of the conspirator Varro Murena (and so the brother-in-law of Maecenas). Juvenal (*Sat.* 7.94) later held him up as an example of bygone munificence to poets.

68. Quinctius: *Epist.* 1.16.

*PIR*¹ Q 39; *RE* 24:1105–1106 no. 62. A wealthy friend, possibly a senator, to whom Horace addressed a verse letter about self-knowledge. He may be identical with Quinctius Hirpinus (69 below).

69. Quinctius Hirpinus: *Carm.* 2.11.

*PIR*¹ Q 39; *RE* 24:1105–1106 no. 62. A coeval and host of Horace who received an ode on the *carpe diem* theme. *Hirpinus* in line 1 may be an ethnic adjective rather than a cognomen (Quinctii are numerous in the region of the Hirpini); in either case, this man may be identical with Quinctius (68 above), but the nomen is widespread.

70. Quintilius: *Carm.* 1.24, *Ars* 438–452, Hieron. *Chron.* 165 a Helm.

*PIR*¹ Q 25; *RE* 24:899–902 no. 5. A friend of Vergil (VERGIL 40) whose death (in 23 according to Jerome) elicited an ode of condolence. Though praised in the *Ars* as a judicious critic of poetry, he is not named among Horace's ideal readers at *Serm.* 1.10.81–90. The scholiasts identify him as an *eques,* Quintilius Varus of Cremona; it is not impossible, though not likely, that Quintilius is the same man as Varus (90 below).

71. Roscius: *Serm.* 2.6.34–35.

PIR: no entry; *RE* 1A:1116 no. 3. An otherwise unknown friend or acquaintance who requested Horace's support in a legal transaction.

72. ?(P.) Rupilius Rex: *Serm.* 1.7.

RE 1A:1231–1232 no. 10. A fellow member of Brutus' cohort during the civil war whose litigation before Brutus' tribunal in Asia is the subject of an unflattering satire. The scholiasts identify him as a proscribed ex-praetor P. Rupilius, and senatorial Rupilii of the late Republic are otherwise attested. But Horace's man is often identified with a P. Rupilius known as a *publicanus* in Bithynia (Cic. *Fam.* 13.9.2 = 139 SB).

73. Sabinus: *Epist.* 1.5.27–28.

*PIR*¹: no entry, but compare S 23; *RE:* no entry, but compare 1:1598–1599 no. 21. A supper guest of Horace and a mutual friend of Horace and Manlius Torquatus. There is nothing but an undistinctive cognomen to connect him with homonymous friends of Vergil (VERGIL 41) and of Ovid (OVID 50).

74. (C.) Sallustius Crispus: *Carm.* 2.2.

*PIR*¹ S 61; *RE* 1A:1955–1956 no. 11; *eques*. Recipient of an ode applauding his wise use of wealth. A partisan of Antony before Actium, Sallustius afterward became a trusted agent of Augustus, serving alongside and eventually replacing Maecenas. His liberality also attracted the notice of Crinagoras (*Anth. Plan.* 40 = Gow-Page *Garland of Philip* 1:220, no. 36).

75. ?Sarmentus: *Serm.* 1.5.51–70.

PIR[1] S 144; *RE* 2A:25. A *scurra* and a *scriba* traveling with a diplomatic party which Horace, Vergil, and other friends of Maecenas accompaned in the early 30s. The scholiast on Juv. *Sat.* 5.3 identifies him as an Etrurian-born freedman of Maecenas who acquired equestrian status along with a position as quaestorian *scriba*. Sarmentus was also a favorite of Augustus. Horace gives no hint of a personal relationship with him, though they were linked by their clerkships and friendship with Maecenas. (VERGIL 42)

76. Scaeva: *Epist.* 1.17.

PIR[1] S 184, compare *PIR*[2] L 322; *RE* 2A:343 no. 2. A young friend who receives advice on courting the rich. Pseudo-Acro identifies him as Lollius Scaeva *eques Romanus,* but the scholiasts have conflated *Epist.* 1.17 and 18, to Scaeva and Lollius respectively.

77. Septicius: *Epist.* 1.5.26.

PIR[1] S 300; *RE* 2A:1557 no. 2. An otherwise unknown supper guest of Horace and a mutual friend of Horace and Manlius Torquatus.

78. Septimius: *Carm.* 2.6, *Epist.* 1.9, and Suet. *Vita Hor.* p. 297.28–30 Roth.

PIR[1] S 306; *RE* 2A:1560 no. 3. A young friend for whom Horace wrote a letter of recommendation to Tiberius and a mutual friend of Horace and Augustus. Porphyrio identifies him as an *eques* and a *commilito* of Horace (the latter by a mistaken inference from *Carm.* 2.6.8). See also Titius (84 below).

79. (L.) Sestius (Quirinalis): *Carm.* 1.4.

PIR[1] S 436; *RE* 2A:1885 no. 3; *cos.* 23. A host of Horace and a wealthy man who received an ode on springtime and mortality. Like Horace, Sestius had taken the side of Brutus in the civil war; he was rehabilitated after Philippi and eventually admitted to the friendship of Augustus.

80. ?Sosius I: *Epist.* 1.20.2 and *Ars* 345.

PIR[1] S 555; *RE* 3A:1176 no. 1. One of the booksellers who marketed Horace's poems. The scholiasts identify the Sosii as two brothers; their occupation suggests that they were Greek. It is possible but not evident that they had a personal as well as a business relationship with Horace.

81. ?Sosius II: see the preceding entry.

82. Servius (Sulpicius Rufus): *Serm.* 1.10.86.

PIR: no entry; *RE* 4A:860–862 no. 96; R. Syme *CQ* 31 (1981): 421–427; senator. One of a group of prominent contemporaries whom Horace claimed as sympathetic readers in the mid-30s. Servius should be the son of Servius Sulpicius Rufus, *cos.* 51. He is evidently the father of the Sulpicia whose verses are preserved in the Tibullan corpus and the brother-in-law of Messalla Corvinus; he may be the poet mentioned by Ovid at *Tr.* 2.441–442 and by Pliny at *Epist.* 5.3.5.

83. *Terentia: Carm.* 2.12.13–28 with Pseudo-Acro there and on *Serm.* 1.2.64–66; compare Pseudo-Acro on *Epodi* 3.21 and Porphyrio on *Epodi* 14.13.

PIR[1] T 76; *RE* 5A:716 no. 96. Maecenas' wife from at least 22 to 16, and said by Pseudo-Acro to be the true identity of the *domina* Licymnia who in an ode to Maecenas is celebrated for her beauty, singing, grace, and fidelity in love. It is not inconceivable that Horace would have used a pseudonym to create an eroticized portrait of a contemporary noblewoman, but the authority of Pseudo-Acro is too weak to establish it; Licymnia may be the courtesan she appears to be.

84. *Titius: Epist.* 1.3.9–14.

PIR[1] T 195; *RE*: no entry. A young poet friend traveling with Tiberius' entourage in the East in about 20. Pseudo-Acro gives him the double nomen Titius Septimius, evidently conflating him with the Septimius whom Horace commends to Tiberius in *Epist.* 1.9. He may be related to Munatius (46 above) and to Munatius Plancus (47 above). In the absence of other clues, the nomen is too common to argue identity with a like-named friend of Tibullus (TIBUL-LUS 7), and it is still less certain that he should be connected with the Rufus whom Ovid mentions as a lyric poet (OVID 49).

85. (C.) *Trebatius (Testa): Serm.* 2.1.

PIR[1] T 228; *RE* 6A:2251–2261 and Suppl. 7:1619–1622 no. 7. A legal expert whom Horace consulted about problems of writing satire. Trebatius had been a protégé of Cicero and a confidential agent of Caesar, and he was a preeminent legal authority under Augustus. The scholiasts identify him as an *eques* and author of books on civil law and religion.

86. (M. Valerius) *Messalla Corvinus: Serm.* 1.6.42 (not certainly Messalla Corvinus), 1.10.29 and 85, *Carm.* 3.21, *Ars* 371, and Servius Auctus on Verg. *Aen.* 8.310.

PIR[1] V 90; *RE* 8A:131–157 and 2389–2390 no. 261; *cos.* 31. An aristocrat, orator, and man of letters whom Horace claimed as a sympathetic reader in the mid-30s and displayed in an ode of the next decade as his dinner guest. Messalla had studied in Athens when Horace was there and like him had chosen Brutus' side in the civil war, but he nevertheless became a pillar of the Augustan establishment. His other literary connections include Maecenas and Pollio as well as Tibullus (TIBULLUS 8) and the other poets of the Tibullan Corpus, Ovid (OVID 58), Vergil (VERGIL 48), Valgius Rufus (88 below), Sextilius Ena, the *Ciris* poet, and perhaps the poet of *Catalepton* 9.

87. frater Messallae: *Serm.* 1.10.85.

RE 7:1003–1005 no. 18; senator. One of a group of prominent contemporaries whom Horace claimed as sympathetic readers in the mid-30s. Messalla's only known *frater* is an older half-brother, L. Gellius Publicola (*cos.* 36), like Messalla a partisan of Antony in the 30s; he is the Gellius attacked by Catullus.

88. (C.) Valgius (Rufus): *Serm.* 1.10.82 and *Carm.* 2.9.

PIR[1] V 169; *RE* 8A:272–276 no. 7; *cos.* 12. A fellow poet whom Horace named as a sympathetic reader in the mid-30s and later urged to redirect his poetic activity from plaints of love to the victories of Augustus. Valgius was also associated with the poet Cinna and with Messalla Corvinus (86 above). (VERGIL 50)

89. (L.) Varius (Rufus): *Serm.* 1.5.40 and 93, 1.6.55, 1.9.23, 1.10.43–44 and 81, 2.8.21 and 63–64, *Carm.* 1.6.1, *Epist.* 2.1.245–247, *Ars* 53–55, and Hieron. *Chron.* p. 166 e Helm.

PIR[1] V 194; *RE* 8A:410–413 no. 21. The poet Varius along with Vergil had arranged for Horace's introduction to Maecenas in 38, and a few months later the three friends accompanied Maecenas on one of his diplomatic journeys. In about 35 Horace praised Varius as the greatest contemporary writer of epic and claimed him as a sympathetic reader of his own satires. Varius is again held up as the ideal representative of epic in the following decade; Horace does not allude to his success with tragedy. Though best known for his relationship to Vergil (VERGIL 51), he was also associated with Philodemus and Cinna the poet. He is probably too old to be the poet Varius whom Ovid mentions (OVID 60).

90. Varus: *Carm.* 1.18.

PIR[1] Q 25; *RE* 24:899–902 no. 5. Recipient of a drinking ode and probably Horace's host at Tibur. His identification as a Quintilius Varus by manuscript superscriptions is compatible with a medieval tradition that labeled an Augustan ruin at Tibur as the estate of Quintilius. But if Varus is the same man as 70 above, his death is memorialized six poems later in the same book. He cannot be the newly restored exile Pompeius (Varus?), 64 above, or (in view of *Serm.* 1.3.130–132) the jurist and consular Alfenus Varus (VERGIL 53). The cognomen is too common to warrant much confidence in any identification.

91. (P.) Vergilius (Maro): *Serm.* 1.5.39–104, 1.6.54–55, 1.10.44–45 and 81, *Carm.* 1.3, 1.24.10–12, *Epist.* 2.1.245–247, *Ars* 53–55, Mart. *Epigr.* 8.18.5–6, Servius Auctus on Verg. *Aen.* 8.310, Pseudo-Acro on *Serm.* 1.3.31, Hieron. *Chron.* 165 a and 166 e Helm, Donatus Auctus *Vita Verg.* p. 30.43–45 Brummer = p. 360.143–362.146 Bayer.

PIR[1] V 279; *RE* 8A:1021–1506 no. 7. Vergil had befriended Horace by the year 38, when he and Varius arranged for his introduction to Maecenas, and some months later the three friends accompanied Maecenas on a diplomatic journey. In the same period Horace praised Vergil as a master of the bucolic genre and claimed him as a sympathetic reader of his own satires. A decade later he addressed a *propempticon* and a *consolatio* to Vergil; a literary dialogue in which Maecenas cast Horace and Vergil as interlocutors along with himself and Messalla probably dates from the same period. Horace's latest references, written probably after Vergil's death in 19, exalt him as a classic of modern poetry. See also the following entry. (OVID 61, PROPERTIUS 21, TIBULLUS 10)

92. Vergilius: *Carm.* 4.12.

PIR[1] V 274; *RE:* no entry. Recipient of a bantering invitation to a drinking-party in which he is dubbed the "cliens nobilium iuvenum." Both ancient and modern scholars are divided about identifying Vergilius as the poet. Nothing said about him suggests the poet, however, and though the poem cannot be dated, the book in which it appears was published well after the poet's death.

93. Vinnius: *Epist.* 1.13.

PIR[1] V 452; *RE* 9A:150–151 no. 1. Recipient of a verse letter instructing him to deliver a parcel of poems to Augustus. He is identified in the manuscript superscriptions as Vinnius Asellus; Pseudo-Acro identifies him alternately as Vinnius Asellus or C. Vinnius Fronto. He is otherwise unknown.

94. ?(M. Vipsanius) Agrippa: *Serm.* 2.3.185–186, *Carm.* 1.6, and *Epist.* 1.12.1 and 26.

PIR[1] V 457; *RE* 9A:1226–1275 no. 2; *cos.* 37, 28, and 27. Augustus' coadjutor was complimented as a popular official in the late 30s and as a successful warrior in the 20s. But apart from these references to public services, there is no sign in his well-documented career that he had personal ties with Horace or any other poet. (VERGIL 55)

95. Viscus Thurinus: *Serm.* 1.9.22, 1.10.83, and 2.8.20.

PIR[1] V 408; *RE* 8A:1998 no. 68. Horace claimed to enjoy the literary approbation of *uterque Viscorum* in the mid-30s, and he mentioned a Viscus as the steady companion of Varius and Maecenas during the same period. Pseudo-Acro identifies the two men as both brothers and senators, adding that their father Vibius Viscus chose to remain an *eques* although he was wealthy and enjoyed the friendship of Augustus. The rare cognomen *Viscus* is found only in conjunction with the nomen *Vibius* in *CIL;* a L. Vibius Viscus Macrinus is attested as a senator in the middle of the first century A.D. Horace's approving reader is probably the critic Viscus addressed in a papyrus fragment attributed to Cornelius Gallus (frag. 4, line 3, *FPL* p. 130 Büchner). (VERGIL 56)

96. Viscus II: *Serm.* 1.10.83. See the preceding entry.

Appendix 2B: Connections of Ovid

The great majority of Ovid's friends are known to us from his references to them in poems he wrote late in life. The following list is therefore strongly biased toward friends of his maturity. The principal uncertainty concerns the thirty-odd persons in his catalog of contemporary poets in *Pont.* 4.16: in most cases it is not clear whether he is claiming them as friends or simply naming them as colleagues. He took pains not to reveal the identity of most recipients of the *Tristia,* and for the most part I have not speculated about them. Finally, this list does not include all members of the palace family who are complimented in the poems because by the close of the Augustan period such compliments by themselves are unlikely to indicate personal acquaintance (even though Ovid's downfall in A.D. 8 probably did have something to do with friendships at court).

1. (Aemilius) Macer: *Tr.* 4.10.43–44.

*PIR*² A 378; *RE* 1:567 no. 86. The poet of the *Ornithogonia* and the *Theriaca,* whom Ovid heard recite when Macer was old and Ovid young; Macer died in 16 according to Jerome. It is uncertain whether he is the same man as Macer II (30 below); he cannot be Tibullus' friend Macer (TIBULLUS 4). (VERGIL 1)

2. Albinovanus Pedo: *Pont.* 4.10, 4.16.6, and Sen. *Cont.* 2.2.12.

*PIR*² A 479; *RE* 1:1314 no. 5 and Suppl. 7:834 no. 2b. A fellow poet and erstwhile comrade to whose loyalty Ovid appealed in a letter of A.D. 14. He is plausibly identified with a Pedo who participated as a cavalry officer in Germanicus' German campaign the following year. His unusual nomen suggests that he is related to Horace's young friend Albinovanus Celsus (HORACE 2).

Albius Tibullus: see Tibullus.

3. ?Annaeus Seneca: Sen. *Cont.* 2.2.8–12, 7.1.27, and *Suas.* 3.7.

*PIR*² A 616; *RE* 1:2237–2240 no. 16; *eques.* The elder Seneca followed Ovid's performances when Ovid still practiced declamation; they may have been connected through a mutual friendship with Iunius Gallio (26 below).

4. Arellius Fuscus: Sen. *Cont.* 2.2.8.

*PIR*² A 1030; *RE* 2:635–637 no. 3. Ovid's preceptor in rhetoric in the 20s. A Greek of Asiatic origin, Arellius was one of the most celebrated declaimers of the age, both in Greek and in Latin.

5. Atticus: *Am.* 1.9, *Pont.* 2.4 and 2.7.

*PIR*² A 1333; *RE* 2:2239 no. 2. Known only from Ovid, Atticus was a valued literary adviser for at least two decades prior to Ovid's exile, and during the exile he received letters appealing for support. The dearth of detail about him and the ordinariness of his cognomen balk efforts to identify him with other known Attici.

6. (M. Aurelius) Cotta Maximus (Messalinus): *Pont.* 1.5, 1.7.31–34, 1.9, 2.2.99–100, 2.3, 2.8, 3.2, 3.5, and 4.16.41–44. *Pont.* 3.8, to "Maximus," may be to

Cotta or to Paullus Fabius Maximus (18 below); some of the *Tristia* to unnamed recipients are surely directed to Cotta (as perhaps 4.5).

PIR² A 1488; *RE* 2:2490–2491 no. 111, compare 110; *cos.* A.D. 20. Messalla Corvinus' younger son, with whom Ovid claimed an attachment dating from Cotta's infancy; he received six or more letters from exile which celebrate his distinction as an orator, mention his poetry, and encourage him to work on Ovid's behalf. An outspoken friend of the regime during his lifetime, he was later instanced by Juvenal (*Sat.* 7.95) as a munificent friend of poets.

7. Bassus: *Tr.* 4.10.47–48.

PIR² B 82; *RE* 3:107 no. 3. An iambic poet belonging to a group with whom Ovid associated in his youth. Bassus is plausibly identified with the like-named friend of Propertius (PROPERTIUS 4), but there are no grounds for linking him with the Bassus whom Horace mentions (HORACE 9).

8. Brutus: *Pont.* 1.1, 3.9, and 4.6.

PIR² B 171; *RE:* no entry. A sympathizer to whom Ovid sent a collection of his exilic poems; he is described as an orator with a record of vigorous prosecution. Ovid's friend is possibly but not probably to be identified with the obscure declaimer Bruttedius Brutus.

9. ?Camerinus: *Pont.* 4.16.19.

PIR² C 366; *RE* 3:1429 no. 1. Named in a catalog of contemporary poets as the author of a sequel to the *Iliad*. He may be Q. Sulpicius Camerinus, *cos.* A.D. 9 and scion of a noble family with literary interests (Juv. *Sat.* 7.90).

10. ?Capella: *Pont.* 4.16.36.

PIR² C 403; *RE* 3:1505 no. 2. Named in a catalog of contemporary poets as a writer of elegiac distichs, but otherwise unknown.

11. Carus: *Pont.* 4.13 and 4.16.7–8.

PIR² C 455; *RE* 3:1631–1632 no. 1. An otherwise unknown poet friend from whom Ovid sought assistance when he became the educator of Germanicus' sons Nero and Drusus.

12. (Cassius) Salanus: *Pont.* 2.5.

PIR² C 520; *RE* 3:1744 no. 86. An acquaintance whom Ovid encouraged to put his sympathy for Ovid into action. Salanus was an intimate of Germanicus, whom he had instructed in rhetoric and continued to train as an adult.

13. Celsus: *Pont.* 1.9.

PIR² C 638; *RE* 3:1882 no. 2. A friend of modest means and standing who had shared the favor of Cotta Maximus (6 above) and whose death Ovid lamented in about A.D. 13. Since he is not identified as a poet and his name is common, there is little to support an identification with Horace's friend Albinovanus Celsus (HORACE 2).

14. Cornelius Fidus: Sen. *Dial.* 2.17.1.

　　*PIR*² C 1360; *RE* 4:1312 no. 153. Ovid's son-in-law.

15. (Cornelius) Severus: *Pont.* 4.2 and 4.16.9.

　　*PIR*² C 1452; *RE* 4:1509–1510 no. 369. A friend and fellow poet whose work (on Roman historical themes) Ovid asked to have sent to him in Tomis. (*Pont.* 4.2.3 appears to preclude his identification with 51 below.)

16. ?Cotys: *Pont.* 2.9 (see also Rhoemetalces, 46 below).

　　*PIR*² C 1554; *RE* 11:1554 no. 2.8. A Thracian prince, son of King Rhoemetalces, to whom Ovid wrote extolling his martial and poetic prowess and begging him to keep Tomis safe from barbarian incursions. It is doubtful that Ovid had any prior acquaintance with him. Much earlier, Cotys was the subject of a poem by Antipater of Thessalonica (*Anth. Plan.* 75 = Gow-Page *Garland of Philip* 1:40, no. 48).

17. ?(Domitius) Marsus: *Pont.* 4.16.5.

　　*PIR*² D 153; *RE* 5:1430–1432 no. 66. Named in a catalog of contemporary poets, apparently as a writer of epic. Marsus is universally identified as the epigrammatist Domitius Marsus. (TIBULLUS 2, VERGIL 14)

18. (Paullus) Fabius Maximus: *Pont.* 1.2, 3.3, and 4.6.9–14. The Maximus of *Pont.* 3.8 may be either this man or Cotta Maximus (6 above).

　　*PIR*² F 47; *RE* 6:1780–1789 no. 102; *cos.* 11. A noble whose house Ovid had frequented before his exile and whose marriage he had celebrated in an epithalamium. Maximus received two or three letters from Tomis extolling his lineage and his oratory and urging him to intercede for Ovid with Augustus; a late poem laments his death in A.D. 14. Maximus was married to Augustus' cousin Marcia (32 below). Three decades earlier he had been a friend of Horace (HORACE 25).

19. ?Fontanus: *Pont.* 4.16.35.

　　*PIR*² F 461; *RE* 6:2841 no. 1. Named in a catalog of contemporary poets as a singer of the loves of satyrs and naiads, but otherwise unknown.

Germanicus: see Germanicus Iulius Caesar.

20. ?Gracchus: *Pont.* 4.16.31.

　　*PIR*² G 196; *RE* 2A:1371–1374 no. 41. Named in a catalog of contemporary poets as a tragedian. He is probably the Gracchus known as the author of an *Atalanta* and a *Thyestes,* and he may be the aristocrat Sempronius Gracchus, whose affair with Augustus' daughter Julia was exposed in the year 2.

21. ?Grattius: *Pont.* 4.16.34.

　　*PIR*² G 220; *RE* 7:1841–1846 no. 2. Named in a catalog of contemporary poets as the author of a didactic poem on hunting, of which over 500 lines are extant.

22. (Q.) Horatius (Flaccus): *Tr.* 4.10.49–50.

PIR[2] H 198; *RE* 8:2336–2399 no. 10; *eques.* The poet of the *Odes,* of which Ovid says he attended recitations in his youth. (TIBULLUS 3, VERGIL 21)

23. [Germanicus (Iulius Caesar)]: (selected references) *Pont.* 2.1.49–68, 2.5.41–76, 4.5.25–26, 4.8.21–88, *Fasti* 1.3–26, 63–64, and 285–286.

PIR[2] I 221; *RE* 10:435–464 no. 138; *cos.* A.D. 12 and 18. The prince whom Tiberius had adopted at Augustus' insistence received two letters from Ovid (*Pont.* 2.1 and 4.8) and the dedication of the *Fasti.* But the way in which Ovid appeals to him (especially at *Pont.* 4.8.81–82) and his preference for working through intermediaries show that they were not personally acquainted.

24. C. Iulius Hyginus: Suet. *Gr.* 20.2.

PIR[2] I 357; *RE* 10:628–651 no. 278. A freedman and librarian of Augustus and a prolific scholar who Suetonius says was "familiarissimus Ovidio poetae," though Ovid nowhere mentions him by name. It has been suggested on tenuous grounds that Hyginus is the unnamed recipient of *Tr.* 3.14 who is asked to give Ovid's books a haven in Rome and to excuse any defects they may contain.

25. ?(Iulius) Montanus: *Pont.* 4.16.11–12.

PIR[2] I 434; *RE* 10:681–682 no. 364. Named in a catalog of contemporary poets as an author of epic and elegiac works. Montanus is the long-lived Iulius Montanus who had frequented Vergil's recitations (VERGIL 23) and lived to experience both the favor and the displeasure of Tiberius.

26. (Iunius) Gallio: *Pont.* 4.11 and Sen. *Suas.* 3.7.

PIR[2] I 756; *RE* 10:1035–1039 no. 77; *senator.* A coeval and long-time friend of Ovid, from whom he received a *consolatio* on the death of his wife. Known mainly as a declaimer, Gallio had enjoyed the friendship of Messalla Corvinus and perhaps some relationship with Maecenas early in his career.

27. ?Largus: *Pont.* 4.16.17–18.

PIR[2] L 111; *RE* 12:837 no. 5. Named in a catalog of contemporary poets as the author of an epic on Antenor's migration to north Italy, but otherwise unknown.

28. ?Lupus: *Pont.* 4.16.25–26.

PIR[2] L 419; *RE* 13:1852 no. 10. Named in a catalog of contemporary poets as the author of an epic on the return of Menelaus and Helen to Sparta, but otherwise unknown.

29. Macer I: *Am.* 2.18, *Pont.* 2.10 and 4.16.6.

PIR[2] M 13a; *RE* 21:2276–2277 no. 92; P. White, *CQ* 42 (1992): 210–218. A fellow poet and long-time friend with whom Ovid had once traveled in Asia and Sicily and with whom he sought to renew communication from Tomis; Macer was also related in some way to Ovid's third wife and may have been a senator. The commonness of the cognomen makes it uncertain whether he is to be identified with Macer II (30 below) or with Tibullus' like-named friend (TIBULLUS 4). He cannot be either Aemilius Macer (1 above), who died in 16, or Pompeius Macer, son or grandson of Theophanes of Mytilene and a prominent equestrian official of Augustus' reign. His kinship with Ovid's wife and authorship of a Latin epic preclude a Greek background.

30. ?Macer II: Quint. *Inst.* 6.3.96.

PIR[1] P 472; *RE* 21:2276–2277 no. 92. Author of a *carmen tetrastichon* from which Ovid lifted verses to create a satiric cento attacking bad poets (who conceivably included Macer). His identity cannot be further determined, but see 1 and 29 above.

31. ?(C. Maecenas) Melissus: *Pont.* 4.16.30.

PIR[2] M 38; *RE* 15:532–534. Named in a catalog of contemporary poets as a comedian. Melissus was an Italian-born freedman of Maecenas who had been appointed by Augustus to organize the library of the Porticus Octaviae. In addition to creating comedies of a new type which he called *trabeatae,* he produced a voluminous series of anecdotal writings. (VERGIL 26)

32. Marcia: *Fasti* 6.802–809, *Tr.* 1.6.25–28, *Pont.* 1.2.137–142, and 3.1.78.

PIR[2] M 257; *RE* 14:1605–1606 no. 120. The wife of Paullus Fabius Maximus (18 above), whom Ovid praises for her nobility, beauty, and talent. Ovid's third wife had belonged to the entourage of Marcia, a tie to which Ovid appealed in letters to Maximus though he did not write directly to Marcia. Marcia was also a confidante of Livia.

33. ?Marius: *Pont.* 4.16.24.

PIR[2] M 290; *RE* 14:1810–1811 no. 8. Named in a catalog of contemporary poets as an adept of every genre, but otherwise unknown.

34. ?Numa: *Pont.* 4.16.10.

PIR[2] N 196; *RE* 17:1253 no. 3. Named as a writer of epic in Ovid's catalog of contemporary poets, but otherwise unknown.

35. ?*Passer: Pont.* 4.16.33. (N.B.: the line containing this reference is variously transmitted in the manuscripts and stands under suspicion of being corrupt.)

No entry in *PIR* or *RE*. If the text is sound and if Passer is a proper name, he is named as a bucolic writer in Ovid's catalog of contemporary poets.

36. Sex. Pompeius: *Pont.* 4.1, 4.4, 4.5, and 4.15.

PIR[1] P 450; *RE* 21:2265–2267 no. 62; *cos.* A.D. 14. A rich benefactor who had helped Ovid during his journey into exile and who received four letters entreating further support; the letters also compliment him on his consulate and allude to his connections in the palace, especially with Germanicus. Pompeius was later praised as a generous friend of *studia* by Valerius Maximus (4.7 *ext.* 2).

37. (C. Pomponius) Graecinus: *Am.* 2.10, *Pont.* 1.6, 1.10.37, 2.6, and 4.9.

PIR[1] P 540; *RE* Suppl. 14:440–441 no. 46c; *cos.* A.D. 16. A long-time comrade who pursued unspecified *studia* and *artes ingenuae* in the intervals of a military and administrative career. Graecinus assumed a coolness after Ovid's fall which Ovid tried to thaw in three letters written between A.D. 12 and 16, the last celebrating Graecinus' installation as consul. See also the following entry.

38. (L. Pomponius) Flaccus: *Pont.* 1.10 and 4.9.57–88 and 119–120.

PIR[1] P 538; *RE* Suppl. 14:439–440 no. 46a; *cos.* A.D. 17. The brother of Graecinus (37 above), Flaccus too received a plaintive letter from Ovid in about A.D. 13, but drew no further letters when shortly afterward he was serving as legate in the Danube region. Three years later Ovid made complimentary remarks about his exploits against the Getae and his upcoming consulate in a last letter to Graecinus.

39. Ponticus: *Tr.* 4.10.47–48.

PIR[1] P 587; *RE* 22:26–27. A writer of epic and one of the poets with whom Ovid remembers consorting in his youth. Ponticus is plausibly identified as the poet friend of Propertius (PROPERTIUS 17).

40. M. Porcius Latro: Sen. *Cont.* 2.2.8.

PIR[1] P 638; *RE* 22:233–235 no. 49. A professor of oratory whose performances the young Ovid used to frequent and whose *sententiae* he sometimes adapted in his poems.

41. ?Priscus I: *Pont.* 4.16.10.

PIR[1] P 714; *RE* 23:3 no. 1. One of a pair of like-named writers *(uterque Priscus)* named in a catalog of contemporary poets among the writers of epic. The name is common, but it has often been suggested that one of the two poets may be the *eques* Clutorius Priscus who composed a lament on the death of Germanicus and perished for a premature lament on the demise of Tiberius' son Drusus (Tac. *Ann.* 3.49.1).

42. ?Priscus II: *Pont.* 4.16.10.

See the preceding entry.

43. ?Proculus: *Pont.* 4.16.32.

PIR[1] P 740; *RE* 23:74 no. 1. Named in a catalog of contemporary poets as an imitator of Callimachus, but otherwise unknown.

44. (Sex.) Propertius: *Tr.* 4.10.45–48.

PIR[1] P 752; *RE* 23:758–796 no. 2. The elegist, whose recitations Ovid frequented as a youth and whom along with Ponticus and Bassus Ovid describes as comrades. (VERGIL 39)

45. ?Rabirius: *Pont.* 4.16.5.

PIR[1] R 1a; *RE* 1A:28–29 no. 7. Named in Ovid's catalog of contemporary poets as a writer of epic, Rabirius is represented only by fragments, including some from an epic on Augustus' defeat of Antony at Alexandria.

46. ?Rhoemetalces: *Pont.* 1.8.16–24, 2.9.38–46, and 4.7.25–26.

PIR[1] R 50; *RE* 1A:1003–1004 no. 1. The aged king of Thrace and father of the prince Cotys (16 above); though Ovid extols his valor against invading hordes, it is unlikely that he and Ovid were personally acquainted. (Most authorities believe that Rhoemetalces was already dead when Ovid wrote and that *Pont.* 1.8.16–24 and 4.7.25 concern the son rather than the father.)

47. Rufinus: *Pont.* 1.3 and 3.4.

PIR: no entry, but compare *PIR*[1] V 394; *RE:* no entry, but compare 8A: 1979–1981 no. 48; R. Syme, *History in Ovid* (Oxford, 1978), pp. 83–87. A friend to whose message of consolation Ovid responded with two letters of his own and a copy of his poem on Tiberius' Pannonian triumph; Rufinus appears to be a man of letters and possibly a poet. His name has prompted attempts to link him with a Vibius Rufinus known as a botanical writer and with a C. Vibius Rufinus who governed Germany in A.D. 43–45, but a cognomen remains the only trait they have in common.

48. Rufus I: *Pont.* 2.11.

PIR[1] R 131; *RE* 1A:1204 no. 1. A notable of Fundi and the *avunculus* of Ovid's third wife, whom Ovid thanked for looking after his affairs in Rome. Nothing in the letter suggests a connection with any other known Rufus.

49. ?Rufus II: *Pont.* 4.16.27–28.

PIR[1] R 130; *RE:* no entry. Named in a catalog of contemporary poets as the author of lyrics in Pindar's manner. The choice of genre has prompted suggestions that this Rufus may be the lyric poet Titius whom Horace knew (HORACE 84), since Titii Rufi of this period are known; but both Titius and Rufus are very common names. There is nothing to connect Ovid's poet with the Titius whom Tibullus knew (TIBULLUS 7).

50. Sabinus: *Am.* 2.18.27–34 and *Pont.* 4.16.15–16.

PIR[1] S 23; *RE* 1A:1598–1599 no. 21. A long-time friend recently deceased in A.D. 16; Sabinus wrote companion poems to some of Ovid's *Heroides* and a calendar poem. He shares a common cognomen and nothing else with friends of Horace (HORACE 73) and of Vergil (VERGIL 41).

51. Severus: *Pont.* 1.8.

No entry in *PIR* or *RE*. A well-to-do former comrade who received a letter recalling all that the exiled Ovid missed about life in Rome. (*Pont.* 4.2.3 appears to preclude identification of this man with 15 above.)

52. (P.) Suillius (Rufus): *Pont.* 4.8.

PIR[1] S 700; *RE* 4A:719–722 no. 4; senator. The husband of Ovid's step-daughter, Suillius received a letter asking him to intercede with Germanicus at about the time he became Germanicus' quaestor.

53. [Tibullus]: *Am.* 3.9 and *Tr.* 4.10.51–52.

PIR[2] A 484; *RE* 1:1319–1329 no. 12; *eques.* Although Tibullus was the subject of an elegiac lament by Ovid and although both poets were protégés of Messalla Corvinus, Ovid's comment at *Tr.* 4.10.51–52 appears to preclude the possibility that he and Ovid were personally acquainted. (HORACE 3, VERGIL 47)

54. ?Trinacrius: *Pont.* 4.16.25. (N.B.: *Trinacrius* here may not be a personal name, but an ethnic attached to the noun *auctor.*)

No entry in *PIR* or *RE*. Named in a catalog of contemporary poets as the author of a *Perseis,* but otherwise unknown.

55. ?Turranius: *Pont.* 4.16.29.

PIR[1] T 295; *RE* 7A:1440 no. 3. Named in a catalog of contemporary poets as a tragedian. Both senatorial and equestrian Turranii are on record during this period, but no definite link can be drawn between the tragedian and any of them.

56. ?Tuscus: *Pont.* 4.16.20.

PIR[1] T 306; *RE* 7A:1491–1492 no. 1. Named in a catalog of contemporary poets as author of a poem on "Phyllis," who may be either the mythical heroine or Tuscus' pseudonymous mistress. It has often been thought that Ovid's Tuscus is the friend to whom Propertius assigns the pseudonym "Demophoon," though Propertius gives no indication that his friend is a poet (PROPERTIUS 20).

57. Tuticanus: *Pont.* 4.12, 4.14, and 4.16.27.

PIR[1] T 314; *RE* 7A:1611–1612 no. 2. A long-time partner in Ovid's poetic activities who produced in his own right an epic *Phaeacis* and who received two of Ovid's letters from exile. Ovid indicates that Tuticanus also pursued an equestrian or senatorial career, and a senatorial family of this name is attested during the first century B.C. Tuticanus' name may lurk behind the corrupt ascription of a quatrain in the *Greek Anthology* (*Anth. Pal.* 5.49 = Page *Further Greek Epigrams,* pp. 60–61).

58. (M. Valerius Messalla Corvinus): *Tr.* 4.4.3–6 and 27–34, *Pont.* 1.7.27–30, 2.2.1 and 97–98, 2.3.69–78, and 3.5.7.

PIR[1] V 90; *RE* 8A:131–157 and 2389–2390 no. 261; *cos.* 31. An aristocrat to whom Ovid had attached himself by 15 at the latest and whom he credits with encouraging his early endeavors in poetry. Ovid wrote a poem on the occasion of Messalla's death in A.D. 8 or 12 and later extolled his nobility and eloquence in letters to his sons (6 above and 59 below). It is sometimes suggested that the "Lygdamus" poems of the Tibullan corpus are Ovidian and that their presence in the Corpus Tibullianum reflects his early connection with Messalla. (HORACE 86, TIBULLUS 8, VERGIL 48)

59. (M. Valerius Messalla) Messalinus: *Pont.* 1.7, 2.2, and 2.3.79–80; Messalinus must be the unnamed recipient of *Tr.* 4.4 as well.

PIR¹ V 93; *RE* 8A:159–162 no. 264; *cos.* 3. Messalla Corvinus' elder son, with whom Ovid by his own account had a weaker connection than with the other son (6 above). In three letters written between A.D. 11 and 13 Ovid tries to make the best of their acquaintance, complimenting Messalinus on his military and civil distinctions and urging him to use his eloquence and his intimacy with Augustus on Ovid's behalf. (TIBULLUS 9)

60. ?Varius: *Pont.* 4.16.31. (N.B.: as often with this name, some manuscripts read *Varus*.)

PIR¹ V 202; *RE* 8A:425–426 no. 3. Named in a catalog of contemporary poets as a tragedian. This Varius is often identified with L. Varius Rufus, the friend of Vergil (VERGIL 51) and Horace (HORACE 89) and the author of a *Thyestes* produced in 29. But that identification would make Varius almost a generation older than the other poets in Ovid's catalog, and the name is common.

61. [(P.) Vergilius (Maro)]: *Tr.* 4.10.51.

PIR¹ V 279; *RE* 8A:1021–1506 no. 7. The poet of the *Aeneid,* whom Ovid says that he saw but did not have occasion to know as a young man. (HORACE 91, PROPERTIUS 21, TIBULLUS 10)

62. ?Vestalis: *Pont.* 4.7.

PIR¹ V 302; *RE* 8A:1776–1778. Vestalis was a centurion and district administrator attached to the Roman army of the lower Danube, where he received a letter from Ovid praising his valor during a siege by Getic marauders. He is known only from Ovid, and it is unlikely that Ovid had any prior acquaintance with him.

63. P. *Vinicius*: Sen. *Cont.* 10.4.25.

PIR¹ V 446; *RE* 9A:119–120 no. 8; *cos.* A.D. 2. Vinicius is said to have been a "summus amator Ovidi" by the elder Seneca, but the fondness meant is evidently literary, not personal (compare *Cont.* 7.3.8).

Appendix 2C: Connections of Propertius

Except for Hostia and Ovid, Propertius' connections are known solely from his poems, which yield scant information about them. A quarter of the following entries are persons mentioned in the Cornelia elegy (4.11), undoubtedly written to gratify some living recipient, though it is impossible to know who that person was or whether it was anyone mentioned in the poem. Persons known only by pseudonyms are not registered, though these include some of Propertius' closest friends (Lynceus, Lycotas, and perhaps Panthus; for Demophoon, see 20 below).

Aelia Galla: see Laelia Galla.

1. ?L. Aemilius Paullus: Prop. 4.11.63–64, 85–96.

> *PIR*² A 392; *RE* 1:580 no. 115; *cos.* A.D. 1. A young son whom Cornelia commits to the care of his father (3 below) in the valedictory Propertius has her speak on the occasion of her death.

2. ?M. Aemilius Lepidus: Prop. 4.11.63–64, 85–96.

> *PIR*² A 369; *RE* 1:561–563 no. 75; *cos.* A.D. 6. A young son whom Cornelia commits to the care of his father (3 below) in the valedictory Propertius has her speak on the occasion of her death.

3. ?Paullus Aemilius Lepidus: Prop. 4.11.

> *PIR*² A 373; *RE* 1:565–566 no. 82; *cos.* 34, *cens.* 22. Widower of Cornelia and principal addressee of the valedictory Propertius has her utter from beyond the tomb. After Cornelia's death he married Augustus' niece the younger Marcella.

4. Bassus: Prop. 1.4.

> *PIR*² B 82; *RE* 3:107 no. 3. A companion whose praise of other beauties elicited a poem on the unsurpassable beauty of Cynthia; it may be implicit that Bassus too is a poet. He is universally identified with the poet whom the young Ovid knew (OVID 7). But there is no basis for connecting him with the Bassus whom Horace mentions (HORACE 9).

5. ?M. Claudius Marcellus: Prop. 3.18.

> *PIR*² C 925; *RE* 3:2764–2770 no. 230; *aed.* 23. Augustus' nephew and son-in-law, whose untimely death in 23 elicited from Propertius a poem deploring the frailty of human hopes. (HORACE 19, VERGIL 9)

6. ?Cornelia: Prop. 4.11.

> *PIR*² C 1475; *RE* 4:1597 no. 419. An aristocratic matron whose death elicited from Propertius an elegy in the form of a valedictory from the mouth of Cornelia herself. Efforts to define her place within her *gens* have been impeded by the abundance of contemporary Cornelii and the obscurity of their interrelationships. Her death is usually dated to the year 16, when a P. Cornelius Scipio who might be the consul she identifies as her brother is recorded in the *fasti*. But the brother could be the consul of 18, P. Cornelius Lentulus Marcellinus, in which case her death would be slightly earlier.

7. ?Cornelius: Prop. 4.11.65–66.

> *PIR*² C 1438, compare 1395; *RE* 4:1438 no. 333, compare 4:1391 no. 233; R. Syme, *The Augustan Aristocracy* (Oxford, 1986), pp. 245–253; senator. A brother whom Cornelia compliments on reaching the consulate in the funeral elegy

Propertius has her utter. He is most often identified as P. Cornelius Scipio, consul in 16, but could be the consul of 18, P. Cornelius Lentulus Marcellinus. Either man should be approximately Propertius' coeval.

8. Gallus I: Prop. 1.5, 1.10, 1.13, and 1.20.

No entry in *PIR* or *RE*. A young aristocrat and close friend whose amatory pursuits partly overlap with Propertius' own. The last poem to Gallus is a short mythological narrative offered in token of friendship, but there is no indication that Gallus is himself a poet. If *nobilitas* and *priscae imagines* at 1.5.23–24 imply consular ancestry, and if it derives from Gallus' father rather than his mother, and if his cognomen was borne before him by others in the family, he may be related to L. Caninius Gallus (*cos.* 37). But identification would be baffled if any of these assumptions were incorrect, and the cognomen is very common. Propertius' aristocratic friend cannot be Vergil's friend Cornelius Gallus (VERGIL 11).

9. ?Gallus II: Prop. 1.21.

No entry in *PIR* or *RE*. On the evidence of the most inscrutable poem in the Propertian corpus, Gallus was a soldier mortally wounded as he fled from the battle of Perusia in 40. That he had some relationship to Propertius is an inference from the fact that Propertius devotes a sympathetic poem to him, but he is otherwise unknown.

10. Hostia: Apul. *Apol.* 10.

PIR[2] H 231; *RE* 8:2517 no. 6. "Hostia" is given on the authority of Apuleius as the true name of Propertius' pseudonymous mistress Cynthia. This datum has often been combined with details Propertius gives about an unnamed woman he invites to become his lover in 3.20, who belongs to a *fortunata domus* and is descended from a *doctus avus*. The *avus* has been thought to be the poet Hostius, known as the author of a *Bellum Histricum* written a hundred years earlier.

11. ?Iulia: Prop. 3.18.12 and 4.11.59–60.

PIR[2] I 634; *RE* 10:896–906 no. 550. Augustus' daughter is twice noticed in Propertius' poems. An elegy on the death of Augustus' son-in-law (5 above) cites as one of his distinctions his connection with the house of Augustus. And in the elegy for Cornelia (6 above), Propertius has Cornelia boast that she has been deemed worthy to be Julia's (half) sister.

12. Laelia Galla: Prop. 3.12. (N.B.: *Aelia* is the modern vulgate for a reading given as *L(a)el(l)ia* by all manuscripts of Propertius at 3.12.38; the text was emended solely in order to connect Propertius' Galla with a known family.)

PIR[2] A 294; *RE* 1:539 no. 173. The youthful wife whom Propertius' friend Postumus left behind as he embarked on military service. Laelia Galla is otherwise unknown, but in the guise of Aelia Galla she is generally identified as a relation of Aelius Gallus, Prefect of Egypt in the years 26 and 25.

13. C. Maecenas: Prop. 2.1 and 3.9.

*PIR*² M 37; *RE* 14:207–229 no. 6; *eques*. Propertius boasted of gaining the favor of Maecenas (whose closeness to Augustus he celebrates) and meditated on his advice about pursuing grand poetic themes. As a resident of the Esquiline (3.23.24, 4.8), Propertius was perhaps a neighbor of Maecenas. (HORACE 40, VERGIL 25)

14. ?Octavia: Prop. 3.18.11–14.

*PIR*² O 66; *RE* 17:1859–1868 no. 96. Augustus' sister, whose son Marcellus' death in 23 elicited a poetic lament in which Propertius highlights Octavia's role in managing her son's career. (HORACE 53, VERGIL 31)

15. P. Ovidius Naso

*PIR*² O 180; *RE* 18:1910–1986 no. 3; *eques*. For Propertius' connection with Ovid, see OVID 44. (HORACE 58, TIBULLUS 5, VERGIL 34)

16. Paetus: Prop. 3.7.

No entry in *PIR* or *RE*. An otherwise unknown younger friend of Propertius, scion of a not prosperous Italian family, who drowned while sailing to seek his fortune; Propertius made his death the subject of a cautionary elegy.

17. Ponticus: Prop. 1.7 and 1.9.

*PIR*¹ P 587; *RE* 22:26–27. A fellow poet whom Propertius urged to abandon an epic on Eteocles and Polynices and to record in verse his new-found experience of love. Ponticus must be the poet whom the young Ovid knew (OVID 39).

18. Postumus: Prop. 3.12.

*PIR*¹ P 672; *RE* 22:986–987 no. 5. Recipient of a poem chiding him for leaving behind a young wife (12 above) for the sake of a military adventure in the East. Postumus' link with Propertius, the presumed connections of his wife, and the generally complimentary tone of the poem have encouraged speculation that Postumus may be the senator C. Propertius Postumus known from an Augustan inscription (*ILS* 914). But Propertius does not intimate that Postumus is a kinsman, the cognomen Postumus is of no use in establishing family connections, the senator's *cursus* gives no indication that he saw army service outside Rome, and his tribe is not the tribe of Propertius' town or region. Propertius' friend cannot be the Postumus who received a Horatian ode at about the same time (HORACE 66): Horace's friend should be older.

19. ?Scribonia: Prop. 4.11.31 and 55–57.

*PIR*¹ S 220; *RE* 2A:891–892 no. 32; R. Syme, *The Augustan Aristocracy* (Oxford, 1986), pp. 247–249. The mother both of Augustus' daughter (11 above) and of the Cornelia who is the subject of a Propertian elegy (6 above); in it Propertius has Cornelia ask her mother to bear witness that her life has been without blemish. Scribonia was briefly the wife of Augustus in 40–39, but

Cornelia was the product of one of two earlier unions which remain to be clarified.

20. *Tuscus*: Prop. 2.22 and Ov. *Pont.* 4.16.20.

PIR[1] T 306; *RE* 7A:1491–1492 no. 1. Propertius 2.22 is addressed to a pseudonymous friend "Demophoon" about whom no details are given, but whose name recalls a mythical son of Theseus who wooed and abandoned a Thracian princess, Phyllis. Ovid later names among the poets of his generation a Tuscus (OVID 56) who gained renown for his "Phyllis"; she should be either the heroine, whose tale Tuscus will have retold in verse, or Tuscus' own mistress, celebrated under the pseudonym of Phyllis in his love poems. Many have drawn the tenuous conclusion that she is the mistress and that Propertius used "Demophoon" as a matching pseudonym for Tuscus. If "Demophoon" really is Tuscus, "Phyllis" must have enjoyed an unusually prolonged career as his mistress.

21. ?P. Vergilius Maro: Prop. 2.34.61–80, Don. *Vita Verg.* 30 Hardie, Donatus Auctus p. 30.43–45 Brummer = pp. 360.143–362.146 Bayer.

PIR[1] V 279; *RE* 8A:1021–1506 no. 7. In his most fulsome tribute to any poet, living or dead, Propertius praised Vergil's *Eclogues* and *Georgics* and foretold the greatness of the Aeneas epic then in progress (notice in this connection Sen. *Suas.* 3.5). Propertius also resided on the Esquiline, where Vergil kept a townhouse (Prop. 3.23.24, 4.8, Don. *Vita Verg.* 13 Hardie). (HORACE 91, OVID 61, TIBULLUS 10)

22. (Volcacius) Tullus: Prop. 1.1, 1.6, 1.14, 1.22, and 3.22.

PIR[1] V 624; *RE* Suppl. 9:1837 no. 17. A wealthy young aristocrat whom despite his youth Propertius treated with deference and who received from him more poems than anyone else. Though Propertius frequented his house in Rome, he declined an invitation in 30 or 29 to tour Asia with the entourage of Tullus' *patruus,* the proconsul L. Volcacius Tullus. A few years later Propertius urged his friend to return from Asia in order to marry and embark upon a senatorial career. Tullus is known only from Propertius.

Appendix 2D: Connections of Tibullus

The following list presupposes that Tibullus is the author of books 1 and 2 of the *Corpus Tibullianum* but of nothing else in it, except perhaps 3.19.

Aemilius Macer: see Macer.

1. Cornutus: Tib. 2.2, 2.3.1.

PIR[2] C 1507, compare C 34; *RE* 4:1635 no. 2. A recently married coeval for whom Tibullus wrote a birthday poem; he cannot be certainly identified with any other Cornutus of the period. A possible candidate is the M. (Caecilius) Cornutus attested as a colleague of Messalla Corvinus in the college of Arval

Brethren in 21 and 20, but Arval priests are generally older and more distinguished than Tibullus' friend appears to be.

2. ?Domitius Marsus: Domitius Marsus frag. 7, *FPL* p. 111 Morel = 143 Büchner.

    *PIR*² D 153; *RE* 5:1430–1432 no. 66. A quatrain by the epigrammatist lamenting the deaths of Tibullus and of Vergil may but need not indicate that Marsus and they had been friends. (OVID 17, VERGIL 14)

3. *Q. Horatius Flaccus*

    *PIR*² H 198; *RE* 8:2336–2399 no. 10. For Horace's possible connection with Tibullus, see HORACE 3. (OVID 22, VERGIL 21)

4. Macer: Tib. 2.6.1–6.

    No entry in *PIR* or *RE*. An erstwhile comrade in amatory pursuits who received a poem on the occasion of his departure for army service. The cognomen is too common to encourage identification with any other known bearer of the name. Tibullus' friend is often but mistakenly identified with the poet Aemilius Macer, who is reported to have died in Asia in 16. Tibullus gives no indication that Macer is a poet; he is surely not writing about someone fifty years old or more; and Asia proper in this period was not a theater of military operations. A less unlikely candidate would be the Macer who is Ovid's friend (OVID 29).

5. [P. Ovidius Naso]: Ov. *Am.* 3.9, *Tr.* 4.10.51–55.

    *PIR*² O 180; *RE* 18:1910–1986 no. 3. Although Ovid wrote an elegy on Tibullus' death and like Tibullus was a protégé of Messalla Corvinus, his comment at *Tr.* 4.10.51–52 rules out the possibility of a relationship with Tibullus. (HORACE 58, PROPERTIUS 15, VERGIL 34)

6. Plania: Apul. *Apol.* 10.

    PIR: no entry; *RE* 20:2187. "Plania" is given on the authority of Apuleius as the true name of Tibullus' pseudonymous mistress Delia. The name would imply that she was a Roman citizen of at least freedwoman status.

7. Titius: Tib. 1.4.73–76.

    *PIR*¹ T 195; *RE*: no entry. A friend whose marriage, evidently recent, Tibullus says has forestalled the presentation of a poem about the love of boys. He shares a not uncommon nomen with a poet friend of Horace (HORACE 84), but nothing indicates that he was a poet and he should be a little older than Horace's friend. Titius has also been linked with a poet Rufus mentioned by Ovid who may or may not be a Titius Rufus (OVID 49).

8. M. Valerius Messalla Corvinus: Tib. 1.1.53–54, 1.3.1–4 and 55–56, 1.5.31–34, 1.7, 2.1.31–36, 2.5.119–120, *Vita Tib.* p. 171 Lenz-Galinsky = 112 Luck.

    *PIR*¹ V 90; *RE* 8A:131–157 and 2389–2390 no. 261; *cos.* 31. Tibullus took part in Messalla's campaign against the Aquitani in 27 and may have accompanied him to Cilicia, Syria, and Egypt on an earlier tour of duty. After 27 he composed pieces in honor of Messalla's birthday and of his son's adlection into the college of *quindecimviri*. Compliments in other poems celebrate Messalla's past exploits as a warrior but never touch on his eminence in oratory. (HORACE 86, OVID 58, VERGIL 48)

9. ?M. Valerius Messalla Messalinus: Tib. 2.5.1–2, 17–18, 115–118, compare 1.7.55–56.

PIR[1] V 93; *RE* 8A:159–162 no. 264; *cos.* 3. Messalla Corvinus' son, whose installation in the college of *quindecimviri* elicited a poem that is more a compliment to the father than a sign of Tibullus' association with the son. (OVID 59)

10. ?P. Vergilius Maro: Domitius Marsus frag. 7, *FPL* p. 111 Morel = 143 Büchner.

PIR[1] V 279; *RE* 8A:1021–1506 no. 7. An elegiac quatrain by Domitius Marsus describes Tibullus as sent by Death to be the *comes* of Vergil in the underworld. The language may indicate that the two poets had been friends in life, or it may simply emphasize the quickness with which the death of one followed the death of the other. (HORACE 91, OVID 61, PROPERTIUS 21)

Appendix 2E: Connections of Vergil

Information about Vergil's connections is notoriously poor since his poems contain few mentions of his friends and contemporary testimony about them is thin. The sources which purport to know most belong to late antiquity or even later and must be regarded warily even when the particulars they relate are not manifestly fantastic. Entries for which I consider the sources dubious are indicated below, but many scholars would advocate a higher level of skepticism than I have shown.

Sources which duplicate information contained in earlier or more trustworthy sources and scholia which are no more than paraphrases of primary texts have generally been ignored. The set of names enumerated by Horace at *Serm.* 1.10.81–84 presents a special problem. They are most obviously, of course, friends of Horace. But since Horace may have wanted them to be seen as members of a coterie around Maecenas and since Vergil is one of them, I have listed them as (questionable) associates of Vergil.

1. *Aemilius Macer*: Filargirius on *Ecl.* 5.1, Filargirius and *Schol. Bern.* on *Ecl.* 7, *Schol. Bern.* on *Ecl.* 9, *Vita Monacensis* p. 57.51 Brummer = p. 334.53 Bayer, and *Vita Noricensis* p. 55.34 Brummer = p. 342.35–36 Bayer.

PIR[2] A 378; *RE* 1:567 no. 86. An older contemporary and a fellow poet

from the north (Verona), said on weak authority to have been Vergil's friend in
the 40s. But there is nothing intrinsically improbable about the friendship. Vergil is known to have borrowed lines from Macer's poems, and Macer was later
associated with Ovid (OVID 1).

2. *M. Antonius:* Filargirius on *Ecl.* 2 and 3 and *Vita Monacensis* p. 57.27–31
Brummer = p. 332.28–32 Bayer; compare *Schol. Bern.* on *Ecl.* 2.43.

RE 1:2595–2614 no. 30; *cos.* 44. The triumvir is identified in late commentaries as one of the men behind the masks of the *Eclogues* and more fantastically
in a late *vita* as Vergil's owner by marriage, who took him to Egypt as a *consili-
arius.*

3. ?Aristius Fuscus: Hor. *Serm.* 1.10.83.

*PIR*² A 1048; *RE* 2:906 no. 2. A *grammaticus* named by Horace along with
Vergil and others as possibly belonging to a literary coterie around Maecenas
(HORACE 7).

4. [Q. Asconius Pedianus]: Filargirius on *Ecl.* 3.104–105.

*PIR*² A 1206; *RE* 2:1524–1527 no. 3. A critic with whom Vergil is said to
have discussed the riddle of *Eclogues* 3.104–105. Asconius was a bona-fide Vergilian scholar, but he was born a decade after Vergil's death. Filargirius' note is
as bogus as the companion claim regarding Cornutus (13 below).

5. *C. Asinius Gallus:* Donatus Auctus *Vita Verg.* pp. 25.42–26.4 Brummer =
p. 356.71–73 Bayer.

*PIR*² A 1229; *RE* 2:1585–1588 no. 15; *cos.* 8. The son of Asinius Pollio (6
below), whose identification in late sources as a friend of Vergil results from a
confusion with *Cornelius* Gallus.

6. C. Asinius Pollio: (selected references) Verg. *Ecl.* 3.84–89, 4.11–14, 8.6–13
(uncertain), Apul. *Apol.* 10, Macr. *Sat.* 3.7.1, Hieron. *Chron.* 171 e Helm, Don.
Vita Verg. 9 and 19 Hardie, Donatus Auctus p. 22.32–33 Brummer = p. 354.49–
50 Bayer, p. 25.36–42 Brummer = pp. 354.65–356.71 Bayer, Servius *Vita Verg.*
p. 22.22–25 Hardie, *Vita Monacensis* p. 57.50–55 Brummer = p. 334.52–57
Bayer, Servius on *Ecl.* 2.1, 4.1, Servius Auctus on *Ecl.* 4.11, 8.10, 8.12, and 9.11,
Filargirius on *Ecl.* 3.88; compare Servius on *Aen.* 2.7, 6.554, 11.183.

*PIR*² A 1241; *RE* 2:1589–1602 no. 25; *cos.* 40. Hailed by Vergil as an admirer
of the *Eclogues* and a poet in his own right, Pollio was also the recipient of
Vergil's prophecy that the year of his consulship would witness the birth of a
wonder-child who would reinstate the Golden Age. (One interpretation which
sprang up within a generation of Vergil's lifetime held that the child was Pollio's
son, 5 above.) If Pollio rather than Augustus is the anonymous addressee of
Eclogue 8, he is lauded for exploits which have earned him a triumph (in 39)
and credited with instigating Vergil to write. In the late 40s Pollio was operating
as an Antonian army leader in and around northeast Italy; commentators of late

antiquity offer divergent stories of how he helped protect Vergil's lands from triumviral confiscations and speak of other *beneficia* he is supposed to have conferred. Pollio was earlier associated with the poets Catullus and Cinna (20 below) and with Vergil's friend Gallus (11 below), and he cultivated relations with many other literary figures after his retirement from active politics in 39. But the Asinius Pollio whom Servius cites as a commentator on Vergil may not be the consular, but a much later critic. (HORACE 8)

7. *Ballista:* Don. *Vita Verg.* 17 Hardie, *Vita Focae* p. 32.41–48 Hardie, Servius *Vita Verg.* p. 21.10–13 Hardie, Filargirius on *Ecl.* 1 *pr.*

RE 2:2829 no. 1. A schoolmaster by day and brigand by night whose demise is said to have inspired Vergil's first couplet; the *Vita Focae* depicts Ballista as the poet's own schoolmaster.

8. ?Q. Caecilius Epirota: Suet. *Gr.* 16.

*PIR*² C 42; *RE* 3:1201 no. 53. A freedman protégé of Vergil's friend Gallus (11 below) during the 30s; after Gallus' death he opened a school whose curriculum featured works of Vergil and other new poets. That Caecilius was a personal friend of Vergil as well as of Gallus is likely but not demonstrable.

9. ?M. Claudius Marcellus: Verg. *Aen.* 6.860–886, Don. *Vita Verg.* 32–33 Hardie, Servius on *Aen.* 6.861.

*PIR*² C 925; *RE* 3:2764–2770 no. 230; *aed.* 23. Augustus' nephew and son-in-law, whose death in 23 elicited a tribute which Vergil read before Augustus and Marcellus' mother Octavia. (HORACE 19, PROPERTIUS 5)

10. ?L. Cocceius Nerva: Hor. *Serm.* 1.5.28, 32, and 50.

*PIR*² C 1223; *RE* 4:130–131 and Suppl. 7:90 no. 12. See HORACE 22.

11. C. Cornelius Gallus: (selected references) Verg. *Ecl.* 6.64–73, 10, Don. *Vita Verg.* 19 Hardie, Servius on *Ecl.* 10.1, 10.46, *G.* 4.1, Probus, introduction to *Ecl.*, p. 328.2–5, 329.3–5 Thilo-Hagen, *Vita Monacensis* p. 57.50–54 Brummer = p. 334.52–57 Bayer, Filargirius on *Ecl.* 1 *pr.,* 3 *pr.,* 5.73, 7 *pr.* and 67, 9, and 10.

*PIR*² C 1369; *RE* 4:1342–1350 no. 164; *eques.* A fellow poet depicted as enjoying the special favor of the divine patrons of song; his tribulations as a poet of love are the theme of the *Tenth Eclogue,* which incidentally discloses that he had taken up service as a soldier. Vergilian lives and commentaries of late antiquity assign Gallus a role in protecting Vergil's property during the late 40s; the latest sources make them schoolmates a decade earlier. But Gallus leaves his first sure trace in the historical record in 43, as a protégé of Asinius Pollio (6 above). He soon attached himself to the young Augustus and emerged from the civil war as the first Roman governor of Egypt, but in 27 or 26 he was driven to suicide after incurring Augustus' displeasure. According to Servius, he was the subject of a tribute in Vergil's *Fourth Georgic* which was eliminated at Augustus' behest after Gallus' disgrace. See also 13 below.

12. *Q. Cornificius: Schol. Ver.* on *Ecl.* 7.22, Filargirius on *Ecl.* 2, 3, 5, 7 and 8, and Donatus Auctus *Vita Verg.* p. 32.3–4 Brummer = p. 364.191–194 Bayer.

   RE 4:1624–1630 no. 8; E. Rawson, *CQ* 28 (1978): 188–201; senator. A fellow poet who in late Vergilian lore generally figures as a rival of Vergil but sometimes as a friend. Though the sources lack credit, there is nothing improbable about the association. Cornificius had been a friend of Catullus; in the civil war he was at first a Caesarean partisan, but died fighting on the side of the senate in 41. See also 13 below.

13. [Cornutus]: Filargirius and *Schol. Bern.* on *Ecl.* 3.105.

   *PIR*² A 609; *RE* 1:2225–2226 no. 5. An alleged source who reported hearing from Vergil the true explanation of the riddle propounded at *Ecl.* 3.104–105. Since the Vergilian commentator L. Annaeus Cornutus lived too late to have been personally acquainted with Vergil, the name is often emended, either to Cornificius, a reading found in some manuscripts of the Filargirius commentary, or to Cornelius, on the assumption that Cornelius Gallus or Cornelius Balbus the younger is meant. But it is more likely that the testimony of Filargirius here is simply unreliable, as in the companion note about Asconius Pedianus (4 above).

14. ?Domitius Marsus: Domitius Marsus 7, *FPL* p. 111 Morel = 143 Büchner.

   *PIR*² D 153; *RE* 5:1430–1432 no. 66. A quatrain lamenting Vergil's death in 19 together with Marsus' tie to Maecenas may but need not imply that Marsus was a friend of Vergil. (OVID 17, TIBULLUS 2)

15. *Epidius: Vita Bern.* p. 67.6–11 Brummer = p. 248.3–7 Bayer.

   RE 6:59 no. 2. Teacher of oratory at Rome in whose school Vergil allegedly became acquainted with Augustus. That Epidius taught the young Augustus is known from Suet. *Gr.* 28.1; that he taught Vergil at the same time has been doubted in view of the seven-year age difference between Vergil and Augustus and the weak authority of the source.

16. Eros: Don. *Vita Verg.* 34 Hardie.

   *PIR*² E 87; *RE:* no entry. A freedman and copyist of Vergil.

17. Flaccus: Don. *Vita Verg.* 14 Hardie, Filargirius on *Ecl.* 5.20; *Schol. Bern. Ecl.* 5 *pr., Anth. Lat.* 778 Riese; compare Pseudo-Acro on Hor. *Carm.* 1.24.1.

   *PIR*¹ V 277; *RE:* no entry. A brother of Vergil who died in early manhood, and who some ancient commentators believed was commemorated by Vergil under the figure of Daphnis in the *Fifth Eclogue*.

18. ?C. Fonteius Capito: Hor. *Serm.* 1.5.32 and 38.

   *PIR*² F 469; *RE* 6:2847 and Suppl. 3:528 no. 20; *cos.* 33. See HORACE 26.

19. ?Heliodorus: Hor. *Serm.* 1.5.2.

See HORACE 29.

20. ?C. Helvius Cinna: Verg. *Ecl.* 9.35–36.

RE 8:225–228 no. 11; *trib.* 44. A poet from north Italy (Brixia), who the goatherd Lycidas of the *Ninth Eclogue* says excels him in musical talent. In the 50s Cinna was associated with both Catullus and Asinius Pollio (6 above), but he died in 44 and so could not have been alive at the time of Vergil's tribute.

21. Q. Horatius Flaccus

*PIR*² H 198; *RE* 8:2336–2399 no. 10; *eques*. For the relationship between Vergil and Horace, see HORACE 91. (OVID 22, TIBULLUS 3)

22. C. Iulius Caesar Augustus: (selected references) Verg. *Ecl.* 1.6–10 and 42–45 (uncertain), 8.6–13 with scholia (uncertain), *G.* 1.24–42, 498–501, 2.170–172, 3.12–48, 4.559–562, *Aen.* 1.286–296 (uncertain), 6.789–807, 7.601–606, 8.675–728, Hor. *Epist.* 2.1.245–247 (with Pseudo-Acro), [Verg.] *Cul.* 1–10, 25–41, Pliny *HNat.* 7.114, Tac. *Dial.* 13.1–2, Claud. *carm. min.* 40.23, Macr. *Sat.* 1.24.10, Prisc. *GL* 2:533.13 Keil, Don. *Vita Verg.* 12, 21, 27, 31–32, 35, 37–38, 41 Hardie, Servius *Vita Verg.* p. 22.17–23 and 27–31 Hardie, and notes on *Ecl.* 3.74, 10.1, *G.* 4.1, *Aen.* 4.324, 6.230, 6.861, Servius Auctus on *Ecl.* 9.11, *Vita Probiana* p. 27.14–16 Hardie, *Vita Bern.* p. 67.6–11 Brummer = p. 248.3–9 Bayer, Donatus Auctus *Vita Verg.* pp. 21.37–22.33 Brummer = pp. 350.5–354.50 Bayer, p. 23.38–39 Brummer = p. 354.55–56 Bayer, p. 25.22–25 Brummer = p. 354.59–63 Bayer, pp. 28.34–29.1 Brummer = p. 360.118–130 Bayer, p. 31.5–29 Brummer = p. 362.151–171 Bayer, p. 31.32–36 Brummer = p. 364.175–179 Bayer, p. 32.9–46 Brummer = pp. 366.201–368.241 Bayer.

*PIR*² I 215; *RE* 10:275–381 no. 132. Augustus is commonly recognized in the anonymous *iuvenis* of the *First Eclogue* who guarantees the shepherd Tityrus possession of his holding; if Tityrus represents Vergil, the poem takes the relationship back at least to the late 40s. Lives and commentaries of late antiquity add abundant but discordant particulars about Augustus' role in the seizure and restitution of Vergil's property during the triumviral confiscations. The *Culex* and some very late sources (Donatus Auctus and the *Vita Bernensis*) stretch his acquaintance with Vergil back to a time when both are said to have been schoolmates, despite a seven-year difference in their ages. The least problematic evidence begins with roughly the last decade of Vergil's life. In the *Georgics* Vergil paid lavish tribute to Augustus, who summoned him for a private reading of the work in 29. (According to Servius, Augustus later pressured Vergil to excise from book 4 all mention of a protégé and functionary who had fallen out of favor.) Palace readings are again attested for parts of the *Aeneid,* which also accorded a place of honor to Augustus. Fragments are extant of letters between Augustus and Vergil, and several sources allude to large gifts from Augustus. In 19, while en route to the East, Vergil encountered Augustus at Athens and was traveling with him when he fell fatally ill. His will named Augustus heir to the second largest share of his estate. Contrary to the poet's expressed desire that any unfinished work be suppressed, Augustus had Varius and Tucca put in order and publish the draft of the *Aeneid* Vergil had entrusted to them. (HORACE 31)

23. ?Iulius Montanus: Don. *Vita Verg.* 29 Hardie.

*PIR*² I 434; *RE* 10:681–682 no. 364. A poet who had heard and admired Vergil's recitations of his poetry. (OVID 25)

24. *T. Lucretius Carus: Vita Monacensis* p. 56.9 Brummer = p. 330.9 Bayer; *Vita Noricensis* p. 54.10 Brummer = p. 340.5 Bayer, *Vita Gud.* I p. 56.14–15 Brummer = p. 252.16 Bayer.

RE 13:1659–1683 no. 17. The poet of the *De rerum natura,* identified in late lives as the brother of Vergil's mother Magia (27 below).

25. C. Maecenas: Verg. *G.* 1.2, 2.39–46, 3.40–45, 4.1–5, Hor. *Serm.* 1.5.39–104, 1.6.54–55, 1.10.81, Sen. *Suas.* 1.12, 2.20, 3.5, *Laus Pis.* 230–237, Sen. *Epist.* 101.13, Calp. *Ecl.* 4.160–163, Martial 1.107.4, 7.29.7, 8.55, 12.3, Don. *Vita Verg.* 13, 20, 27, 37, and 44 Hardie, Servius *Vita Verg.* p. 22.22–27 Hardie, Servius on *Ecl.* 2.15, Servius Auctus on *Ecl.* 5.55, *Aen.* 8.310, Filargirius on *Ecl.* 6.20, *Schol. Bern.* on *Ecl.* 6.17, *Vita Probiana* p. 27.9–10 Hardie, *Vita Monacensis* p. 57.50–54 Brummer = p. 334.52–55 Bayer, Donatus Auctus p. 31.36–41 Brummer = p. 364.179–184 Bayer, p. 32.18–19 Brummer = p. 366.210–211 Bayer.

*PIR*² M 37; *RE* 14:207–229 no. 6; *eques.* Vergilian lives of late antiquity carry Maecenas' friendship with Vergil back to the late 40s or early 30s when he helped protect property imperiled by triumviral resettlement; Maecenas is also said to have introduced Vergil to the future Augustus at this time. Vergil had certainly gained Maecenas' friendship by about 38, when he introduced Horace to him. A year or so later, he and other literary friends accompanied Maecenas on a leisurely diplomatic mission. At the end of the decade he addressed the *Georgics* to Maecenas, who he says instigated the work, and he and Maecenas arranged for Augustus to hear a reading of it when he returned to Italy in 29. Vergil eventually owned a townhouse on the Esquiline near Maecenas' estate there. Several sources offer confused particulars about slave-boys or slave-girls of Maecenas of whom Vergil was enamored. Maecenas was one of the heirs named in Vergil's will, and he continued to be a zealous promoter of the poet's work and reputation after Vergil's death in 19. (HORACE 40, PROPERTIUS 13)

26. C. Maecenas Melissus: Don. *Vita Verg.* 16 Hardie.

*PIR*² M 38; *RE* 15:532–534. A contemporary who recorded a personal reminiscence of Vergil. Melissus is plausibly identified as Maecenas' freedman, active as a *grammaticus,* imperial librarian, and comic playwright. (OVID 31)

27. Magia (Polla?): Don. *Vita Verg.* 1–3, 14 Hardie, [Verg.] *Cat.* 8, *Vita Probiana* p. 26.2, 27.18 Hardie, *Vita Focae* p. 31.11–19 Hardie, *Vita Monacensis* p. 56.6–14 Brummer = p. 330.5–14 Bayer; compare *Schol. Bern.* on *Ecl.* 5.22 (the name *Maia* generally appears in place of *Magia* in later sources).

    RE 14:442 no. 21. Vergil's mother, the daughter of a *viator* and small landholder in the region of Mantua; she is said to have survived into Vergil's early adulthood and to have married a second time.

28. ?Messius Cicirrus: Hor. *Serm.* 1.5.51–70.

    *PIR*² M 517; *RE* 15:1244 no. 6. See HORACE 44.

29. ?Murena: Hor. *Serm.* 1.5.38.

    *PIR*¹ T 74; *RE* 5A:707 no. 92; senator. See HORACE 48.

30. *Musa:* [Verg.] *Cat.* 4.

    *PIR*² O 18; *RE* 17:1851–1852 no. 73. A gifted *iuvenis* to whose friendship the poet of *Catalepton* 4 asks to be admitted. The only other Musa who can be connected with Vergil is an Octavius Musa mentioned in Vergilian commentaries: Servius Auctus at *Ecl.* 9.7 says that he was a triumviral surveyor who expropriated Mantuan territory; Filargirius at *Ecl.* 8.6 says that he was a Mantuan magistrate who alienated the commissioner in charge of expropriations. Musa and Octavius Musa are generally amalgamated with Octavius I (32 below) and Octavius II (33 below).

31. ?Octavia: Don. *Vita Verg.* 32 Hardie, Servius on *Aen.* 6.861; Donatus Auctus p. 27.6–7 Brummer = p. 356.90–91 Bayer, compare *Vita Monacensis* p. 57.27–31 Brummer = p. 332.28–30 Bayer.

    *PIR*² O 66; *RE* 17:1859–1868 no. 96. Marcellus' mother, who attended a palace recitation at which Vergil read his tribute to her deceased son; according to the interpolated version of Donatus' life, she rewarded Vergil lavishly on that occasion. (HORACE 53, PROPERTIUS 14)

32. ?Octavius I: Hor. *Serm.* 1.10.82.

    *PIR*² O 18; *RE* 17:1851–1852 no. 73. Named by Horace with Vergil and others as possibly belonging to a literary coterie around Maecenas (HORACE 54). The name is very common, but this man is generally conflated with Musa (30 above) and with Octavius II (33 below).

33. *Octavius II:* [Verg.] *Cat.* 11.

    *PIR*² O 18; *RE* 17:1851–1852 no. 73. A writer of history whose death from drink is lamented in *Catalepton* 11. The lines may be (but are not necessarily) a mock-epitaph, in which case Octavius' demise may be only a jocular fiction. If that is the case, then the historian could be Octavius I (32 above), as is usually thought. It is less likely that he is (Octavius) Musa (30 above).

34. [P. Ovidius Naso]

    *PIR*² O 180; *RE* 18:1910–1986 no. 3; *eques*. For Ovid's non-relationship with

Vergil, see OVID 61. (HORACE 58, PROPERTIUS 15, TIBULLUS 5)

35. Parthenius: Macr. *Sat.* 5.17.18.

PIR[1] P 99; *RE* 18:1895–1899 no. 15. A contemporary Greek poet resident in Rome who is said to have been Vergil's *grammaticus* in Greek, and from whom Vergil later borrowed in his own poetry. Parthenius offered literary assistance to Vergil's friend Gallus (11 above), and may have had connections with Cinna (20 above) and Asinius Pollio (6 above) as well.

36. Philodemus: Philod. *PHerc. Paris.* 2 as read by M. Gigante and M. Capasso, *SIFC*, 3 ser., 7 (1989): 4, *PHerc.* 1802 (*Vol. Herc. Coll. Altera* 1:92, col. 11, line 3) as read by A. Körte, *RhM* 45 (1890): 173.

RE 19: 2444–2482 no. 5; T. Dorandi, *ANRW* 2.36.4:2328–2368. An Epicurean philosopher and epigrammatist from Gadara resident in south Italy. A newly deciphered fragment of his *De adulatione* contains an allocution to Vergil along with Plotius, Varius, and Quintilius, confirming the restoration of Vergil's name in a long-known fragment addressing Varius, Quintilius, and someone whose name begins with "V-". Vergil's association with Philodemus was facilitated by his frequent sojourns in Campania; Vergil's teacher Siro (45 below) was also a friend of Philodemus (known from *PHerc.* 312, see M. Gigante, *A&R* 28 [1983]: 36). (HORACE 62)

37. Plotia Hieria: Don. *Vita Verg.* 9–10 Hardie, Servius on *Ecl.* 2.15 *(Leria)*, 3.20, Filargirius on *Ecl.* 6.20 *(Seria)* and *Schol. Bern.* on *Ecl.* 6.17 *(Iera)*.

PIR[1] P 397; *RE* 21:610 no. 21. A possibly illusory love interest of Vergil's. According to the Donatan life, "Plotia Hieria" was rumored to have had a liaison with Vergil while married to his friend Varius (51 below), though she herself later told the Vergilian scholar Asconius Pedianus that the story was false. Servius at *Ecl.* 3.20 knows a version of the story which he thinks arose from a fanciful interpretation of a passage in the *Eclogues*. Other sources (including Servius himself at *Ecl.* 2.15) speak of Vergil's passion for a certain "Leria," "Seria," or "Iera," who is identified as either a slave of Maecenas or the consort of Varius.

38. Plotius Tucca: (selected references) Philod. *PHerc. Paris.* 2 as read by M. Gigante and M. Capasso, *SIFC*, 3 ser., 7 (1989): 4, Hor. *Serm.* 1.5.40, 1.10.81, Don. *Vita Verg.* 37 and 40 Hardie, *Vita Probiana* p. 27.11–12 Hardie, Servius *Vita Verg.* p. 22.29–31 Hardie (compare the scholia on *Aen.* 2.566, 4.436, 5.871, 7.464), scholia on Persius *Sat.* 2.42, Hieron. *Chron.* p. 166 e Helm, [Verg.] *Cat.* 1, Donatus Auctus p. 28.4–10 Brummer = p. 358.103–110 Bayer, pp. 30.43–31.1 Brummer = pp. 360.143–362.146 Bayer.

PIR[1] P 394; *RE* 21:1266–1267 no. 17a. A fellow poet of Cisalpine origin who was associated with Vergil from the late 40s down to Vergil's death in 19. Together with Varius, Plotius is said to have readied the still unfinished *Aeneid* for publication at the behest of Augustus. (HORACE 63)

39. ?Sex. Propertius

PIR[1] P 752; *RE* 23:758–796 no. 2. For Propertius' relationship with Vergil, see PROPERTIUS 21. (OVID 44)

40. Quintilius (Varus?): Philod. *PHerc. Paris.* 2 as read by M. Gigante and M. Capasso, *SIFC*, 3 ser., 7 (1989): 4, *PHerc.* 1802 (*Vol. Herc. Coll. Altera* 1:92, col. 11, line 3) as read by A. Körte, *RhM* 45 (1890): 173, Hor. *Carm.* 1.24, Hieron. *Chron.* 165 a Helm, schol. on Hor. *Ars* 438, *Vita Probiana* p. 27.11–12 Hardie, Servius on *Ecl.* 5.20, *Vita Monacensis* p. 57.50–55 Brummer = p. 334.52–57 Bayer, p. 58.62–67 Brummer = p. 334.64–70 Bayer. (N.B.: in late sources Quintilius is intermittently confused with Quintilius Varus the Augustan general, Alfenus Varus, and Varius.)

PIR[1] Q 25; *RE* 24:899–902 no. 5. A fellow north Italian (from Cremona) who together with Varius and Plotius was associated with Vergil from at least the late 40s onward; his death, which Jerome dates to 23, prompted Horace to address a *consolatio* to Vergil. Late lives and commentaries say that Vergil studied philosophy with Quintilius under Siro (45 below), and Quintilius is addressed along with Vergil, Varius, and Plotius Tucca in Philodemus' *De adulatione* (36 above). Quintilius was an *eques* according to Porphyrio on Hor. *Ars* 438. (HORACE 70)

41. *Sex. Sabinus:* [Verg.] *Cat.* 5.5–6.

No entry in *RE*. An otherwise unknown intimate (perhaps a lover) to whom the "Vergil" of *Catalepton* 5 bids farewell as he prepares to take up the study of philosophy with Siro. Sabinus' existence is uncertain, his name is common, and there is little reason to seek for links with the Sabinus of Horace (HORACE 73) or of Ovid (OVID 50).

42. ?Sarmentus: Hor. *Serm.* 1.5.51–70.

PIR[1] S 144; *RE* 2A:25. See HORACE 75.

43. *?Selius:* [Verg.] *Cat.* 5.3. (N.B.: *Selius* is an emendation in a line which is seriously corrupt.)

RE: no entry, but compare 2A:1309 nos. 1 and 3. One of the *scholastici* whom the "Vergil" of *Catalepton* 5 renounces as he prepares to take up the study of philosophy with Siro; the context might (but probably does not) imply that Selius had previously been Vergil's teacher. The emendation owes its inspiration to Cicero's mention (*Acad. pr.* 2.11) of two brothers Selius who in the early 80s were disciples of the Academic Philo.

44. Silo: Don. *Vita Verg.* 14 Hardie.

PIR[1] V 282; *RE*: no entry. A younger brother of Vergil who died in boyhood.

45. Siro: [Verg.] *Cat.* 5.8–10, 8.1–2, Servius on *Ecl.* 6.13 and *Aen.* 6.264, *Vita Focae* p. 33.63–64 Hardie, Donatus Auctus *Vita Verg.* pp. 32.46–33.1 Brummer = p. 368.242–243 Bayer (the text here reads *Silo*).

RE 3A:353–354; G. D'Anna in *Enciclopedia Virgiliana* (Rome, 1984–1991), 4:893–895. An Epicurean philosopher under whom Vergil and Quintilius studied in south Italy; the "Vergil" of *Catalepton* 8 speaks of having taken over a small house and property of Siro's. Siro was also associated with Philodemus (36 above).

46. *?Tarquitius*: [Verg]. *Cat.* 5.3–4. (N.B.: *Tarquitius* is an emendation in a line which is seriously corrupt.)

RE 4A:2392–2394 no. 7. One of the *scholastici* whom the "Vergil" of *Catalepton* 5 renounces as he prepares to take up the study of philosophy with Siro; the context might (but probably does not) imply that Tarquitius had previously been Vergil's teacher. Of shadowy identity and date, Tarquitius is known as an author who transcribed books of Etruscan sacred lore into Latin.

47. ?Tibullus
For the possible relationship of Vergil and Tibullus, see TIBULLUS 10. (HORACE 3, OVID 53)

48. M. Valerius Messalla Corvinus: Servius Auctus on *Aen.* 8.310, [Verg.] *Ciris* 54, *Cat.* 9; compare Sen. *Suas.* 2.20.

PIR¹ V 90; RE 8A:131–157 and 2389–2390 no. 261; *cos.* 31. One of the interlocutors with Vergil and Horace in a dialogue written by Maecenas and possibly an auditor of recitations by Vergil. The notice Messalla attracts in the *Appendix Vergiliana* may also point to a tradition that he was Vergil's friend. (HORACE 86, OVID 58, TIBULLUS 8)

49. Valerius Proculus: Don. *Vita Verg.* 37 Hardie, *Vita Probiana* p. 27.18 Hardie; compare *Schol. Bern.* on Verg. *G.* 3.18.

PIR¹ V 118; RE 8A:213 no. 318. Vergil's younger half-brother, whom he named heir to half his estate.

50. ?C. Valgius Rufus: Hor. *Serm.* 1.10.82.

PIR¹ V 169; RE 8A:272–276 no. 7; *cos.* 12. Named by Horace along with Vergil and others as possibly belonging to a literary coterie around Maecenas. (HORACE 88)

51. L. Varius Rufus: (selected references) Philod. *PHerc. Paris.* 2 as read by M. Gigante and M. Capasso, *SIFC*, 3 ser., 7 (1989): 4, *PHerc.* 1802 (*Vol. Herc. Coll. Altera* 1:92, col. 11, line 3) as read by A. Körte, *RhM* 45 (1890): 173, Verg. *Ecl.* 9.35, Hor. *Serm.* 1.5.39–93, 1.6.54–55, 1.10.81, *Epist.* 2.1.245–247, *Ars* 55, Mart. *Epigr.* 8.18.5–8, Quint. 10.3.8 (*Varius* here is an emendation of *Varus*), Don. *Vita Verg.* 10, 37–42 Hardie, *Vita Probiana* p. 27.11–12 Hardie, Hieron.

Chron. p. 166 e Helm, Porphyrio on Hor. *Carm.* 1.6, [Verg.] *Cat.* 7.1, Donatus Auctus p. 28.4–10 Brummer = p. 358.103–110 Bayer (compare Servius on *Aen.* 2.566, 4.436, 5.871, 7.464). (N.B.: Varius is intermittently confused with Alfenus Varus and Quintilius Varus in late sources.)

PIR[1] V 194; *RE* 8A:410–413 no. 21. A fellow poet associated with Vergil from at least the late 40s down to Vergil's death in 19. He shared with Vergil the dedication of Philodemus' *De adulatione* (36 above), probably when late sources say that he was studying with Vergil in south Italy; in the early 30s they were still residing in Campania. The goatherd Lycidas of the *Ninth Eclogue* is made to praise Varius as a singer superior to himself. Varius was named among Vergil's heirs and was said to have been charged by Augustus with readying the *Aeneid* for publication; he was later cited as a source of details about Vergil's life. He is probably not the poet Varius to whom Ovid refers (OVID 60). (HORACE 89)

52. ?*Varro:* [Verg.] *Cat.* 5.3. (N.B.: for *Varro* the text reads *Vario;* the whole line is seriously corrupt.)

RE Suppl. 6:1172–1277 no. 84; senator. One of the *scholastici* whom the "Vergil" of *Catalepton* 5 renounces as he prepares to take up the study of philosophy with Siro; the context might (but probably does not) imply that Varro had been Vergil's teacher. If the emendation is correct, the reference would be to the scholar M. Terentius Varro, on whose antiquarian writings Vergil is known to have drawn.

53. Varus: Verg. *Ecl.* 6.6–12, 9.26–29, Don. *Vita Verg.* 19 Hardie and p. 16.278–279 Brummer = p. 236.288–289 Bayer, Servius on *Ecl.* 6.6, Servius Auctus on *Ecl.* 6.6, 9.10, Filargirius on *Ecl.* 1 *pr.* and 8.6. (N.B.: in late sources Varus is intermittently confused with Quintilius Varus and Varius.)

PIR[1] A 379; *RE* 1:1472–1474 no. 8. A military figure to whose exploits Vergil paid tribute and whom he linked with the fortunes of Mantua in the era of triumviral expropriations. Ancient and modern authorities identify him, probably correctly, with the jurist Alfenus Varus, *cos.* 39; what military role he could have played remains unclear. According to the scholia on Hor. *Serm.* 1.3.130 he was like Vergil a north Italian (from Cremona). There is no basis but a common cognomen for connecting him with Horace's friend Varus (HORACE 90).

54. Vergilius: Don. *Vita Verg.* 1, 14 Hardie, *Vita Focae* p. 31.6–8 Hardie, [Verg.] *Cat.* 8, *Vita Monacensis* p. 56.6 Brummer = p. 330.5 Bayer, *Vita Noricensis* p. 54.4 Brummer = p. 340.4–5 Bayer. (N.B.: in late lives Vergil's father is named *Stimichon* or *Istimicon.*)

No entry in *RE*. The poet's father, who according to late sources rose from being a potter or wage laborer to become an agricultural proprietor; the Donatan life reports that he survived into Vergil's early manhood. The "Vergil" of

Catalepton 8 speaks of bringing his father to live on Siro's former property near Naples.

55. ?M. Vipsanius Agrippa: Verg. *Aen.* 8.682–684, Servius on *Aen.* 1.292, Servius Auctus on *G.* 3.29, Don. *Vita Verg.* 44 Hardie (*Vipsanius* here is an emendation of *Vipranius*).

PIR[1] V 457; *RE* 9A:1226–1275 no. 2; *cos.* 37, 28, and 27. Vergil paid tribute to Agrippa's role at Actium in book 8 of the *Aeneid,* and the scholiasts detect implicit compliments in two other passages. The M. Vipsanius (assuming that *Vipranius* has been correctly emended) who accused Vergil of being a "novae cacozeliae repertor" is probably not the general, who avoided using his nomen, but a critic (compare Isid. *Orig.* 1.22.2). Although several poets allude to Agrippa, there is no hint in his well-documented career of personal ties with any of them. (HORACE 94)

56. ?Viscus I: Hor. *Serm.* 1.10.83.

PIR[1] V 408; *RE* 8A:1998 no. 68. One of a pair *(uterque Viscorum)* whom Horace names with Vergil and others as possibly forming a literary coterie around Maecenas (HORACE 95). A Viscus is associated with Vergil's friend Varius at Hor. *Serm.* 1.9.22–23 and 2.8.20–21 and is saluted in a papyrus fragment attributed to his friend Gallus (frag. 4, line 3, *FPL* p. 130 Büchner). Pseudo-Acro identifies the two Visci as brothers and senators.

57. ?Viscus II: Hor. *Serm.* 1.10.83.
    See the preceding entry.

APPENDIX 3

Iubere *and Literary Requests*

Among the many words which serve to denote the making of a literary request, the verb *iubere* merits special attention for two reasons. It happens to occur in some of the contexts in which debate about Augustus' role vis-à-vis the poets has been most intense (Verg. *Ecl.* 8.11, *G.* 3.40, Prop. 3.9.52), and there is a peculiarity to its use that has perhaps not been fully appreciated.

Here are the passages known to me in which a form of *iubere* is used in speaking about literary instigation:

1. Cic. *Att.* 2.4.3 = 24 SB (Atticus to Cicero).
2. Cic. *Att.* 13.47 = 339 SB (Atticus to Cicero).
3. Cic. *QFr.* 3.6(8).3 = 26 SB (Cicero's brother Quintus to Cicero).
4. Verg. *Ecl.* 6.9, referring to 4–5 (the god Apollo to Vergil).
5. Verg. *Ecl.* 8.11 (Asinius Pollio or Augustus to Vergil).
6. Verg. *G.* 3.41 (Maecenas to Vergil).
7. Prop. 3.3.16 (imaginary: "quis te / carminis heroi tangere iussit opus?").
8. Prop. 3.9.52 (Maecenas to Propertius, in future).
9. Hor. *Epist.* 2.2.63 (unnamed literary friend to Horace).
10. Ov. *Am.* 2.1.3 (the god Amor to Ovid).
11. Sen. *Cont.* 1 *pr.* 3 (Seneca's sons to Seneca).
12. Pliny *HNat.* 25.7 (Pompey to his freedman Lenaeus; I owe this reference to Robert Kaster).
13. Stat. *Silvae* 1 *pr.* p. 1.19 Courtney, in the apparatus (the emperor to Statius).
14. Mart. *Epigr.* 2.6.1 (Martial's literary friend Severus to Martial).
15. Mart. *Epigr.* 4.17.1 (a fictitious literary friend to Martial).
16. Mart. *Epigr.* 11.42.3 (Martial's literary friend Caecilianus to Martial).
17. Pliny *Epist.* 6.15.2 (the senator Iavolenus Priscus to the *eques* Passennus Paulus).
18. Fronto *Ad Verum Imp.* 2.3.1, p. 125.16 van den Hout (Fronto to the

emperor—Verus seeks from Fronto a literary treatment of his current campaign, and offers in turn to write up a *commentarius* for Fronto, "ut iubes").

19. Marius Plotius Sacerdos GL 6:496.11 Keil (Uranius, a *vir clarissimus* and the father of a *contubernalis* of Sacerdos, to Sacerdos).

20. Marius Plotius Sacerdos GL 6:497.1 Keil (Maximus and Simplicius to Sacerdos).

21. Donatus *Vita Verg.* 37 Hardie (Augustus to Plotius and Varius).

22. Ausonius *Praefationes* 3.9 Green (the emperor to Ausonius).

23. Ausonius *Epigrammata* 7 Green, in the *titulus* (the emperor to Ausonius).

24. Ausonius *Cento nuptialis,* prefatory letter p. 133.8–9 Green (the emperor to Ausonius).

25. Palladius *De insitione* preface (Pasiphilus to Palladius).

26. Priscian GL 2:194.2 Keil (Julianus, a literary friend and consular, to Priscian).

27. [Probus] GL 4:219.3, 8, and 12 Keil (Caelestinus to the author).

Clearly the examples are numerous enough that it is fair to characterize *iubere* as being a conventional term in such contexts. They also bear out two points made in Chapter 3, that it is the recipient rather than the initiator of a request who resorts to peremptory terms to characterize it, and that peremptory language does not necessarily correlate with superior status. For each entry in the list, I have indicated who initiates the request, and while the initiator often does enjoy superior status or wield greater authority than the recipient of the request, that is evidently not the case in nos. 1, 2, 3, 9, 11, 15, and 18.

But what is more important about the use of *iubere* is that (as with "tell" and "bid" in English) the nuance of command which it conveys is significantly weaker than in other Latin verbs meaning "order" or "command." This is reflected in the fact that whereas *iubere* occurs widely in reference to requests of all sorts, its dictionary partners *imperare* and *praecipere* have almost no currency in such contexts. What *iubere* echoes when used by the recipient of a request is not utterances like "I charge you" or "I order you," but the use of a simple imperative. At the beginning of *Amores* 2, Ovid says that the god of love bade him write the poems of book 2 as well as book 1; he refers to the words of Amor spoken at 1.1.24: "quod canas, vates, *accipe* opus." At the beginning of *Aeneid* 2, Aeneas says to Dido, "Queen, you bid me to revive an unspeakable sorrow"; he refers to the words with which Dido brings book 1 to a close: "immo age et a prima, *dic*, hospes, origine nobis / insidias . . ." In *Epistles* 1.7.14 Horace says that the Calabrian peasant offers his pears and bids his guest to eat. In the dialogue which illustrates the scene, the peasant's command is given three times, once with a word for "please" ("vescere sodes"), once as a simple imperative ("at tu, quantum vis, tolle"), and once as a suggestion ("non invisa feres pueris munuscula parvis"). As is evident particularly in the last example, the use of an imperative by no means suffices to establish duress, pressure, or the like.

Bibliographical Note

A good analytical survey of studies on the interdependence of Roman literature, society, and politics does not exist and could not be assembled in the space available here. But some direction can be offered to readers who wish to know what has been written in this area and how it diverges from the line taken in the present work. With two exceptions all references below are to sources available in English. For the most part the selection is also slanted to books rather than articles and to recent studies which include good bibliographies. This sampling will quickly point the way to reading that can lead as far as anyone has time and inclination to follow.

The most accessible handbook account of the late Republic and early principate is H. H. Scullard, *From the Gracchi to Nero: A History of Rome 133 B.C.–A.D. 68*, currently in its 5th edition (London and New York, 1982). But the classic treatment is *The Roman Revolution* by Ronald Syme (Oxford, 1939), whose influence on the present study runs deeper than the surface polemic might suggest. A good discussion of the structure of Roman society can be found in G. Alföldy, *The Social History of Rome,* trans. D. Braund and F. Pollock (London and Sydney, 1985).

On the subject of literature in its societal context, nothing has superseded the descriptive amplitude of L. Friedlaender, *Roman Life and Manners under the Principate,* trans. J. H. Freese, L. A. Magnus, and A. B. Gough (London and New York, 1908–1913); the sections on Roman society in volume 1 and on the theater and music in volume 2 are worth reading, as well as the section on belles-lettres in volume 3. Kenneth Quinn in "The Poet and His Audience in the Augustan Age," *ANRW* 2.30.1 (Berlin and New York, 1982), pp. 75–180, addresses many of the topics discussed above in Chapter 2. Jasper Griffin traces links between the repertoire of poetry and a wide variety of contemporary mores in *Latin Poets and Roman Life* (London, 1985); Elizabeth Rawson describes the role played in literary society by writers other than poets in *Intellectual Life in the Late Roman Republic* (Baltimore, 1985). At the moment, however, the social background of Roman literature is being studied most intensively by Italian scholars, whose approaches are well represented in the gargantuan compilation *Lo spazio letterario di Roma antica,* ed. G. Cavallo, P. Fedeli, and A. Giardina (Rome, 1989–1991). The papers that parallel the argument of this book are in the first three volumes, dedicated respectively to production, circulation, and reception of texts.

The relationship of Roman poetry to the elite is examined under the heading of patronage in *Literary Patronage in Greece and Rome* by B. K. Gold (Chapel Hill, 1987) and in several papers of a collection she organized, *Literary and Artistic Patronage in Ancient Rome* (Austin, 1982). How far the concept of patronage is applied to social interaction generally by Latin writers is the subject of two philological inquiries by P. A. Brunt, *"Clientela"* and *"Amicitia* in the Late Roman Republic," both in *The Fall of the Roman Republic and Related Essays* (Oxford, 1988). Richard Saller draws on sociological studies of parallel institutions in other societies in his *Personal Patronage under the Early Empire* (Cambridge, 1982). A sociological perspective also informs many of the papers assembled by Andrew Wallace-Hadrill in *Patronage in Ancient Society* (London and New York, 1989). For a direct impression of the sociological literature on patronage, one may consult a recent monograph and two sets of collected papers: S. N. Eisenstadt and L. Roniger, *Patrons, Clients and Friends: Interpersonal Relations and the Structure of Trust in Society* (Cambridge, 1984); *Friends, Followers, and Factions: A Reader in Political Clientelism,* ed. S. W. Schmidt, J. C. Scott, C. Landé, and L. Guasti (Berkeley and Los Angeles, 1977)—see especially the papers by Gouldner, Hall, Landé, Mayer, and Wolf; and *Patrons and Clients in Mediterranean Societies,* ed. E. Gellner and J. Waterbury (London, 1977)—especially the papers by Gellner, Silverman, and Waterbury. Since in recent years the study of patronage in Roman society has been so strongly influenced by sociologists, it may be worth noting a bias with which they approached the subject. The study of patron–client relations burgeoned in the 1960s and 1970s as sociologists looked beyond the macro-political structures which had been their dominant concern to the social role of smaller groups. Yet patronage attracted their attention in part because it too had a significant political dimension. Not until the 1980s did sociologists (in conjunction with social psychologists) give comparable effort to exploring the less power-oriented phenomenon of friendship, and the insights of this newer wave of research have yet to be carried over into the study of Roman social relations. A good book with which to start is G. Allan, *Friendship: Developing a Sociological Perspective* (London, 1989).

It is now conventional to analyze personal relations of any sort as forms of exchange, but the two pioneers of this approach were P. M. Blau, *Exchange and Power in Social Life* (New York, 1964) and G. C. Homans, *Social Behavior: Its Elementary Forms,* rev. ed. (New York, 1974). For an analysis of networks and circles as chains of exchange, see J. Boissevain, *Friends of Friends: Networks, Manipulators and Coalitions* (Oxford, 1974).

For background to the literary history traced in Chapter 4, two excellent resources are B. Weinberg, *A History of Literary Criticism in the Italian Renaissance* (Chicago, 1961) and A. F. B. Clarke, *Boileau and the French Classical Critics in England (1660–1830)* (Paris, 1925). Many studies have been published of politics and the press in eighteenth-century England; a recent one is by J. M. Black, *The English Press in the Eighteenth Century* (Philadelphia, 1987), but there is still good value in L. Hanson, *The Government and the Press 1695–1763* (Oxford, 1936).

An immense bibliography has accumulated around the subject of politics in Augustan poetry. D. Little compiled a list of much that had appeared down to about 1975 and grouped the titles helpfully by poet and opus in *ANRW* 2.30.1 (Berlin and New York, 1982), pp. 350–370. The papers in two recent collections (and papers they cite) go some way to bring discussion up to the present: *Poetry and Politics in the Age of Augustus,* ed. A. J. Woodman and D. A. West (Cambridge, 1984) and *Between Republic and Empire: Interpretations of Augustus and His Principate,* ed. K. A. Raaflaub and M. Toher (Berkeley and Los Angeles, 1990). To the extent that poetry can be seen as a medium comparable to public art and architecture, one can draw on Paul Zanker's analysis of the way Augustus used images to communicate an ideology: *The Power of Images in the Age of Augustus,* trans. A. Shapiro (Ann Arbor, 1988).

Much has been written, particularly in the last twenty-five years, that is relevant to the discussion of the empire theme in Chapter 6. Heading the list are *Imperialism in the Ancient World,* ed. P. D. A. Garnsey and C. R. Whittaker (Cambridge, 1978)—especially Brunt's paper "*Laus Imperii*"; C. Nicolet, *Space, Geography, and Politics in the Early Roman Empire,* trans. H. Leclerc (Ann Arbor, 1991); and J. S. Richardson, "*Imperium*

Romanum: Empire and the Language of Power," *JRS* 81 (1991): 1–7. To appreciate the historical currents which led poets to their intimations of Augustus' divinity, one cannot do better than read L. R. Taylor, *The Divinity of the Roman Emperor* (Middletown, 1931) and S. Weinstock, *Divus Iulius* (Oxford, 1971). The most recent account of Augustus' cult in Rome and Italy is D. Fishwick, *The Imperial Cult in the Latin West: Studies in the Ruler Cult of the Western Provinces of the Roman Empire,* Études préliminaires aux religions orientales dans l'empire romain 108 (Leiden and New York, 1987–). The edifices raised by Augustus and his peers are catalogued and described in S. B. Platner and T. Ashby, *A Topographical Dictionary of Ancient Rome* (Oxford, 1929). E. Nash provides pictures of what is extant and references to archaeological studies in *Pictorial Dictionary of Ancient Rome,* 2nd ed. (New York and Washington, 1968), but for more up-to-date information one must consult the sections on Augustan buildings in *Kaiser Augustus und die verlorene Republik,* ed. W.-D. Heilmeyer (Mainz, 1988).

Notes

1. The Poet as Companion and Protégé

1. That the lines on Servilius' companion are a self-portrait is reported by Gell. *NA* 12.4.5 on the authority of Aelius Stilo.

2. For expressions like *vivere cum* and *convictus*, see Cic. *Arch.* 6, *Pis.* 68, Hor. *Serm.* 1.6.47, Ov. *Tr.* 1.8.29, Suet. *Vita Ter.* p. 292.9–10 Roth; for *usus* and *uti*, see Ov. *Tr.* 3.6.19, *Pont.* 4.3.15, Suet. *Vita Ter.* p. 293.29 Roth, *Vita Hor.* p. 297.27 Roth.

3. For some other examples of *domus*, compare Hor. *Serm.* 1.9.49, Ov. *Tr.* 4.4.33, *Pont.* 1.2.136, 1.7.68, 2.2.1, Mart. *Epigr.* 4.40.2; for *lares* and *Penates*, Ov. *Pont.* 1.7.58, *Laus Pis.* 218, Mart. *Epigr.* 12.2.11; for *limen*, Hor. *Epist.* 1.18.73, *Laus Pis.* 82 and 110, Mart. *Epigr.* 10.58.12, 12.18.4; for *ianua*, Ov. *Pont.* 1.7.54; for *atria*, Mart. *Epigr.* 4.40.1, 5.20.5, 12.2.10; for *mensa*, Ov. *Pont.* 1.2.130, Suet. *Vita Hor.* p. 297.21 Roth.

4. For example, Ov. *Tr.* 1.8.31–32, *Pont.* 2.4.9–10, 4.3.13–14.

5. The whole section down to line 58 is relevant to the distinction of *seria* and *lusus*. For other passages which present relations with the great in similar terms, compare Enn. *Ann.* 268–286 Skutsch = 234–251 Vahlen, Hor. *Carm.* 3.8, *Laus Pis.* 137–208, Mart. *Epigr.* 4.8, 4.14, Stat. *Silvae* 4.4.46–77, 4.5.49–60.

6. I set aside the one case in which writing could be a gainful occupation in and of itself: dramatic writers of course earned an income by selling scripts (though even this occupation did not presuppose a fixed schedule of work). I also exclude from the category of fixed employment military or provincial tours of service, since these were temporary (and often undertaken precisely in order to keep great friends company). These qualifications aside, I am aware of four exceptions to the generalization that poets did not have regular occupations which supported them. In addition to selling scripts, Plautus is said to have maintained himself at various points by manual labor, by work as an actor or theater technician, and by commercial ventures (Gell. *NA* 3.3.14, Hieron. *Chron.* p. 135 h Helm); Pacuvius in addition to selling scripts is said to have

found employment as a painter (Hieron. *Chron.* p. 142 e Helm, with Pliny *HNat.* 35.19); Horace after the debacle at Philippi apparently obtained a position as *scriba quaestorius* (Suet. *Vita Hor.* p. 297.8–9 Roth, with Hor. *Serm.* 2.6.36–37); and the hapless Florus lived by teaching school in Spain *(Vergilius orator an poeta)*. Plautus and Florus are so far removed from the normal career paths of Roman poets that they hardly impinge on the present argument about sharing the pastimes of the rich. The relevant point to make is that since they found no entrée into genteel society, the problem of balancing remunerative employment with social commitments did not arise for them. Pacuvius and Horace, on the other hand, evidently did succeed in combining both. We know almost nothing about Pacuvius' painterly career or his commitments in society, and so it is fruitless to inquire how he managed both concurrently; perhaps painting was only an occasional sideline. The truly puzzling exception is Horace, who apparently held on to his clerical position for several years after becoming Maecenas' friend (*Serm.* 2.6.36–37) and perhaps never resigned it, which does seem to contradict the presumption that attachment to the rich precludes regular employment elsewhere. Yet the *scriptus quaestorius* may have entailed only minimal or intermittent duties. Comments about lackadaisical performance on the part of the *apparitores* (Cic. *Verr.* 3.184, Frontin. *Aq.* 101.2) and inscriptions which show a tendency for them to hold multiple appointments have often been taken as indicating that the apparitorial posts could be treated as sinecures. Certainly Horace always conveys the impression (most notably at *Serm.* 1.6.111–129) that apart from social obligations, his time was his own.

7. I take it for granted that, one case apart, writing poetry was not in itself a gainful endeavor, since even today, with advantages like copyright protection, royalties, and mass markets which were unknown to their Roman counterparts, most poets find that their writing does not yield a livelihood. The only specialty which ancient sources suggest was potentially remunerative was writing for the stage: "scaena est lucrosa poetae," observes Ovid at *Tr.* 2.507. By the end of the first century B.C., that meant writing either mimes or librettos for pantomimes (Sen. *Suas.* 2.19, Juv. *Sat.* 7.82–87), genres with which only a handful of the poets known to us had anything to do.

8. The equestrian census requirement is often mentioned, as for example at Pliny *HNat.* 33.32, Pliny *Epist.* 1.19.2, Juv. *Sat.* 14.323–326. For evidence documenting the equestrian status of Horace, Tibullus, and Ovid, see the appropriate entries in Appendix 1.

9. I have borrowed the 6 percent figure from R. Duncan-Jones, *The Economy of the Roman Empire: Quantitative Studies,* 2nd ed. (Cambridge, 1982), who takes it as the standard return on investment in land (see especially p. 33, note 3). The rate of interest charged on money out at loan could be higher.

10. Cic. *Cael.* 17. The 30,000 figure was cited by the prosecutor at Caelius'

trial as the epitome of profligate living; Cicero maintained that the true figure was only 10,000.

11. Suet. *Jul.* 38.2, Caes. *BCiv.* 3.21.1, Cass. Dio 42.51.1 and 48.9.5. Compare also Plut. *Sulla* 1.6 (a story presupposing two rents of 2,000 and 3,000 in the late second century B.C.).

12. My translation equivocates over the amount. The manuscripts read "terna milia *aeris*," which should mean "three thousand asses" (worth 750 sesterces) per month. Because that figure seems implausibly low and because the *sestertius* had generally displaced the *as* as the typical unit of reckoning, editors tend to eject *aeris*, understanding "sesterces" instead. I do not know from what statistical evidence it can be shown that Nepos' figure is impossible; that it is astonishingly low Nepos himself realizes, because immediately afterward he adds "atque hoc non auditum, sed cognitum praedicamus: saepe enim propter familiaritatem domesticis rebus interfuimus."

13. Nicholas Horsfall made this point to me.

14. The other passages in which Cicero discusses Marcus' living arrangements are *Att.* 14.16.4 = 370 SB, 15.15.4 = 393 SB, 15.20.4 = 397 SB, 16.1.5 = 409 SB.

15. In alphabetical order, Quintilian's thirty-one are: Accius, (Aemilius) Macer, Afranius, (Albinovanus) Pedo, (Albius) Tibullus, Caecilius (Statius), Caesius Bassus, (C. Valerius) Catullus, (C. Cornelius) Gallus, Cornelius Severus, Ennius, (M. Furius) Bibaculus, Horace, Lucan, Lucilius, Lucretius, (T. Maccus) Plautus, Ovid, Pacuvius, Persius, Pomponius Secundus, Propertius, Rabirius, Saleius Bassus, Serranus, Terence, (M. Terentius) Varro, (P. Terentius) Varro Atacinus, Valerius Flaccus, Varius, and Vergil (Quint. 10.1.85–100). All but two of them are listed in Appendix 1, where the evidence for their social status is set out. The two not listed in the appendix are Serranus (10.1.89) and Saleius Bassus (10.1.90). Serranus is scarcely more than a name to us—in Quintilian's text, in fact, an emended name, restored with the help of two fleeting references elsewhere to a Serranus who was poetically active during the first century A.D. but whose status is unknown. Saleius Bassus is slightly better known as a poet of the mid to late first century A.D., but his status too is undetermined.

16. For the connection with Cicero, see Cic. *Fam.* 10.32.5 = 415 SB, and probably 10.31.6 = 368 SB; for Gallus' role on the expropriation commission, Don. *Vita Verg.* 19 Hardie and Servius Auctus on Verg. *Ecl.* 9.10; for his army service, Verg. *Ecl.* 10.44–45.

17. Out of many possible examples, a few must suffice. Cato in Cicero's *De senectute* is made to refer to Ennius as "familiaris noster" (sec. 10); Laelius in the *De amicitia* speaks of Terence as "meus familiaris" (sec. 89) and of Pacuvius as "hospes et amicus meus" (sec. 24). Porcius Licinus, writing about Terence's relationship with Laelius and Scipio, recalls the period when Terence "se amari ab his credit," *FPL* frag. 3, p. 45 Morel = 58 Büchner. Lucretius tells Memmius

that he is prompted to write by the "sperata voluptas / suavis amicitiae," 1.140–141. Writing to Horace, Maecenas declares, "ni te visceribus meis, Horati, / plus iam diligo, tu tuum sodalem nimio videas strigosiorem," Suet. *Vita Hor.* p. 297.13–15 Roth; Horace calls Maecenas "dulcis amicus," *Epist.* 1.7.12. Speaking of Augustus' ties with Vergil and Varius, Horace says "dilecti tibi Vergilius Variusque poetae," *Epist.* 2.1.247. Pliny on hearing of Martial's demise writes "ut amicissimum defunctum esse doleo," *Epist.* 3.21.6.

18. The claim to a proper schooling gets particularly heavy emphasis from Horace, who as a freedman's son had the hardest time establishing credentials in society. At *Serm.* 1.6.76–78 he says that his father went out of his way to guarantee him an upper-class education: "sed [me] puerum est ausus Roman portare docendum / artis quas doceat quivis eques atque senator / semet prognatos."

19. The code which is signified by evocations of the *dignus amicus* in Horace (*Serm.* 1.6.52–64, *Epist.* 1.7.22–24, 2.1.245–247) and in the *Laus Pisonis* (128–137, 218) is expounded by Cicero at *Amic.* 62–81; see also *Off.* 1.45–46.

20. In this connection it is worth pointing out a difference between Cicero's discussion of friendship in the *De amicitia* and Aristotle's discussion in book 8 of the *Nicomachean Ethics.* Both Aristotle and Cicero acknowledge the possibility of friendship between unequal partners. But for Aristotle, who analyzes friendship in terms which partly anticipate (and partly inspired) modern exchange theory, inequality is a fundamental complication which necessitates distinctions between kinds of friendship. Cicero, on the other hand, can present friendship as a more or less uniform phenomenon by focusing on the *studia, mores,* and *officia* which unite the partners rather than on status differences which divide them. It can probably be taken for granted that, to the eyes of Romans, the two parties to a friendship would rarely have looked like equals.

21. Gifts consisting clearly or possibly of money are mentioned in connection with Vergil at Don. *Vita Verg.* 13 Hardie, Mart. *Epigr.* 8.55.9–11, and Donatus Auctus p. 27.6–7 Brummer = 356.90–91 Bayer; with Varius at Mart. *Epigr.* 8.55.21; with Horace at *Epod.* 1.31–32 and *Epist.* 1.7.15 and 39; with Ovid at *Tr.* 4.5.7–8, *Pont.* 4.1.23–24, and 4.5.37–38; with Domitius Marsus at Mart. *Epigr.* 8.55.21 and 23–24; with Martial at Pliny *Epist.* 3.21.2.

22. For Augustus' generosity to Vergil, see Hor. *Epist.* 2.1.245–247 with Pseudo-Acro's note, Don. *Vita Verg.* 12 Hardie, *Vita Probiana* p. 27.14–16 Hardie, and Servius on *Aen.* 6.861. For Augustus' gifts to Varius, see Hor. *Epist.* 2.1.245–247, Pseudo-Acro's comment there, and an errant manuscript notation about Varius' *Thyestes,* "Lucius Varius cognomento Rufus Thyesten tragoediam magna cura absolutam post Actiacam victoriam Augusti ludis eius in scaena edidit pro qua fabula sestertium deciens accepit" (for text and discussion, see H. D. Jocelyn, "The Fate of Varius' *Thyestes,*" *CQ* 30 [1980]: 387–400). Augustus is also said to have given money to Horace at Suet. *Vita Hor.* p. 297.34 Roth and

to an anonymous poet at Macr. *Sat.* 2.4.31. Among Augustus' successors, Tiberius gave to Clutorius Priscus (Tac. *Ann.* 3.49.1 and Cass. Dio 57.20.3), Nero to "Loukillios" (*Anth. Pal.* 9.572.7–8), Vespasian to Saleius Bassus (Tac. *Dial.* 9.3), and Marcus Aurelius to Oppian (*Suda* 4:547.17–29 Adler; see also A. Westermann, *Biographoi: Vitarum scriptores Graeci minores* [Braunschweig, 1855], pp. 64.18 and 66.22–23). Julius Caesar had set an example before Augustus with his gift to Laberius (Macr. *Sat.* 2.7.8).

23. The only evidence I know that might suggest regular payments to a literary figure (though not to a poet) is Suet. *Gr.* 20.2. Suetonius there cites an assertion by the consular Clodius Licinus that the librarian and scholar Hyginus was "liberalitate sua quoad vixerit sustentatus." Since Suetonius and Tacitus use the verb *sustentare* when speaking of a fixed annual subsidy at *Ves.* 17 and *Ann.* 13.34.1 respectively, it is possible that Clodius Licinus' assistance took a similar form. If so, Hyginus' social status as a freedman is surely relevant to the arrangement. But Robert Kaster points out to me that at *Tib.* 46 Suetonius uses *sustentare* in a context that expressly excludes money payments, and suggests that the passage about Hyginus may mean no more than that he received shelter and sustenance by being taken into Licinus' household.

24. Mart. *Epigr.* 2.91–92, 3.95.6, 9.97.5–6; for the link between paternity and eligibility for legacies, compare Juv. 9.87–90. Note that more than a century and a half earlier the Greek poet Archias had been accustomed to benefit in wills made by Roman friends (Cic. *Arch.* 11).

25. As Seneca says at *Ben.* 4.40.4, "quidam, cum aliquod illis missum est munusculum, subinde aliud intempestive remittunt et nihil se debere testantur; reiciendi genus est protinus aliud invicem mittere et munus munere expungere"; Seneca's comments at *Ben.* 2.31–34 and 6.41 are also relevant.

26. For example, Pers. *prol.* 12–14, Calp. *Ecl.* 4.23–28, Mart. *Epigr.* 5.36, Juv. 7.36–97. Apart from poems directed to the emperors, the only Latin text I know in which the recipient of verse is explicitly asked for money in return is Phaed. 3 *epil.* 8–27—a book presented by one Greek freedman to another.

27. That Maecenas gave Horace the Sabine farm is implied at Hor. *Carm.* 2.18.11–14 and stated by the scholia there and by Porphyrio on Hor. *Epodi* 1.31. Mark Antony gave land to the poet Anser according to Servius on Verg. *Ecl.* 9.36, and Martial describes property he was given by his countrywoman Marcella at *Epigr.* 12.31. For fantasies, see Calp. *Ecl.* 4.152–155, Mart. *Epigr.* 1.55, 8.18.9, 11.18.

28. Poets who attached themselves to the entourage of military commanders include Ennius (Cic. *Arch.* 27, *Tusc.* 1.3, *Brut.* 79), Archias (Cic. *Arch.* 11), Tibullus (Tib. 1.7, *Vita Tib.* p. 171 Lenz-Galinsky = 112 Luck) and the trio of unknowns to whom Horace writes at *Epist.* 1.3. Poets who accompanied officials on peacetime duty include Catullus (10.5–13, 28.7–10), probably Ovid (*Pont.* 2.10.22–29) and perhaps Cinna (Catull. 10.29–30); Petronius assigned his

fictional character Eumolpus a tour of duty with a quaestor in Asia (*Sat.* 85.1). Propertius declined a place in a governor's entourage (Prop. 1.6).

29. At least formally, the emperor was the source of most posts to which we hear of poets gaining access during the principate. Augustus offered Horace a secretaryship in the palace (Suet. *Vita Hor.* p. 297.17–23 Roth), and Ovid's poet friend Carus was a palace tutor (Ov. *Pont.* 4.13.47–48). Literary talent seems to have helped earn Seneca's friend Lucilius entry into a procuratorial career (see especially Sen. *Epist.* 19.3), and won Seneca himself his role as Nero's mentor (Tac. *Ann.* 12.8.2). Juvenal claims at *Sat.* 7.88–92 that honorary commissions in the army were among the few chances poets had of improving their fortunes; it is generally believed that Martial's equestrian tribunate (*Epigr.* 3.95.9–10) was just such an appointment.

30. Hor. *Carm.* 1.1.2, Ov. *Pont.* 1.6.13–14, *Laus Pis.* 244–245, Juv. 7.22–23, and *Anth. Lat.* 445.5 Riese = 443.5 SB.

31. The economic coloring of *praesidium* is particularly clear at *Laus Pis.* 244–245, Juv. 7.22–23, Cic. *Amic.* 46, and Val. Max. 4.7. *pr.* Compare also the distinction Cicero draws at *Off.* 1.58 between the material resources which constitute the *praesidia vitae* and the human intercourse which gives life its full meaning.

32. Hor. *Epist.* 1.1.103, Ov. *Pont.* 4.1.36, *Laus Pis.* 244; that monetary support is implied is clearest in the passage from the *Laus Pisonis* and in Juvenal's inversion of the standard expression at *Sat.* 14.112.

33. For *arx* in this context, see *Anth. Lat.* 405.5 Riese = 401.5 SB; Cic. *Phil.* 8.24 proves that it was already a cliché in Cicero's time. For *columen*, see Hor. *Carm.* 2.17.4; this too was already a cliché by Cicero's time (*Phil.* 13.26).

34. For Ovid's *opus* metaphor, see *Pont.* 4.1.23–36 and compare Arist. *Eth. Nic.* 9.7.2–4 1167b31–1168a5. The metaphor is not peculiar to Ovid: see *Eleg. Maec.* 150 and *Epic. Drusi* 39. For phrases like *tuus poeta*, see Hor. *Epist.* 1.7.11, Ov. *Tr.* 5.7.22, *Pont.* 4.15.38; Crinagoras seems to have coined a Greek equivalent at *Anth. Pal.* 6.229.6 = Gow-Page, *Garland of Philip* 1:200 no. 4. For the correlative *poeta meus*, see Sen. *QNat.* 4A.2.2, though Seneca may have in mind spiritual rather than material benefits to Lucilius, as at *Epist.* 34.2.

35. Many texts concerning *beneficia* allude to gifts specifically intended to boost the capital worth and social position of the recipient: Val. Max. 4.7.5, *ILS* 1949, Sen. *Ben.* 3.3.2, 3.9.2–3, 3.12.2, 3.14.3, 4.11.6, *Laus Pis.* 109–111, Valla's scholia on Juv. 5.109, Mart. *Epigr.* 4.67, 5.19.10, 5.25, 12.6.9–11, 14.122, Pliny *Epist.* 1.19.

36. Horace acclaims Maecenas as both *decus* and *praesidium* at *Carm* 1.1.2, and as *decus* and *columen* at *Carm.* 2.17.4; see also *decus* and *tutela* at *Laus Pis.* 243–244 and *honor* and *arx* at *Anth. Lat.* 405.5 Riese = 401.5 SB. Such pairs are stereotypical: compare *praesidium/decus* at Lucr. 2.643, *ornamentum/praesidium* at Cic. *Fam.* 3.10.9 = 73 SB, *ornamentum/arx* at Cic. *Phil.* 8.24, and *praesidium/*

ornamentum at Pliny *Epist.* 6.18.2. *Decus* and related words can of course be used in salutations by themselves, as at Verg. *G.* 2.40 and Prop. 2.1.74.

37. The sense of this couplet, which closes the poem, is more than usually compressed; the translation expresses my understanding of it, but interpretations differ considerably.

38. For texts which illustrate the convention of the *carmen iussum,* see Catull. 65 and 68.9–14 as well as the citations collected in Appendix 3. For the *carmen promissum,* see Hor. *Epod.* 14.7, *Ars* 45, [Verg.] *Ciris* 47. For the *iudicium* that important friends pass on poems shown to them, see Hor. *Serm.* 1.10.81–90, 2.1.83–85, *Epist.* 1.4.1, Ov. *Fasti* 1.19–20, *Tr.* 4.4.29–30, *Pont.* 2.2.103–104, 2.4.13–18, 4.12.25–28, Phaed. 3 *prol.* 62–63, Calp. *Ecl.* 4.52, Mart. *Epigr.* 4.86, 5.80.10–13, 6.1, 7.28, 9.26, 12 *pr.,* Stat. *Silvae* 2 *pr.* p. 31.1–3 Courtney, and Pliny *Epist.* 4.14.

39. For language extolling the great friend as a source of *ingenium,* compare "te sine nil altum mens incohat," Verg. *G.* 3.42; "crescet et ingenium sub tua iussa meum," Prop. 3.9.52; "dux ingenii," Ov. *Pont.* 2.3.78, 4.12.23; "fax studii," Ov. *Pont.* 1.7.28; "tu facis ingenium," Mart. *Epigr.* 12.3.5. Prayer language is used at Tib. 2.1.35–36, Verg. *G.* 2.39–44, Ov. *Fasti* 1.3–26, *Laus Pis.* 216–218.

40. That the inspiration metaphor has to do with choice of subjects is most explicit in Propertius 2.1.1–16, though here it is the *amica* rather than the *amicus* who is said to quicken the poet's *ingenium.*

41. For *ponere,* see Ov. *Pont.* 3.6.52, 4.12.1; for *inserire,* see Mart. *Epigr.* 4.31.4; for *texere,* see *Panegyricus Messallae* 5 and 211 and (in reference to a prose work) Cic. *Att.* 13.12.3 = 320 SB.

42. See the complaint at *Laus Pis.* 115–127 about the uses to which most Roman gentlemen put their adherents.

43. So common was it for Roman socialites to dabble in verse that Juvenal later treats it as a characteristic dodge of the rich: they never feel they owe anything to real poets because they profess to be first-rate talents themselves (*Sat.* 7.36–39). Poets are no less abundantly represented among the society friends of Martial and Statius than they are among those of Horace and Ovid.

44. For some glimpses of what went on, see Catull. 50.1–6, Ov. *Pont.* 3.5.39–40, Stat. *Silvae* 3 *pr.* p. 60.3–6 Courtney, 4.6.1–16, Mart. *Epigr.* 9.89, 10.58.1–6.

45. The progress of this lost opus is chronicled in Cic. *QFr.* 2.14.2 = 18 SB, 2.16.3–4 = 20 SB, 3.6.3 = 26 SB, 3.7.6 = 27 SB.

46. Two comments may be offered here about the term *officia,* which most often serves to characterize actions that friends do for each other, whether they are literary friends or friends in general. The first is that the word has little in the way of abstract or metaphysical content clinging to it. Corresponding to its etymology (*ops + facere*), it denotes the performance of concrete actions, specific interventions of work or help. In most contexts its sense is closer to "functions,"

"gestures," or "practical services" than to "duties" or "obligations." The second point is that *officia* is one in a set of Latin words which mirror the relative statuses of those performing acts of help or service. The contrasts which Seneca articulates in the following passage are overdrawn, but they have a basis in usage: "sunt enim qui ita distinguant: quaedam beneficia esse, quaedam officia, quaedam ministeria. beneficium esse quod alienus det (alienus est qui potuit sine reprehensione cessare); officium esse filii, uxoris, earum personarum quas necessitudo suscitat et ferre opem iubet; ministerium esse servi, quem condicio sua eo loco posuit ut nihil eorum quae praestat inputet superiori" (*Ben.* 3.18.1; though Seneca does not include it, *obsequium* belongs to the same system of oppositions). It is another sign of the basic parity of friends that *officium* is the word most often used to designate their actions vis-à-vis each other, even when a social superior acts on behalf of a lesser friend. Words like *obsequium* and *ministerium,* on the other hand, are rarely applied to interactions between those who profess to be friends.

47. I offer only a minimal sampling of texts, biased where possible toward relationships in which poets figure. For *rex*, see Hor. *Epist.* 1.7.37, 1.17.43, Stat. *Silvae* 3.2.92, and Juv. *Sat.* 7.45; for *dominus*, see Petr. 57.2, Mart. *Epigr.* 2.68.2, 4.67.4, and Juv. *Sat.* 5.137; for *patronus*, see Cic. *Planc.* 69, *Fam.* 6.7.4 = 237 SB, 7.29.2 = 264 SB, Hor. *Epist.* 1.7.92, Porph. on Hor. *Carm.* 1.36.8, and Serv. on Verg. *Ecl.* 3.84; for *cliens*, see Hor. *Carm.* 4.12.15, *Laus Pis.* 119, Mart. *Epigr.* 10.10.11, and Porph. on Hor. *Epod.* 1.1; for *parasitus*, see Lucilius 717 Marx, Suet. *Vita Hor.* p. 297.21 Roth; Juv. *Sat.* 1.139 and 5.145; for *scurra*, see Hor. *Serm.* 2.7.36, *Epist.* 1.18.2–4, and Pliny *Epist.* 9.17.1; for *servus* and *servire*, see Hor. *Serm.* 2.5.99, 2.7.81–82, Ov. *Pont.* 4.8.66, Mart. *Epigr.* 2.18.7, 2.32.7, and 10.56.1.

48. In literary sources it is unusual during this period to find the word *patronus* applied (outside forensic contexts) to one who takes up the cause of an *individual.* But probably this lacuna reflects the quirkiness of our documentation rather than a decline in the patronage of individuals. As has been noted countless times, Latin literary sources mirror elite concerns. Romans of the upper class had reason to dwell on their role as public speakers both because oratory had been the whole point of their education and because it was one of their chief modes of interaction with peers. They were preoccupied about slaves because they depended on large staffs of slaves to organize their day-to-day existence and because they often retained economic and other interests in slaves they freed. They flaunted their patronage of towns and guilds because the adherence of mass organizations in the capital and of whole communities beyond enhanced their image as important persons. Aid to sundry petitioners, on the other hand, had nothing remarkable about it when the recipients were of such lowly estate that they could properly be tagged as clients. The reason that Ro-

man gentlemen are not more often identified as *patroni* in relation to individual *clientes* may thus be that the sources pay little heed to their transactions with low-status persons generally. This seems a more likely explanation than that in transactions with individuals which our sources do report they were exercising patronal functions, but were nevertheless not labeled *patroni* because that would have grated on the sensitivity of the other party. It is true that *patronus* is a proud word, and for that reason it might conceivably have been eschewed in direct discourse between patron and client. But since it was the *vox propria* for a social role, there would have been no reason for third-party speakers (or writers) to avoid it. Furthermore, the word *cliens* grated in the same way as *patronus* (see Cic. *Off.* 2.69, Sen. *Ben.* 2.23.3), yet that word (in the universalizing plural) is amply attested; much the same can be said of the word *rex*. There is also a second factor which limits the number of contexts in which *patronus* gets applied to individuals. In Roman society an important person is usually important by virtue of several roles and attributes at once (for example, as a member of the governing class, as the scion of a noble family, as a wealthy man, as a socialite). Since the possession of clients will rarely be the single most important attribute, *patronus* has little currency as a generic label for one of the *principes viri*.

49. As with *patronus,* there is a perceptible bias in the use of *cliens,* though this time the bias has to do with the distinction between singular and plural rather with the occurrence or non-occurrence of the word. *Cliens* is found more often in the plural than in the singular (and when it does occur in the singular, the individual so qualified is often unidentified). I would suggest that essentially the same screening process operated in both cases. References to single individuals who are identified as *clientes* are infrequent because our sources take little note of transactions with low-status persons, whereas references to *clientes* en masse are common because it is a mark of distinction to have masses of clients.

50. Conversely, Augustine seems to treat *patronus* as a synonym interchangeable with *potens amicus* in *Tractates on the Epistle of John* 10.4: "dicit tibi Deus 'patronum tibi vis facere aut amicum potentem; ambis per alienum inferiorem. Me ama,' dicit tibi Deus, 'non ad me ambitur per aliquem'"; see also Porph. on Hor. *Carm.* 1.36.8, glossing Horace's word *rex* with *patronus.*

51. *Patronus* must long have functioned as a polite appellative if texts like Plaut. *Mos.* 746, *As.* 757, Ter. *Ad.* 456, and Hor. *Epist.* 1.7.92 are valid indicators. What seems to change is that whereas the term once typified the parlance of low-status persons like slaves, freedmen, and prostitutes in discourse with their betters, in the later empire respectable and even important persons made free with it.

52. This is strikingly evident in the most detailed account we have of Roman

patronage. According to Dionysius of Halicarnassus (*Ant. Rom.* 2.10.1–2), patrons advise clients and assist them in various transactions, while it is the clients who provide financial aid to the patrons.

2. GROUP ATTACHMENTS

1. *Grex* and *cohors* perhaps come closest to expressing that idea, though neither has much currency in the context of literary relationships: see Ter. *Eun.* 1084, Cic. *Amic.* 69, *Att.* 1.14.5 = 14 SB, 6.1.10 = 115 SB, and Hor. *Epist.* 1.9.13 for *grex;* Suet. *Cal.* 19.2, *Nero* 5.1, *Gal.* 7.1, *Vita Luc.* p. 299.22 Roth, Tac. *Ann.* 1.29.2 and 6.9.2 for *cohors amicorum* (a phrase which echoes the quasi-military appellation for the staff of a Roman official abroad). *Contubernium* may refer to a broad circle of friends, but it is used just as often of a connection between two people (thus exhibiting the same sort of ambiguity as our word "company" in the phrase "the company of"); the same is true of *convictus*. Except in business contexts, *societas* is an abstract rather than a collective noun ("social intercourse" rather than "a society"); *sodalitas* and *sodalicium* when they function as collective nouns are rarely if ever applied to strictly social groups, nor is *collegium* so applied. Other words do not even remotely approximate the overtones of words like English "group" or "circle." *Comitatus* and *agmen* ("entourage" and "file") describe masses in movement, made up of those who troop after a great man as he goes about in public. *Clientela* draws attention to the status difference between him and his dependents; *caterva* and *turba* are obviously somewhat disparaging. To be sure, it was not beyond the power of the Latin language to express the idea of group friendship: compare, for example, Cic. *Off.* 1.56, "nihil est amabilius nec copulatius quam morum similitudo bonorum; in quibus enim eadem studia sunt, eaedem voluntates, in iis fit ut aeque quisque altero delectetur ac se ipso, efficiturque id quod Pythagoras vult in amicitia, ut unus fiat ex pluribus" (Cicero has recourse to Pythagoras' formula again at *Amic.* 92). Nevertheless, discussion of this aspect is far less common than discussion of two-party relationships.

2. Hence the most groveling and desperate among Cicero's correspondents ventures to dub him the "patronus omnium" (Cic. *Fam.* 6.7.4 = 237 SB).

3. Pollio's presence at a recitation sponsored by Messalla is documented by Sen. *Suas.* 6.27; for Messalla and Maecenas' discussion of Vergil, see Sen. *Suas.* 2.20; Maecenas' literary symposium is known from Servius Auctus on Verg. *Aen.* 8.310. Some have argued that the Messalla of this piece must be Messalla Rufus, the consul of 53, chiefly on the grounds that Corvinus (born probably in 64 B.C.) was too young a man to have foisted on him the sentiment that wine "brings nimble eyes, makes all things more lovely, and restores the delights of sweet youth." Let those who have reached their forties decide this point for themselves. Horace when barely forty-five already bewails the passing of youth

(*Epist.* 1.1.1–9, 1.7.25–28), and Macrobius contends that, for a woman at least, thirty-eight is an age "vergens in senium" (*Sat.* 2.5.2).

4. For documentation, see the entries under the appropriate names in Appendixes 2A (for Horace), 2E (for Vergil), and 2B (for Ovid).

5. Our knowledge of Sarmentus' background derives from a scholium to Juvenal *Sat.* 5.3. It should be noted, by the way, that Sarmentus is a *scurra* (*Serm.* 1.5.52), that similar characters (Servilius Balatro and Vibidius) turn up in Maecenas' train again at *Serm.* 2.8, and that Gabba (whose association with Maecenas is documented by Plut. *Amat.* 16 [759 F-760 A]) and "Iortios" (an associate known from the *Suda,* 2:200.2 Adler) are further examples of the type. Clearly Maecenas enjoyed this sort of company, which should allay any temptation to think that conversation at his table was unrelievedly literary.

6. Many readers have felt that Horace's relationship to Propertius was positively hostile, on the basis of *Serm.* 1.9 and *Epist.* 2.2.95–101, which they take as directed against Propertius. A similar but I believe wholly unpersuasive inference is sometimes drawn from *Carm.* 4.4.18–22 regarding Horace's relationship with Domitius Marsus, because these lines seems to belittle the legend of the Amazons, and Marsus wrote an *Amazonis.*

7. Don. *Vita Verg.* 11 and 13 Hardie. This information is partly borne out by two anecdotes. When Vergil joined the party whose trip to Brundisium is chronicled in *Serm.* 1.5, he did not start from Rome, like Horace, but met the others where the Appian Way first approached Campania (lines 39–44). And several years later, when he read the *Georgics* to Augustus, the rendezvous took place not in Rome but once more in Campania, at Atella (Don. *Vita Verg.* 27 Hardie). At both times Vergil must have been residing in the south.

8. The malice of companions is the leading theme of *Serm.* 1.3 (note especially lines 58–61, "hic fugit omnis / insidias . . . / cum genus hoc inter vitae versemur, ubi acris / invidia atque vigent ubi crimina"), and the theme surfaces also at 1.4.78–103, 1.10.78–80, *Epist.* 1.3.30–36, 1.14.37–38, and 1.18.10–20 and 67–85. For witnesses other than Horace, see Sen. *Ben.* 6.34, Pliny *Epist.* 2.6.2, 7.28.3, Juv. 3.119–125, and Lucian *De mercede conductis* 17, 26, and 39–40.

9. We do not know what poems Ovid had in mind when he said that his early work was written under the aegis of Messalla (*Pont.* 2.3.77–78). But given the known facts of his poetic development, there can be no reasonable doubt that this portion of his oeuvre consisted of love poetry. One hypothesis holds that it is actually preserved in the *Corpus Tibullianum,* under the pseudonym of Lygdamus.

10. To the poetry produced under Messalla's aegis we must add the work of Sextilius Ena, for whom Messalla sponsored a recitation; Sextilius' poem was on a Roman historical theme (Sen. *Suas.* 6.27). If one had to take the *Ciris* and

Catalepton 9 into account as well, it would be still harder to define a unified Messallan thematic.

11. For Maecenas' prose style, see Sen. *Epist.* 114, Quint. 9.4.28, Suet. *Aug.* 86.2, and Macr. *Sat.* 2.4.12; the poetic fragments are collected in *FPL* pp. 101–103 Morel = 131–134 Büchner.

12. The political investment of Sabin(i)us Tiro, who dedicated a work on horticulture to Maecenas (Pliny *HNat.* 19.177), is also open to question.

13. For instances of Maecenas' press-agentry on behalf of Vergil, see Sen. *Suas.* 1.12 and 2.20. For efforts by Messalla and his son Cotta Maximus on Ovid's behalf, see *Tr.* 4.4.31 and *Pont.* 3.5.43. For Pliny's efforts, see *Epist.* 1.16, 4.27, 5.17, 6.21, and 8.12.

14. *Laus Pis.* 223–242 and 253–258, Mart. *Epigr.* 7.97 and 12.2.9–15, Stat. *Silvae* 2 pr. p. 32.27–29 Courtney, and Pliny *Epist.* 9.25.3.

15. Some good examples are Cic. *Fam.* 7.5.3 = 26 SB, 13.3 = 315 SB, 13.17.3 = 283 SB, 13.19.3 = 285 SB, 13.24 = 290 SB, Pliny *Epist.* 2.13 and 7.31.

16. Cic. *Fam.* 7.6 = 27 SB documents the start of the relationship with Caesar, and references to Trebatius scattered through the *Letters to Atticus* show what it had become by the 40s. For a more intricate hopscotch toward Caesar's favor by an ambitious Greek writer, see Cic. *Fam.* 13.16 = 316 SB.

17. Suet. *Vita Hor.* p. 297.17–24 Roth, and Sen. *Cont.* 10.5.21.

18. Pliny *Epist.* 7.7–8 and 7.15, and Stat. *Silvae* 4.4.20–21. Compare also the triangular relationship between Rubellius Plautus, Cornelius Laco, and Piso Licinianus to which Tacitus alludes at *Hist.* 1.14.1.

19. Mart. *Epigr.* 4.82, 5.80, 7.68, and 10.93. The Secundus to whom Martial asks Severus to show his poems in 5.80 may be the Caecilius Secundus who turns up three years later in 7.84.

20. Val. Max. 4.7 ext. 2, Hor. *Serm.* 1.6.54–62, *Epist.* 1.18.76–85, and *Serm.* 1.9. For a parallel movement involving Greek friends of Augustus, see Strabo 14.5.4 (670).

21. There are three other cases in which it could be argued that Horace has ties to both a father and a son, though that is not the view generally taken. (1) At *Serm.* 1.1.10.83, Horace refers to *uterque Viscorum*. Since Pseudo-Acro supplies particulars about a father and two sons here, it is possible that Horace has in mind the father and one son, though the scholiast thinks he is referring to the two brothers. (2) At *Epist.* 1.18.60 Horace instances a detail about the *paternum rus* of Lollius Maximus which may imply that he was personally acquainted with Lollius' father; moreover the possibility cannot be entirely ruled out that this Lollius Maximus is a son of the consular M. Lollius of *Carm.* 4.9. (3) The Munatius of *Epist.* 1.3.31 might be a son of the consular L. Munatius Plancus of *Carm.* 1.7. Otherwise, Horace gives no indication that paternal connections played any part in acquainting him with his many friends in their twenties or

younger (Aelius Lamia, Albinovanus Celsus, Iullus Antonius, Paullus Fabius Maximus, Iccius, Julius Florus, C. Marcius Censorinus, Scaeva, Septimius, and Titius).

22. That Messalinus' fancied triumph is meant to recall Messalla's real triumph is made clear by *ipse* at 2.5.117; note also that in 2.5.119 Tibullus expects to maintain his relationship with Messalla even after Messallinus is grown.

23. At the end of the next century (the only other point at which we have comparable data about poets' relationships), the picture is similar. Out of an assortment of some 140 friends, Martial takes note of persons who belong to different generations of the same family twelve times. Yet only two cases are significant. Martial seems acquainted with Camonius Rufus and his father (*Epigr.* 6.85 and 9.74), and with Faustinus and his son Marcellinus (*Epigr.* 3.6, 6.25, and 7.80). But none of his other references suggest that he is on familiar terms with both parties. At *Epigr.* 8.66 Martial congratulates the senatorial poet Silius Italicus on the consulate of his son Decianus, and at *Epigr.* 9.86 he commiserates over the death of Silius' younger son Severus (who cannot be identical with Martial's friend Severus, given *sui* at 9.86.1 and the reemergence of Severus in *Epigr.* 11.57). He congratulates Munatius Gallus on a distinguished match made by his daughter at *Epigr.* 10.33, and at *Epigr.* 7.40 he condoles with Claudius Etruscus on the death of his aged father, an imperial freedman who had been discharged and was living in internal exile until shortly before his death. Most of the other references involve parents of very young children (*Epigr.* 1.114, 1.116, 4.45, 5.6.6, 5.56, 6.27, and 6.38), and the two remaining (*Epigr.* 10.98.3 and 12.62.14) are wholly uninformative.

Among the eighteen *privati* who receive Statius' *Silvae* the situation is still clearer, since the poet generally divulges more information about his friends than Martial does. The one family in which his contacts unmistakably spanned the generations was domiciled in his own home territory on the Bay of Naples and had a Greek background like his own. Statius was on close terms with Pollius Felix and his wife Polla (*Silvae* 2.2, 3 *pr.*, 3.1, 3.5.103, 4.8.13–14 and 57–58); he knew Pollius' daughter and son-in-law Julius Menecrates, whom he congratulated on the birth of their third child (*Silvae* 4.8); and he at least kept himself informed about the military career of Pollius' son (*Silvae* 4.8.12). In the other four cases in which he alludes to sons or fathers of his friends, there can be no question of a personal relationship. The sons of Vitorius Marcellus (*Silvae* 4.4.70–77) and of Vibius Maximus (*Silvae* 4.7) were young children; Vettius Crispinus' father (*Silvae* 5.2.30–67) had been dead for at least a couple of years before Statius wrote to the son, and despite a long account of the father's career, Statius claims no personal tie with him; and the father of Claudius Etruscus (*Silvae* 3.3) was that same freedman to whom Martial refers, who died shortly after a period of exile.

24. The brother of Messalla referred to at *Serm.* 1.10.85 is presumed to

be his half-brother Gellius Poplicola; the Visci mentioned at *Serm.* 1.10.83 are probably brothers, but (as indicated in note 21) conceivably they could be father and son.

25. The evidence for Horace's relations with Tiberius and Drusus is collected under the respective entries in Appendix 2A.

26. *Epist.* 1.20.2. Apart from the five instances discussed, Horace occasionally refers to brothers of people honored in his poems (namely, the brother(s) of Aelius Lamia at *Epist.* 1.14.7, of Lollius Maximus at *Epist.* 1.18.63, and of Proculeius at *Carm.* 2.2.6), but nothing in those contexts suggests that he stood on familiar terms with them.

27. See the entries for C. Pomponius Graecinus and L. Pomponius Flaccus in Appendix 2B. Shortly after Ovid's letter to Flaccus was written, Flaccus was posted as legate to the lower Danube region where Ovid was interned, yet at least in verse, Ovid attempted no further contact with him (compare *Pont.* 4.9.75–88 and 119–120).

28. See in Appendix 2C the entries for Cornelia, Cornelius, L. Aemilius Paullus, and M. Aemilius Lepidus.

29. Evidence from the end of the first century A.D. again runs parallel. The corpus of Martial's epigrams reveals only three pairs of brothers of which both parties have ties to Martial: Domitius Tullus and Lucanus (*Epigr.* 1.36, 3.20.17, 5.28.3, and 9.51; these brothers are known to have maintained an exceptionally close relationship, on which see Pliny *Epist.* 8.18), the poets Turnus and Scaevus Memor (*Epigr.* 11.9–10), and Unicus and his brother (*Epigr.* 12.44, perhaps the clearest instance to be found of lateral recruitment within a family). Statius twice refers to brothers of his friends (the brother of Claudius Etruscus at *Silvae* 3.3.145–155 and the brother of Crispinus at *Silvae* 5.2.65 and 75), but appears to have no relationship with them.

30. Compare "me / *cum magnis* vixisse invita fatebitur usque / invidia," *Serm.* 2.1.75–77, and Horace's advice to Scaeva about getting ahead, "*principibus placuisse viris* non ultima laus est," *Epist.* 1.17.35.

31. For Propertius' friends, see 1.1.25–38, 1.11.25, 2.4.13, 2.25.39–44, 3.8.21, 3.21.15, and 3.24.9; the *amici* are probably implicit in Propertius' anonymous second-person addresses (as at 2.1.1, 2.8.2, 3.11.1 and 8, 3.13.1) and in some of his allusions to what contemporaries say about him (as at 2.14.12, 2.17.11, 2.24.1–10, 2.26.21–22, and 3.25.1–2). For Lygdamus' milieu, see [Tib.] 3.5.1 and 29–34, 3.6.9–18 and 43–46.

32. Hor. *Serm.* 1.4.129–39; see also 1.3.69–75 and 139–142, 1.6.69–70.

33. Alfenus Varus from Cremona (schol. Hor. *Serm.* 1.3.130–32); Plotius Tucca from Cisalpine Gaul (schol. Pers. *Sat.* 2.42); and Quintilius (Varus?) from Cremona (Hieron. *Chron.* p. 165 a Helm and schol. Hor. *Ars* 438). The *origo* of Varius Rufus is not known, but he is constantly associated with Vergil and Tucca, and the Patavine Asconius was supposedly in a position to report having

had a conversation with Varius' wife or mistress Plotia (Don. *Vita Verg.* 10 Hardie). Aemilius Macer and C. Helvius Cinna, who may have been friends with Vergil though a connection cannot be proved, were also from the north. Macer was Veronese (Hieron. *Chron.* p. 166 g Helm), and Helvius Cinna came probably from Brescia, where the nomen is well attested (note also Cinna frag. 9, *FPL* p. 89 Morel = 115 Büchner). In addition to regional ties they shared, Quintilius, Plotius, and Varius were study companions of Vergil in south Italy: see the *Vita Probiana* p. 27.10–12 Hardie, Serv. on *Ecl.* 6.13, and now above all Philod. *PHerc. Paris.* 2 as deciphered by M. Gigante and M. Capasso in *SIFC,* 3 ser., 7 (1989): 4.

34. Horace's stay in Athens overlapped with that of L. Calpurnius Bibulus and M. Valerius Messalla Corvinus (Cic. *Att.* 12.32.2 = 271 SB) and perhaps of Torquatus too, if he is identical with the (Manlius) Acidinus Cicero mentions in the same context. Fellow partisans of Brutus included Bibulus (App. *BCiv.* 4.162, 4.434–436, and 4.575) and Messalla (App. *BCiv.* 4.159–162, 4.575, Plut. *Brut.* 40–41, and Vell. Pat. 2.71.1), as well as that chronic rallier Dellius (Sen. *Suas.* 1.7), Pompeius (Hor. *Carm.* 2.7.1–5), and Sestius (App. *BCiv.* 4.223, Cass. Dio 53.32.4, and Crawford *RRC* 1:515, no. 502). Two more possibilities are Calpurnius Piso, if the recipient of the *Ars* is the consul of 23 (see Tac. *Ann.* 2.43.2), and Torquatus, if Horace's friend is the Aulus Torquatus of Nepos *Att.* 11.2 or a son.

35. Ovid writes to his (third) wife's son-in-law P. Suillius Rufus (*Pont.* 4.8), to her uncle Rufus (*Pont.* 2.11), and to Macer who was another kinsman (*Pont.* 2.10.10). This woman had belonged to the entourage of Augustus' aunt Atia (*Pont.* 1.2.139) and then to the entourage of Atia's daughter Marcia: she thus reinforced Ovid's ties with Marcia and her husband Paullus Fabius Maximus (Ov. *Pont.* 1.2.136–150, 3.1.75–78, and *Fasti* 6.809). As the daughter of Atia and confidante of Livia (Tac. *Ann.* 1.5.1–2), Marcia may for her part have opened certain doors at court—to those glittering friends whose acquaintance Ovid later regretted having made (*Tr.* 3.4.4–8), for example, and to members of Germanicus' entourage like Albinovanus Pedo, Carus, Cassius Salanus, and perhaps Sextus Pompeius. (Suillius Rufus was also closely connected with Germanicus at this period.)

36. In this regard, two texts which can be interestingly juxtaposed are Hor. *Epist.* 1.7, documenting the transition of a dependent to free agency, and Ov. *Pont.* 1.9, describing a dependent who did not make the transition.

37. For the details of Horace's relationships with these men, see Appendix 2A.

38. For the role of the school in molding poets, one of the prime texts is Suet. *Gr.* 11.2 on Valerius Cato, "peridoneus praeceptor maxime ad poeticam tendentibus ut quidem adparere vel his versiculis potest, 'Cato grammaticus Latina Siren / qui solus legit ac facit poetas.'" See also *Gr.* 16.3 for a verse

describing another *grammaticus* as "tenellorum nutricula vatum" (though Suetonius seems not to understand this verse as referring to pupil-poets). The rudiments of a poetic vocation are linked with school experience by Ovid (*Tr.* 4.10.15–30), the *Ciris* poet (44–45), and Juvenal (*Sat.* 1.1–18); Pliny remembers having tried his hand at tragedy at the age of fourteen (*Epist.* 7.4.2), and a contemporary of Pliny's won the prize for Latin poetry at the Capitoline Games when he was thirteen (*ILS* 5178).

39. For the *chorus* metaphor, see Hor. *Carm.* 4.3.15, *Epist.* 2.2.77, Ov. *Tr.* 5.3.52, *Pont.* 3.4.68, and Stat. *Silvae* 2.7.23; see also *manus* at Hor. *Serm.* 1.4.141, *turba* at Prop. 3.1.12 and Ov. *Tr.* 5.3.47, and *cohors* at Stat. *Silvae* 1.2.249. Ovid speaks of a poetic *foedus* at *Pont.* 2.5.60, 2.9.63, and 4.13.43, of a *ius sodalicii* at *Tr.* 4.10.46, and of *sacra* at *Pont.* 2.9.64, 2.10.17, 3.4.67, and 4.8.81. Statius calls himself the *collega* of another poet at *Silvae* 1 pr. p. 2.23 Courtney.

40. Verg. *Ecl.* 3.84–91, 9.32–36; the contrastive effect is due at least partly to the amoebean style of the two poems.

41. *Epod.* 6, 10, *Serm.* 1.2.1–4, 1.3.1–19 and 85–89, 1.4, 1.9.21–25, 1.10, 2.1, 2.5.40–41, *Epist.* 1.4.3, 1.19, 2.1, 2.2.87–108, *Ars* 295–304, 382–384, and 408–437. The asperity which pervades the first book of *Satires* drops off appreciably once Horace has become established himself.

42. Suet. *Jul.* 55.3; for the situation, compare Quint. *Inst.* 7.2.24.

43. Diod. Sic. 1.3.8 and 1.4.2–3. Presumably Diodorus is alluding to private libraries, like the one Lucullus made available to visiting Greek savants (Plut. *Luc.* 42). But Rome also acquired its first public library during Diodorus' sojourn there.

44. Philodemus' comment survives in a papyrus fragment of his *On Rhetoric,* 2:145 Sudhaus, frag. 3, lines 8–15.

45. Lucan's *salticae fabulae* are known from the *Vita Luc.* p. 336.19 Hosius; Statius' pantomimes are mentioned by Juvenal at *Sat.* 7.86–92. For stage adaptations of Vergil's poems, see Tac. *Dial.* 13.2, Suet. *Nero* 54, Don. *Vita Verg.* 26 Hardie, Macr. *Sat.* 5.17.5, and Serv. *Ecl.* 6.11; for adaptations of Ovid's poems, see *Tr.* 2.519–520, 5.7.25–28. Pliny discloses that some of his poems were adapted for public performance (*Epist.* 7.4.9), and Hor. *Serm.* 1.10.17–19 can be taken as establishing the same for poems of Calvus and Catullus.

46. Hor. *Serm.* 1.2.1–11, 1.3.1–19 and 129–130, 1.4.72, 1.9.25, 1.10.17–19, 78–80, and 90–91. For simplicity's sake I have ignored the apparently unresolvable question of whether the singer variously introduced as Tigellius, Hermogenes, and Tigellius Hermogenes is one or two persons. If two men are in fact to be distinguished, they are nevertheless both singers, and the second is almost certainly to be seen as the freedman and professional inheritor of the first. The *Satires* also mention another singer (1.10.79 and 90) and a dancer (2.6.72), and it should be noted that the obnoxious interlocutor of *Serm.* 1.9 also boasts of being a singer and a dancer (24–25).

47. *Epigr.* 3.4.7–8; the motif recurs in *Epigr.* 5.56. Since singers often composed their own material, it was easy for poets to see them as practicing an art in competition with their own.

48. *Via* in line 20 I interpret as the *Via Sacra,* taking the setting to be the same as that of Hor. *Serm.* 1.9.1. Ovid enumerates his favorite haunts again at *Pont.* 1.8.35–38, and a similar list emerges from the itinerary Catullus follows in the search for a friend which he recounts in poem 55.

49. The clearest evidence that bookshops served as gathering places dates from the second century A.D. (Gell. *NA* 5.4, 13.31, and 18.4), but that function seems already implied by Hor. *Serm.* 1.4.71–72 and, on one interpretation, by Catullus 55.4. For socializing in public libraries the earliest evidence again comes from the second century (Gell. *NA* 11.17 and 13.20.1), though Mart. *Epigr.* 12 *pr.* line 11 Lindsay = p. 395.11 SB may be relevant, and we have a pretty vignette of users congregating in a *privately* owned library during the first century B.C. (Plut. *Luc.* 42).

50. "Cum Livius Andronicus bello Punico secundo scribsisset carmen, quod a virginibus est cantatum, quia prosperius respublica populi Romani geri coepta est, publice adtributa est ei in Aventino aedis Minervae, in qua liceret scribis histrionibusque consistere ac dona ponere; in honorem Livi, quia is et scribebat fabulas et agebat," Fest. pp. 446.29–448.4 Lindsay. Although it is generally assumed that this passage points to one *collegium* incorporating both *scribae* and actors, the text does not seem to exclude the possibility that there were two *collegia.*

51. "[Accius poeta] Iulio Caesari amplissimo ac florentissimo viro in conlegium poetarum venienti numquam adsurrexit, non maiestatis eius immemor, sed quod in conparatione communium studiorum aliquanto se superiorem esse confideret. quaproper insolentiae crimine caruit, quia ibi voluminum non imaginum certamina exercebantur," Val. Max. 3.7.11.

52. The inscription of Cornelius Surus has recently been republished with an improved reading, a photograph, and full references to earlier discussion by S. Panciera, "Ancora sull'iscrizione di Cornelius Surus magister scribarum poetarum," *BCAR* 91 (1986): 35–44 (a reference for which I am indebted to Nicholas Horsfall). As read by Panciera the text runs: "[Cor]nelius P. l. Surus, / [nome]nclator, mag(ister) / [Capito]linus (quinquies) a(nnis) (nouem), / [mag(ister)? s]utorum, praeco / [ab ae]rario ex tribus / [decuri]eis, mag(ister) scr(ibarum) poetar(um) / [ludos] fecit in theatro lapidio, / [ac]cens(us) co(n)s(ulis) et cens(oris)." The inscription has been dated chiefly by its reference to a *theatrum lapidium,* which should put it after the building of Pompey's theater in 55 B.C. and (less certainly) before the last decade of the century, by which time the city could boast three stone theaters. The epigraphic style is said to be consistent with a Caesarean or Augustan date. The only other indication of date is that among the charges which comprise his *cursus,* Surus lists the position

of *accensus censoris,* without identifying which censor he served. After 22 B.C. the censorship was reserved to the emperor and members of his family (except for one powerful *privatus* who served as Claudius' censorial colleague in A.D. 47). If one can assume that Surus would have named the censor he served had it been anyone so grand as an emperor or prince, his appointment should belong in or before the year 22. Even if this criterion is valid, however, it does not necessarily yield a terminus complementary to the reference to the stone theater: Surus could as easily have been *accensus censoris* before 55 B.C. as after.

53. It may be that the industrious Surus was a *poeta* of consummate art, but the odds are rather that the qualification was not difficult to meet. It is even conceivable that he was not a *poeta* by any definition: there are *collegia* in which it is clear that not every member and more particularly not every officer practiced the titular occupation.

54. Except for the enigmatic *aedes Camenarum* of Pliny *HNat.* 34.19, which is also (and for the same reason) taken to be a reference to the Temple of Hercules of the Muses, and Juvenal's *aedes Musarum et Apollinis* at *Sat.* 7.37, where the context indicates that the temple is metaphorical.

55. I say this fully accepting that the information which Porphyrio and Pseudo-Acro furnish about other passages is often of great value. But that cannot be the case at *Serm.* 1.10.38. The relevant part of the note in the Porphyrio commentary reads as follows: "[Horatius] ait se id genus carminis scribere quod Meci Tarpae arbitrio non subiciatur. nam hi fere qui scaenae scribebant ad Tarpam hunc velut emendatorem ea adferebant. *Quae neque in aede sonent:* In aede Musarum, ubi poetae carmina sua recitabant." Holder, following Pauly, distinguished these as separate observations and transposed them. They constitute alternative and partial explanations: the situation is either that poets used to recite poems in the temple of the Muses, or that poets who wrote for the stage used to submit their scripts for criticism to Tarpa. One explanation corresponds to Porphyrio's note on *Epist.* 2.2.94, where Horace refers to poets in a temple but makes no mention of Tarpa, and the scholiast comments, "significat autem aedem Musarum, in qua poetae recitabant." The other part of the note points unmistakably to a different Horatian passage, *Ars* 387, in which Horace advises a would-be tragedian to submit his efforts to Maecius (Tarpa) the judge, but says nothing about competing in a temple. In the truncated version of the commentary which has come down to us, Porphyrio's note at *Ars* 387 ("Maecius perdiligens carminum fuit aestimator") now bears no resemblance to his comment at *Serm.* 1.10.38. But all the details in this part of his note on the *Satires* passage are clearly based on what Horace says in the *Ars:* that is where Porphyrio gets the nomen Maecius, the idea that Tarpa is an *emendator,* and the certainty that Horace is talking about tragic poets only; hence also the sudden disappearance of a recitation context in this portion of the note. There is every reason to conclude that Porphyrio did not understand the passage from the

Satires and had no independent information about it. Instead, remembering two other passages of Horace which sounded partly relevant, he explained *Serm.* 1.10.38 in terms of them. Since it is only at *Serm.* 1.10.38 and not in the other two passages that Horace seems to be talking about a poetic competition before a judge, Porphyrio is therefore a useless guide to the circumstances of that competition.

The Pseudo-Acronian scholia have little to say about what is going on in the temple scene apart from what they derive from Porphyrio. They are more preoccupied with the temple itself, which is identified in successive stabs as the Temple of Apollo, a Mouseion or Athenaeum, or the Temple of the Muses. Since none of these assertions is fleshed out with the least bit of historical or topographical detail, there is no reason to think that we have here anything but a run of uninformed guesses.

But although the comments by Porphyrio and Pseudo-Acro can confidently be discounted, I must register a qualm about the note by the Commentator Cruquianus: "Metius Tarpa fuit iudex criticus, auditor assiduus poematum et poetarum in aede Apollinis seu Musarum quo convenire solebant poetae suaque scripta recitare; *quae nisi a Tarpa aut alio critico, qui numero erant quinque, probarentur, in scenam non deferebantur.*" What is reported in the italicized part of the note has no parallel in any other source and no foundation in Horace's text. So long as the authenticity of the Cruquius scholia remains unsettled, the possibility must be left open that the scholiastic tradition did after all have access to independent information at this point, though apparently not about the temple.

56. Admittedly we do not know much. Apart from whatever it is that *Serm.* 1.10.38 tells us, Cic. *Fam.* 7.1.1 = 24 SB identifies Spurius Maecius as the man who selected the works staged in Pompey's theater in 55, and Horace at *Ars* 387 opines that a would-be writer of drama would do well to try out his work on Maecius. The problematic Cruquius scholium on Hor. *Serm.* 1.10.38 also connects Tarpa with the stage.

57. Two other considerations may be relevant here, but unfortunately they pull in different directions. If we could know for certain that the poets' guild held competitions in the first place, we would have reason to hypothesize that the competitions were limited to tragedy, comedy, and mime. It was for contributions to the public good in the form of public performances that the poets first gained official recognition in the third century B.C. (Festus pp. 446.29–448.4 Lindsay), and even afterward, it must have been primarily their public poetry which guaranteed them continuing rights of organization as a *collegium*. However, it is also worth bearing in mind that a pre-production scrutiny of dramatic scripts (if such was the practice) need not necessarily have been conducted under the auspices of the poets' guild. Magistrates in charge of the festivals may have preferred to select their own experts, as Terence found when he submitted a script (Suet. *Vita Ter.* p. 292.28–34 Roth). For that matter, they may

have chosen to bypass advisers altogether and to commission pieces directly from playwrights (see Macr. *Sat.* 2.6.6). Frequent and important as the *ludi scaenici* were, we know next to nothing about preparations for them.

58. For *certare* in such contexts, see Hor. *Epist.* 1.19.11, Verg. *Ecl.* 5.8–9, *Laus Pis.* 223, and Stat. *Silvae* 1.2.248, and for *vincere*, Hor. *Epist.* 1.4.3, 2.1.59, Ov. *Tr.* 2.381, 3.7.20, and *Panegyricus Messallae* 200. For the crowning metaphor, see Hor. *Serm.* 1.10.49, *Carm.* 1.1.29, *Epist.* 1.3.25, 1.19.26, and 2.2.96. For *iudex* as "connoisseur," see Hor. *Epist.* 1.4.1, Prop. 2.13.14, Ov. *Tr.* 1.1.45, 3.7.24, and the papyrus fragment attributed to Cornelius Gallus, *FPL* frag. 4.5 Büchner.

59. A passage of the *Ars* may offer one further argument against the idea that Tarpa presided over a formal competition. In lines 385–390 Horace advises an aristocrat's son to take his tragedy to Tarpa, and it is clear that what he has in mind is not a private consultation, but a recitation *(in Maeci auris)* in a public forum (implied by the verb *descendat*): a situation very similar, in other words, to the situation implied at *Serm.* 1.10.38. It is hard to believe that Horace would advise a young blueblood to pit himself against others under conditions in which he risked losing face.

60. To wit, Livius Andronicus (Festus p. 446.29–30 Lindsay), Accius and Julius Caesar Strabo (Val. Max. 3.7.11), Cornelius Surus (note 52), and Martial and his friend Canius Rufus (Mart. *Epigr.* 3.20). It has been suggested on the basis of *Serm.* 2.6.36–37 that Horace makes a seventh. Horace there identifies himself as a *scriba,* by which he might conceivably mean *scriba poeta,* as (perhaps) in the Surus inscription. But the more common view is that Horace means *scriba quaestorius* and is referring to the clerkship which Suetonius says he acquired after Philippi (*Vita Hor.* p. 297.9 Roth). The context does not decide one way or the other.

61. Hor. *Epist.* 1.20.1–12, *Ars* 372–373, Mart. *Epigr.* 1.2, 1.113, 1.117, 4.72, and 13.3.

62. Hor. *Epist.* 2.1.214–218, 2.2.92–94, Ov. *Tr.* 3.1.59–72, *Pont.* 1.1.5–10, Mart. *Epigr.* 5.5 and 12.2.7–8.

63. For contemporary poets in the schools, see Suet. *Gr.* 16.3, Hor. *Serm.* 1.10.74–75, *Epist.* 1.20.17–18, Pers. *Sat.* 1.29–30, and Stat. *Theb.* 12.815. Horace's comment is found at *Epist.* 2.1.84–85.

64. Seneca does not specify the date, but Pollio would have had little time for a literary career before his ostentatious withdrawal from politics in 39; his endeavors as a dramatist and as a historian demonstrably belong after that year.

65. Among myriad references to poetic recitations, these vignettes give the best picture of what took place: Sen. *Suas.* 6.27, Pers. *Sat.* 1.13–27, Sen. *Epist.* 122.11–13, Tac. *Dial.* 9.3–4, Pliny *Epist.* 1.13, 4.27, 5.17, 6.15, 6.17, 8.12, Juv. *Sat.* 1.1–13, 7.39–47, and 82–87. Evidence about the setting in which recita-

tions took place is complicated by the difficulty of differentiating among the various situations to which the term *recitare* is applied in our sources. Nevertheless, in those cases where we can discern that the recitation involves a single poet reading his work to a general audience, if a setting is specified, it is predominantly a great man's mansion: Sen. *Suas.* 6.27, Tac. *Ann.* 3.49.1, *Dial.* 9.3, Mart. *Epigr.* 4.6.4–5, Pliny *Epist.* 8.12.2, Juv. *Sat.* 1.12 and 7.40. Poems which had been adapted for performance by singers or dancers were of course presented in theaters, and the emperor Nero elected to recite his poetry in a theater (Suet. *Nero* 10.2, Cass. Dio 62.29.1, and Tac. *Ann.* 16.4.2), but these are obviously exceptional cases. For one thing, they feature principals who either were or considered themselves experts in the art of performance. Other references to theater recitation (Hor. *Epist.* 1.19.41–42, Tac. *Dial.* 10.5, and possibly Stat. *Silvae* 5.2.160–163; Petr. *Sat.* 90.5 and Gell. *NA* 18.5.1–4 concern theater recitations outside Rome) are so scarce and uninformative that we cannot tell whether it was a typical venue or not. Temples and probably the new state libraries contained open areas suitable for use as auditoriums, and it is not impossible that poets sometimes gave readings there. Horace envisions a temple setting for what is apparently a serial recitation at *Serm.* 1.10.38, and perhaps also at *Epist.* 2.2.91–101. But in fact we cannot verify a single case in which a solo performance before an invited audience took place in a temple or public library. Given the indications we have, we must conclude that such performances most often took place in the town houses of the elite. This domestic ambience is one of the elements which differentiate the Roman practice of recitation from the Greek practice of epideixis. It is not unlikely, however, that some reciters—socially prominent dilettanti, for example, and perhaps a handful of well-established popular poets—were capable of drawing audiences too large for a private salon. Their performances may well have been staged in larger public buildings.

66. Horace imputes a sense of literary noblesse oblige to Augustus at *Epist.* 2.1.214–218, but the preeminent spokesman of that outlook is the younger Pliny: *Epist.* 1.13, 3.15.2, 3.21.3, 5.17.6, 6.17.5, and 8.12.1; see also Statius on Manilius Vopiscus "qui praecipue vindicat a situ litteras iam paene fugientes," *Silvae* 1 pr. p. 2.24–25 Courtney.

67. See Sen. *Suas.* 6.27, Pliny *Epist.* 6.15.2 and 4, and Tac. *Dial.* 9.3. The fact that invitations were issued suggests not only that recitations were attended by a more diverse group than those who would normally frequent a sponsor's home, but that in practice admission may have been open to anyone. If the reciter was free to invite whomever he pleased, the domestic staff would have had little idea whom to let in and whom to keep out (unless we want to suppose that people waved invitations as they entered). Another reason for thinking that admission was unrestricted is that the sources often use language suggesting that

a general public attended recitations: *populus* (Ov. *Tr.* 4.10.57–58, Pers. *Sat.* 1.15, Pliny *Epist.* 5.3.11, 7.17.11–12), *urbs* and *volgus* (Juv. *Sat.* 7.83–86), and *homines* (Sen. *Cont.* 4 *pr.* 2).

68. For habitués of the recitation circuit, see Pliny *Epist.* 1.13.5 and 8.12.2; attendance by other poets is indicated at Don. *Vita Verg.* 29 Hardie, Sen. *Suas.* 6.27, Ov. *Tr.* 4.10.49–50 (if Ovid is speaking of public recitation here), and Juv. *Sat.* 1.1–13. Pliny's characterization of recitation audiences in *Epist.* 1.13 suggests that they were likely to include a few philistines.

69. For hecklers, see Don. *Vita. Verg.* 43 Hardie, Sen. *Epist.* 122.11–13, Pliny *Epist.* 6.15.2; for walk-outs, see Sen. *Suas.* 6.27 and Suet. *Vita Luc.* p. 299.24–25 Roth; see also the similar incident which occurred during a declaimer's performance, Sen. *Cont.* 2.4.12–13.

70. Notice Pliny's own effusive response to a reading at *Epist.* 5.17.4–5, and the fact that his specific comments on a recitation have to be canvassed after the performance by letter, *Epist.* 3.15.

71. Suetonius' monograph on the *grammatici* treats some half dozen who were prominent in Rome during the Augustan period (*Gr.* 15–22), and sporadic references to their activities continue until we have Gellius' expansive picture of a literary milieu a century and a half later in which they are omnipresent (for example, Gell. *NA* 2.3.5, 3.16.16, 4.1, 5.4.2, 6.17, 7.6.12, 8.10, 14.5, 15.9, 16.6, 18.7, 19.10.7, 19.13.4, and 20.10).

72. A partial list can be quickly compiled from a few sources. Seneca the Elder reports on performances by approximately three dozen Greek declaimers, most of whom he seems to have encountered in Rome on the same circuit as the Latin rhetors and declaimers he heard; they are readily identified with the help of the prosopography in H. Bornecque, *Les déclamations et les déclamateurs d'après Sénèque le père* (Lille, 1902). At least three of the poets excerpted in the *Greek Anthology* visited or resided in Rome at some point during Augustus' ascendancy (Antipater of Thessalonica, Crinagoras of Mytilene, and Diodorus of Sardis), and a half-dozen others may also have visited there during the same time (Alpheus of Mytilene, Antiphilus of Byzantium, Apollonides, Bassus, Philodemus, and Thallus). The major works of Greek prose which have survived from this period were all written by authors residing at least temporarily in Rome: Diodorus Siculus' universal history, Dionysius of Halicarnassus' rhetorical studies and his history of early Rome, and Strabo's geography. The names of many other Greek writers and intellectuals can be assembled from A. Hillscher, *Hominum litteratorum Graecorum ante Tiberii mortem in urbe Roma commoratorum historia critica, Jahrbuch für classische Philologie,* Supplementband 18 (Leipzig, 1892); G. W. Bowersock, *Augustus and the Greek World* (Oxford, 1965); and now (apropos of Greek contemporaries of Vergil in Rome) N. Horsfall, *Virgilio: L'epopea in alambicco* (Naples, 1991), pp. 39–41. Some active at Rome between the death of Caesar and the death of Augustus include Anaxilaus of Larissa, Apollodorus

of Pergamum, Areus of Alexandria and his sons Nicanor and Dionysius, Athenaeus of Seleucia, Athenodorus of Tarsus, Caecilius of Caleacte, Habron, Isidore of Charax, Nestor of Tarsus, Nicolaus of Damascus, the mime writer Philistio, Theodorus of Gadara, Thrasyllus of Alexandria, the historian Timagenes, the younger Tyrannio, and Xenarchus of Seleucia.

73. No *grammatici* are known among the friends of Propertius or Tibullus. Among Horace's friends only one man, Aristius Fuscus, can be identified as a *grammaticus;* Horace also offers a reminiscence of his old schoolteacher Orbilius, though it is not a fond one. Ovid refers once to the poet and *grammaticus* Melissus in a catalogue of poets but does not name Hyginus, though he and Hyginus are said to have been friends; whether his friend Carus can be considered a *grammaticus* is uncertain. Vergil, whose poems make very few references to friends, mentions no *grammatici* among them, though he is said to have had personal ties with Melissus and Parthenius and may have been acquainted with Aristius Fuscus and Caecilius Epirota as well. (For the sources, see the appropriate names in Appendix 2A, 2B, and 2E.)

As for Greek friends, again, Propertius and Tibullus are not known to have had any. Horace introduces into his poems the rhetor Heliodorus and the doctor Antonius Musa, who were certainly Greek, and also the rancher Pompeius Grosphus, the epicure Catius, and a pair of booksellers, the brothers Sosius, some or all of whom may have been Greek. Ovid honors Rhoemetalces and Cotys, two Hellenized Thracians ruling in the region where he was interned, but otherwise omits to speak of any Greeks including his rhetoric teacher Arellius Fuscus. No Greeks figure among the handful of contemporaries Vergil names in the canonical poems, but the philosopher Siro is addressed in the *Catalepton,* and evidence external to the poems associates Vergil with Parthenius, Philodemus, and (by a fortuitous conjunction) the rhetor Heliodorus. (Sources may be found under the appropriate names in Appendix 2.)

3. REQUESTS AND PRESSURE

1. For example, Cic. *Att.* 2.4.3 = 24 SB, 2.12.3 = 30 SB, 2.14.2 = 34 SB, 4.6.3 = 83 SB, 13.13.2 = 321 SB, 14.17.6 = 371 SB, 16.13a(b).2 = 424 SB, *Fam.* 3.9.3 = 72 SB, 7.1.6 = 24 SB, Pliny *Epist.* 5.8, 7.12, 8.15, 9.11, 9.18, and 9.25.

2. Cic. *Fam.* 3.9.3 = 72 SB, 5.12 = 22 SB, 9.8 = 254 SB, Pliny *Epist.* 1.3.4–5 and 7.33.

3. Cic. *Fam.* 8.3.3 = 79 SB and 12.16.4 = 328 SB.

4. Note also *hortari* and *excitare* in *QFr.* 2.14[13].2 = 18 SB, though it is not clear that these verbs refer precisely to Quintus' solicitation about the epic.

5. Cicero uses the same word in speaking of pressure from his younger brother, "epistulam hanc convicio efflagitarunt codicilli tui," *QFr.* 2.10[9].1 = 14 SB.

6. For further details about the usage of *iubere,* see Appendix 3.

7. See for example Cic. *Fam.* 3.9.3 = 72 SB, 8.3.3 = 79 SB, 12.16.4 = 328 SB, and *Att.* 12.12.2 = 259 SB.

8. Prop. 2.17.28, Ov. *Tr.* 3.4b.67–68, 4.5.11–12, Mart. *Epigr.* 4.31 and 5.15.

9. *Auct. ad Her.* 1.1, Varro *Rust.* 1.1.2, Quint. *Inst.* 1 *pr.* 1–3, and Tac. *Dial.* 1.1–2.

10. For letters requesting information, see Cic. *Att.* 12.5b = 316 SB, 12.23.2 = 262 SB, 13.30.2 = 303 SB, Pliny *Epist.* 4.30, 7.27, and 8.14. Horace and Crinagoras produce poetic adaptations of the form in *Epist.* 1.15 and *Anth. Pal.* 9.559 = Gow-Page *Garland of Philip* 1:218 no. 32. For some examples of epistolary responses to such requests, see Pliny *Epist.* 3.5, 5.13, 6.16, 6.20, and 9.13.

11. For Caesar see Cic. *Att.* 13.26.2 = 286 SB and 13.50.1 = 348 SB; for Varro, *Att.* 4.16.2 = 89 SB and 13.12–16 = 320–323 SB; for Hortensius, *Att.* 4.6.3 = 83 SB; for Brutus, *Att.* 13.12.3 = 320 SB and 13.21a.1 = 327 SB.

12. Cic. *Att.* 13.44.1 = 336 SB.

13. For protreptic messages to other writers, see *Epist.* 1.3, 2.10, and 5.10. Disinterested motives are attributed to another friend of letters, Titinius Capito, at *Epist.* 8.12.1: "colit studia, studiosos amat fovet provehit, multorum qui aliqua componunt portus sinus gremium, omnium exemplum, ipsarum denique litterarum iam senescentium reductor ac reformator."

14. See the texts cited in Chapter 1, note 39.

15. Apart from poems (for which see the texts cited in Chapter 1, note 38), the promise motif occurs also in connection with prose works: see Cic. *Fam.* 3.9.3 = 72 SB, 3.11.4 = 74 SB, Cic. *Fam.* 9.8.1 = 254 SB, 12.16.4 = 328 SB, Sen. *Cont.* 9 *pr.* 1, Pliny *Epist.* 1.2.1 and 5.10.

16. For poems, see the references in Chapter 1, note 38; for prose works, see Cic. *Att.* 15.1a.2 = 378 SB, 16.11.1 = 420 SB, Pliny *Epist.* 1.2, 3.13, 8.19.2, and Justinus *Epitome Trogi pr.* 6.

17. Cic. *Att.* 2.1.2 = 21 SB, 12.6a.1 = 243 SB, 13.12.2 = 320 SB, 13.19.2 = 326 SB, 16.2.6 = 412 SB, 16.3.1 = 413 SB, Ov. *Tr.* 3.14, Mart. *Epigr.* 3.5, 5.5, 7.26, 7.97, 12.2.15, and Stat. *Silvae* 2 *pr.* p. 32.27–29 Courtney.

18. Catull. 1, Verg. *Ecl.* 6.6–12, Mart. *Epigr.* 3.2, 9.58, and Stat. *Silv.* 4 *pr.*

19. Admittedly the possibility exists that Cicero planned to supply guidelines later on, when he wrote up the *commentarii* that would contain the raw materials for Lucceius' history (*Fam.* 5.12.10).

20. For the remark to Atticus, see *Att.* 13.45.2 = 337 SB; for the representation to Brutus, see *Tusc.* 1.1 and 5.121; for that to Matius, *Fam.* 11.27.5 = 348 SB.

21. There is one partial exception: Horace's *Letter to Augustus* can be set beside an extract from the letter in which Augustus solicited it (Suet. *Vita Hor.*

p. 298.2–11 Roth). But since this is a case of prompting by the emperor, discussion of it is reserved to Chapter 5.

22. Cic. *Brut.* 132. Quintus Cicero supplied his brother with details for the epic on Caesar's British campaign (Cic. *QFr.* 2.14[13].2 = 18 SB), but that and Catulus' memoir are the only clear examples I have found of *commentarii* provided to poets. Cicero had evidently given up on Archias and Thyillus (Cic. *Att.* 1.16.15 = 16 SB) by the time he composed the memoir of his consulate described at *Att.* 1.19.10 = 19 SB, and I assume that what he sought from Posidonius (*Att.* 2.1.2 = 21 SB) was not poetry but historical prose.

23. Quint. *Inst.* 10.1.85–91.

24. Cic. *Arch.* 19 (Marius), 21 (Luculli), *Att.* 1.16.15 = 16 SB (Metellus), *Arch.* 28, 31, *Att.* 1.16.15 = 16 SB (Cicero).

25. Strabo 14.5.14 (674) and *Suda* 4:164.5–7 Adler.

26. *Anth. Pal.* 9.428 = Gow-Page, *Garland of Philip* 1:12 no. 1.

27. Cic. *Arch.* 18 and Strabo 14.5.14 (674).

28. Catull. 36.1; see also 95.3, if the reference there is to an epic.

29. In this paragraph I have followed the current parlance according to which the *recusatio* is a poem refusing an invitation to write epic, usually on grounds of a Callimachean aesthetic which exalts small, carefully wrought poems over big, flaccid poems. But that is an artificial restriction of the term. It is true that most *recusationes* are directed toward epic, probably because war and conquest stimulated a demand for epic. But this literary sub-type is the product of a distinctively Roman setting in which poets were closely involved in the life of their society friends. The refusal is regularly addressed to an interested party, as Callimachus' pronouncements were not, and the kind of invitation that is refused necessarily varies with the taste of those parties. There are *recusationes* which have nothing to do with epic, like Catullus 65 and 68, Horace *Epist.* 2.2, and *Ciris* 1–47, or even with poetry (see Hirtius' letter, *BGal.* 8 *pr.* 1).

30. Statius indicates that three of his *Silvae* were written on request (1.2, 2.7, and 3.4, according to statements in the prefaces of the respective books), and Martial says the same about some of his epigrams (*Epigr.* 9.89 and 11.42). The best case in which prompting can be deduced from a common recipe consists of the parallels between Stat. *Silvae* 4.6 and Mart. *Epigr.* 9.43. Other parallel pairings involve Stat. *Silvae* 1.2 and Mart. *Epigr.* 6.21, *Silvae* 1.5 and *Epigr.* 6.42, *Silvae* 2.7 and *Epigr.* 7.21–23, *Silvae* 3.4 and *Epigr.* 9.11–13 and 16–17, and *Silvae* 4.6 and *Epigr.* 9.43.

31. See the preceding note for examples.

32. For example, Plaut. *Aul.* 478–535, *Cur.* 466–485, *Men.* 571–597, and *Miles* 685–700.

33. "Neque enim notare singulos mens est mihi / verum ipsam vitam et mores hominum ostendere," Phaed. 3 *prol.* 49–50; "adgnoscat mores vita leg-

atque suos," Mart. *Epigr.* 8.3.20, and "hoc lege, quod possit dicere vita 'meum est,'" 10.4.8.

34. Some of the signs which post the steady popularity of satire are (1) Pers. *Sat.* 1.67–68, on satirical themes as subjects for fashionable poetry in Persius' day; (2) Mart. *Epigr.* 4.29.7 and Quint. *Inst.* 10.1.94 on the vogue for Persius' own satires more than a generation after his death; (3) the note in Valla's scholia on Juv. *Sat.* 1.20, registering the enthusiasm for the satirist Turnus at the court of the Flavian emperors; and (4) Ammianus Marcellinus 28.4.14, on the philistinism and sloth of the late fourth-century aristocracy, whose only reading consists of Juvenal and the titillating biographies of Marius Maximus.

35. Hor. *Serm.* 1.1.24–26 (the schoolteacher analogy), 1.4.1–5 (the social reformer), and 1.1.13–14 and 120–121 (the pedant).

36. In *Serm.* 2.7, apart from the tone, the slave's obviously self-interested motive for haranguing his master further undercuts the integrity of the message.

37. Drinking parties: Prop. 2.33b, 2.34, Ov. *Am.* 1.4 and 2.5; journeys: [Tib.] 3.9 = 4.3.11–14, Prop. 2.26.29–58, 4.3.45–48, Ov. *Am.* 1.9.9–14 and 2.16.17–32; birthdays, sickness, and bereavement: [Tib.] 3.10–12 = 4.4–6, Prop. 3.10, Ov. *Am.* 2.6, 2.13, and 3.1.57.

38. [Tib.] 3.1, Prop. 1.8b.40, Ov. *Am.* 3.1.57–62, and *Ars* 2.281–286.

39. Inspiration: Tib. 2.5.111–112, Prop. 2.1.1–16, 2.30b.40, and Ov. *Am.* 2.17.34; promise of fame: Prop. 2.5, 2.11, 3.2.17–26, 3.24.4, Ov. *Am.* 1.3.25–26, 1.10.59–60, and 2.17.27–34.

40. In addition to Ovid's *Ars,* Tib. 1.4, 1.6.9–42, 1.8, Prop. 1.10, 1.20, 2.18a.1–4, 3.3.47–50 (compare Hor. *Serm.* 2.5, *Epist.* 1.17 and 1.18).

41. Tib. 2.4.1–6, [Tib.] 3.19 = 4.13.22, Prop. 2.23.23–24, 2.25.11, 3.11.1–4, 3.15.10, 3.17.41, Ov. *Am.* 3.11.12, and *Ars* 2.228; see Chapter 1, note 47, for the slavery metaphor in relation to the leaders of society.

42. For Livia, see Vell. Pat. 2.130.5, Tac. *Ann.* 5.2.2, and Cass. Dio 57.12.2; for Octavia, Plut. *Ant.* 54.4 and Vitr. 1 *pr.* 2; for Antonia, Joseph. *AJ* 18.143 and 179 and Suet. *Cal.* 15.2; for Julia, Macr. *Sat.* 2.5.1–6.

4. The Political Perception of Augustan Poetry

1. The Greek loan-word *aula* is current as a term for the imperial court by the turn of the first century A.D.: see Mart. *Epigr.* 7.40.1, 9.36.10, 9.79.7, Tac. *Hist.* 1.7.3, 1.13.4, and 2.95.2.

2. R. P. Le Bossu, *Traité du Poëme Epique* (Paris, 1675); the copy I consulted was printed at Paris in 1693.

3. I quote from W. J.'s second edition (London, 1719). Of course, the literary avant-garde in England knew Le Bossu, as they did other French critics, before he was translated.

4. "Intentio Vergilii haec est, Homerum imitari et Augustum laudare a par-

entibus," Servius *pr. Aen.* 1:4.10–11 Thilo-Hagen; compare Ti. Claudius Dona-tus, "[Vergilius] talem enim monstrare Aenean debuit, ut dignus Caesari, in cuius honorem haec scribebantur, parens et auctor generis praeberetur," *pr.* 1:2.20–21 Georgii. Servius (or Servius Auctus) finds allusions to Augustus at *Aen.* 1.292, 1.294, 3.274, 3.276, 3.280, 3.501, 4.234, 5.45, 5.556, 5.568, 6.69, 6.612, 6.230, 7.170, 7.606, 7.762, 8.361, 8.686, 8.721, and 8.728.

5. Servius on *Aen.* 2.557, 2.135, 3.46, 2.683, 10.800, and 6.668.

6. For example, in book 1, chap. 10, book 2, chaps. 7, 14, and 18, and book 4, chap. 9.

7. Some remarkable documents of this operation are printed in volume 5 of the *Lettres, instructions et mémoires de Colbert*, ed. P. Clément (Paris, 1868). See especially the list of "gratifications faites par Louis XIV aux savants et hommes de lettres français et étrangers de l'année 1664 à l'année 1683" (pp. 466–498) and the letters to Colbert from his liaison with the Republic of Letters, Jean Chapelain (pp. 587–650).

8. Notice, for example, the parade of Italian learning put on by René Rapin in his *Comparaison d'Homere et de Virgile* (1668) and *Reflexions sur la poëtique et sur les ouvrages des poëtes anciens et modernes* (1674).

9. As in the formulation by Jacopo Mazzoni, "Io dunque stimo, che la facultà civile fosse quella, che ritrovò non solamente l'uso della Poesia: ma che appresso considerasse la norma, e la regola dell'Idolo poetico," *Della difesa della comedia di Dante distinta in sette libri* (Cesena, 1588), sec. 64 of the *Introduttione e sommario*. By the time Rapin wrote his *Reflexions sur la poëtique*, the doctrine had become a commonplace: "En effet, la Poësie étant un Art, doit être utile par la qualité de sa nature, et par la subordination essencielle, que tout Art doit avoir à la Politique, dont la fin génerale est le bien publique," sec. 7 of the "Reflexions en géneral," *Oeuvres du P. Rapin* (The Hague, 1725), 2:115.

10. Giason Denores, *Discorso intorno a que' principii, cause et accrescimenti che la comedia, la tragedia et il poema eroico ricevono dalla filosofia morale e civile e da' governatori delle republiche*, in *Trattati di poetica e retorica del Cinquecento*, ed. B. Weinberg, vol. 3 (Bari, 1972), pp. 376–377. Directly or indirectly, Denores appears to be the source of much else in Le Bossu besides the idea that epic teaches citizens to cherish the prevailing regime.

11. Few topics have generated so much contention among historians of early modern England as the organization, impact, and continuity of the first political parties. But whether the crucial divisions were between Whig and Tory or Court and Country or between hybrids of these factions, or whether these party labels merely disguised economic interests or the ambitions of individuals, no one would dispute the particular fact which is relevant to my argument: that Englishmen of the eighteenth century habitually spoke as though party considerations directly affected political behavior.

12. James Ralph, *The Case of Authors by Profession or Trade* (London, 1758),

p. 29; the term "political writer" figures on page 33. It already had the same sense twenty years earlier in the title of the pseudonymous pamphlet by "Marforio," *An Historical View of the Principles, Characters, Persons etc. of the Political Writers in Great Britain* (London, 1740).

13. *The Works of John Dryden*, vol. 5: *Poems: The Works of Virgil in English, 1697*, ed. W. Frost and V. A. Dearing (Berkeley and Los Angeles, 1987), p. 281.28–32.

14. Ibid., 5:283.29–30. I illustrate the collapse of Le Bossu's bipartite moral from Dryden because the Vergil translation was a literary landmark. But the shrinkage is already apparent in the paraphrase offered a year earlier by another early champion of Le Bossu, the critic John Dennis: see *The Critical Works of John Dennis*, ed. E. N. Hooker (Baltimore, 1939), 1:55–59.

15. Joseph Spence, *Polymetis: Or, an Enquiry concerning the Agreement between the Works of the Roman Poets, and the Remains of the Antient Artists. Being an Attempt To Illustrate Them Mutually from One Another* (London, 1747), p. 18. Spence had formed his view of the *Aeneid* many years earlier: the manuscript of an unpublished lecture delivered at Oxford in 1730 bears the title "On Vergil's Aeneid. That it was a Political Poem" (according to H. D. Weinbrot, *Augustus Caesar in "Augustan" England: The Decline of a Classical Norm* [Princeton, 1978], p. 65, n. 24.).

16. *Joseph Spence: Observations, Anecdotes, and Characters of Books and Men Collected from Conversation*, ed. J. M. Osborne (Oxford, 1966), 1:229–230.

17. C. G. Heyne (ed.), *P. Virgilii Maronis Opera* (Leipzig, 1767), 1:116 (note that this is Heyne's *first* edition of Vergil). The works which he had in mind were presumably Joseph Warton et al., *The Works of Virgil in Latin and English* (London, 1753), 1:17–18; Lewis Crusius, *The Lives of the Roman Poets* (London, 1726), 1:72–73 and 94; and John Martyn, *The Georgicks of Virgil with an English Translation and Notes* (London, 1746), p. vii (I owe the verification of this last reference to Nicholas Horsfall).

18. *Works of Dryden*, 5:18.32–19.8. I am not familiar enough with seventeenth-century England to know if Chetwood's idea might have been related to the state of agriculture after the English Civil War.

19. H. J. G. Patin, *Études sur la poésie latine* (Paris, 1868–1869), 1:61–62.

20. Ibid., 1:63.

21. W. S. Teuffel, *Geschichte der römischen Literatur*, 4th ed., rev. L. Schwabe (Leipzig, 1882), pp. 430–431. W. Y. Sellar brought the interpretation into his article on Maecenas in the ninth edition of the *Britannica*, vol. 15 (1883), pp. 194–195.

5. Literary Initiatives from Augustus' Side

1. For the emperor's control over the state libraries, see Hor. *Epist.* 2.1.216–217, Tac. *Ann.* 2.83.3, Suet. *Tib.* 70.2, and *Anth. Pal.* 7.158 (a reference I owe

to Nicholas Horsfall); he could also order removal of an author's work, Ov. *Tr.* 2.8, 3.1.59–82, and Suet. *Cal.* 34.2. For sponsorship of performances, see Ov. *Tr.* 2.509–511, the notice about production of Varius' *Thyestes* (Chapter 1, n. 22), Suet. *Vita Hor.* p. 297.36–37 Roth, *Aug.* 89.1, and *Claud.* 11.2. For the emperor's role in the imperial poetry competitions, see Stat. *Silvae* 4.2.60–67 and Florus *Vergilius orator an poeta* chap. 1.8–9 Jal.

2. Brutus, C. Claudius Marcellus, Q. Caecilius Metellus Pius Scipio, and Q. Fabius Maximus had all solicited monographs on family history from Atticus, according to Nep. *Att.* 18.3–4.

3. See the extracts quoted at Suet. *Claud.* 4.6, Quint. *Inst.* 1.6.19, and Suet. *Aug.* 86.3 and 86.2 respectively.

4. Quoted at Macr. *Sat.* 2.4.12; the poem which was at least in part the target of his gibes is preserved at *FPL* frag. 2, p. 101 Morel = 132 Büchner.

5. Suet. *Aug.* 85.2 and Macr. *Sat.* 2.4.2.

6. The address to Agrippa and Maecenas is known from Plut. *Comp. Dem. et Cic.* 3.1. Unlike some earlier leaders, but like his adoptive father, Augustus did not present his story to some man of letters who might give it the definitive gloss.

7. For Augustus' presence at performances by declaimers, see Sen. *Cont.* 2.4.12 and 10.5.21; for Cordus' reading, Suet. *Tib.* 61.3; for Vergil's readings, Don. *Vita Verg.* 27 and 32 Hardie and Servius on *Aen.* 4.324.

8. At *Dial.* 13.2 Tacitus refers to Augustus' letters to Vergil as though there were a series of them; at *Sat.* 1.24.11 Macrobius quotes from a letter to Augustus which begins "ego vero frequentes a te litteras accipio"; and fragments of two letters are preserved by Priscian (*GL* 2:533.13 Keil) and Donatus (*Vita Verg.* 31 Hardie). The Suetonian life of Horace refers to a series of letters from Augustus to Horace and quotes from several (pp. 297–298 Roth).

9. *Opinari* in the third person more often means "to state as one's opinion" than "to think." Note especially Suet. *Claud.* 3.2, where a reference to what Augustus "opinatus sit" is backed up with quotes from his letters; see also Suet. *Aug.* 51.2. Another sign that Suetonius is quoting here is the awkward way in which the *opinatus* clause is inserted between "usque adeo probavit" and the result clause.

10. Augustus' request for the *Aeneid* is less cogently attested than his requests to Horace. It is not mentioned in Donatus' life of Vergil, the most circumstantial account, which is thought to incorporate much of the material transmitted by Suetonius. The only sources which do state that Vergil's subject was suggested to him by the emperor are the Servian life (p. 22.27–28 Hardie) and the first Gudian life (p. 61.41–42 Brummer = 254.43–44 Bayer). Their credibility is undermined by the schematic way in which they present the stages of Vergil's literary career (the *Eclogues* are proposed by Pollio, the *Georgics* by Maecenas, and the *Aeneid* by Augustus). Ovid, speaking to Augustus, calls the epic *tua Aeneis* at *Tr.* 2.533, but he may have in mind the rescuing of the poem by

Augustus after Vergil's death. According to Calpurnius (*Ecl.* 4.158–163) and Martial (*Epigr.* 8.55), it was Maecenas who suggested the *Aeneid*.

11. "Aeneida prosa prius oratione formatam digestamque in XII libros particulatim componere instituit, prout liberet quidque, et nihil in ordinem arripiens," Don. *Vita Verg.* 23 Hardie. Vergil evidently chose not to share this prose sketch with Augustus. In answer to the latter's request for either a *hypographe* or an excerpt, Vergil said that he had nothing—in metrical form, presumably—polished enough to send, but he kept quiet about the precis: "de Aenea quidem meo, si mehercle iam dignum auribus haberem tuis, libenter mitterem, sed tanta inchoata res est ut paene vitio mentis tantum opus ingressus mihi videar, cum praesertim, ut scis, alia quoque studia ad id opus multoque potiora impertiar," Macr. *Sat.* 1.24.11. Or it may be that at the time of Augustus' inquiry Vergil had not yet written the prose draft.

12. The nearest analogue to Macrobius' story of Augustus and the Greek poet is the story Cicero tells about Sulla and the *poeta de populo* at *Arch.* 25.

13. For Augustus' employment of the geographer, see Pliny *HNat.* 6.141; for Nero's employment of centurions, see Sen. *QNat.* 6.8.3 and Pliny *HNat.* 6.181.

14. Cass. Dio 53.2.6–7 with 53.11; for another passage in which Dio assumes the possibility of orchestration, see 53.19.3.

15. Cic. *Att.* 12.40.2 = 281 SB. The other letters alluding to the memorandum, arranged in chronological order according to Shackleton Bailey's edition, are 13.26.2 = 286 SB, 12.51.2 = 293 SB, 12.52.2 = 294 SB, 13.1.3 = 296 SB, 13.2 = 297 SB, 13.27.1 = 298 SB, 13.28.2–3 = 299 SB, 13.31.3 = 302 SB, and 13.7 = 314 SB. A similar episode comes to light at *Att.* 13.50 = 348 SB.

16. Throughout the letters Cicero refers to Atticus' contacts as *isti,* 12.51.2 = 293 SB, 13.1.3 = 296 SB, 13.27.1 = 298 SB, 13.31.3 = 302 SB, and 13.7 = 314 SB. The persons meant are almost certainly Oppius and Balbus; Balbus later prevailed on one of Caesar's lieutenants to write a final installment of the *Gallic War.*

17. Cicero alludes to Caesar's expectations at *Att.* 13.28.3 = 299 SB, "ille vero potius non scripta desideret quam scripta non probet."

18. See especially his comments at *Att.* 12.51.2 = 293 SB and 13.27.1 = 298 SB.

19. For the problems, see *Att.* 13.27.1 = 298 SB and 13.28.3 = 299 SB. Cicero's letter may thus have been an early example of that strategy of optative discourse which came into vogue with the principate: praiseworthy actions and intentions which bear no relation to an emperor's actual behavior are nevertheless imputed to him in hopes of inducing him to adopt them. The technique is adumbrated by Pliny at *Epist.* 3.18.3.

20. Zosimus 2.6 and Phlegon, *FGrHist* 257, F 37.5.2. These and other sources for the Secular Games are collected in G. B. Pighi, *De ludis saecularibus populi Romani Quiritium,* 2nd ed. (Amsterdam, 1965), where the oracle can be found on pp. 56–57.

21. It is possible but not provable that the singing of the hymn represented another modification in the program. Only one authority, reported at second hand by a source (Pseudo-Acro on Hor. *Saec.* 8) whose reliability is hard to gauge, states that a hymn was featured in pre-Augustan celebrations of the games. But the hymn per se is less notable than the composition of the chorus which rendered it. A chant and a procession by twenty-seven maidens was a remedy which the priests had recommended on numerous occasions to avert the threat of dire happenings during the Republic. But the games of 17 B.C. were the first occasion, so far as is known, on which twenty-seven boys participated in the ritual. Choruses are chosen to coddle the sensibility of the god to whom they sing. The institution of the boys' chorus may be a consequence of the role which Apollo was given in Augustus' Secular Games. Note the distinction which Horace draws in verses 34–36 of the *Hymn:* "supplices audi, pueros, Apollo; / siderum regina bicornis, audi, / Luna, puellas" and the similar distinction in *Carm.* 1.21.1–2.

22. Compare "di, probos mores docili iuventae, / di, senectuti placidae quietem" at lines 45–46 and "quindecim Diana preces virorum / curat et votis puerorum amicas / applicat auris" at 70–72.

23. For references to prayers by Augustus and the priests, see lines 49–52 and 70–71. Horace does not allude to prayers that were offered during the ceremonies by Roman matrons and by Agrippa.

24. Horace's only concessions to golden-age imagery are in lines 57–60, where he speaks of the "return" of Fides and kindred tutelaries, and in 67–68, where he speaks of the prorogation of the Roman state into another lustrum and a *melius aevum.*

25. The frame of reference for lines 57–60 is set by the personifications Horace invokes. Unlike *probi mores* and *quies* in 45–46, they are official values, relating to the responsibilities of citizens toward the state or vice versa. Fides, Honos, and Virtus had long been hypostasized as deities of Republican Rome; the cornucopia too was a familiar motif on Republican coinage. Augustus was chiefly responsible for elevating Pax to her position as a tutelary of the state, but Caesar had already taken the first steps. Pudor, however, did not have a niche in the civic pantheon, unless Horace intended an equation with Pudicitia.

26. Horace himself in other contexts often portrays Augustus as the author of Rome's prosperity: *Carm.* 4.2.37–40, 4.5.5–38, 4.14.41–52, and 4.15.4–24.

27. Cass. Dio 54.18.1. The birth of Lucius and Augustus' adoption of him and his brother are the first two events Dio treats under the year 17; the Secular Games are the fifth.

28. Notice that, by contrast with Horace's *Hymn,* the coinage celebrates Actian Apollo in the following year: Sutherland-Carson, *RIC,* rev. ed., 1:69, nos. 365–366.

29. The prayers which Augustus offered at successive points during the proceedings are recorded in the *acta, ILS* 5050 = Pighi (above, n. 20), pp. 108–119

(for new fragments of the *acta* that have accrued since Pighi, see L. Moretti, *RPAA* 55–56 [1982–1984]: 361–379). It is instructive to set them beside Horace's poem: Augustus' petition to the Moerae, to Jupiter, and so on through Apollo and Diana follow exactly the same formula.

30. Allusions to this campaign are strewn through many sources, but the fullest accounts of it may be found in Cass. Dio 54.22, Strabo 4.6.9 (206), 7.1.5 (292), and Vell. Pat. 2.95; for Drusus' part in it, see also *Epic. Drusi* 15–16, 175, 385–386, and Flor. *Epit.* 2.22.

31. Notice that except for the first-person verb *distuli* in line 21, Horace has entirely suppressed his own persona in *Carm.* 4.4, by contrast for example with *Carm.* 1.37 and *Epod.* 9, where he cultivates a personal perspective on the events he celebrates.

32. With no great confidence, at the crux in lines 17–18 I have translated Bentley's "videre *Raetis* bella sub Alpibus Drusum gerentem Vindelici"; the manuscripts and Porphyrio give *Raeti,* which Shackleton Bailey daggers. Rhaeti and Vindelici are described in ancient sources as different peoples who inhabit neighboring Alpine regions, but I have not been able to disentangle them in relation to this campaign.

33. Notice that nothing is made of Drusus' youth in the *second* poem (*Carm.* 4.14), which treats of Tiberius' and Drusus' exploits together.

34. It is of some interest as showing the independence of Horace's approach that he does not breathe a word about Augustus' wife Livia, who was Drusus' mother. Contrast the line taken by whoever wrote the *Epicedion Drusi* when Drusus died six years later. Livia has the featured role, with lesser billing given to other members of the court—Augustus, Tiberius, Antonia, Octavia, Marcellus, and Agrippa. Out of nearly 500 lines, exactly four (162, 331, and 451–452) touch on Drusus' Claudian ancestry.

35. Horace never refers directly to the *clades Lolliana,* though it was on his mind both in the *Lollius Ode* (*Carm.* 4.9) and at *Carm.* 4.2.33–36.

36. There will be some discrepancy between what Suetonius says and what Horace wrote no matter what view one adopts. On the interpretation proposed here, Suetonius will have learned from a reliable source that Augustus requested a poem in honor of Drusus, but will then have generalized his statement so that it covered both poems in the Horatian corpus which have to do with the Vindelician war. For what it is worth, this view is corroborated by those shambling authorities Pseudo-Acro and Porphyrio, who identify *Carm.* 4.4 but not 4.14 as the product of the emperor's request.

37. I should register here that I am discounting the assertion of Junius Filargirius (in his comment on Verg. *Ecl.* 6.3) that it was Augustus who ordered Vergil to write his shorter poems. So far as I am aware this claim has found no credit with Vergilian scholars, who in fact rarely mention it. Filargirius has simply extracted his information from *Ecl.* 6.3–5 ("Cynthius . . . admonuit: 'pastorem

. . . oportet . . . deductum dicere carmen'"), after postulating that Cynthius (= Apollo) is a cover name for Augustus.

38. Similar bargains are offered to prospective benefactors at *Laus Pis.* 214–219 and *Panegyricus Messallae* 201–211.

39. Actually, lines 40–42 contain a twofold reference back to the opening lines. *Altum* corresponds to "via qua me possim tollere humo" in 8–9 and *intactos* is meant to contrast with "omnia iam vulgata" in 4.

40. It may be worth pointing out that three of the four occurrences of the name "Caesar" in the *Epodes* are clustered in this one poem.

41. The equation of lyric poetry and love poetry emerges clearly in the opening lines of *Carm.* 4.1, which Horace wrote when he found himself in spite of all involved with lyrics again. Notice also the connection Horace draws between *Venus* and *carmina* when he explains to Florus why he has written no poems he can send, *Epist.* 2.2.24–25 and 55–57.

42. Fragments of Maecenas' own writings suggest his fondness for sensual themes. Note especially the praise of wine put into the mouth of a character in his *Symposium,* "idem umor ministrat faciles oculos, pulchriora reddit omnia, et dulcis iuventae reducit bona," cited by Servius Auctus on Verg. *A.* 8.310, and the lubricious description "feminae cinno crispat et labris columbatur incipitque suspirans, ut cervice lassa fanantur nemoris tyranni" quoted by Sen. *Epist.* 114.5.

43. See Cic. *Fam.* 9.8.1 = 254 SB (Cicero to Varro, presenting a dialogue in which Varro had been given a speaking part): "puto fore ut, cum legeris, mirere nos id locutos esse inter nos, quod numquam locuti sumus; sed nosti morem dialogorum." See also Cic. *Att.* 13.19.5 = 326 SB.

44. Those who suppose that Horace's satire represents an encounter with an official spokesman might wish to differentiate between the situation there and the situation presented in some other texts. When Quintus Cicero urges his brother to compose an epic in honor of Caesar (*QFr.* 2.14[13] = 18 SB), do we conclude that he is representing Caesar? When Pliny encourages a poet to persevere with an epic on Trajan (*Epist.* 8.4), do we conclude that he is acting as Trajan's agent? The question might even be raised about the role of Horace himself: was Augustus' own laureate doubling as a recruiter of talent when he advised Valgius to write poems in praise of the emperor's victories (*Carm.* 2.9)?

45. Such is the delicacy of poets' talk that one cannot always tell when they mean to be committing themselves to a definite position. But the following cases seem to belong to the category I have described: Hor. *Carm.* 1.6 (a refusal), 2.12 (a refusal), 3.25 (a promise?), 4.2 (a refusal), 4.15 (evidently a refusal in lines 1–4, possibly a promise in 25–32), *Epist.* 2.1.250–259 (a refusal), Verg. *E.* 8.7–11 (a promise, but probably addressed to Pollio rather than to the future Augustus), *G.* 3.46–48 (a promise; the temple allegory in lines 13–36 has also been interpreted as a promise), Prop. 2.1 (a refusal), 2.10 (a promise), 2.34.55–94 (a refusal?), Ov. *Tr.* 2.323–338 (a refusal), and *Culex* 8–10 (a promise?).

46. Though as Robert Kaster has remarked to me, if the bulk of Augustus' appeals to poets garnered only *recusationes,* the influence he exerted does not look particularly effective.

47. The slight connection Agrippa was once thought to have had with the literary milieu has come in recent years to seem illusory. Donatus' life of Vergil (sec. 44 Hardie) reports a (harsh) evaluation of Vergil's style by an otherwise unidentified Marcus Vipranius. Editors have usually emended *Vipranius* to the more familiar nomen *Vipsanius* and have thus encouraged identification of the critic as Marcus Vipsanius Agrippa. But (1) there is no objective reason to judge the text corrupt; (2) the great general does not fit comfortably into the Donatan context, which is a cento of strictures on Vergil culled from critics all equally obscure; and (3) even if the emendation were correct, it would be doubtful that a Marcus Vipsanius should be identified as Agrippa, who was notorious for having discouraged use of his nomen. That Agrippa kept his distance from the poets fits his characterization by Pliny as a "vir rusticitati propior quam deliciis" (*HNat.* 35.26). Even more remarkable than his distance from Roman literati is the fact that he (unlike Tiberius a few years later) evaded the attention of Greek poets during his long sojourn in the East.

48. For his self-effacing attitude, see Cass. Dio 53.23.2–4; for the triumphs declined, Cass. Dio 48.49.4 (38 B.C.), 54.11.6 (19 B.C.), and 54.24.7 (14 B.C.).

49. Don. *Vita Verg.* 35–41 Hardie. That story of Augustus' intervention was current within a century after Vergil's death is shown by Pliny *HNat.* 7.114; it may be implicit in Ovid's use of the phrase *tua Aeneis* when speaking to Augustus at *Tr.* 2.533.

50. We are free to imagine any number of ways in which Augustus might have struck down the document which blocked him, from an enactment asserting the nation's patrimonial rights over works of the spirit to administrative chicanery. Yet it must be recognized that the legal barriers which protected the poet's wishes did not require much of an assault. The only sanction a legatee faced for failing to comply with a testamentary condition was forfeiture of his legacy to the heirs. The worst that threatened Varius and Tucca, therefore, was the necessity of restoring the papers or their value. And they faced no challenge at all unless proceedings were initiated by the heirs, who were none other than Vergil's half-brother, Augustus, Maecenas, and the legatees themselves.

51. Our source for the burning of the *Metamorphoses* is Ovid himself, *Tr.* 1.1.117 and 1.7.11–26. For other acts of literary piety on the part of survivors, see Suet. *Claud.* 11.2, *Gr.* 8.3, Probus *Vita Pers.* p. 39.42–45 Clausen, and Pliny *Epist.* 2.10.

Perhaps we should allow for one other factor in judging Augustus' intervention. It is generally believed that the Donatan report of Vergil's end derives ultimately from reminiscences which we know Varius wrote about him. If that is so, it served Varius' purpose to play up the element of coercion by Augustus, which absolved him of responsibility for taking a step which demonstrably corresponded with his own preferences regarding the *Aeneid.*

52. This inference is strengthened by the chilly reception with which Crassus' actions were greeted at two other points in his campaign. In addition to the rebuff over the *spolia opima,* his right to assume the title *imperator* was evidently contested (Cass. Dio 51.25.2), and there was no hoopla over his recovery of a Roman standard lost to the enemy in fighting some years earlier (Cass. Dio 51.26.5).

53. For earlier examples of Augustus' lucky finds in the priestly archives, see Cass. Dio 47.18.6 and 48.44.2.

54. The temple restoration can be dated only indirectly by reference to the death of Atticus, who had suggested it to Augustus and who died in 32 (Nep. *Att.* 20.3).

55. Livy does dwell on one facet of the emperor's activity for the sake of a conceit toward which he is building. Augustus' pious care of sacred buildings has assimilated him to the status of a temple intimate, whose witness to temple furnishings is as sacrosanct as the furnishings themselves. To "take away" (*subtrahere,* 4.20.7) that testimony would be tantamount to temple robbery (which is the literal meaning of *sacrilegium,* ibid.).

As regards the inscription, historians often take Livy to task for having failed to verify it. But in his convoluted statement, which goes to remarkable lengths to distinguish between the inscription and the witness to the inscription, perhaps we should recognize a hint that the relic had perished as soon as it was found, and that all now depended on the word of the eyewitness.

56. Whatever may be the case with the breastplate and the inscription, the criteria which Augustus applied ("ea rite opima spolia habentur quae dux duci detraxit, nec ducem novimus nisi cuius auspicio bellum geritur," 4.20.6) were not ad hoc fabrications. Though Varro denied that the *spolia opima* could be taken only by a *dux,* it is clear from the context of his discussion (cited in Festus' entry under *spolia opima,* pp. 202.14–25 and 204.1–19 Lindsay) that he was combating a view well established before the year 29 B.C.

57. The earlier date is that given in Jerome's chronicle, p. 164 c Helm; the later by Cass. Dio 53.23.5–7.

58. Few will subscribe to the solution Servius propounds for this dilemma, though he prosecutes it throughout his commentary on the *Tenth Eclogue:* "licet [Vergilius] consoletur in ea Gallum, tamen altius intuenti vituperatio est" (because the poem portrays the degradation of Gallus' affair with Lycoris, and because it contains a covert hit at Antony).

59. For sympathetic references to Gallus during Augustus' lifetime, see Prop. 2.34.91–92, Ov. *Am.* 1.15.29–30, 3.9.63–64, *Ars* 3.334, 3.537, *Rem.* 765, *Tr.* 2.445–446, and 4.10.53.

60. In the first of his two statements Servius says that the excised portion ran

from the middle of book 4 to the end. But his account of what replaced it contains a discrepancy which has been used by some to whittle down the extent of the *laudes Galli*. In the note at *Ecl.* 10.1 Servius says that Vergil substituted the Aristaeus tale, which does take up half the book, from lines 315 to 558. But at *G.* 4.1 he calls the replacement section the Orpheus tale; within the Aristaeus tale there is a story about Orpheus which occupies only about a hundred lines, from 453 to 547.

61. Gell. *NA* 6.20. Notice that Gellius is not overly impressed by the commentator's claim: "ea res verane an falsa sit, non laboro." Notice also that the detail descended in garbled form to Servius, who used a variant version of it in his note on *Aen.* 7.740 (but not later at *G.* 2.225, although his proximate source Donatus evidently retailed it there).

62. If one chooses to *accept* Servius' report, however, it may be well to have clearly in mind a necessary corollary. In that case, the supposition that Maecenas prescribed the plan of the *Georgics* must be false, since such a plan can hardly be supposed to have envisioned a half-book devoted to the praises of Gallus.

63. For the source see Chapter 1, n. 22.

64. "Aere gravi donatus est, id est massis: nam sic et Livius argentum grave dicit, id est massas," says Servius at *Aen.* 6.861, evidently struggling to make sense out of information which baffles him. The interpolated manuscripts of the Donatan life offer a variation according to which Octavia counted out 10,000 sesterces per line in return for Vergil's tribute to her son (p. 27.6–7 Brummer = 356.90–91 Bayer).

65. The extract gives no clue to the time of writing, since Augustus could have claimed to be "occupatissimus et infirmus" at almost any point in his career. Some readers have assumed, presumably because the arrangement is discussed by letter, that Augustus was abroad at the time, probably in Spain, and therefore writing between late 27 and early 24 B.C. This assumption has no reliable foundation. The extract is from a letter, not to Horace, but to Maecenas, who had to be approached diplomatically if he was to relinquish his claims on Horace's company. Augustus may well have preferred to write out what he had to say. He had in any case a strong preference for written over oral communication (Suet. *Aug.* 84.2), and he certainly wrote letters to Nepos when he and Nepos were both in Rome. I would be amazed if anyone who knew Horace seriously imagined that he could have been induced to accept a position overseas.

66. For persons acting as literary assistants, compare Suet. *Claud.* 41.1, *Gr.* 10.2 and 6, Hor. *Epist.* 1.8.2, 2nd Quint. *Inst.* 10.1.128. Friends also took on positions as schoolmasters (Pliny *Epist.* 4.13.10), assessors (Juv. *Sat.* 3.162), and estate managers (Hor. *Epist.* 1.12).

67. See the assertion of the speaker at Livy 39.16.8 and compare Livy 4.30.11,

25.1.10–12, and 40.29.13–14. The books which figure in the last-mentioned passage are a partial exception in that they did not belong to a religious cult but were found buried in a chest which bore the inscription of King Numa. Accounts differ concerning what these books contained, but all agree that they were considered a threat to established Roman religion. (The main sources apart from Livy 40.29 are Pliny *HNat.* 13.84–88 and Plut. *Numa* 22.2–8.)

68. The expulsion is known only from a brief note in Jerome's chronicle, p. 163 k Helm; the note gives no other clue to Anaxilaos' offense other than to identify him as a *magus* as well as a philosopher.

69. For philosophers, see Ath. *Deipn.* 12.547A, Gell. *NA* 15.11.1–2, and Plut. *Cato Mai.* 22.4–5; for rhetors, Suet. *Gr.* 25.1; for astrologers, Val. Max. 1.3.3 and (during the triumvirate) Cass. Dio 49.43.5.

70. The principal texts on which our knowledge of these *maiestas* trials is based are Suet. *Aug.* 55, Cass. Dio 56.27.1, Tac. *Ann.* 1.72, and Suet. *Cal.* 16.1. Even the spare account given in this paragraph is not without its difficulties, since the trial and book burning alluded to by Seneca the Elder at *Cont.* 10 *pr.* 4–8 would seem to have predated the trial of Cassius Severus.

71. For example, we do not know the author, date, circumstances, or (with one exception) the original provisions of the *lex Iulia de maiestate.* We have no connected account of the precedent-setting Augustan case or cases to show us how the law whose provisions we do not know was made to cover written and spoken words; the scattered references we do have to these early cases are often difficult to harmonize with one another. We do not know to what extent remedies for libel were available under existing civil and criminal law before Augustus began prosecuting it under the *lex Iulia.*

Even the date of the first prosecution for literary *maiestas* is uncertain. But four incidents help to delimit the years in which libel was becoming a politically sensitive issue: (1) During a period of unrest in A.D. 6, unknown malcontents posted anti-government tracts which prompted a senatorial investigation (Cass. Dio 55.27.1–3). (2) One anonymous author who was successfully tracked down had circulated a scurrilous letter purporting to be by Augustus' wayward grandson Agrippa Postumus. The letter is probably related to the banishment of Postumus in A.D. 7 (Suet. *Aug.* 51.1 and Cass. Dio 55.32.2). (3) Under the year A.D. 32 Jerome notes that Cassius Severus died in the twenty-fifth year of his exile (p. 176 b Helm). Jerome's dates are frequently inaccurate, but for what it is worth, his note implies that Cassius' prosecution for *maiestas* took place in A.D. 8. (4) In the year A.D. 12, Augustus ordered an investigation which resulted in the burning of some defamatory leaflets and the punishment of the authors (Cass. Dio 56.27.1).

72. Covert authorship is part of the gravamen in the cases mentioned by Cass. Dio 55.27.2 and 56.27.1, and Suet. *Aug.* 51.5 and 55. It is not known,

however, whether the writings for which Labienus and Cassius Severus were prosecuted had been put about anonymously—though in the latter case, Tac. *Ann.* 1.72.4 *(quoque)* may imply that they had been.

73. Cass. Dio 54.30.4; an anecdote reported by Quint. *Inst.* 6.3.78 seems to imply a similar curb on oratory.

74. *Tr.* 3.8.39–40 and 4.10.98. At one point (*Tr.* 3.6.33–34) Ovid seems to imply that his action could have been construed as an effort to obtain a bribe.

75. The date is deduced from Tac. *Ann.* 4.71.4. As with Ovid's deliction, there is no narrative account of the Julia affair, which means that we are largely in the position of trying to amalgamate one unknown with another.

76. Lines 171–228 date the appearance of book 1 of the *Ars* to the year 2 or 1 B.C., and some scholars have supposed that this was the date of a *second* edition.

77. For the continuing availability of Ovid's works generally, see for example *Tr.* 3.14.9–10. Ovid's statements about their availability in the public libraries are ambiguous. At *Tr.* 3.1.59–82 he speaks of being barred from the libraries, but that may be only the treatment he anticipates rather than a sanction actually imposed. At the start of the same poem he writes as though he has the option of seeking access to the libraries for his books, and at *Pont.* 1.1.5–10 he says he does not submit his books for fear that they *might* be refused.

78. "Demi iussa . . . Arte," *Tr.* 2.8. That is the reading of the oldest manuscripts, but the text has been disputed. At *Tr.* 1.1.68 there is another allusion to a penalty of some sort, "quas meruit, poenas iam dedit illud opus." At *Tr.* 3.1.65–66 Ovid assumes that whatever the status of his other works, the *Ars* will certainly not be found in the libraries.

6. Poetic Approaches to Political Themes

1. Polyb. 1.1.5–1.2, the fragment of Aemilius Sura lodged in the text of Vell. Pat. at 1.6.6, *Oracula Sibyllina* 3.158–161, Dion. Hal. *Ant. Rom.* 1.2, Strabo 17.3.24 (839), Pompeius Trogus passim, Ov. *Met.* 15.426–436, and often afterward.

2. See the Index of Types in Crawford *RRC,* 2:859–878, under the entries "diadem," "globe," "sceptre," and "Victory."

3. For the language, see *Auct. ad Her.* 4.13, Cic. *Verr.* 2.4.81, *Dom.* 90, and *Phil.* 6.19.

4. Cic. *Balb.* 16, *Sest.* 129, and Plut. *Pomp.* 45.6–7.

5. The theme is first sounded in Greek poetry, Lycoph. *Alex.* 1226–1230 and perhaps Melinno (Lloyd-Jones and Parsons, *Supplementum Hellenisticum,* pp. 268–269, no. 541), if that mystifying poem is a Hellenistic product, then fleetingly in Lucretius 3.836–837 and in lines 66–67 of the extract which Cicero quotes from the poem on his consulate at *Div.* 1.21 (*FPL* p. 70 Morel = 84 Büchner). The long preamble of Catullus' eleventh poem, in which he extols the readiness of two comrades to follow him to the ends of the earth, is devoid

of patriotic sentiment, but it may nevertheless owe something to nationalistic poetry of the Late Republic. The extremities which Catullus names (the Indians, Hyrcanians, Arabs, Scythians, and Parthians; the Nile and the Rhine; Britain) are exactly those trumpeted in imperial contexts later on.

6. The chronology of Vergil's *Eclogues* has become the subject of controversy in recent years, largely in consequence of an unresolved dispute about the identity of the unnamed addressee of the *Eighth Eclogue*. I side with those who believe that the collection was completed in or soon after 39 B.C. rather than with those who down-date its appearance to the mid-30s.

7. But Meliboeus' pointed observation may not be original with Vergil. Compare Flor. *Epit.* 2.2.3 on Tiberius Gracchus: "depulsam agris suis plebem miseratus est, ne populus gentium victor orbisque possessor laribus ac focis suis exsularet," together with Plut. *Ti. Gracchus* 9.5.

8. This poem *could* have been written at any time between the battle of Philippi and the elimination of Antony; theoretically, therefore, it could even precede Vergil's *First Eclogue*. But in the absence of counterindications, the odds that a poem written between 42 and 31 predates a poem written between 43 and 39 are less that that it was written afterward. The chronological context most often suggested for the *Seventh Epode* is the struggle with Sextus Pompey during the middle 30s.

9. *Paneg.* 187; Isocrates was doubtless influenced by such passages as 7.145 in Herodotus' history of the war between Greece and Persia. Not that so simple an idea requires a literary warrant: compare Tac. *Ann.* 1.49.

10. I subscribe to a conventional date for the *Panegyricus,* taking lines 121–134 as describing Messalla's inauguration as consul in January, 31 B.C. The poem must have been written soon after that date—in any case, before Messalla's Aquitanian triumph in 27, which if it had already taken place would have made the sentiment expressed in lines 136–138 extremely gauche.

11. Lines 106–117 can only refer to the campaign described by App. *Ill.* 16–28, Cass. Dio 49.35–38, and Strabo 4.6.10 (207).

12. For commanders other than Augustus who are glorified in post-Actian verse, see Tib. 1.7.1–8 and [Verg.] *Catal.* 9.3–6 and 51–54, both concerning Messalla. Hor. *Epist.* 1.16.25–29, in which it is said that the theme of "bella pugnata terra marique" is recognized as property belonging to Augustus, suggests that the period in which other leaders could be allowed to overshadow Augustus was over by about 20 B.C. But poets continued to extol the advance of Roman dominion without always mentioning Augustus: for example, Tib. 2.5.57–60, Verg. *Aen.* 6.851–853, Prop. 3.1.15–16, 4.3.7–10, Ov. *Fasti* 1.85–88, 2.683–684, and 4.255–256; in prose, notice Dion. Hal. *Ant. Rom.* 1.2–3.

13. This is clear from his plea to be included in Messalla's circle at lines 190–211; compare also 35–38.

14. For Alexander in the schools, see *Auct. ad Her.* 4.31 and Sen. *Suas.* 1 and 4.

15. For example, Man. 1.898–902, 4.764–766, and even the unromantic Horace, *Carm.* 3.3.53–56. The identification of empire and cosmos is particularly prominent in later writers like Lucan and Seneca, for whom empire took on negative overtones. It should be noted that the author of the *Panegyric* was not the first author to imagine the empire in relation to the cosmos. Cicero had compared them at *Rep.* 6.16–22, but to opposite effect, using the vastness of the cosmos to argue the smallness of the empire.

16. See Verg. *G.* 2.170–173, 3.16–33, 4.560–562, and Hor. *Serm.* 2.1.10–15—a passage which purports to represent, not Horace's own voice, but a style of speaking then in vogue. There is a parallel development in the use of the epithet *magnus:* it is not applied to Augustus in poetry of the triumviral period, but turns up all of a sudden right after Actium (Verg. *G.* 2.170, 4.560, Hor. *Serm.* 2.5.64, *Carm.* 1.12.50, Prop. 2.1.26, 2.7.5, and 2.31.2). *Magnus* often has strong martial overtones, as can be seen in most of the passages just cited (and also in Catull. 11.10, *Panegyricus Messallae* 176, [Verg.] *Catal.* 9.3); comparisons with Pompey the Great may have been in the back of people's minds.

17. Contemporaries at any rate interpreted the triumph of 29 in global terms: note the parade of captured nations at Verg. *Aen.* 8.722–728, and the language used at *G.* 3.32–33 and Prop. 3.9.53. For Pompey's triumph in 61, see note 4 above. For Caesar's quadruple triumph in 46, see Suet. *Jul.* 37.1 and Cass. Dio 43.19.1.

18. For the map and the portico, see Pliny *HNat.* 3.17 and 6.139, Cass. Dio 55.8.4, the *Divisio orbis terrarum* (in *Geographi Latini minores* Riese, p. 15); Strabo alludes to the map without precisely identifying it at 2.5.17 (120).

19. This idea is most explicit at Ov. *Met.* 15.877–879, *Tr.* 4.9.19–24, and 4.10.128, but emerges earlier at Hor. *Carm.* 2.20.13–20. It is closely related to the idea that the permanence of the empire will guarantee literary renown through time, Hor. *Carm.* 3.30.7–9, Verg. *Aen.* 9.446–449 (here linked with Augustus), Ov. *Am.* 1.15.25–26, and *Tr.* 3.7.50–53.

20. Hor. *Carm.* 1.29, Tib. 1.1.49–55, 2.6.1–6, Prop. 3.5.1–18, 3.12, and 4.3.

21. For predictions by poets in their capacity as *vates,* see Hor. *Carm.* 1.12.49–60, 1.35.29–32, 3.5.2–4, 4.2.33–36, Prop. 3.1.15–16, 3.4.1–6, 3.12, 4.6.77–84, Ov. *Ars* 1.177–180, *Tr.* 4.2, *Pont.* 3.4.87–114. For vaticinations by gods *vel sim.,* see Hor. *Carm.* 3.3.40–56, Tib. 2.5.57–60, Verg. *Aen.* 1.278–288, 4.229–231, 6.791–807 and 851–853, 8.722–728, Ov. *Met.* 15.431–452 and 829–831, *Fasti* 1.515–517, 3.29–38, 4.827–834, and 6.359–360. That prophecies of conquest were poetic fixtures even before the Augustan period seems indicated by Lycoph. *Alex.* 1226–1230, by Horace's parody of the form at *Serm.* 2.5.62–64, and by Tibullus' use of it to compliment someone other than the emperor at 1.7.1–6.

22. Verg. *G.* 2.170–172, 3.16–36, *Aen.* 6.794–800, 7.602–606, 8.722–728, Prop. 2.10.13–18, and 4.3.

23. There is also a Greek epigram by Crinagoras, *Anth. Pal.* 6.161 = Gow-Page *Garland of Philip* 1:204 no. 10, on the young Marcellus' return from the Cantabrian expedition.

24. Ov. *Ars* 1.177–228. A Greek poet, Antipater of Thessalonica, has an epigram on the same occasion, *Anth. Pal.* 9.297 = Gow-Page *Garland of Philip* 1:40, no. 47.

25. Ovid says (*Pont.* 2.5.25–34 and 3.4.3–6) that he also composed a longer piece on the triumph which is not extant.

26. Ov. *Pont.* 1.8.11–19 and 4.7. In addition to those events treated by Roman poets there are a couple treated only by Greek poets: the Thracian war of 12–10 B.C. conducted by L. Calpurnius Piso (Antipater *Anth. Pal.* 9.428 = Gow-Page *Garland of Philip* 1:12, no. 1 was written to introduce a now lost epic on this campaign) and an imperfectly identified victory by Germanicus (Crinagoras *Anth. Pal.* 9.283 = Gow-Page *Garland of Philip* 1:214, no. 26).

27. The two ideas are connected at Hor. *Carm.* 3.14.14–16, 4.5.25–28, 4.14.43–44, 4.15.17–24, *Epist.* 2.1.2, Prop. 3.11.55–66, 4.6.37, Ov. *Fasti* 1.529–532, and 5.587–588.

28. Horace invokes it again at *Carm.* 3.5.1–4; it is not present in Propertius or Vergil, but is ubiquitous in Ovid's later work, as for example at *Met.* 15.858–860 and *Fasti* 2.131–138.

29. The only echoes of the formula *senatus populusque Romanus* in passages concerned with Augustus are at Hor. *Carm.* 4.14.1, Verg. *Aen.* 8.679, and Ov. *Fasti* 2.127.

30. Ov. *Fasti* 2.130 and 132. In this case Ovid was actually anticipated by subjects of the Roman empire in the East. Almost immediately after Augustus received the title *pater patriae* from the Roman senate in 2 B.C., it was expanded in some Greek inscriptions to "Father of His Country and of the Entire Human Race" (for example, *IGRR* 4, no. 1756.101), presumably because eastern subjects of Augustus felt they were not covered by the umbrella of a *pater patriae*. It is possible that the Greek formula influenced Ovid's but just as likely that it did not. For another Republican title transposed into Ovidian imperialese, see *princeps imperii* at *Tr.* 2.219.

31. References in contemporary poetry exhibit a clear-cut pattern: when Augustus is described as a ruler, it is almost always in context of the empire (*regnare*: Hor. *Carm.* 1.12.52; *tenere terras*: Hor. *Carm.* 3.14.15–16; *regere orbem*: Hor. *Carm* 1.12.57, Ov. *Tr.* 5.2.50, Man. 1.8; *regere imperium*: Ov. *Tr.* 2.166, *Pont.* 3.3.61; *regere terras*: Ov. *Tr.* 4.2.10; *coercere terras*: Ov. *Pont.* 3.3.61; *movere terras imperiumque*: Ov. *Pont.* 2.2.64; *arbiter imperii*: Ov. *Tr.* 5.2.47; *frena imperii capere*: Ov. *Pont.* 4.13.27–28; *frena imperii moderari*: Ov. *Pont.* 2.9.33; *frena imperii tenere*: Ov. *Fasti* 1.532; *orbis paret*: Ov. *Tr.* 5.8.26; *terra sub Caesare*: Ov. *Pont.*

1.2.99; *dominus terrarum:* Ov. *Pont* 1.9.36, 2.8.26; *imponere iugum terris:* Man. 4.550; *mundum regere* and *terrae imperare: ILS* 137.6–7), rarely in a Roman context (*regere Italiam:* Verg. *Aen.* 4.230; *patriae rector:* Ov. *Tr.* 2.39; *Roma sub Caesare:* Man. 1.925; *regere nos: ILS* 137.7). The difference in tone is particularly noticeable where both Rome and her empire are mentioned together, as at Ov. *Fasti* 1.531–532, "et penes Augustos patriae tutela manebit: / hanc fas imperii frena tenere domum," and *Tr.* 5.2.47–50, "arbiter imperii, quo certum est sospite cunctos / Ausoniae curam gentis habere deos, / o decus, o patriae per te florentis imago, / o vir non ipso, quem regis, orbe minor." Cicero had commented on the tendency to avoid terms expressing authority in political discourse of the Republic (*Rep.* 1.64).

32. See *Anth. Pal.* 9.224.6 = Gow-Page *Garland of Philip* 1:212, no. 23, 9.297.1 = Gow-Page *Garland of Philip* 1:40, no. 47, 9.307.4 = Gow-Page *Garland of Philip* 1:300, no. 5; *Les inscriptions grecques de Philae,* ed. E. Bernand (Paris, 1969), 2:78, no. 142.2 and 4; Lloyd-Jones and Parsons, *Supplementum Hellenisticum,* p. 496, no. 982.8.

33. For example, *Auct. ad Her.* 4.13, Lucr. 3.836–837, Cic. *Verr.* 2.4.81, *Planc.* 11, *Dom.* 90, and *Phil.* 6.19.

34. Notice that Ovid later reinvented almost the same argument at *Tr.* 2.213–238.

35. Tac. *Ann.* 1.11–12, Cass. Dio 57.2; Tacitus uses the terms *imperium* and *respublica* interchangeably, while Dio speaks only of the empire. In this case we can be sure that Tacitus and Dio are reporting the substance of things actually said and not merely reconstructing the debate in their own terms, because Strabo, who was writing not long after Tiberius' accession, brings up the same argument in connection with it, 6.4.2 (288). Dio indeed implies at 56.39.5 that the argument was current even earlier, when Augustus was still alive.

36. But Scipio as praised by Ennius at *Var.* 23–24 Vahlen very nearly qualifies, and Julius Caesar would surely have qualified if only the poetry of the 40s had survived.

37. *Red. Sen.* 8, *Red. Pop.* 11, *Sest.* 144; compare the elder Pliny's much-quoted apothegm "deus est mortali iuvare mortalem," *HNat.* 2.18.

38. *Panegyricus Messallae* 7–17, Hor. *Carm.* 1.26.11, Ov. *Pont.* 1.2.147–148, 1.9.35–36 and 49, Stat. *Silvae* 1.4.19–37; compare also the frequent use of the verb *venerari* in place of *colere,* Tib. 1.5.33, Ov. *Pont.* 1.2.49, 1.7.7, 2.2.1, and *Ciris* 18.

39. For the goddess-mistress, see Catull. 68.70, Ov. *Am.* 1.7.32, 2.11.44, 2.18.17, and 3.2.60; for sacred imagery in other contexts, Plaut. *As.* 712–716, *Cap.* 863–864, *Pseud.* 327, Hor. *Serm.* 2.6.52, *Epist.* 1.19.43, Prop. 3.9.46, Ov. *Am.* 1.6.16, *Ars* 3.489–490; Cic. *Nat. D.* 2.32, *Att.* 4.16.3 = 89 SB, *Rep.* 1.18, *De Or.* 1.106, and 2.179.

40. The most famous statement of this doctrine is to be found at Cic. *Rep.* 6.13–16. In this sense, even Augustan poets sometimes acknowledge the possibility of apotheosis for others besides Augustus, as at Hor. *Carm.* 3.2.21–22, Prop. 3.18.33 (Claudius Marcellus), and Man. 1.758–804.

41. Poets often allude to the divinity of Julius Caesar, and less often to the father-son relationship between him and Augustus, but in only a handful of passages do they bring both elements into conjunction and identify Augustus as the son of a god. The earliest references are Verg. *Aen.* 6.792 and 8.681, followed by Prop. 4.6.59–60, and then *Eleg. Maec.* 178, Ov. *Met.* 15.745–860, *Fasti* 2.144, 3.157–160, and Man. 1.9. Only one of these passages expressly says that Caesar's divinity spills over onto Augustus, and that point is made in the form of a conceit, at Ov. *Met.* 15.760–761.

42. The decree is reported at Cass. Dio 51.19.7, and the libation is mentioned at Hor. *Carm.* 4.5.31–36 and Ov. *Fasti* 2.635–638. It is noteworthy that the first time such a libation is mentioned in Augustan poetry (at Tib. 2.1.27–32), it is an honor tendered to the *privatus* Messalla Corvinus.

43. *Fortuna Redux:* Aug. *Anc.* 11.1, Cass. Dio 54.10.3; *Pax Augusta:* Aug. *Anc.* 12.2; Lares Compitales: Ov. *Fasti* 5.145–146 and numerous inscriptions referring to the Lares Augusti (for example *ILS* 3612–3623); the cult innovation is evidently connected with Augustus' administrative reorganization of the city, Suet. *Aug.* 30.1 and 31.4 and Cass. Dio 55.8.6–7; compare Pliny *HNat.* 3.66.

44. The respective texts being the prefaces to Vergil's own *Georgics* 1 and 3, and App. *BCiv.* 5.546.

45. See for example *Acts of the Apostles* 14.11–13, 28.6, Vell. Pat. 2.107.2, and Mart. *Epigr.* 5.3.

46. See, for example, *OGI* 56.33–34, 90.47, 339.35–36, and 383.132–33. What the Greek texts and the Vergilian passage have in common is that the recipient of monthly sacrifices is a living man who is both ruler and benefactor. Monthly cult per se is not unknown among Romans, though it is not particularly common: see Tib. 1.3.34, Suet. *Gal.* 4.3, Probus on Verg. *G.* 1.10.

47. This conviction should be registered as a minority view: many critics believe that the babe of the *Fourth Eclogue* is a flesh-and-blood relative of Augustus, and still more believe that the story of Daphnis in the *Fifth Eclogue* is an allegory constructed around Julius Caesar.

48. I accept as the only firm foundation for dating the *Georgics* the information that Vergil read them to Augustus on four successive days in the summer of 29 B.C. (Don. *Vit. Verg.* 27 Hardie). I assume that the poem was more or less finished at that time, and came into circulation soon afterward. Lines 28–31 of book 3 prove that the proem of that book cannot have been written before 30 B.C. I assume that the proem of book 1, which introduces the poem as a whole, was written no earlier.

49. Hercules is again the implicit model at the very end of the *Georgics*, 4.560–562: "Caesar dum magnus ad altum / fulminat Euphraten bello victorque volentis / per populos dat iura viamque adfectat Olympo."

50. As Servius explains on line 33 (and as Ov. *Met.* 2.195–197 and Germ. *Arat.* 547–549 and 623–644 confirm), Vergil has at this point had recourse to an eleven-sign version of the zodiac which was competing with the twelve-sign version which became standard. In the eleven-sign version, Scorpio occupied the space of *two* signs, his body and tail forming one, and his pincers *(chelae)* the other. In the twelve-sign version, Scorpio's two pincers are the balance pans of Libra. The clash between the two theories opened up a sector of the zodiac which Vergil could appropriate for panegyrical purposes, and that was no doubt his primary consideration in placing Augustus' sign where Libra's should have been (later on, at line 208, Libra is back in possession of the spot). But Vergil may also have been thinking of Augustus' date of birth (September 23), which would normally have made Libra his horoscope. If that is the case, however, Vergil chose not to follow Augustus' own idea of his relationship to the stars. It is a notorious fact that the emperor promoted Capricorn as his sign (Suet. *Aug.* 94.12, Man. 2.507–509), which was already being displayed on his coins in the 20s.

51. If one may compare great and grotesque, Vergil's conceit in the proem of the *Georgics* bears a passing resemblance to the approximately contemporary forecast in the *Panegyricus Messallae* of Messalla's exploits in the anti-world (lines 135–176). Both poets are striving to eke out a triumphalist vein sorely depleted by hyperbole.

52. Martial prowess is one (though only one) aspect of Augustus hinted at in line 28, where Vergil imagines the world binding myrtle round its new god's brow. The wreath of myrtle was an emblem of victory, particularly of victories won with little loss of life: see Pliny *HNat.* 15.125–126 and Gell. *NA* 5.6.20–23.

53. Compare Lucr. 2.9–10, 3.3–4, 6.27–28, Cic. *Fin.* 1.57. All these passages are concerned with Epicurus' revelations about the principles of human action, which are not unrelated to a knowledge of the cosmos. But Vergil's language about "the way" is perhaps closer in spirit to that in the opening of Parmenides' famous poem, Diels-Kranz *Vorsokr.* 28 B 1.

54. Despite Servius' assurances that Augustus himself bore the name Quirinus, I take "Quirinus" here to mean Quirinus, military patron of the Roman state, just as the name is used at Prop. 4.6.21, "altera classis erat Teucro damnata Quirino" (of Antony's fleet at Actium), and Mart. *Epigr.* 10.26.1–4, "Vare . . . Ausonio frustra promisse Quirino / hospita Lagei litoris umbra iaces" (to a centurion).

55. "Demissa ab Iove gens" in line 35 emphasizes the descent of the Trojan nation from Zeus through Dardanus, rather than the descent of the Julian family

from Venus; for the Trojans named, compare the similar list (in a nationalistic context) at *Aen.* 6.650.

56. Two texts which probably imply the existence of temples as early as the 20s are Vitr. *De arch.* 5.1.7 and *ILS* 110; compare also Cass. Dio 53.27.2–4. For festivals (none datable so early), see *ILS* 5531 (Iguvium), Suet. *Aug.* 98.5 (Naples), *CIL* 9.4395 (Foruli), and *NSA* 8 (1932): 129 (Aufidena).

57. Note *ego . . . mecum* (10), *deducam* (11), *referam* (12), *ponam* (13), *mihi* (16), *ego* (17), *agitabo* (18), *mihi* (19), *ipse* (21), *feram* (22). For the profusion of first-person elements, compare Enn. *Ann.* 34–50 Skutsch = 35–51 Vahlen, Plaut. *Mil.* 387–392, and (closer in feeling to the Vergilian passage) Prop. 4.6.1–10.

58. Although Vergil does not use the word *dedicare* in *G.* 3.11–16, I would suggest that the concept underlies his treatment. From its predominant use in relation to temples and altars and other sacral objects, *dedicare* was transferred to literary contexts, where it tended to retain a religious coloration until it finally faded into the formula of book-dedication. One of the earliest and most vivid metaphorical applications occurs in Vergil's contemporary Vitruvius, at *De arch.* 9 *pr.* 16 (through their reading of the *Annales,* lovers of literature have the *simulacrum* of Ennius "in suis pectoribus dedicatum"); compare Sen. *Cont.* 1 *pr.* 10.

59. For the talismanic power of the Palladium, see Cic. *Scaur.* 48, Livy 5.52.7, 26.27.14, and Ov. *Fasti* 6.428; the threat to the temple of Vesta in lines 15–16 thus points ahead to the phrase "ruentis imperii" in 25–26.

60. The chief evidence that has been mustered in this connection consists of (1) two dedications, one to "Augustus Mercurius" by tradesmen of Cos (A. Maiuri, *Nuova silloge epigrafica di Rodi e Cos* [Florence, 1925], no. 466) and another to "Mercurius Augustus" by a freedman *vici magister* in Rome (*CIL* 6.283; other inscriptions honoring "Augustus Mercurius" appear to be post-Augustan); (2) a series of inscriptions from Pompeii (*CIL* 10.884–923) which have been interpreted as showing that certain slave or freedman *ministri* originally associated with Mercury were later reconstituted as *ministri* of Augustus Mercurius; and (3) some half-dozen reliefs, coin-types, and gems bearing representations of Mercury which are thought to show physiognomical resemblances to Augustus, or images of Augustus which are accompanied by the caduceus. But this mélange of documentation does not add up to evidence of a popular cult. The pictorial items are devoid of legends that date, identify, or explicate them, and their purported resemblances to portraits of Augustus depend very much on the eye of the beholder. The caduceus had been appearing on Roman coins for two centuries before Augustus, and not just as an attribute of Mercury, but as a more generalized emblem of peace and prosperity. As for the Pompeian inscriptions, only one (*CIL* 10.888) actually names both Augustus and Mercury together, and it is not clear from the abbreviated text whether the functionaries named are *ministri* of "Augustus Mercurius," or *ministri* of Augustus making a

dedication to Mercury (in *CIL* 10.885 and 886, "Merc." is certainly dative). The inscriptions from Rome and Cos do clearly identify Augustus with Mercury, but even they do not establish that the identification was widespread. The tradesmen and the *magister* represent a Greek rather than a Roman mentality; moreover, they belong to a mercantile milieu in which Mercury was traditionally regarded as a patron god and in which he may easily have acquired associations that did not carry over to the population at large.

61. Cic. *Har.* 62. In the same passage, Cicero goes on to contrast the stage fiction with Roman notions about intercourse between gods and men, and elsewhere (*Man.* 41 and *QFr* 1.1.7 = 1 SB) he treats the belief that the gods visit earth in human form as typically Greek.

62. *Ridens* corresponds to Homer's "laughter-loving" (as at *Il.* 3.424 and 4.10), and for Iocus and Cupido, compare Hes. *Theog.* 201; Horace's description of Apollo is adapted from *Il.* 15.308 and perhaps *Od.* 11.128.

63. *Hymn. Hom. Ap.* 22–24, *Ven.* 9–11, 14.3–5; compare Hes. *Theog.* 926.

64. The purification of Orestes: Aesch. *Eum.* 282–283, 445–452, 578, 620–625; of the Danaids: Apollod. *Bibl.* 2.22; of Ixion: Schol. Ap. Rhod. 3.62.

65. Commentators on lines 13–20 tend to explain them by reporting flood stories from the annals of Tiberology. No doubt Horace was aware of inundations in real life which sometimes swamped the Forum, but he cannot have been describing anything so experiential when he wrote "retortis . . . violenter undis," "ire deiectum monumenta . . . templaque," and "se . . . iactat."

66. The phrase is Aristophanes' (*Pax* 393), but the idea goes all the way back to Homer (*Il.* 24.334–335); it is expressed also in the standing epithet *eriounios*.

67. Hor. *Carm.* 3.3.9–12 and 3.14.1–4; the comparison with Hercules is perhaps implicit in "finire quaerentem labores" at *Carm.* 3.4.39, and it has often been thought to play a part in Vergil's Hercules narrative in *Aeneid* 8.

68. At *Aen.* 1.289–290 Jupiter predicts Augustus' apotheosis after his career on earth; at 6.791 Anchises styles him as *divi genus;* at 8.680–681 he is shown on Aeneas' shield with a halo of fire; and at 9.642 he is presumably included among the *dei* of whom Iulus is to be the progenitor.

69. These two poems, together with 4.6.60 and another reference to Augustus' descent from Venus at 4.1.46, seem to be Propertius' only contributions to the divinity theme. On the basis of lines like "vix timeat salvo Caesare Roma Iovem," 3.11.66, and "Caesar / dum canitur, quaeso, Iuppiter ipse vaces," 4.6.13–14, it is sometimes thought that he goes further, and exploits the conceit of a parity between Augustus and Jupiter. But that is a misconception. As may be seen from similar turns at 2.13.16 and 2.34.18, he is using a form of hyperbole which has nothing to do with the ruler cult, and which is on record as early as Plautus; see *As.* 414–415, *Cas.* 323–324, *Mos.* 242–243, *Ps.* 265–267, and *Rud.* 1361.

70. As indicated by the query a newsmonger supposedly puts to Horace, "o bone, nam te / scire, deos quoniam propius contingis, oportet, / numquid de Dacis audisti?" *Serm.* 2.6.51–53 (a poem of about 30 B.C.); compare the complaint of the man who cannot get Horace to circulate his poems publicly, "Iovis auribus ista / servas," *Epist.* 1.19.43–44.

71. Horace also resorts to the "we" mode when predicating divinity of Augustus at *Carm.* 3.5.1–4.

72. *Met.* 15.840–851, *Fasti* 3.699–704, and *Pont.* 4.13.17–26.

73. Verg. *Aen.* 8.97–368, Tib. 2.5.23–38 and 55–60, Prop. 4.1.1–38, 4.2.1–10, 4.4.1–14, and 4.9. A couple of decades later Ovid produced passages in the same vein at *Ars* 1.101–134 and 3.113–120, and there are many scattered through the *Fasti*. There is of course a much larger number of passages which deal with the ethos of early Rome, but I am concerned here only with those which also emphasize topography.

74. The relevant portion of Lucretius is book 5, lines 783–1457. This contribution had already been amalgamated with the stockpile of poetic motifs by the time of Horace *Serm.* 1.3.97–112.

75. The *Antiquitates rerum humanarum et divinarum* in 41 books, *De vita populi Romani* in 4 books, *De gente populi Romani* in 4 books, the *Liber tribuum*, the *Aetia*, the *Liber urbanarum rerum*, and *De familiis Troianis*. In addition to these explicitly antiquarian investigations, Varro's *Logistoricon* and his works on language, literary history, and law also delved into the Roman past.

76. According to Augustine, *De civ. D.* 6.3, Varro devoted nine books of the *Antiquitates* to *loci* (six in connection with *res humanae* and three in connection with *res divinae*). That category is also announced as the organizing principle for book 5 of the *De lingua Latina*: "in hoc libro dicam de vocabulis locorum et quae in his fiunt" (5.10).

77. For example, "quid inter hos Ioves intersit et eos, qui ex marmore, ebore, auro nunc fiunt potes animadvertere et horum temporum divitias et illorum paupertates," Non. 162.15–18 Mercier (1:239 Lindsay), "haec aedis, quae nunc est, multis annis post facta sit. utique omnia regis temporibus delubra parva facta," Non. 494.7–9 Mercier (3:792 Lindsay), both cited from the *De vita populi Romani*, and August. *De civ. D.* 4.31, "[Varro] dicit etiam antiquos Romanos plus annos centum et septuaginta deos sine simulacro coluisse. 'quod si adhuc,' inquit, 'mansisset, castius dii observarentur.'" Varro's antiquarian works also advertised his antipathy toward foreign cults (see Serv. Auct. on *Aen.* 8.698, with Tert. *Ad Nat.* 1.10.17), a bias which is sometimes echoed in the poets' excursions on early Rome, Verg. *Aen.* 8.185–188 and Prop. 4.1.17–18.

78. Compare Tib. 2.5.33–36 and Varro *Ling.* 5.44 and 156; Propertius appears to give a different etymology for *Velabrum* at 4.9.5–6. Vergil's story of Aeneas' visit to the Palatine invokes two etymologies attested in Varro, for *Argi-*

letum (*Aen.* 8.345–346, compare Varro *Ling.* 5.157) and *Thybris* (*Aen.* 8.330–332, compare Varro *Ling.* 5.30). The poems also rely on a number of etymologies for which Varronian parallels are not on record.

79. The date of book 1 is established by a digression at 1.19.3 in which Livy notes that in the year 29 B.C. Augustus closed the gates of the Temple of Janus for the second time in Rome's history. Livy uses the new name "Augustus" which the emperor took in 27 B.C., and he does not yet know about a third closing of the gates which took place in 25 or 24 B.C. (or for that matter about the reopening of the gates later in 27, on the occasion of Augustus' departure for the Spanish campaign, Oros. 6.21.1).

80. The epigram by the poets' coeval Domitius Marsus is printed in most editions of Tibullus and in *FPL* p. 111 Morel = 143 Büchner.

81. The hypothesis that Tibullus had heard recitations of work in progress from the *Aeneid* is not per se impossible. Propertius had some knowledge, though not very accurate knowledge, of Vergil's epic in the 20s (Prop. 2.34b.61–66), and it is well attested that Vergil gave readings from his poems (for example, Gell. *NA* 6.20.1, Don. *Vita Verg.* 29 and 43 Hardie, and Serv. on *Ecl.* 6.11 and *Aen.* 4.323). The problem is that there is no evidence pointing to recitations from book 8 or from any other part of the second half of the *Aeneid* before Vergil's death.

82. The closest parallel that has been cited is between *Aen.* 8.46, "hic locus urbis erit, requies ea certa laborum," and Tib. 2.5.56, ". . . hic magnae iam locus urbis erit." But the line in *Aeneid* 8 is under strong suspicion of being a gloss imported from book 3.

83. For the date of both buildings, see Cass. Dio 51.22. The Curia Julia is one of the elements Propertius brings into his juxtapositions of primeval and modern at 4.1.11 and 4.4.13.

84. Cass. Dio 51.19.1. For the location (beside the Temple of the Deified Julius), see E. Nash, *Pictorial Dictionary of Ancient Rome,* 2nd ed. (New York, 1968) 1:92 and the more recent information by E. Nedergaard, "Zur Problematik der Augustusbogen auf dem Forum Romanum," in *Kaiser Augustus und die verlorene Republik,* ed. W.-D. Heilmeyer (Mainz, 1988), pp. 224–239.

85. Cass. Dio 48.42.4–6, 49.42.2, and Suet. *Aug.* 29.5, respectively.

86. The date of Augustus' restoration (probably by 32 B.C. and certainly by 27 B.C.) is fixed by Nep. *Att.* 20.3 and Livy 4.20.7. Propertius devoted one of his antiquarian poems (4.10) to the Temple of Jupiter Feretrius.

87. Cass. Dio 54.4. Vergil may be alluding to this temple at *Aen.* 8.352–354, and Propertius at 4.1.7.

88. Suet. *Aug.* 30.2, probably from the spoils of Egypt; compare Cass. Dio 51.22.3.

89. For the location and layout of the temple area, see G. Carettoni, "Die Bauten des Augustus auf dem Palatin," in *Kaiser Augustus,* ed. Heilmeyer

pp. 263–267, with further sources cited there. The Temple of Apollo with its associated structures comes up for mention in Augustan poetry more often than any other urban monument: it is evoked at the beginning of the poem (2.5) which contains Tibullus' sketch of early Rome, and it figures as a point of reference in one of the sketches by Propertius (4.1.3); it is also mentioned at Hor. *Carm.* 1.31, *Saec.* 65, *Epist.* 1.3.17, 2.1.216–217, 2.2.94 (this reference is not certain), Prop. 2.31, 4.6.11–12, Verg. *Aen.* 6.69–70 (implicit), 8.720, Ov. *Am.* 2.2.3–4, *Ars* 1.73–74, 3.119, 3.389–390, *Tr.* 3.1.59–68, *Fasti* 4.951. Augustus' house was under construction at the same time as the Temple of Apollo. He was purchasing lots for it in 36 B.C. (Cass. Dio 49.15.5, Vell. Pat. 2.81.3), and it was evidently complete by 27 B.C., when the senate decorated its portal (Cass. Dio 53.16.4, Aug. *Anc.* 34.2); for the site and layout, see the article by Carettoni. Suetonius at *Aug.* 72.1–2 stresses the plainness of Augustus' original residence on the Palatine and his preference for simple furnishings throughout his life, but he probably does not mean that the house in which Augustus lived as *princeps* was built on a modest scale. The testimony about Augustus' purchases of multiple lots together with the excavated remains suggest that it was grand at least by contemporary standards, and that is also the impression one gets from allusions to it by Propertius at 2.16.19–20 and Ovid at *Ars* 3.119 and *Tr.* 3.1.33–34.

90. Vitr. *De arch.* 1 pr. 2. Most accounts of Vitruvius assume publication of the *De architectura* in the 20s or thereabouts. It is worth emphasizing here that Vitruvius' dedication illustrates exactly the kind of motivation which I think often led the poets to their themes: he observed the emperor's words and actions and then without any apparent prompting tried to lend his work a relevant coloration.

91. Note that it is a visitor and a non-Roman, Strabo of Amaseia, who extols the sights of the Campus Martius over those of the city center, 5.3.8 (236).

92. Suet. *Aug.* 31.3. The Arval Brethren were functioning again by 20 B.C. (the latest possible date for the inscription which first attests them, *CIL* 6.32338). That Augustus revived the colleges of the Fetials and the Sodales Titii is deduced mainly from their sudden reemergence in Augustan inscriptions, but the Fetials were also put on show in a ritual staged in 32 B.C. (Cass. Dio 50.4.5).

93. For the revival, see Suet. *Aug.* 38.3; for the itinerary, Dion. Hal. *Ant. Rom.* 6.13.4, Cass. Dio 55.31.2, and *De Vir. Ill.* 32.3.

94. For the poets' awareness of the influx of new wealth, see Prop. 3.9.27–28, Ov. *Am.* 2.9.17–18, and *Ars* 3.114.

95. For the pontificate, see Nic. Dam., *FGrHist.* 90 F 127 (9) and Vell. Pat. 2.59.3; for the patriciate, Nic. Dam., *FGrHist.* 90 F 128 (35) and Cass. Dio 45.2.7; for the urban prefecture, Nic. Dam., *FGrHist.* 90 F 127 (13).

96. Nic. Dam., *FGrHist.* 90 F 127 (17 and 19) and Suet. *Aug.* 8.1.

97. Nic. Dam., *FGrHist.* 90 F 130 (48), Suet. *Jul.* 83.2.

98. Nic. Dam., *FGrHist.* 90 F 130 (53, 113, 115, 117) and Vitr. *De arch.* 1 *pr.* 2.

99. Octavian's aborted matches involved the daughter of Servilius Isauricus (Suet. *Aug.* 62.1), Antony's stepdaughter (Suet. *Aug.* 62.1, Plut. *Ant.* 20.1, and Vell. Pat. 2.65.2), and Scribonia (Suet. *Aug.* 62.2, Cass. Dio 48.16.3, App. *BCiv.* 5.222). For Antony's taunt about the Getic princess, see Suet. *Aug* 63.2.

100. Octavia's marriage: App. *BCiv.* 5.273, 5.278, and Cass. Dio 48.31.3; Marcellus' engagement: Cass. Dio 48.38.3; Julia's engagement: Suet. *Aug.* 63.2 (Suetonius reports this as an allegation by Antony, who further alleged that Julia was subsequently offered to the king of the Getae).

101. See Cic. *Phil.* 9 and 14, Val. Max. 5.2.10, Cass. Dio 46.38.2 and 46.51.4. Apparently more public funerals were proclaimed in the year 43 than in any year of Roman history before or after.

102. Cass. Dio 48.33.1. The attention which he invited at the first shaving of his beard a year later ought perhaps to be compared (Cass. Dio 48.34.3).

103. Compare the ugly reaction of the aristocracy when the *novus homo* Agrippa received a state funeral years afterward, Cass. Dio 54.29.6—and Agrippa was the country's most illustrious general, and had been three times consul.

104. For the proscribed guardian, see App. *BCiv.* 4.47 and Suet. *Aug.* 27.1; for a motive, compare Nic. Dam., *FGrHist.* 90 F 126 (3).

105. For some examples, see App. *BCiv.* 4.136, 5.217–218, 5.267–271, and 5.303 for mediation by Antony's mother Julia; 5.291 and 303 regarding Sextus Pompey's mother Mucia; and 4.136 and 5.390–397 regarding Octavia. Other examples are to be found in the tales of the proscriptions, the most detailed of which is contained in the *Laudatio Turiae* (*ILS* 8393). Compare also Appian's story of the matrons' embassy when they were singled out for a special tax, *BCiv.* 4.135–146.

106. Plut. *Pomp.* 53.5–6, Cass. Dio 39.64, Livy *Per.* 106, App. *BCiv.* 2.68, Vell. Pat. 2.47.2. Though Caesar later exploited popular feeling about Julia (Plut. *Caes.* 55.4 and Cass. Dio 43.22.3), he probably did not instigate the obsequies in the Campus Martius. Her death was sudden, following childbirth, and Caesar at the time was far away, in Gaul if not still in Britain (for the date, see Cic. *QFr.* 3.1.17 and 25 = 21 SB, and Sen. *Dial.* 6.14.3). Furthermore, there are good parallels for such an initiative by the urban throng: compare especially the incident told by Cassius Dio at 48.53.4–6.

107. *Epic. Drusi* 351–352. Items from the palace also gained coverage in the capital gazette, Suet. *Aug.* 64.2, *Tib.* 5, *Cal.* 8.2, Cass. Dio 48.44.4 and 57.12.2.

108. Gell. *NA* 15.7.3; in the letter Augustus indicates that he is writing on his sixty-fourth birthday.

109. For the Paphlagonian oath, see *OGI* 532.9–11. For the new Spanish oath, see J. Gonzalez, "The First Oath pro salute Augusti Found in Baetica,"

ZPE 72 (1988): 113–127; the text is given on p. 113 and the relevant lines are 8–11. Gonzalez dates the inscription to 6 or 5 B.C. Fragments of a Samian oath published by P. Herrmann in *MDAI(A)* 75 (1960): 70–84 may include the children of Augustus, and may date from 6 or 5 B.C. An earlier text which is in one respect similar should probably not be brought into the discussion. According to the *acta* of the Secular Games of 17 B.C., Augustus prayed that the gods would be propitious "p. R. Quiritibus, XVvirum collegio, mihi, *domo, familiae*," ILS 5050.99 = Pighi (Chapter 5, n. 20), p. 114. But the matrons who participated in the ceremonies evidently uttered the same formula (line 130), which appears to be traditional: see Cato *Agr.* 141.2 and Suet. *Aug.* 58.2.

110. For the coins, see Sutherland-Carson, *RIC,* rev. ed., 1:72, no. 404. The legend, however, refers to the moneyer, leaving the images unaccompanied by comment.

111. Cass. Dio 53.30.1–2, Vell. Pat. 2.93.1. Seneca states as a matter of fact that Marcellus was "praeparatus successioni," *Dial.* 11.15.3; compare 6.2.3.

112. Commentators on Horace often assert that *Carm.* 1.12 was written to celebrate Marcellus because a four-stanza parade of illustrious Romans closes with a reference to the *fama Marcelli,* followed by another to the *Iulium sidus* (lines 45–48). In the context of a heroic catalog, however, there can be no doubt that the surface reference of *fama Marcelli* must be to the third-century Marcellus, winner of the *spolia opima* and conqueror of Syracuse, who duly figures in comparable catalogs elsewhere (Verg. *Aen.* 6.855–859 and Man. 1.788). Any compliment to Augustus' teenage nephew would be subliminal at best. Note that the treatment of Marcellus is one of many instances in which Greek poets exhibit an entirely different alignment toward the palace: Crinagoras of Mytilene addressed epigrams to him on two occasions during his lifetime, *Anth. Pal.* 6.161 and 9.545 (= Gow-Page *Garland of Philip* 1:204 nos. 10 and 11).

113. If, as is likely, Octavia took up residence in the house of Augustus after her divorce by Antony (see Plut. *Ant.* 57), Marcellus must have been raised there. And in that case Propertius' phrase "amplexum Caesaris esse focos" is fuzzy, conflating his status as Augustus' son-in-law with his prior status as a member of the household.

114. The *Epicedion Drusi* and the *Elegiae in Maecenatem* are both controversial texts, as regards dating and much else. I personally would be prepared to accept the consequences of dating them by the events they commemorate, but for the purposes of my argument about the succession theme, that is perhaps beside the point. What is important is that their perspective on the dynasty does not represent attitudes that can be dated *earlier* than the last decade of the first century B.C.

115. Suet. *Claud.* 1.5. Since the author of the *Epicedion* addresses himself to Livia above all, it would be possible to hypothesize that his silence about

Gaius and Lucius was deliberate: they were not heirs and successors of *her* line.

116. In fact line 174 echoes phrases addressed to aristocratic parents by earlier poets, Tib. 1.7.55–56 and Hor. *Ars* 24.

117. Perhaps Ovid also counts on the looseness of the term *princeps*. Though preeminently an appellation for Augustus, it was applied also to other members of the imperial house, if the *Epicedion Drusi* is a reliable index of usage in the last decade of the century: see lines 261, 285, 303, 352, and 356.

118. "Succedatque suis orbis moderator habenis: / quod mecum populi vota precantur idem," Ov. *Pont.* 2.5.75–76. References to the succession in the *Fasti* are difficult to date, because these books were at least partially revised after the death of Augustus. Consequently it is not certain whether such passages as *Fasti* 4.859–860 ("cuncta regas et sis magno sub Caesare semper, / saepe etiam plures nominis huius habe") were composed before or after Tiberius' accession.

119. For example, *Tr.* 2.57 and 155–166, 5.2.51–52, 5.5.61–62, 5.11.25–26, and *Pont.* 2.8.41–42.

120. See Tac. *Ann.* 1.3.2 and Cass. Dio 54.27.1 and 55.9.

121. In extant poetry there is one positive or more precisely neutral reference, at Hor. *Serm.* 1.5.33. During his lifetime, Antony had in his entourage two poets who presumably portrayed him favorably, Anser (Servius on Verg. *Ecl.* 9.36) and Boethus of Tarsus (Strabo 14.5.14 [674]), and after his death he figured as a character in a civil war epic by Rabirius, who allowed him a sympathetic utterance to consummate his death scene (*FPL* frag. 2, p. 121 Morel = 153 Büchner). But none of this has anything to do with his being Augustus' brother-in-law.

122. The only poets who advert to Agrippa's domestic link with Augustus are the author of the *Epicedion Drusi* (67–69) and Ovid in the *Ars* (3.391–392); both texts belong to the last decade of the century and postdate Agrippa's demise.

123. *Epist.* 1.3.1–2, 1.8.2 and 14, 1.9, 1.12.26–27, and 2.2.1.

124. The only allusion is in the appellation "Claudius Augusti privignus" at Hor. *Epist.* 1.3.2.

125. See Sen. *Dial.* 6.2.5, on poems honoring Marcellus. Domitius Marsus' epigrams on Augustus' mother Atia are probably relevant, if they could be dated.

Index of Augustan Persons

Index of Passages

The following register notes passages quoted or discussed in the text (but quotations of isolated phrases have generally been excluded).